HOLLYWOOD MADONNA

HOLLYWOOD LEGENDS SERIES
CARL ROLLYSON, GENERAL EDITOR

HOLLYWOOD MADONNA
Loretta Young

Bernard F. Dick

UNIVERSITY PRESS OF MISSISSIPPI • JACKSON

www.upress.state.ms.us

The University Press of Mississippi is a member of the Association of American University Presses.

Copyright © 2011 by University Press of Mississippi
All rights reserved
Manufactured in the United States of America

First printing 2011

∞

Publisher: University Press of Mississippi, Jackson, USA
Authorised GPSR Safety Representative: Easy Access System Europe - Mustamäe tee 50, 10621 Tallinn, Estonia, gpsr.requests@easproject.com

Library of Congress Cataloging-in-Publication Data

Dick, Bernard F.
Hollywood Madonna : Loretta Young / Bernard F. Dick.
    p. cm. — (Hollywood legends series)
Includes bibliographical references and index.
ISBN 978-1-61703-079-6 (cloth : alk. paper) —
ISBN 978-1-4968-6160-3 (paperback) — ISBN 978-1-61703-080-2 (ebook)
1. Young, Loretta, 1913–2000. 2. Motion picture actors and actresses—United States—Biography. I. Title.
    PN2287.Y6D53 2011
    791.4302'8092—dc22
[B]   2010053734

British Library Cataloging-in-Publication Data available

For Ned Comstock

CONTENTS

Preface ix

1. Life without Father 3
2. The Creation of Loretta Young 10
3. LORETTA TALKS! 18
4. Sacrificial Wives, Shop Girls, and Proud Proletarians 26
5. Loaned Out 39
6. Last Days at Warner's 48
7. Darryl Zanuck's Costume Queen 53
8. The Men in Her Life 65
9. Heeding the Call of the Wild 71
10. The Great Lie 79
11. Return from the Ashes 88
12. Addio, Darryl 103
13. The Price of Freedom 112
14. Loretta Goes to War 125
15. "Age cannot wither" (but Hollywood Can) 132
16. Thrice Blessed: A Reunion, a Replacement, and an Oscar 139
17. The Return to Fox—and Zanuck 154
18. Slow Fade to Small Screen 163
19. Radio Days 170
20. Another Medium, Another Conquest 186
21. The Road to Retirement 207
22. A New Life 218
23. The Last Reel 230

Notes	245
Filmography	256
Major Radio Appearances	259
Major Television Appearances	261
Index	262

PREFACE

My family entered the television age in February 1954, when *The Loretta Young Show* was in its first season. Then, my only interest was live television. I delighted in *Studio One* and *Robert Montgomery Presents*, which brought theatre into our parlor, along with missed cues, flubbed lines, and camera gaffes that actually enhanced the immediacy of the experience. Filmed television was movies; live television, even variety shows, like *The Ed Sullivan Show* and *The Perry Como Show*, were theatre. My mother watched *I Love Lucy* and *The Loretta Young Show*. I did not—then.

I knew who Loretta Young was. I probably saw her before 1944, but my earliest memory of Loretta Young is a scene from *And Now Tomorrow* (1944) that lodged itself in my memory. (Little did I know at the time that I would be writing her biography.) It is the scene when Loretta, now hearing-impaired, awakens to the sight of a rain-streaked window. But there is no sound. She knows she should hear the impact of the rain against the glass, but cannot. I had no idea what a subjective camera or a POV shot were, but I shared Loretta's fear, reflected in a face that, still beautiful, had taken on a kind of delicately expressed alarm, devoid of histrionics and panic—the sort of expression one would expect from a well-bred woman facing the first crisis in her life. I also had fond memories of *The Farmer's Daughter*, and, as the product of a Catholic grade school education, of *Come to the* Stable, in which Loretta's Sister Margaret corresponded to the kind of nun with whom I was familiar: the nun who uses her gentle, and often wily, powers of persuasion to accomplish her end—always, of course, for the greater glory of God.

Because my mother rhapsodized about *The Loretta Young Show*, I decided to watch it with her, but just once—or so I thought. I was mesmerized by Loretta's much touted entrance, in which she executed a 180-degree turn while closing the door—her dress seeming to rotate with her—and then breezed into the living room where she purred her welcome. My first thought was, "How phony!" But after I saw a few more episodes,

I knew that what might have seemed like artifice was Loretta's special form of theatre. It wasn't live, but she made it seem as if it were, particularly with that iconic entrance so reminiscent of the way a star makes her first appearance in a Broadway play. But that was Loretta—a star doing a star turn.

In 1954, I did not appreciate the historic significance of *The Loretta Young Show*, unaware that it was the first truly successful (it ran eight seasons) attempt at anthology television—not a show that used the sitcom format, in which the stars play the same characters in each episode—but one following the repertory model, in which the star appears in a different vehicle each week. If asked how to define *The Loretta Young Show* in 1954, I would have said: "Thirty-minute movies." That's how they struck me. And, in a sense, I think my original definition holds true: They were truncated movies.

I had not thought much about Loretta over the years until the mid-1990s when Judy Lewis, her daughter by Clark Gable, published *Uncommon Knowledge*, in which Lewis divulged the details of her birth, the result of a liaison between the unmarried Loretta and the married Gable while they were filming *The Call of the Wild* (1935). I thought I was reading a treatment for a woman's picture, with a cover-up that seemed like something out of an unwed mother movie of the 1930s—Loretta as Stella Dallas. Judy's Loretta Young was not the plucky Katie of *The Farmer's Daughter* or the saintly Sister Margaret. There was a real person, in some ways a tragic one, behind the Loretta Young who glided through the door, ready to offer another character from a repertory that seemed to defy categorization.

I knew then that I wanted to tell Loretta's story, but from a different perspective, focusing on the woman and her films. It is impossible to separate the artist from the art when it is the art that reveals the artist. The films, beginning with *Laugh, Clown, Laugh* (1928), which made a star out of a fifteen-year-old newcomer, present a gradual efflorescence of a talent that was too often mistaken for Hollywood glamour or heavenly beauty. I have chosen to interweave Loretta's films with her life in, I think, the right proportion. Since so many of her 1930s films are inaccessible except to fans of Turner Classic Movies (TCM), I have synopsized the plots for readers unfamiliar with these movies, but interested in seeing their place in her career.

I have chosen a form of documentation familiar to readers of trade books, one that uses neither parenthetical documentation nor the raised footnote/endnotes format *of The Chicago Manual of Style*. Readers interested in the source of a particular statement need only consult this book's notes section, in which the documentation appears page by page. A few words taken from a statement or quotation are followed by notation of their source.

I was privileged to meet Judy Lewis, and I hope I have done her mother justice. And for the movie lover, I trust I have done the same.

I would also like to acknowledge my gratitude to the following: Grover Crisp, vice president, Asset Management and Film Restoration, Sony Pictures; actor Douglas Dick, who appeared with Loretta in *The Accused* (1948); Craig Fuller, associate editor, Utah Historical Society; Barbara Hall, Special Collections, the Margaret Herrick Library; Mother Dolores Hart, mother abbess, Abbey of Regina Laudis; Kristine Krueger of The National Film Information Service (NFIS); the staff of Fairleigh Dickinson University's Metro Campus library, especially reference librarian Kathleen Stein-Smith, MaryAnn Sena, and Deborah Daniele; Terry Salomonson, Audio Classics Archive; veteran publicist Walter Seltzer; and biographer Donald Spoto.

I have made use of the following special collections:

The Margaret Herrick Library, Fairbanks Center for Motion Picture Study
Loretta Young Clippings File
Paramount Collection
Jane Ardmore Papers
Gladys Hall Collection
Lux Radio Theatre Collection
Hollywood Women's Press Club Records
Hal Wallis Collection
University of Southern California (USC), Cinema-Television Library
Hedda Hopper Collection
Warner Bros. Archives
MGM Collection
Constance McCormick Collection
Louella Parsons Collection
Twentieth Century-Fox Collection
Universal Collection
International Pictures Collection
The George Burns and Gracie Allen Collection
Hal Humphrey Collection

I owe a special debt to my wife, Katherine Restaino, for her assistance and encouragement; to Judy Lewis, for providing so much relevant information in *Uncommon Knowledge* about her mother's family background; and to Anthony Greco, for locating many of Loretta's difficult-to-find films of the 1930s.

Finally, I want to thank Ned Comstock, the ultimate archivist at the University of Southern California's Cinema and Television Library, who always succeeds in turning the burden of research into the joy of discovery.

Teaneck, New Jersey
August 2010

HOLLYWOOD MADONNA

CHAPTER 1

Life without Father

Loretta Young and director Frank Borzage had something in common besides *Man's Castle* (1933), the only film (and one of Loretta's best) that they made together: Both hailed from Salt Lake City, Utah. Loretta could have been born in any number of places. Her parents, Gladys Royal and John Earle Young, met in Denver, where they were married in 1907. Her sister, Polly Ann, was born there on 25 October 1908. In 1910, John Earle Young, who worked as an auditor for the Denver and Rio Grande Western Railroad, was transferred to Salt Lake City, and Gladys was required to relocate. It was not the ideal time to do so; she was pregnant again and scheduled to deliver in July. En route, Gladys went into labor in Salida, Colorado, in the heart of the Rockies; fortunately, Salida was a stop on the Denver and Rio Grande, and it was there that Elizabeth Jane Young (later known professionally as Sally Blane) was born on 11 July. Elizabeth Jane was not even in Salida long enough to have any memories of the town; once Gladys was able to travel, she and her children, now numbering two, continued on to Salt Lake City. Still, Salidans regard "Sally Blane" as one of their own.

Catholicism played a major role in Gladys's life. In 1908, a year after her marriage, Gladys, then twenty, converted to Roman Catholicism, unaware that she had married a man whose wooden leg proved no deterrent to women. Young exuded a potent masculinity that mocked the essence of seduction, which is usually slow and subtle until the moment of total surrender. In Young's case, the ritual was unimportant. Gazes locked, loins throbbed, and bodies conjoined. Gladys knew the scenario, having seen her husband in action, but she believed—at least for a time—in remaining faithful to her marriage vows, which pledged couples to remain together "for better or worse." But the worse was yet to come.

Gladys was the force that kept the family from splintering when her husband's promiscuity resulted in a cycle of separations followed by promises that were never kept. Gladys's father, Robert Royal, differed from her husband only in degree. Gladys's father was born in Tennessee; her mother, Fanny, in Missouri; and Gladys herself in Los Angeles. Even so, Gladys acquired the airs of a genteel Southern lady, even as her graciousness belied her resilience and adaptability. Robert Royal was not meant to be a father, much less a father of three daughters. After Fanny died of appendicitis, Royal abandoned his family. Gladys was then five. Loretta was four when Gladys initiated the first of several separations from John Earle Young that culminated in desertion and divorce. Loretta came from a family where husbands failed their wives and children, abandoning them when supporting them became too onerous or when other women proved more desirable than their own wives.

By the time Gladys was twenty-six, she was the mother of four. When the third child arrived, the Youngs had their own home where, on 6 January 1913, Gretchen Young was born, followed by her brother John a year later on 7 October 1914. "Gretchen" did not become "Loretta" until she was fifteen and on the brink of stardom. But to her family she was always Gretchen, whom her sisters dubbed "Gretch the Wretch" owing to her aggressiveness.

According to the studio biographies, which are often more like hagiographies, Loretta was born on Hollywood Avenue, the address an implicit harbinger of things to come. In this case, the biographies were partially correct. The Youngs did live on Hollywood Avenue, but not in 1913. According to the 1914 *Salt Lake City Directory*, they lived at 288 J. Street, within walking distance of what was then the city's commercial and business center. The houses on J Street ranged from baronial to cottage-size, the latter most likely the kind in which the Youngs lived. Theirs was a respectable neighborhood, where residents included a large number of businesspersons.

In 1915, the Youngs were at a different address: 1422 Hollywood Avenue. John was now working as a clerk for the Oregon Shortline Railroad Company. Hollywood Avenue was about four miles from the center of the city in what would now be considered the suburbs. Exactly why the Youngs moved is difficult to say, yet the move was part of a sequence of relocations: sometimes within a city, at other times to another state. Possibly the Youngs—or at least Gladys—thought Hollywood Avenue would provide a better environment for the children, since the area was still somewhat rural. The family was not at that address very long, yet it was the only one that Loretta remembered, having no recollection of J. Street. She obviously gave the Hollywood Avenue address to studio publicists, who invested it with a significance that it never really had.

Loretta rarely spoke about Salt Lake City. By the time she was four, she was living in Los Angeles with her mother and siblings. When Gladys could no longer endure her husband's infidelities, which made a mockery of their marriage vows, it was relocation time again. She and the children moved to Los Angeles, which became their permanent home.

Gladys had a reason for bringing her children to Los Angeles in 1917. Her sister, Charlene, lived there with her husband, Ernest Traxler, a production manager and minor director (e.g., *Caleb Piper's Girl* and *Go Get Em, Gerrity*, both 1919) at Famous Players-Lasky, the precursor of Paramount. To supplement their income, Charlene took in boarders, and Traxler found extra work for their three-year-old daughter. Since his sister-in-law's children were attractive, Traxler found them work, too. John, for example, was often cast as Wallace Reid's son. No sooner had Gladys and her family arrived in Los Angeles than Traxler, who had connections at other studios, managed to get the children cast as extras in Universal's *Sirens of the Sea* (1917), a retelling of the Lorelei legend with the four-year-old Loretta as a nymph. Loretta knew nothing about nymphs or the Lorelei, nor did it matter. She was exposed to the excitement of on-location shooting; besides, she was paid the munificent sum of $3.50 for doing relatively little.

In 1917, Universal released films in three, then four, categories in order of prestige: Jewels (later Super Jewels), Bluebirds, and Red Feathers. *Sirens* was a Jewel, requiring location filming, which took place on Catalina Island and the Channel Islands (now part of Channel Islands National Park) off the coast of Southern California. The Young children were only used in the Catalina exteriors. Still, it must have been thrilling for them to board the ferry to Catalina (probably from Long Beach), even if they did not understand the reason for the excursion. To them, it was a holiday; they donned funny clothes and stood in front of an odd piece of equipment that bore no resemblance to anything they had ever seen. Yet the experience left an impression on both Loretta and Elizabeth Jane, who had been exposed, however briefly, to the magic of movies.

The atmosphere, hectic but exciting, was a welcome diversion from their uneventful lives. The children would not have phrased it that way; they would have just called it "fun." But it was also fun that in a few years, show business would bring both sisters much more than $3.50. Meanwhile, Loretta was at her uncle's studio, Famous Players-Lasky, where she played the "anonymous child" in *The Primrose Ring* (1917), starring Mae Murray, who became a short-lived fairy godmother. Roles in *The Only Way* (1919), *White and Unmarried* (1921), and *The Sheik* (1921) followed.

When Loretta was seven, her aunt, also an extra at Famous Players-Lasky, rushed home and told Loretta to head over to the studio, which happened to be just across the street. A child was needed for a scene in *The Only Way*. Loretta had been making mud pies and arrived with her face splattered with mud, only to be told to come back after she washed her face. When she did, she was placed on a strange looking table and told to cry. The scene worked. *The Only Way* is a lost film, but if it ever resurfaces, Loretta can be seen as the "child on operating table."

At seven, she had no idea that the star of *The Only Way*, Fannie Ward, had been a popular actress on both the New York and London stages before making her film debut in 1915. Cecil B. DeMille, who followed the theatre scene, cast Ward against type in *The Cheat* (1915), in which she was obviously too old (forty-three) to play the young wife who loses money in the market and is forced to negotiate a loan from an ivory dealer (Sessue Hayakawa), whose terms are quite simple: She must pay with sex. When she is able to repay the loan, he retaliates by ripping her dress and branding her. The film was a hit, with Ward and Hayakawa receiving high praise for their performances. His film career lasted longer than hers, which petered out in the early 1920s, after which Ward played vaudeville.

During the filming of *The Only Way*, Ward sensed that there was something exceptional about Loretta, who did not strike her as a mere extra. But Ward was too busy promoting her own career to advance Loretta's. Now forty-seven, Ward knew her Hollywood days were drawing to a close, and she did not have any intention of living vicariously through a protégé. Besides, Ward still had her fans, who could see her on the stage, if no longer on the screen.

It was quite the opposite with Mae Murray, who was immediately attracted to the "anonymous child" in *The Primrose Ring*. Loretta personified the kind of daughter Murray envisioned for herself but could never have. Murray was now on her third husband, director Robert Z. Leonard, whom she married in 1918 and divorced seven years later. Like her previous two marriages, the one with Leonard was also childless. Murray would eventually have a son by her fourth and last husband. Meanwhile, to fill the void in her life, Murray implored Gladys to allow Loretta to live with her and Leonard and enjoy the privileges that affluence could bring. Gladys, knowing it would be "one less mouth to feed," agreed, and Loretta, with the Traxler's youngest child, Charlene, as her companion, become part of the Leonards' household.

Five-year-old Loretta had never seen such elegance: a beautifully furnished home, servants, a new wardrobe for herself, and, to cap it off, ballet lessons. But Cinderella's golden coach reverted to a pumpkin, when, according to Loretta's daughter, Judy Lewis, Murray wanted Loretta to move to the East Coast with her and her husband. Gladys refused, either because her maternal instincts prevailed or possibly because she sensed that Murray's obsession with Loretta was a sign of mental instability, as later proved to be the case. If Murray and Leonard had any real notion of leaving Los Angeles, they soon abandoned it. Murray worked steadily in Hollywood, racking up a total of thirty-one films between 1918 and her swan song in 1931. Loretta resumed her mundane life. But achieving Murray's lifestyle became Loretta's goal. Eventually, her prosperity would surpass Murray's.

Loretta's brother John had even better luck when Ida and Angus Lindley offered to take him into their home. Again, Gladys agreed, but not to a permanent arrangement. John, who was never close to his mother, resented the matriarchal household in which he lived. Once Gladys realized the extent of John's disaffection, she untied the apron strings and gave him his freedom. John was then eight. The break was permanent, and eventually John Royal Young changed his name to John Lindley.

Gladys's son was the youngest male to exit her life. She may not have realized how easy it is for a child to transfer affection from a parent to a patron who can offer a substitute for parental love along with a charmed life. But what else could Gladys do? She knew that the family's survival depended on her. In imitation of her sister, she borrowed money from a local priest and opened a boarding house of her own. Many of Gladys's boarders were actors, and their presence made Loretta increasingly aware of a world that she knew she would enter. The boarding house also served another purpose: The income it generated enabled Gladys to send her children to Catholic schools, the only kind that she would consider.

Since Gladys was particularly concerned about Loretta's education—perhaps because she sensed her daughter's star quality—Loretta was taken out of one school and enrolled in another. She stayed only for very brief periods at St. Brendan's and Sacred Heart Convent School (now Sacred Heart Academy) before Gladys discovered Ramona, in Alhambra, California, eight miles from downtown Los Angeles and founded in 1899 by the Sisters of the Holy Name of Jesus and Mary. At Ramona, Loretta endeared herself to the nuns, who found her candor refreshing. When one of them gently admonished her for her mediocre grades, Loretta replied—with an innocence reinforced by self-confidence—that she did not need good grades because she was going to be a movie star. Once Loretta did achieve star status, the studios made much of her being "convent educated."

School required Loretta to take a brief hiatus from the movies. Unlike Polly Ann, who attended high school, Loretta's formal education ended with her graduation from Ramona. There is a gap in her filmography from 1921 to 1927. Loretta must have started grade school around 1918, and even though she had bit parts in three movies (one in 1919, two in 1921), she only had to work for an hour or two. But once she left Ramona, she averaged three and four movies a year, maintaining the same revolving door schedule throughout the 1930s, as she exited one film and entered another. The pace began to decelerate in the 1940s and wound down in 1953, after which a new vista opened up for her: television.

In 1920, Gladys knew she had to do something about her marriage, now one in name only. A chastened and repentant John Earle Young briefly rejoined his family in Los Angeles. But his reformation was short-lived. He continued to cheat on Gladys, who finally realized he was incorrigible. There would be no more separations and tearful returns. Like Robert Royal, once he realized there was no hope of reconciliation John Earle Young abandoned his family,.

Gladys felt she had no other choice but to file for divorce. It was a wrenching decision for a devout Catholic. However, priests were frequent dinner guests at the Young home. Loretta's sisters recalled one such priest, Father John Ward, who advised Loretta to "acknowledge what you have and use it." Perhaps it was he or another priest—for example, the one who loaned Gladys money for the boarding house—who told Gladys that, under the circumstances (desertion, ignorance of her husband's whereabouts), a civil divorce is permissible only if followed by a Church annulment after establishing that there is no possibility of reconciliation. In Gladys's case, there was none; thus, she could remain a Catholic and even remarry. And in 1923, Gladys married one of her boarders, George Belzer.

Remarriage resulted in both a new home and another child, Georgiana, born in 1924. By 1936, Belzer realized he was not the head of his family. His entrepreneurial wife had taken up interior decorating; his stepdaughter Elizabeth Jane, now known as Sally Blane, while not a star, was a recognizable name; and Loretta was a major star at Twentieth Century-Fox. Raised to think of the husband as provider and the wife as "help mate," Belzer knew that, as a lowly accountant, he could not compete with women whose jobs were more lucrative than his own. By 1936, his marriage was over. And Gladys, now pushing fifty, knew her marrying days were over. She had her career, and Loretta and Sally had theirs. More importantly, Gladys had her faith.

Gladys was never meant to be a wife, only a mother. She may not have known what a feminist was, but in her own way she was one. She transformed herself from a lothario's wife into an interior decorator with an eye for color and detail that won her clients. Even Loretta profited from her mother's expertise when she wanted the right set for her iconic entrance on her television show. Gladys would have been an ideal wife for a man who could bask in the reflected glory of his wife's success without feeling any diminution of his manhood. But in the early years of the twentieth century, such males were rare. And, as far as Gladys was concerned, they were not missed. Loretta, too, was meant for motherhood, not marriage. If her first husband, Grant Withers, dubbed her "the steel butterfly," he did so because she was not destined for anyone's net. Steel is an alloy, hard and durable. And so was Loretta Young.

CHAPTER 2

The Creation of Loretta Young

In Hollywood, both past and present (but more commonly past), myth and fact have mingled indiscriminately. Myth is elevated to the level of truth, while facts are given a mythic makeover, so that what was drab and ordinary acquires a glossy overlay, like lacquered wood.

But there are facts that are verifiable. Norma Jean Baker did not become Marilyn Monroe in the same way Esther Blodgett (Janet Gaynor) become Vicki Lester in *A Star is Born* (1937) by picking up her paycheck and discovering that she had been renamed. Although Marilyn has inspired an ever-burgeoning mythology, there was nothing mythic about her name change. Ben Lyons, Fox's casting director, was obsessed with the Broadway star, Marilyn Miller. He believed Norma Jean was a "Marilyn." But what about the last name? Alliterative names, or names with liquid consonants (l, m, n, r), always had cachet. When Norma Jean mentioned that Monroe was her grandfather's surname, Norma Jean Baker became Marilyn Monroe. How Gretchen Young became Loretta Young is another matter: There is the received version, which seems plausible, and the alternative one, which is less so.

The received version: In her autobiography, Colleen Moore recalled the time she was making *Her Wild Oat* (1927) at First National. Among the extras, was "the most beautiful little girl I had ever seen." "Little" was not the right word: Loretta was then fourteen. Like Mae Murray, Moore was enchanted by Loretta who, even as a teenager, had the look of a fairy child. Moore arranged for a screen test and was elated with the results. So was First National, but the studio was not happy with Loretta's teeth, which were too obtrusive. Braces were recommended, to be followed by dental work. But Loretta remained a bit toothy until the early thirties, when her perfectionism—perhaps enhanced by creative dentistry—completed what nature had left unfinished.

Moore, not incidentally, also took credit for the name change: "I named her after the most beautiful doll I had ever had: Loretta." Loretta, who appeared in two films that starred Moore, was unbilled in both. The second was *Naughty but Nice*, released in June 1927, six months before *Her Wild Oat*, which premiered at the end of the year. In all likelihood, the former film made Moore aware of Loretta.

Moore may not have known that shortly after Loretta's one-day stint in *Naughty but Nice*, she was at Paramount playing a supporting role in *The Magnificent Flirt*, filmed between March 6 and March 27, 1928, but released in June of that year. Loretta's days as an extra had ended, as her Paramount salary showed: She received $633 for three weeks of work. Now billed under the name that Moore had given her, Loretta played Denise Laverne, the daughter of the glamorous Florence Laverne (Florence Vidor), a widow whose flirtatiousness sets the plot in motion: the mother is wooed by a bachelor, the daughter by his nephew. As in a typical boudoir comedy, true love travels a rocky road: The bachelor jumps to the conclusion that Florence is a cocotte when he sees her embracing his nephew, little knowing that she is expressing her happiness about the younger man's engagement to her daughter. But soon the ground levels off, and the two couples embark on a smooth journey into a world where marriages are made not in heaven, but on Mount Olympus.

Moore may have renamed her, but after *The Magnificent Flirt*, Loretta was no longer anyone's protégée. Indeed, she even surpassed her patron. Although Moore proved she was a serious actress in such films as *So Big* (1925), *Lilac Time* (1928) and finally *The Power and the Glory* (1933), the public and critics preferred Colleen Moore, the embodiment of the 1920s flapper, who was wholesomely sexy, but neither as voluptuous nor as brash as Clara Bow. Loretta even became more versatile than Moore, taking on roles seemingly unrelated to her persona and proving that a star's screen image is a composite of many faces, each of which can be superimposed on a character. The script determined the face, and Loretta's portrait gallery continued to grow.

The alternative version of Gretchen Young's metamorphosis is suspect, even though it comes from one of Hollywood's premier directors. In his autobiography, Mervyn LeRoy (*Little Caesar*, *I Am a Fugitive from a Chain Gang*, *Waterloo Bridge*, etc.), recalled the time he phoned the Young home, inquiring about the availability of Sally Blane for his film, *Too Young to Marry* (1931). Sally, Gladys informed him, was working in another film; however, Gladys had a daughter who was available and more attractive than Sally. Even then Gladys knew which of her daughters would achieve stardom. LeRoy was an outstanding director, who launched the Warner Bros. gangster cycle with *Little Caesar* (1930). His memory is another matter. LeRoy wrote that when he took one look at the teenager in his office, he knew automatically that she was no Gretchen: "And so Loretta Young was born that day in my office. She was my first discovery."

Here the story bifurcates. According to Loretta's daughter, LeRoy did call the Young residence, asking to speak not to Sally Blane, but to Polly Ann Young. However, Loretta was the one who answered the phone, claiming that her sister was on location, and then asking demurely, "Will I do?" "He must have been very surprised when a fourteen-year-old arrived in his office, but he hired her anyway, as an extra in a movie starring Colleen Moore." The phone call is not the issue; one could easily imagine Gladys promoting Loretta or Loretta promoting herself. But which sister did LeRoy want, and for what film? Polly Ann had a paucity of credits; she was unbilled in all but two of the seven films she made between 1929 and 1931. By contrast, Sally had appeared in 63 films between 1917 and 1930. LeRoy must have phoned about Sally, who would have been unavailable, going from picture to picture and ending up with sixteen credits in 1931 alone. But Loretta as an extra in a Colleen Moore film directed by Mervyn LeRoy? Loretta appeared in two 1927 Colleen Moore movies, neither of which was directed by LeRoy. The only film LeRoy made with Moore was *Oh, Kay!* (1927), in which none of the Young sisters appeared. LeRoy wrote that the film he phoned about was *Too Young to Marry* (1931), based on *Broken Dishes*, the play that brought Bette Davis to Hollywood. The movie version starred Loretta and Grant Withers. In 1931, neither Loretta nor Sally was working as an extra; for *Marry*, Loretta received $2,750; Withers, $1,650. When it was released in May 1931, Loretta had been going by her new name for three years. Furthermore, Loretta and Withers met when they were cast in *Second Floor Mystery*, released in April 1930 and directed by Roy Del Ruth. (Loretta fell madly in love with Withers, and the couple eloped in January 1930, divorcing the following year.)

Who called whom, when, and about what film? If it was *Too Young to Marry*, the phone call would have been made in fall 1930, with LeRoy inquiring about Sally Blane, not Polly Ann Young. If it was *Naughty but Nice*, the call would have been made in early 1927, and the caller was most likely the director, Millard Webb, or his designee. Assuming there was such a call (and it's hard to imagine anyone calling about an extra), Loretta, then fourteen, would have answered the phone in the same way, purring, "Will I do?" in a voice bound to get her an interview. And if the call were intended for Sally, the film would not have mattered. Loretta came first.

The sisters were fiercely competitive. Loretta had just started at First National when she discovered that Sally was making $65 a week at Paramount. Loretta immediately demanded the same—and got it. Of the two, Loretta was Gladys's favorite. When Loretta received her weekly check, she immediately handed it over to her mother; Sally, on the other hand, only gave Gladys two-thirds of hers. When Sally's son was mauled by a dog, the damage to one of his eyes was so severe that doctors thought he might lose it. Instead of comforting her distraught sister, Loretta shrugged: "If he loses it, he loses it. That's up to God." Loretta and Sally appeared together in *The Show of Shows* (1929), a tedious musical revue designed to showcase First National's talent roster, which included Louise Fazenda, Bea Lillie, Lupe Velez, John Barrymore, and Myrna Loy. Chester Morris introduced a number called "Sister Acts" that featured, among others, Loretta and Sally in a Parisian setting, cavorting as mademoiselles and performing as if they were seasoned professionals. Each sister vied for the spotlight, which played no favorites; theirs was, after all, a "sister act."

Even as a teenager, Loretta understood the importance of self-promotion. She was not so much interested in being an actress as being a star, yet she became both. Stars have their own code of ethics: survival at any cost, even at the expense of a sibling. "It's not personal, just business," Loretta might have reasoned. Besides, it was God's will. Blane did not fare badly. She worked steadily throughout the 1930s. With the advent of television, she easily adjusted to her sister's new medium, appearing in a few episodes of *The Loretta Young Show*, in addition to other series that gave her a new life, even if it was on the tube.

Exactly when audiences became aware of a newcomer named Loretta Young depends on when they saw First National's *The Whip Woman*, *The Head Man*, and *Scarlet Seas*; or MGM's *Laugh, Clown, Laugh*; or Paramount's *The Magnificent Flirt*. All of the films were released within a few months of each other in 1928: *Woman* in January, *Clown* in April, *Flirt* in June, and *Head Man* in July. *Scarlet Seas* opened in New York on 31 December and went into wide release the following year. "Loretta Young" was becoming increasingly familiar. In *The Whip Woman*, she was merely billed as "the Girl"—but at least she had a credit. In the others, she played a character: Denise Laverne in *Flirt*, Carol Watts in *Head Man*, and Simonetta in *Clown*.

Of the five, *Clown* was the most important, if for no other reason than its star, Lon Chaney. Although First National's *The Whip Woman* was directed by the indefatigable Allan Dwan, it was virtually ignored. Loretta was cast in it because First National was also Colleen Moore's home studio and the logical one for Loretta. In *Head Man*, Loretta appeared as the daughter of a senator (comic actor Charles Murray) whose bid for the mayoralty is almost sabotaged by the local political machine. The *New York Times* (28 May 1928) reported that in *The Magnificent Flirt*, Loretta responded "nicely" to the "imaginative direction" of H. d'Abbadie d'Arrast. The *Times* (31 December) also observed that as the sea captain's daughter in *Scarlet Seas*, Loretta "spreads pathos," an emotion that came naturally to her.

Although Simonetta in MGM's *Laugh, Clown, Laugh* was Loretta's biggest role to date, the *New York Times*'s formidable film critic, Mordaunt Hall, wrote that "her talent as an actress is not called for to any great extent in this picture." That Loretta even made a film at MGM, the "Tiffany of Studios," with "More Stars Than There Are In the Heavens" emblazoned on the stationery, had to do with the script. *Laugh, Clown, Laugh* required a teenager (Loretta was going on fifteen) to play opposite Chaney. The director, Irish-born Herbert Brenon, may have seen Loretta in *The Whip Woman* and believed she could handle the role; perhaps Moore even used her connections to get Loretta the part. What mattered was credibility. Since *Clown* was one of MGM's last silent films, it required the kind of expressive acting that exponents of the art such as Lillian Gish, John Gilbert, Chaplin, and, of course, Lon Chaney, had perfected.

Although Loretta was a natural actress, the silents were never her forte. Perhaps if she had been given major roles earlier, she might have mastered—and probably would have, given her fierce determination—the art of using her body as her medium of dramatic expression. For Loretta, stardom coincided with the coming of sound. In the beginning, hers was a singsong voice, no different from that of most adolescents who confuse rhythm with accentuation. Loretta may well have had a vocal coach, but more likely, her obsession with perfection drove her to develop a voice that was hailed as a paradigm once it took on the measured cadences of maturity. In the mid 1950s, she was honored for three consecutive years by The American Institute of Voice Teachers for possessing "the finest feminine speaking voice " in television.

MGM envisioned *Laugh, Clown, Laugh* as the successor to *He Who Gets Slapped* (1924), which had a similar circus theme and trio of characters: a clown (Lon Chaney), a bareback rider (Norma Shearer), and a lecherous baron (John Gilbert). Their replacements were a clown (Chaney), a tightrope walker (Loretta), and an amorous but basically decent count (Nils Asther). Like *He Who Gets Slapped*, which was based on a play by Leonid Andreyev, *Clown* was a stage adaptation, inspired by the David Belasco–Tom Cushing drama that starred Lionel Barrymore. MGM purchased the rights shortly after the play opened on 28 November 1923, but preferred to see how *He Who Gets Slapped* fared. When it proved a critical and financial success, *Laugh, Clown, Laugh* went into production.

The film begins with a close-up of a drum inscribed with the name of a company of traveling players: *Ridi, Pagliacci*. The name was inspired by the climax of the great tenor aria, "Vesti la giubba," from Leoncavallo's *Pagliacci*, in which Canio, the head of a similar troupe, prepares for a commedia dell' arte sketch in which his character, Pagliaccio, discovers that he has been cuckolded by his wife, Columbine, who has taken Harlequin as a lover. In Canio's case, art has mocked life: Canio discovers that his wife Nedda is having an affair with Silvio. In the opera, the convergence of life and art brings the performance to a halt, as the crazed Canio stabs Nedda, and then Silvio. The film also ends tragically, but without any murders. Tito (Chaney), the company's head, comes upon an abandoned baby girl, whom he names Simonetta (Loretta) and trains to be a tightrope walker. When Tito discovers that the count is in love with Simonetta, he refuses to stand in their way, even though Simonetta swears that she really loves Tito. In fact, what she feels is a combination of indebtedness and sympathy for a man who can bring happiness to others but not to himself. Tito yields to his death wish. While rehearsing in an empty theater, he imagines he is performing before an audience. He launches into his slide act, scrambling up to a box and onto a wire anchored to the stage. In the past, Tito would coast down the wire as if it were a chute; this time, he crash lands. Chaney plays the scene as if Tito has willed his own death. The closing title is the final line of the opera: "The comedy is ended," a literal translation of *"La commedia è finita."* Fearing that the tragic ending might alienate audiences, MGM shot an alternative in which Tito does not die. It would have been the equivalent of a *Pagliacci* in which Nedda dumps Silvio and returns to Canio. Fortunately, the studio went ahead with the original ending, and audiences concurred. It was a coup for Loretta to receive second billing. But no newcomer could compete with Chaney, who used his body as if it were clay for sculpting and he the sculptor.

The shoot was Loretta's trial by fire. Brenon found her exasperating. Loretta had not yet learned the difference between performing and acting. *The Magnificent Flirt* made no demands on her; she only had to play an ingénue. Loretta had never been thrown into a part where genuine emotion was required. Brenon berated her before the entire company calling her "stupid and useless." Reportedly, he even threw a chair at her. Chaney intervened, and from then on Brenon treated Loretta respectfully. Throughout the shoot, Chaney was as compassionate toward Loretta on the set as Tito was to Simonetta. Nils Asther was similarly helpful. When Loretta was having difficulty expressing her attraction to the count, Asther told her to imagine him as something she truly desired, like a hot fudge sundae. The scene worked. Asther taught Loretta the essence of acting: truth transformed by the imagination into a special form of reality that audiences will accept as the equivalent of life as they know it. If yearning for a sundae can translate into longing, so be it—the audience will see only longing. Tragically, Simonetta's longing was not for Tito, as Chaney acknowledges with one of his many faces.

Loretta's stay at MGM was brief, perhaps because of Brenon's low opinion of her acting, but more likely because the studio was not yet interested in targeting the teenage market. That changed in the thirties when Mickey Rooney, Judy Garland, Freddie Bartholomew, Virginia Weidler, and others became contract players. But by that time, Loretta would have been in her twenties and far too advanced for kid stuff.

Colleen Moore knew the right studio for Loretta: It was her own, First National, where Loretta made six films in 1929 alone. First National, then Associated First National, was founded as a consortium of exhibitors, with production facilities at Burbank, California—an enviable piece of property that did not escape the attention of Warner Bros., particularly after First National's theater chain became the country's largest. Warner's gained control of First National in 1928, moved into the Burbank facility, and released its feature films under the First National banner until the mid 1930s; by then, moviegoers knew the difference between the studio and the label, the latter being no longer necessary. What mattered was appearance of the logo with the WB heraldic design, introduced by a musical fanfare.

Logos meant nothing to Loretta, who may not have been aware that she was being exploited. At sixteen, she was subsisting on a diet of milk shakes to maintain her slender figure. Determined not to gain weight, she took up smoking—a habit that she did not break until well after her career was over. Her day was supposed to end at 5:30 p.m., when she would be driven home. But she would merely go through the front door, exit from the back, and step into another car that would bring her back to the studio, where she would resume filming—often until 3:30 a.m. Inevitably, she had a nervous collapse and was briefly hospitalized, but that eventuality did not deter her; in fact, it spurred her on. Aware of the health problems that could sidetrack a career, she paced herself accordingly. Her salary kept up with the pace: In 1933, Loretta was able to buy a white brick colonial, with hollyhocks and lemon verbena, in Westwood Hills. The home had a curving staircase, ideal for a dramatic descent accompanied by a rustle of taffeta. But Gladys, the interior decorator, envisioned something else, something on the traditional side—perhaps the kind that she yearned for when she married John Earle Young, with four-poster beds, old china, and porcelain. Loretta brought in the money, and Gladys took care of the rest.

CHAPTER 3

LORETTA TALKS!

In 1928, Loretta had only a vague awareness of Joseph P. Kennedy. She might have heard rumors about his relationship with Gloria Swanson (confirmed) or that he was a bootlegger (unproven), but it is hard to imagine that she knew he was the husband of Rose Kennedy, whose father was the colorful and, to some, notorious—Boston mayor, John Fitzgerald, better known as "Honey" Fitz. For Loretta, all that mattered was that she was a contract player at a real studio. What she did not know was that she remained on the studio roster because of Joseph P. Kennedy.

Although remembered primarily as the father of President John F. Kennedy and Senator Robert Kennedy (both assassinated—John in 1963, Robert in 1968), in the post–World War I era Joseph P. Kennedy was a major player in the growing movie business. Always eager to corner the newest market, he set his sights on movies in 1919, when he decided to feature a comic he liked, Fred Stone, in movies that would be distributed through Robertson-Cole (R-C), where he was a board member. But that wasn't enough; his goal was to own a studio, and then to own several studios that he would merge into a conglomerate. Kennedy was thinking of conglomerization long before Hollywood started going corporate in the 1960s.

He began by distributing Universal's films in New England and then "created his own Motion Picture Finance Corporation, a broad umbrella organization to funnel his buying, selling, and producing." When R-C's distribution unit became known as the Film Booking Office (FBO), Kennedy took that over, too. Next, production—and a theater circuit.

FBO's talent roster was hardly first tier, but that didn't matter. The company specialized in B films, the kind that played in theaters throughout side-street America, not in movie palaces. But with the movie craze, star quality was not the important factor; product was all. At best, FBO could offer the public cowboy star Fred Thompson and football player Harold "Red" Grange—and later, the better known Evelyn Brent, Viola Davis, and Bob Steele, the western hero and occasional villain (*The Big Sleep* [1946], which may be the film for which Steele is best remembered). Even in black and white, Steele's eyes photographed as cool grey, capable of alternating between determination and menace.

In 1925 the vaudeville circuit, Keith-Albee-Orpheum (K-A-O), merged with FBO. But that was still not enough. First National had a major theater chain and a roster of popular stars, including Mary Astor, Richard Barthelmess, Colleen Moore, Corinne Griffith, and the German shepherd, Rin-Tin-Tin. Touted as a movie czar, Kennedy dreamed big, imagining a mega conglomerate consisting of Pathé, K-A-O, FBO, and First National. Once Kennedy took control of First National in 1928, he reduced the number of actors by half, from 34 to 17, keeping, among others, Colleen Moore and Loretta.

Why keep Loretta, but not, for example, Mary Astor? Kennedy chose Loretta either because of Moore, whom he had met earlier (and who, no doubt, interceded for her discovery), or because he had seen *Laugh, Clown, Laugh* and was taken with Loretta's beauty, believing that she had the potential for stardom. Certainly he did not choose Loretta because he was attracted to her. Kennedy knew enough not to rob the cradle. Besides, he had Gloria.

Kennedy's draconian cost-cutting and autocratic behavior alarmed some board members, who insisted that an executive committee be formed, making Kennedy accountable. Kennedy threatened to pull out unless he was given complete control. The board did not budge, and Kennedy's reign ended the same year it began, 1928, when Warner Bros. bought First National, acquiring a seventy-acre property in Burbank and a theater circuit. That same year, David Sarnoff, president of the Radio Corporation of America (RCA), which owned the NBC network, began thinking of a way to combine radio, sound film, and live entertainment. His acquisition of FBO and K-A-O—which he found especially attractive because of its theaters—resulted in the formation of RKO Radio Pictures. RKO never acquired its own signature, but was known only for the directors who passed through it, such as Orson Welles (*Citizen Kane, The Magnificent Ambersons*), Merrian C. Cooper (*King Kong*), George Cukor (*Morning Glory*), Howard Hawks (*Bringing Up Baby*), and John Ford (*Mary of Scotland*). Sarnoff's dream of a movie-stage show combination was realized with the opening of Radio City Music Hall right across the street from the RCA building, where NBC was based. When Radio City officially opened in 1932, movies were not part of the bill. That changed in January 1933, when the Music Hall, beloved by generations of moviegoers, and especially tourists, began offering a first run feature and an elaborate stage show—a policy that continued for forty-five years. Despite its name, Radio City Music Hall was not the exclusive home of RKO films, although a great many did open there. Actually, the first film to be shown was *The Bitter Tea of General Yen*, a Columbia release directed by Frank Capra.

Joseph Kennedy was not the visionary Sarnoff was; to Kennedy, the movies were just another investment, another conquest, another acquisition. He lacked the passion that the great studio heads and independent producers—Louis Mayer, Darryl Zanuck, Harry Cohn, Jack Warner, Sam Goldwyn, Hal Wallis—had for moviemaking. Although the moguls were as ruthlessly capitalistic as Kennedy, their love for the business, which required them to present the best (or more often, the second- or third-best) films their studios could make, while at the same time profiting from the revenues they generated. For Kennedy, the movies were just an interlude between business ventures. Thus, Joseph P. Kennedy does not figure prominently in the history of film.

Loretta was probably unaware of Kennedy's departure from First National. What mattered was that *she* was there—and at the studio where Sam Warner, the least heralded of the brothers Warner, realized the potential of the sound film. Sam was the Warner who convinced his brothers to adopt the Vitaphone sound-on-disk system, in which recorded sound was synchronized with celluloid image to produce a "talking picture." The technology, though primitive by contemporary standards, was nonetheless revolutionary. And Loretta was part of the revolution: Her voice was first heard in a film made by the studio that gave birth to the talkies.

When Greta Garbo made her first sound film, *Anna Christie* (1930), the ads proclaimed, "Garbo Talks!" And when she did, it was in a voice that was achingly slow, rising out of the caverns of consciousness—sometimes registering as dreamy, but revealing the soul of a romantic for whom life was a wearisome journey unless it ended in love. But this love was a special kind of love: movie love, delicately photographed and orchestrated, so that the physical is elevated to the spiritual, bodies transformed into souls, and rumpled sheets replaced by a carefully made-up bed.

The press did not react the same way to Loretta's first talkie. At the beginning, there was nothing distinctive about her voice. In *The Squall*

(1929), she spoke like a typical teenager, whose idea of cadence was accenting the right syllables. To look rustic, she was given a wig with braids, which she tugged self-consciously. The director, Alexander Korda, who went on to make far better films (*The Private Life of Henry VIII, Rembrandt, That Hamilton Woman*), left Loretta on her own, concentrating almost exclusively on Myrna Loy, who, although she had lesser billing, not only dominated her scenes but also created a character—which was more than the other actors did.

Based on a play by Jean Bart, for which First National paid $25,500, *The Squall* is set on a Hungarian farm, with most of the actors, including Loretta (but not Loy) sounding like recruits from Central Casting. Loy played Nubi, a Gypsy who ensnares the males of the household, starting with the servant and moving on to the son and finally the father. Moviegoers who knew Loy only from the *Thin Man* series and *The Best Years of Our Lives* might assume she was cast against type. But anyone familiar with her earlier work (e.g., *The Black Watch, The Great Divide, Isle of Escape*) knew that she could play the vamp and project a sensuousness so earthy it was primeval. Stunningly photographed and front lit, her face glowing in close-up, Nubi was a child of nature, as amoral as Bizet's Carmen. Her philosophy is simple: "What can you do when man love you?" The males in the household behave much like animals in heat, looking for any opportunity to steal a kiss or an embrace, as if her provocative dress concealed a fleshy paradise, and her unwashed hair, stringy and oily, gave off an irresistible scent. When Nubi admits to being fifteen, you can believe it, even though at the time Loy was twenty-three. But her untamed hair, serpentine movements, and incantatory delivery of a gypsy song that the males start humming, suggest a teenage Circe. The males don't turn into swine, but they come close to the human equivalent.

By contrast, Loretta was sixteen, and she both looked and sounded her age. Her voice was doughy and expressionless. Some of her line readings were embarrassingly bad ("Oh, grandfather, how can you say that?"), delivered as if she had been over-rehearsed for a high school play. The problem with the portrayal was threefold, owing to the role itself, Korda's fascination with the only character that interested him, and Loretta's inexperience. But Loretta's voice would mature, and her roles would improve.

Within a year, a new Loretta had emerged from the cocoon of pubescence. *Loose Ankles* (1930) opened with a shot of a shapely leg adorned with an anklet. (The title derived from a 1930s song that paid tribute to the "dancing, prancing feet" of dance aficionados.) The leg belongs to Ann (Loretta), and from the way it is being lovingly massaged, it is evident that Ann is one of the idle rich who, in 1930, could afford such pampering. She is also an heiress, who can only come into her legacy if she is free from scandal and finds a respectable husband. Instead, she places a want ad for an "unscrupulous man." A very callow Douglas Fairbanks, Jr. responds, and the rest is plot.

The star was Fairbanks, who received $5,666 in contrast to Loretta's $1,125, which was still, big bucks for a seventeen-year-old in 1930. Loretta's career was burgeoning at First National. *The Road to Paradise* (1930) may have been an inconsequential film, but it revealed Loretta's increasing versatility. She played a dual role: Mary and Margaret. Mary is an orphan (circumstances unexplained) raised by two con men, (Jack Mulhall and Rondo Hatton) who, after discovering that she is a dead ringer for Margaret, a wealthy socialite, recruit her in a plot to burglarize Margaret's town house. The burglary is interrupted by Margaret's arrival. When Margaret is shot (not fatally), Mary risks imprisonment and ministers to her look-alike, who is really her long lost twin, endowed with the same psychic powers (Each twin has a medallion enabling her to read minds). Although *The Road to Paradise* merits, at best, a footnote in Loretta's body of work, her ability to play, even at nineteen, two types of women, embodying the extremes of innocence and experience, attests to growing mastery of her craft. She now knew how to establish a character, react for a close up so that the shot did not look as if it had been edited into the film, and interact with other actors, as if she were not just one of the cast but one of the characters.

Myrna Loy gave Loretta some competition in *The Truth About Youth* (1930). Loretta may have had star billing, but it was Loy who again walked off with the film. Loy was billed fourth as Kara, an exotic dancer who catches the fancy of an orphan, whose guardian (Conway Tearle) is disturbed that his ward, nicknamed "The Imp" (David Manners), is behaving too impishly for a responsible adult. Although engaged to Loretta's character, he is so smitten with Kara that he marries her. Learning that The Imp is not a millionaire, Kara dumps him. To prevent scandal, the guardian convinces everyone that he was Kara's lover. The real revelation—which would have evoked howls if Loretta had not played the final scene with such touching conviction—is her admission that her true love is not the ward, but his guardian. Cuddling up to the fifty-two-year-old Tearle, Loretta further demonstrated her talent for turning dross into silk. She even convinced cynical reviewers that a May-December (or at least May-September) romance was possible. And, to top it all off, she received $4500 for her efforts—$2250 more than Manners.

Of all Loretta's 1930 films, the Samuel Goldwyn production *The Devil to Pay*, was her least impressive. Goldwyn, who had great respect for writers, particularly playwrights, happened to be in London, where he was introduced to Frederick Lonsdale, one of the foremost practitioners of drawing room comedy—the kind that was sophisticated and humane, but not acerbic. Unable to offer Goldwyn a play, Lonsdale provided him with a story that seemed perfect for Ronald Colman, whom Goldwyn had under contract. Dissatisfied with the way filming was proceeding under Irving Cummings's direction. Goldwyn replaced him with George Fitzmaurice; Goldwyn did the same with the female lead, who was another Cummings, Constance. Constance Cummings was a fine actress who, although American born, resided in England. To Goldwyn, however, she did not sound British enough. Loretta inherited the role but could not master the accent. Goldwyn may have assumed, on the basis of her films, that Loretta was the ideal ingénue. She was that, but not as the fiancée of a grand duke. Despite the diction lessons Goldwyn ordered, Loretta was out of her element, although she was thrilled to be working with Colman, the fantasy lover of her girlhood. Rakishly handsome, he moved with masculine grace, wore suits like a second skin, and spoke in a voice that was soothingly urbane. He played William Leeland, the playboy son of a wealthy father, who falls in love with Dorothy Hope (Loretta), the daughter of another wealthy father. Once Dorothy encounters Leeland, the grand duke is only a memory. Complications arise with the appearance of Leeland's ex-lover (Myrna Loy in a minor role). Since this is a Frederick Lonsdale story, the right couples pair off at the end. All that is lacking is a summary curtain line, Lonsdale's specialty. But then, the playwright only supplied the plot, not the script.

Elegantly gowned, Loretta acted with an effervescence that at times threatened to bubble over. But what really detracted from her performance was her smile: She seemed to be smiling with her teeth. Part of the problem was lipstick that extended her lips, instead of just coloring them. Loretta was not meant for elongated lips. In time, she learned to apply lipstick—or insist that it be applied—more subtly and to smile more naturally. But any teenager who goes from film to film (Loretta had seven films in release in 1929, eight in 1930) is bound to encounter a road block, sending her on a detour until she could get back on the main road in a more suitable vehicle. *The Devil to Pay* was her detour. Goldwyn disliked it. But even though the film was not a success, Loretta emerged unscathed. Who would quibble about the performance of a seventeen-year-old with the face of an angel and the form of a wood nymph?

Beau Ideal (RKO, 1931) fared better as *Beau Geste* (Paramount 1939). Loretta was only in the film because she was on loan to RKO. At eighteen, she was unable to express the emotional state of a young woman whose lover is imprisoned in a North African cistern where inmates either die or slit their wrists—details that she (but not the audience) is spared. Her inability to connect with the character is the result of the male-centered script, which details the deliriously implausible story of a man who enlists in the French Foreign Legion to rescue his boyhood friend. The plot is so tightly knotted that the unraveling requires an even greater suspension of disbelief than the entwining. The rescue mission is accomplished, thanks to an Arab woman determined to leave the desert and move on to Paris! Loretta is wasted as the object of both men's affections. She tended to resort to silent screen acting whenever she was saddled with a part to which she could not relate: face averted to suggest reluctance, hand against brow to indicate grief/dismay/despair, and a voice so hysterical that the dialogue was inaudible, perhaps because it was not worth hearing. The problem may also have been her director, Herbert Brenon; this was the second, and last, time she would be working with the chair-thrower. Brenon started in the silents in 1912, winning an Oscar nomination for *Laugh, Clown, Laugh*. He was less successful in the sound era, and although he lived until 1958, his film career ended in 1940. He may well have coached Loretta in the only brand of emotional expression that he understood. Fortunately, Loretta only had a few scenes in *Beau Ideal*, which was not her finest hour—or anyone else's.

No one who makes eight movies in one year, as Loretta did in 1931, can expect an octet of winners. The nadir was the provocatively titled *I Like Your Nerve*, intended as a showcase for Douglas Fairbanks, Jr. Fairbanks's name appears above the title, with Loretta's heading the supporting cast as the stepdaughter of the finance minister of an unnamed Latin American country who attracts the fancy of an American playboy (Fairbanks). His attempts to liberate her from an arranged marriage strain credibility to the breaking point, as the narrative keeps sagging like a rotting tennis net until it collapses in tatters. Except for the playboy's blazer, white pants, and sexy smile, it is hard to know what Loretta's character saw in him. Orry-Kelly, who usually knew how to dress Loretta, designed a wardrobe that may have been chic, but which was more suited to a runway model than a convent-educated virgin, who should have been dressed demurely in a plain skirt and high-necked white blouse set off by a cross. Instead, Loretta looked like a budding fashionista. Even her makeup was ill conceived. If the film were in color, her lips would have photographed as lush red. Her eyes were dramatically lined and her lids visibly shadowed, her hair looking more sprayed than combed. As a contract player, Loretta had no choice but to take the role. After all, that was her job.

"Whoever breaks the Divine Law forfeits the right of way," warns the opening title of *The Right of Way* (1931). The film proves its thesis indirectly. Charles "Beauty" Steele (Conrad Nagel, sounding as effete as Clifton Webb in his heyday),is a cocky lawyer who prides himself on being a showman in the courts. Steele is mired in a loveless marriage and saddled with a debt- ridden brother-in-law, who has stolen money from a trust fund. Attempting to regain the money, Steele is attacked by thugs and tossed into the river, from which he is rescued by a man he has successfully defended. Now an amnesiac, Steele is nursed by a postmistress (Loretta). The inevitable happens: They fall in love, his memory returns—and Steele ends up getting shot by his brother-in-law, who in those pre-code days, when social and sexual mores were loosely enforced, gets away with it. Nagel has a great death scene, envisioning the angel of death dressed in white, whom he asks: "Have we been properly introduced?" Eyes close, hand goes limp, Loretta tears up. Fade Out.

The Right of Way jacks the Enoch Arden story up a notch, asking what might have happened if Enoch had developed amnesia, found his perfect mate, and been murdered. The film is quite the opposite of Tennyson's poem, in which Enoch's wife, Annie Lee, believing him dead, remarries. Upon his return, Enoch takes a last look through the window of her new home, disappears into the night, then tells his tragic story to a tavern owner's widow, and subsequently dies. Nagel overacted at times. Loretta, to her credit, seemed to believe in the script's creaky contrivances. She was effective, even convincing, although the film was not.

CHAPTER 4

Sacrificial Wives, Shop Girls, and Proud Proletarians

Ever since 1906, when the first nickelodeons made their appearance, exhibitors had looked for ways to lure women to their theaters. Initially, these were converted storefronts, which were stuffy and often uncomfortable—particularly those in working class and immigrant neighborhoods. In time, the nickelodeons improved and looked more like typical movie theaters, but they were never on the order of the movie palaces. While the theaters had no problem attracting children, who at least in 1907 comprised a third of the audience, women tended to avoid them, particularly because they seemed disreputable. Once exhibitors realized that female patronage could give their theaters respectability, they wooed these patrons outrageously: A Boston nickelodeon began "offering free admission . . . to women for prenoon shows." Other exhibitors offered women and children half-price admission, a policy that soon became widespread. Throughout the 1930s and 1940s, "dish night" was common in neighborhood theaters; included in the price of admission was a piece of dinnerware—a plate, a cup, a saucer, a gravy boat, a dessert dish. Today, these pieces are antiques, labeled "Depression dishware" and priced accordingly.

With the appearance in 1912 of *Photoplay*, the most popular of the fan magazines, women could enter the magical world of Hollywood. They could read about the stars' favorite recipes, beauty creams, complexion soaps, shampoos, face powders, and lipsticks. They could see pictures of their palatial homes and of the stars themselves dressed informally. Twenty-five cents could get a fan a copy of the February 1939 *Photoplay* with a picture of Claudette Colbert on the cover. Inside, there was something for everyone, including stories about the plight of young women trying to succeed in the movie business, typified by Myrna Loy's tough climb to the top. The issue was well worth a quarter: There was the latest gossip; a preview of spring fashions; candid shots of the stars at a rodeo, playing golf and tennis, and doing calisthenics. Naifs might have assumed that movie people were just plain folks at heart. Others knew better, but that did not stop them from plunking down their quarter.

As the number of female patrons increased, the industry gave them their own genre, the woman's picture—sometimes termed the "three-hankie movie" or "weepie," because they feature women suffering nobly at the hands of nature (consumption in *Camille*, a malignant brain tumor in *Dark Victory*), men (*Rain*, *Autumn Leaves*, in which Cliff Robertson threw a typewriter at a crouching Joan Crawford), a parent (*Now, Voyager*), or a teacher (*The Seventh Veil*). Eventually, a gallery of female character types emerged, and they were not just limited to the woman's picture but transferred easily to other genres. These character types included the virgin (Lillian Gish, Mary Pickford, Doris Day) and the whore (euphemistically called the "hostess," like Bette Davis in *Marked Woman* and Donna Reed in *From Here to Eternity*). But even "the whore" was not a monolithic category: Sometimes she went from sinner to saint and back again (Joan Crawford in *Rain*); sometimes from saint to sinner (Vivien Leigh in *Waterloo Bridge*). There was also the "tart," a cute and perky hooker (Shirley MacLaine in *Irma La Douce*); the high maintenance call girl (Elizabeth Taylor in *Butterfield 8*); the noble whore (Claire Trevor in *Stagecoach*, who helps deliver the baby of a "respectable" woman who otherwise might have died in childbirth); vamps (Theda Bara, Pola Negri); and sex symbols (Jean Harlow, Rita Hayworth, Marilyn Monroe). "Working girls," sometimes called shop girls or department/dime store heroines, were a diverse lot of hoofers (Ruby Keeler in *42nd Street*), secretaries (Jean Arthur in *Easy Living*), servers (Linda Darnell in *Fallen Angel*), and salespersons (Ginger Rogers in *Kitty Foyle*).

Equally significant is the sheer number of films produced during Hollywood's Golden Age (again, not just woman's films) that featured women in a wide range of professions: restaurant chain owner (*Mildred Pierce*), magazine editor (*Lady in the Dark*), journalist (*His Girl Friday*), aviator (*Christopher Strong*), concert pianist (*September Affair*), opera singer (*One Night of Love*), stage actress (*Stage Door*), movie star (*A Star Is Born*), ballet dancer (*The Red Shoes*), commercial artist (*Laura*), high school teacher (*Cheers for Miss Bishop*), college professor (*The Accused*), college dean (*Woman of Distinction*), dress designer (*Daisy Kenyon*), novelist (*Old Acquaintance*), poet (*Winter Meeting*), playwright (*Sudden Fear*), lawyer

(*Adam's Rib*), scientist (*Madame* Curie), athlete (*Pat and Mike*), physician (*The Girl in White*).

Loretta played many of these types, although she was never identified with the woman's film, as were Greta Garbo, Joan Crawford, Bette Davis, and Barbara Stanwyck. Yet, like many actresses in the 1930s and even 1940s, she made a significant number of women's films, two of which have achieved classic status, *Man's Castle* and *Midnight Mary*, and one that should have, *Life Begins*. The significance of the others lies in the mixed messages they sent to women.

Big Business Girl (1931) could have jump-started the woman's movement, particularly after the Constitution was amended in 1920 to grant women the long overdue right to vote. The problem was the denouement, which was another indication of Hollywood's refusal to allow women the related right to choose a career over marriage and explain to a potential mate that she intends to balance both. A woman's only other option was to chant the "woman's place is in the home" mantra, from which Hollywood rarely deviated. Loretta's character, a college graduate, marries a bandleader who goes off to play gigs in Paris while she heads to New York to become a copywriter. She is an instant success, adored by her womanizing boss, who guarantees her access to the executive suite—a rarity in 1930s Hollywood movies where such an elevation was usually contingent upon a woman comprising her virtue. When the husband comes back, the boss sets him up with a hooker (a charmingly brash Joan Blondell) to establish grounds for alimony. But, always faithful to her marriage vows, the wife saves the day and returns to hubby. If women in the 1930s wanted to believe that marriage was preferable to a career, even though they may be superior to their washed out husbands, *Big Business Girl* vindicated their desire. Land a husband and see if he will allow you to pursue a career. Otherwise, resign yourself to shuttling between the bedroom, the kitchen, and the nursery.

Loretta was equally convincing as a member of the working class. It was as if she had been whisked from behind the counter and plopped down in front of the camera. You could actually believe that if Loretta waited on you, you would not have to return the merchandise. She played such a character in the deceptively titled *Play Girl* (1932), looking as if she came straight out of sales. A compulsive gambler (Norman Foster, later to become her brother-in-law) woos and wins her, convincing her that he has a steady job, when he is squandering their money on poker. After becoming pregnant, she learns the truth and demands that he leave. But he returns, repents, and promises to get a job, now that baby makes three.

When Loretta expressed anger and disillusionment, she looked like any woman who discovered that she had been deceived. She delivered her lines with such bitterness that they had a poignant rhythm, each syllable colored with the right emotion. She was an angry shop girl and pregnant wife, whose tolerance had been exhausted. Despite the reconciliation, her character has gone through a cycle of suffering that many women could not have endured. Yet Loretta created a woman of such resilience that audiences knew that, even with her husband's return, she could survive what lay ahead.

There is a line in *Play Girl* that, in retrospect, is prophetic. When Norman Foster proves to be a less than satisfactory lover, Loretta tries to activate his libido: "Come on, Gable, get hot." Little did she know that Gable would "get hot" three years later, and that she would find herself in the same situation as her character.

Play Girl's message was echoed throughout the period: If you land a better job than your husband, give it up if you want to keep him. Or, as the mother of Lola (Loretta) puts it in *Weekend Marriage* (1932), "the man you love is worth all the jobs in the world." The title, *Weekend Marriage*, was titillating but misleading. Loretta was again paired with Norman Foster. They marry, and when she has the opportunity to run her company's St. Louis office, he turns to drink and develops pneumonia. Lola flies back to New York, only to hear her doctor denounce her as a "modern woman." Again, the audience is expected to overlook the husband's inadequacies, ignoring the fact that his wife gets promoted while he loses jobs. Loretta played the final scene as if she believed Lola had made the right choice: Return to your husband and don't rub his nose in his failures. That may have been fine for Lola, but as an actress, Loretta had to breathe credibility into a script that discredited wives who succeeded while their husbands failed. Loretta was not Lola, yet she was so convincing that it seemed she would make the same sacrifice in real life. A script is a script, however unenlightened. *Weekend Marriage* was one of six films she made in 1932. She was expected to make Lola believable, and she did. She had a career to pursue and a mansion to maintain.

They Call It Sin (1932) revealed Loretta's burgeoning ability to balance the extremes of the conventional rich boy/poor girl plot with the excesses of lurid melodrama. She was again directed by Thornton Freeland (*Weekend Marriage*), who this time realized that hers was a face and a figure to which painterly lighting and flattering camera angles could impart an otherworldly beauty. Loretta was now a blonde, back lit so that her hair seemed glazed with silver, and front lit so that her face was translucent. She wore long billowy dresses that ran down her body, curving around the hips and spilling down to her ankles.

A rising executive (David Manners), sent by his prospective father-in-law to check out the Kansas territory, drops in at a church service, where he is immediately attracted to Marion, the organist (Loretta). He even promises that if she is serious about a musical career, she should contact him in New York. That is all Marion has to hear. She takes off for New York, where she discovers that Manners wants the best of both worlds: Marion and his affluent fiancée. When Manners discovers that a predatory producer (Louis Calhern) has hired Marion as a rehearsal pianist, he turns moralist and, along with his doctor-friend (the always reliable George Brent), decides to enlighten her about the producer's intentions (which are strictly dishonorable). By this time Marion has undergone a further transformation. Chicly dressed and brandishing a cigarette holder while sipping champagne, she is now a woman of the world—until the patriarchs sabotage her relationship with the producer, who retaliates by firing her and appropriating the music she has written. When Manners accuses the producer of theft, an argument ensues on the penthouse terrace resulting the producer toppling over the railing

They Call it Sin was an apologia for patriarchy. If Manners had not interfered, the relationship would have unraveled by itself, ending with the producer's disenchantment with Marion, whose overriding ambition was to succeed as a composer. But the film works from the assumption that man knows best, and woman is Adam's rib. Patriarchy triumphs. Only a male can save the day, even though Marion is willing to lie for Manners and tell the police that she caused the accident. Marion doesn't have to. The producer briefly regains consciousness and exonerates Manners before dying. And what about Marion and the doctor, who loves her? After they're married, he may even allow her to continue composing or go back to being a church organist.

The sadly neglected *Life Begins* (1932) was a true woman's film. Unfortunately, it has been virtually ignored because few film historians know of it or have seen it. Originally entitled "Woman's Day," it was a tribute to Warner's refusal to compromise on a script that was never meant for a happy ending. Grace Sutton (Loretta) is married, pregnant, and a murderer. The circumstances of the crime are deliberately vague; apparently, Grace shot a corrupt politician who was trying to frame her.

Loretta's two-piece wardrobe consisted of a drab cloth coat and a floppy hat, replaced with a euphemistically named "hospital gown" after she is admitted to the maternity ward. The ward represents a cross section of women on the eve of delivery: the maternal type, eager to share her experiences and offer words of hope; a show girl (flamboyantly played by Glenda Farrell), who has given birth to twins, intending to put them up for adoption until her motherly instincts get the better of her; an Italian woman who lost her child (and may get one of the twins); and then Grace, forced to decide between abortion and C-section, which would save her child at the expense of her life. She chooses the latter.

Earl Baldwin's script is ingeniously plotted, with enough hints to suggest that Grace could get a suspended sentence and justice would prevail. But he wisely chose a different route—the one to which the film was inexorably heading. *Life Begins* did not cater to audiences hoping for an ending in which mother and child survived. But when a nurse folds up Grace's shawl and removes the chart from her bed—to free it for the next patient—we know what has happened. Wisely, Loretta was given a role in which she could look simultaneously like an angel slumming on earth and a mortal on her way to eternity. Again, it was astonishing that, at nineteen, Loretta could display such a range of emotion. Although she is fearful, she conceals her anxiety from her husband; she is compassionate toward a mental patient who wanders into the maternity ward looking for her "child"; finally, she resigns herself to dying so that life can begin. The final shot is of the title, *Life Begins*, superimposed over Loretta's serene face, implying that she has made the right decision: Life will continue, if not hers, then her daughter's. And from the way her husband cradles the infant in his arms, he believes this, too. *Variety* (30 August 1932) commended Loretta on her convincing performance, noting that she succeeded admirably despite the restrictions of wardrobe and setting. The "must see" reviews did not convince the Academy of Motion Picture Arts and Sciences: *Life Begins* did not receive a single Oscar nomination. But Loretta, now about to turn twenty, had no time to fret. There were more movies to make.

In 1933, she appeared in nine films, one of which was *The Life of Jimmy Dolan*, a tightly constructed melodrama about the boxing world, vividly brought to life by director Archie Mayo. The film was the forerunner of such classics of the ring as *Body and Soul* (1946), *The Set-Up* (1949), and *Champion* (1949). But it was not the *Raging Bull* of 1933. Loretta was cast as Peggy, the generic virgin, with lightened hair and homespun clothes. But it was not her film; in fact she does not appear for the first third of it.

Again Loretta was paired with Douglas Fairbanks, Jr., appearing as the title character. Jimmy Dolan is a prizefighter, who flees a crime scene after accidentally killing a reporter. Dolan goes on the lam, changes his name, rides the rails to Salt Lake City, and ends up at a farm run by Peggy and her aunt (Aline MacMahon, with a respectable Scottish burr), where the two women educate orphans with polio. When niece and aunt cannot meet their mortgage payment, Dolan returns to the ring, and while he doesn't defeat his opponent, he lasts long enough to get the mortgage money. A detective (Guy Kibbee, giving the best performance in the film), in disgrace for having sent the wrong man to the electric chair, attempts to redeem himself by locating Dolan. Just when it seems that Dolan will have to stand trial, the detective turns deliverer. Only the benign Kibbee could perform such a magnanimous gesture. Thus the film does not end, as it should, with Dolan getting a reduced sentence and Peggy agreeing to wait for him until he walks through the prison gates.

The role took little out of Loretta; it was just another movie, this time requiring her to get down and dirty as a farm girl. If *Jimmy Dolan* is remembered, it is not for Loretta, but for the brief appearance of John Wayne, as a visibly nervous boxer counting on the prize money for his family. In his few minutes of screen time, Wayne revealed a vulnerability that he rarely had a chance to exhibit. This was not the first time that Wayne appeared in a film with Loretta. In *Three Girls Lost* (1931), in which Loretta was one of a trio hoping to make it big in Chicago, Wayne played a minor role. The *Los Angeles Times* review (15 June 1931) complimented him on his "nice voice," but noted that he "still needs a few lessons in acting." Fortunately, Wayne never took the review to heart. Once he and John Ford teamed up, his image was carved in celluloid, Hollywood's equivalent of Mount Rushmore. For a time, Loretta and John Wayne, strangely enough, were friendly—or as friendly as she could be with someone with whom she had little in common. The sole connection was his first wife, Josephine Saenz, a friend of Loretta's and a devout Catholic. Since Wayne was not a Catholic, Loretta arranged for the couple to be married at her home on 24 June 1933. A decade later they divorced, Saenz charging "extreme cruelty." Loretta and Saenz remained close, but she never worked again with Wayne.

For Loretta it was back to work, costarring with two actors who revolutionized the crime film, Edward G. Robinson (*Little Caesar* [1930]) and James Cagney (*The Public Enemy* [1931]), and another familiar to moviegoers but not in Robinson or Cagney's league, Warren William. Although

Robinson and Cagney could play more than upwardly mobile gangsters, they had few opportunities to demonstrate their versatility. Robinson displayed an amazing flair for comedy in *The Amazing Dr. Clitterhouse* (1938) and *Larceny, Inc* (1942), but audiences preferred Robinson the heavy. Cagney fared better. He was a superb dancer (e.g., *Taxi!*, *Footlight Parade*, *Something to Shout About*, and, above all, *Yankee Doodle Dandy*, for which he won his only Oscar). He could also exude an air of menace that can still make a viewer uncomfortable. In *Taxi!* (1932), which dramatized the wars waged by a combine against independent taxi drivers who refused to give up their stations, Cagney played a hot-headed cabbie, who would haul off at anyone who looked at him the wrong way. Then cockiness turned to petulance, as the actor's eyes registered a maniacal glee. But he is not the only one with a short fuse. The usually benign Guy Kibbee was cast as an independent driver, whose refusal to relocate results in the loss of his cab when the combine arranges for a truck to crash into it. Enraged, Kibbee shoots the driver and ends up in prison, where he dies.

Although Kibbee's waitress-daughter (Loretta) knows about Cagney's temper, she still marries him. When he is physically abusive, she stands by her man. *Taxi!*, which began on a note of authenticity, degenerates into jaw-dropping disbelief when the mistress of the man responsible for the "accident" that ruined Loretta's father begs her for $100, so she and her lover can leave the country! That she would even make such a request is either unalloyed arrogance or a plot device to suggest that the daughter is a pushover. Initially taken aback, Loretta consents. It's as if she has encountered her mirror image: another woman who, faced with the "love him or leave him" dilemma, chooses the former, as she did herself. The lovers never manage to leave the country. The police arrive, the villain plunges to his death from an open window, and the scales of justice are temporarily balanced, although there is no indication that Cagney has learned to curb his temper—and audiences preferred it that way.

We tend to remember *Taxi!* not for the scenes in which Cagney loses his cool (his behavior is just irksome), but for two others: one in which Cagney s converses with a Yiddish-speaking man in Yiddish; and another, in which the winners of a dance contest are not Cagney and Loretta, who dance like professionals, but the unbilled George Raft and his partner. Both actors were experienced dancers—Raft, sleek and reptilian; Cagney, scrappy and streetwise. But Loretta's performance should not be overlooked. When she had to play a woman of the working class, without a fancy wardrobe and elaborate makeup, she looked and sounded blue collar. The script required her to resolve all the tensions within her character, which was not easy, especially the scene with the mistress. Loretta's sacrificial gesture would have struck audiences as implausible, perhaps even eliciting groans without the right blend of innocence and compassion. That Loretta could combine these emotions in the right proportions is a tribute to her art, which would have been more evident if she had been given better roles. But such was the studio system—particularly Warner's with its assembly line approach to production.

Taxi! and *The Hatchet Man* (1932) were not Loretta's only films with James Cagney and Edward G. Robinson. By the time Warner Bros. had the actors working both sides of the law, Loretta was no longer at the studio. *The Hatchet Man* was not vintage Robinson or Loretta. William Wellman, the director, does not mention it in his autobiography, *A Short Time for Insanity;* Robinson dismisses it in his, *All My Yesterdays;* and Loretta never seems to have expressed an opinion. *The Hatchet Man* may have some historical significance. The David Belasco and Abdullah Amet play that inspired it was a re-creation of the Tong Wars that erupted in various Chinatowns—especially those in San Francisco and Los Angeles—and lasted from the mid 1800s to the 1920s. The tongs were originally secret societies, more like protective agencies than clans, created to protect Chinese immigrants from discrimination and violence. Gradually, they turned into mafia-like organizations with a similar hierarchies and codes of honor. When a tong member was murdered, a hatchet man—the hereditary title for an avenger—would dispatch the victim with a hatchet.

Robinson played the title character. Although he was a graduate of the American Academy of Dramatic Arts, he was not perceived as a "serious" actor and, in fact, was never nominated for an Oscar. Yet in *The Hatchet Man*, he was authentically Chinese in speech and manner. He is assigned to kill a boyhood friend (J. Carrol Naish), who accepts his fate resignedly. (Nash moved and spoke with ritualized staginess, which may have been his or Wellman's idea of the way ethnic Chinese act when faced with death.) But first, Naish has Robinson swear that he will marry his daughter when she comes of age. The daughter is Loretta, unrecognizable in her first scene, in which she appears more metallic than human. Her face looks lacquered rather than made up, resembling a mask with slits for her eerily slanted eyes. Her relationship with Robinson's character is a May-December marriage, which comes apart when Loretta takes a younger lover. The ignominy that her adultery brings on the tong results in Robinson's expulsion and the loss of his business. Meanwhile, the lover turns drug dealer and pimp, whisking Loretta off to China, where she is sold into prostitution. If this turn of the plot seems deliberately sensational, it is historically accurate. The more criminal tongs were drug traffickers and white slavers.

Robinson works his way to China, rescues Loretta, and hurls his hatchet at the wall—the blade landing in the back of the drug-dealing pimp standing behind it. Although *The Hatchet Man* has some historical value in its depiction of the Tong Wars, it is more indicative of Hollywood's indifference to ethnicity and race in the 1930s. Using white actors, however talented, to impersonate Chinese immigrants or even Chinese-Americans reflects the industry's reluctance to groom non-whites for roles requiring ethnic and racial authenticity. That would eventually change, but not for the next three decades. *The Hatchet Man* was Loretta's first, but not her last, ethnic role: On her television series, *The Loretta Young Show*, she portrayed an Asian woman again in "The Pearl" (1956).

Loretta's situation in the 1930s was commonplace: The female lead either outshines the male, or vice versa. In *Employees' Entrance*, it was the latter. Warren William was a competent "B" movie star, best known as Warner's Perry Mason in the 1930s and Columbia's Lone Wolf in the 1940s. As Kurt Anderson, a tyrannical department store manager, William was indisputably the star of *Employees' Entrance* (1933). His Anderson is so satanic that his victims are more pitiable than tragic. The homeless Madeleine (Loretta) takes refuge in the furniture section of the store, where she plans to spend the night in the model parlor. When the predatory Anderson discovers her, she flirts, he is aroused, a dinner invitation follows, and Madeleine is expected to show her gratitude by not resisting when Anderson backs her against a door. A slow fade out indicates that Anderson has made another conquest.

Anderson gets Madeleine a job as a model, which gives Loretta the opportunity to appear in a pre-code bridal gown with an exposed back. Madeleine marries another employee (Wallace Ford), whom Anderson is grooming as his assistant. For Anderson, sex has two functions, neither of which has to do with love: It provides a release of tension and a means of control. Like most womanizers, he regards women—even his own employees-as property, advancing them if they are cooperative, passing them off to other executives when he has finished with them, or firing them when they have outlived their usefulness.

With his hawk-like face, pomaded hair, aquiline eyes, and streamlined figure clothed in black, William was the incarnation of Mephistopheles. Had *Employees' Entrance* been made in 1934, when the production code was being enforced with a vengeance, the resolution would have been dramatically different. As it is, Anderson gets Madeleine drunk and takes advantage of her again in another elliptical fade out. Now a married woman, Madeleine is so overcome with shame that she attempts suicide. Indifferent to the suffering he has caused, Anderson taunts Madeleine's husband into shooting him, but not fatally. The ending is truly pre-code: Anderson, who otherwise would have paid for his transgressions by being reduced to standing on breadlines, survives a coup and returns as the manager, more powerful than ever, employing the same tactics that he used earlier to bolster the store's profits to survive the Great Depression. *Employees' Entrance* was Warren William's film. The script did not allow William to humanize Anderson; instead, he drew on the qualities that made his character succeed in a cutthroat business, when two-thirds of the nation could afford to shop at a department store on the order of Macy's. He regarded the other third as potential employees, provided they could deliver what he wanted.

Loretta fared better in her second film with William Wellman, *Heroes for Sale* (1933). And she would work with him twice more, at MGM (*Midnight Mary*), and finally at Fox (*The Call of the Wild*). Wellman was not the kind of director to discuss his films in detail; he mentions *Heroes for Sale* in his autobiography because it brought him in contact with his future wife, who was working in a Busby Berkeley musical on the next sound stage. Yet *Heroes* was the kind of film that Wellman understood; it was the companion piece to *Wild Boys of the Road* (1933), his take on the Great Depression from the point of view of kids riding the rails and hoping to establish their own utopia. *Heroes* was set in the same period, but within a different context, focusing on the plight of a World War I veteran, Thomas Holmes (Richard Barthelmess), who was never recognized for his heroic capture of a German soldier. Instead, the medal was awarded to a coward, who mustered up enough courage—thanks to a gun—to bring in the prisoner.

Holmes incurs a spinal injury that requires morphine, resulting in addiction and eventual rehab. Once clean, he returns to the workforce and wanders into a friendly luncheonette, where Mary (Aline McMahon) rents him a room on a floor occupied by two other tenants, Hans, a bolshevik inventor, and Ruth, a laundry worker (Loretta). Ruth finds him a job at her laundry, and before long, Holmes has convinced his co-workers to bankroll Hans's new invention, a wringer washer. The owner of the laundry no sooner endorses the invention than he suffers a fatal heart attack. The business is sold, and the new owners think only in terms of cutting jobs and increasing profits. When Ruth is killed during a workers' demonstration, Holmes is accused of being the instigator and sent to prison for five years. His release coincides with the red scare, when real or suspected Communists were being harassed, and in some cases, deported. Forced to join the ranks of the homeless, he meets, of all people (yes, coincidences mount in this film) the coward, who has been reduced to similar straits. As for the resolution—there is none, which is to screenwriter Robert Lord's credit. Holmes has been thrown into the fiery furnace; the refining fire has burned away the past, leaving him transformed and defiantly homeless. Like the narrator in Samuel Beckett's *The Unnamable*, Holmes can say, "I can't go on, I'll go on."

Playing another proletarian, Loretta looked surprisingly authentic, perhaps because the character survived on low-level jobs requiring no marketable skills—which might have been Loretta's fate if she had never become an actress. It was roles like Ruth that revealed her empathy with working class women. She may not have been one herself, but she was an indefatigable worker, subjected to Warner's acrobatic schedule requiring her to bounce from film to film at a pace that even the most energetic teenager would find daunting. Loretta did not need bargain basement clothes and a cosmetic makeover to play Ruth convincingly. Loretta never worked in a laundry, but she understood women who did. She had seen enough of them at her mother's boarding house and on studio lots where they toiled as extras. She absorbed what she experienced, depositing it in a memory bank from which she drew, consciously or otherwise, for her characters. And when she could not connect with a character, she simply used her imagination.

More than *The Hatchet Man*, *Heroes for Sale* was the kind of film with which Wellman identified. From the opening scene on a World War I battlefield, with shellfire, exploding grenades, and rain pouring down on men scrambling into trenches, Wellman's roving camera behaves like another combatant, but impartial enough to avoid the usual Hollywood distinction between the allies and the enemy. Holmes ends up in a German hospital, where a compassionate doctor tells him that his condition will often become so painful that he will need morphine. A lesser director might have made the doctor a devious figure, eager to turn an American into an addict. But the doctor prescribes the only drug he knows to alleviate spinal pain.

When Wellman was directing his kind of film, he framed the shots in such a way as to make them dramatically functional. We see the luncheonette for the first time from the outside, with Mary behind the counter. Rather than cut, Wellman pans to the adjacent building where homeless men congregate. By emphasizing the proximity of the homeless center to the luncheonette, Wellman is not just making a statement about the economic disparity produced by the Great Depression; nor is he trying to avoid another camera set up. The juxtaposition of the two is a form of foreshadowing: Eventually, the homeless will become regular diners, with special privileges.

Heroes for Sale was Wellman's and Lord's film. Wellman understood the subject matter, and Lord, realizing he could not write a pro-communist, or even pro-socialist script, made it easier for Wellman by having the former bolshevik convert to capitalism after his invention makes him a millionaire. But Holmes, who could have shared in the profits, gives the money to Mary, so she can keep the luncheonette open around the clock to feed the unemployed.

Heroes for Sale sends a mixed message: Capitalism helps the needy, but only if a private citizen (not the state) provides the means. What is the answer? Capitalism? Socialism? Philanthropy? A combination of the three? One critic found *Heroes for Sale* politically confused, which it may be. But Warner's, the most pro-Roosevelt of the studios, was really paying homage to the New Deal, exemplified by Tom's magnanimity The only difference is that Tom is a private citizen with his own new deal, based on the time-honored principle of people helping people. How that help is executed—by programs like the Civilian Conservation Corps or the Works Progress Administration, or by a philanthropic gesture—is immaterial as long as there are results. *Heroes for Sale* implies there will be help as long as there are Tom Holmeses.

CHAPTER 5

Loaned Out

At eighteen, Loretta must have had some idea about Columbia Pictures' reputation and its president-production head, Harry Cohn. The studio originated as the CBC Sales Co., the Cs standing for the Cohns, Harry and his brother, Jack, the B, for Joseph Brandt, a lawyer who never practiced law. But Harry had no intention of being part of a triumvirate. By 1924, CBC had become Columbia; by 1932, Brandt, whose health was deteriorating, bowed out. Jack returned to New York, which he preferred to Los Angeles, as vice president for distribution. Harry was the one Cohn associated with the new studio, consolidating his old title, head of production, with his new one, president.

Columbia was located on Gower Street, synonymous with "Poverty Row," where fly-by-night film companies cropped up and disappeared, not far from "Gower Gulch," where actors in cowboy outfits waited for extra work in westerns. Loretta knew little about the film for which she had been loaned out, or its director. The director was Frank Capra, who soon found his place in the pantheon. The film was *Platinum Blonde* (1931). In his autobiography, Capra includes Loretta among the "great cast" that he had assembled, implying that she would have been the star until a decision was made to add some sex in the person of Jean Harlow, whose "breastworks burst their silken confines."

Although Harlow's addition to the cast required some rewriting and a change of title, it did not derail the film. *Platinum Blonde* boosted Loretta's career. For film historians, it is more significant as the first of screenwriter Robert Riskin's collaborations with Capra than for a Harlow sobriquet (derived from a title that was never the writer's first choice). The original title was "Gallagher," the surname of Loretta's character (whose first name is never mentioned). Although Harry Cohn took credit as producer, this was, in every way, a "Frank Capra Production," as was every one of the director's films. By the time "Gallagher" was ready for release in November 1931, it had been retitled *Platinum Blonde*, with the hope of attracting audiences, whose curiosity was piqued by the title character rather than the presence of Loretta, who had yet to acquire a following. Harlow became a sensation after the opening of *Hell's Angels* (1930), in which even the impressive aerial photography could not dim her sheen. Hollywood had discovered a force of nature who needed the right combination of script and director to channel her erotic energy.

Capra might have originally been taken with Harlow's breastworks, but her most distinctive feature was her hair, which looked like spun silver. She was a metallic earth mother with an undulating walk and ungirdled waist, elusive and otherworldly, pursuable but unobtainable. Robert Williams, a promising stage actor whose tragic death a few days after the film's premiere precludes a true assessment of his talent, played Stew Smith, an endearingly cocky reporter assigned to cover a breach of promise suit involving celebrity Ann Schuyler (Harlow). Unaware that his colleague Gallagher is secretly in love with him, Stew becomes so infatuated with Ann that they elope, leaving Gallagher to pine in silence.

Once Stew realizes he is the "Cinderella Man," as the tabloids have christened him—and "a bird in a gilded cage," like the canary in his bedroom—it is only a matter of time before he asserts his independence, prompting Ann to seek a divorce and Stew to admit that he ignored his growing attraction to Gallagher because of his infatuation with Ann. Riskin was too talented a writer to have Stew undergo an epiphany and confess his love for Gallagher. Stew is an aspiring a playwright without a plot, alternating between one exotic setting and another until Gallagher suggests that he write from experience, specifically his most recent one: a rich girl-poor boy whirlwind romance that culminated in a failed marriage. When Stew asks Gallagher how the play should end, she casually, but unconvincingly, explains that the wife should repent, return to her husband, adopt his name, and live in his shabby apartment. From her voice, Stew is now aware of the sadness she has suppressed; he offers his own resolution, in which the hero admits that there was another woman, whose worth he never realized while he was under the spell of the platinum blonde. When Gallagher weeps silently, Stew, compassionate for the only time in the film, takes her in his arms and consoles her. This was the ending audiences wanted—the kind that was unpredictable but indisputably right.

Both Capra and Riskin were committed to elevating the stature of the "little man," the unsung ordinary citizen, insisting that he/she (usually he) merits the same respect granted to royalty. In the opening scene, the vibrant rhythms of the newsroom, with the staccato dialogue, the clacking typewriter keys, and the good-natured banter among the reporters usher us into an egalitarian world, where people of the same class work and occasionally play. In contrast, there is so much empty space in the Schuyler mansion that any sound produces an echo.

As taken as Capra was with Riskin's script, he was equally taken with Harlow; she was a synthesis of moon goddess and earth mother. In the party sequence, Stew and Ann slip away to the garden, retreating into a glass enclosure sprayed with water from a geyser. Their embrace behind water-drenched glass is shot in sensuous chiaroscuro with Harlow's hair as a major source of light. Equally impressive is another scene in which Gallagher, sent to the Schuyler mansion to cover a party for the society page, retires with Stew to the same garden, unaware that Ann is on the terrace above them, looking like a silver-coated statue. Gallagher, in white chiffon, embodies a less ostentatious and more feminine brand of luminosity. The contrast in whiteness—artificial vs. natural—should have resolved Stew's dilemma. Gallagher looked like a woman; Ann, like Pygmalion's statue that has come to life and, at any moment, could revert to marble. Harlow's name may have attracted more moviegoers than Loretta's, yet Loretta, looking at least five years older, held her own. It was a faultless performance in what was essentially a supporting role.

By 1933, Loretta had adjusted to Warner's exit-one-film-enter-another policy. However, her home studio often found her difficult to cast. At times, her beauty obscured her talent, and she found herself playing young women of privilege in picture hats and summery dresses. Significantly, when she was loaned to Columbia for *Platinum Blonde* and especially *Man's Castle*, she could play characters with which she was familiar: members of the working class and the dispossessed. Loretta belonged to neither but encountered both types during the years when her mother ran a boarding house, and later, when Gladys kept moving the family from one neighborhood to another. Loretta's compassion for those less fortunate than herself, intensified by her Catholicism, resulted in two extraordinary performances. It was not merely Loretta's art that made them so memorable. She was fortunate in having two outstanding directors, Capra and Frank Borzage. Borzage—with whom she only worked once—has been labeled the champion of "sublime love," "the poet of the couple," an "uncompromising romantic," and a "consummate dreamer." He was all of these, investing his films with a deep spirituality and sanctifying human relationships as if he were a priest officiating at the union of a man and a woman that is too pure to be validated by marriage (which might be necessary but not the perquisite for love). The faces of the lovers are transfigured, as if nature realized the limitations of studio lighting and decided to add some lumens of its own.

It was cinematographer Joseph August who realized Borzage's vision, painting it in light. If Loretta lived in ancient Rome, she would have been the ideal vestal virgin. As Trina in Borzage's *Man's Castle*, she looked even purer after becoming pregnant by the abusive and irresponsible Bill (Spencer Tracy). But that purity was partly the result of August's lighting, which washed over her face and complemented what lay within.

There was not one false note in Loretta's performance. To watch her wash and iron like a seasoned homemaker, preside over a kitchen stove as if it were her domain, and hear her lyrically ungrammatical speech—reminiscent of Clifford Odets's street poetry—is to see a twenty-year-old actress in total command of her character. That she had had some contact with working women does not entirely explain her performance. She understood the plight of a homeless woman as only an actress can; whether or not she imagined what could have happened to the woman and her family is irrelevant. Hers was that mysterious empathy that an actor feels for a character, resulting in a performance that cannot be explained rationally. Technique? Loretta had it, but she was not a drama school product. Emotional memory? It is difficult to imagine Loretta drawing on any comparable experience; desertion by a father is not the same as homelessness. If, as Hamlet tells Horatio, "There are more things in heaven and earth, Horatio, / Than are dreamt of in your philosophy," there is much in the art of acting that eludes our puny attempts to explain it.

Loretta wore stardom lightly. In 1934, she spoke candidly to a reporter: "I don't feel that I have done anything particularly striking; but I hope to do something really good . . . . After seven years I'm rather well known, however, and I believe very early fame—if you can call it fame—is good for a girl, because she grows up with it and doesn't value it too highly or think it means more than it does." It was her realistic attitude toward success, combined with her faith, that prompted her final remarks in the interview: "Nearly 2000 years ago Christ showed people how to live so that all their problems would be solved."

Cohn was pleased with Loretta's performance in *Platinum Blonde* and wanted her back for *Man's Castle;* however, he did not have the final say when it came to casting. *Man's Castle* was as much a "Frank Borzage Production" as *Platinum Blonde* was a "Frank Capra" one. Borzage must have seen Loretta in any number of films and concluded she was right for Trina. Since Borzage had directed Tracy in *Young America* (1932), he requested him. For Cohn, getting Borzage was a coup, the kind that could expunge the Poverty Row stigma that tainted the studio. *Man's Castle* helped, but the stigma did not disappear until Academy Award night 1935, when Capra's *It Happened One Night* (1934) was awarded five Oscars.

Loretta responded instinctively to Tracy's burly masculinity. She had never costarred with a man like Tracy who, although short, a bit stocky, and not especially handsome, could attract women with his unpretentiousness and virile self-confidence. The same qualities drew Katharine Hepburn to him, even though he often treated her as ungallantly as Bill did Trina. But it was Bill's proprietary attitude that made Trina love him, and it was Tracy's way of expressing affection—sometimes tenderly, other times, chauvinistically—that attracted Trina to him. When Bill threatens to beat Trina, she laughs it off, quoting the opening verses of "Can't Help Lovin' Dat Man" from *Show Boat*: "Fish gotta swim, / Birds gotta fly." She only quotes the beginning; those familiar with the lyrics know that "I gotta love one man / Til I die" comes next. Trina was a one-man woman, which is how Loretta played her. Both she and Bill are victims of the Great Depression, but the difference is that while Bill can con waiters into a meal, Trina is reduced to sitting on park benches, which is how they meet: she, wondering where she will sleep that evening; he, feeding pigeons the popcorn that she eyes hungrily. Bill is an alpha male to the *n*th degree, alternately tender and gruff. He brings Trina to his Hooverville shack, which she turns into a home. Their relationship is not at all sensual, even though when she admits discreetly that she is pregnant, it is obvious that Trina did not reject his advances. She found lovemaking the equivalent of love, not just sex, knowing all the time that Bill was born under a wandering star.

Eventually, he agrees to a marriage performed by an ex-minister, reduced to working as a guard in a toy factory. Desperate for money, Bill becomes involved in an abortive plan to rob the factory. Now a wanted man, he and Trina, in her Victorian wedding gown with its high neck and ruffles (a replica of the one the equally virginal Janet Gaynor wore in Borzage's *Seventh Heaven*), hop a freight. The last scene is pure Borzage, who made a subtle connection between the Holy Family and Bill and Trina with her as yet unborn child, due in December. Trina is lying on a bed of straw, with Bill's head resting on her breast. The camera tracks back, as if the sight is too sacred for profane eyes. The viewer is left with the knowledge that within Trina there is life, and where there is life, there is hope. The final shot is a Nativity tableau: The straw bed, Trina's gown spread out like a fan, and Bill asleep at her breast combine to form a freight car Bethlehem. And if the child is born during their journey, the delivery will take place in a makeshift manager.

Man's Castle was Loretta's defining moment as an actress. "I proved I could really act with that one," she claimed, while at the same time crediting Borzage: "He made you believe your part." Tracy also contributed to Loretta's intensely realistic performance. He was thirteen years older than Loretta, who responded to him as a father figure and potential lover, good for a night on the town. It might be too facile an explanation to say that he was a substitute for her absentee father, whom she barely remembered. Still, she was always attracted to older men, mainly because she thought they would offer her the security that she craved. For Loretta, a salary was no gauge of personal worth, only of personal income. She wanted warmth, affection and above all, a safe haven—"a cleft in the rock of the world," as Blanche DuBois phrased it in *A Streetcar Named Desire*—where she could take refuge when life's problems loomed large for her. As it happened, Loretta ended up solving them herself.

Midnight Mary (1933) was another loan out, this time to MGM, where Loretta had played her first major role in *Laugh, Clown, Laugh*. But she was primarily interested in a film about to go into production at Fox, the studio she would soon be joining. The film was *Berkeley Square* (1933), a time traveler with Leslie Howard re-creating his acclaimed stage role as an American transported to eighteenth-century London. Why Loretta was so obsessed with playing the female lead, which went to Heather Angel, is hard to fathom. Loretta was fond of reading plays, perhaps because she had become so used to screenplays, which, in format, are not that different. What is really puzzling is that she never expressed a desire to work in theater. "She was never interested in the stage, " her daughter recalled. Still, she enjoyed reading Noël Coward and S.N. Behrman because their work epitomized the kind of sophistication to which she aspired. If she had been given the part in *Berkeley Square*, she would be playing another ingénue, but more significantly, one who was overshadowed by Howard, the only name that is even now associated with the film.

In *Midnight Mary* she was at least reunited with William Wellman and starring in a movie that would become a classic product of the heady time before the enforcement of the Production Code in 1934—when a mistress did not have to suffer the wages of sin, men and women cohabited without benefit of marriage, murderers could be acquitted (with the right lawyer), a woman could boast of being a "party girl" without explaining her idea of a party, and morality went unmonitored by watchdogs and censorious moralists. With the inclusion of *Midnight Mary* in WarnerVideo's *Forbidden Hollywood, Vol. Three,* a four-DVD set with Wellman's *Heroes for Sale* and *Wild Boys of the Road, Midnight Mary,* long unavailable, offers proof of what a twenty-year-old natural actress can accomplish with a minimum of training and a maximum of talent.

Although Loretta still fretted about *Berkeley Square,* once *Midnight Mary* opened to flattering notices, she realized that, like everything else in her life, it was part of a divine plan. When filming began in April 1933, Loretta was faced with a challenge: Mary Martin was her most complex role to date. Mary was born in 1910; by the time of the main action she is twenty-three. Although Wellman says nothing about the film in his autobiography (which is not surprising, since *A Short Time for Insanity* is not a life in film, but a life that, coincidentally, involved film), he lavished a great deal of attention on Loretta, particularly on her eyes. She is first seen in a courtroom, where she is on trial for murder; totally disinterested in the proceedings, she thumbs through a copy of *Cosmopolitan,* holding it so close that it masks her face, except for her eyes, which seem larger than usual. In fact, her eyes resemble those of Joan Crawford who, reportedly, had been slated for the role. With fashionably plucked eyebrows and half moons penciled over her eyes, she looks like a woman of the world, although her world is in actuality the criminal underworld. Later, while waiting for the verdict, Mary sits in the county clerk's office, where the dates on the court records books occasion an ingenious flashback sequence, with the camera panning left to right, as Mary's past is reenacted. Orphaned at nine (Loretta plays a convincing nine-year-old with pigtails, scavenging in a dump), Mary is falsely accused of theft and sent to reform school. She emerges as a gangster's moll in the making, awaiting only the right gangster, who materializes in the person of Leo Darcy (Ricardo Cortez), whose mistress she becomes.

Loretta reconciled the two extremes of her character: an essential decency and a cynicism spawned by an unfair legal system that only fed her passion for survival, even if it meant offering herself to Darcy. She knew his weakness for enigmatic women, who could shift back and forth between virgin and whore. Mary's way of snaring a wealthy lover is to gaze at him with playfully seductive but dreamily innocent eyes (brightened by James Van Trees's hagiographic lighting) to signal her availability— but only if she gets her way.

It was a daring performance, all the more because of Loretta's Catholicism. But Loretta also understood Mary's integrity. When a wealthy lawyer, Tom Mannering (Franchot Tone), befriends and then falls in love with her, becoming Darcy's rival, Darcy plans to have him killed, but only succeeds in killing Mannering's close friend (Andy Devine in an unusually sympathetic role). With Mary's shooting of Darcy, the action then returns to the courtroom where a verdict is imminent.

Midnight Mary could easily have been an indictment of capital punishment, which is where it seemed to be heading. Like one of Euripides's plays, *Midnight Mary* required a deus ex machine: Mannering, who barges into the courtroom, claiming to have fresh evidence and demanding a retrial. Exactly what evidence Mannering has, apart from the fact that Mary committed murder to spare his life, is never revealed. But with a lawyer from an illustrious family defending her, Mary not only gets her acquittal but also Mannering. Their fade-out kiss must have convinced cockeyed optimists that "Happy Days Are Here Again" was not just Franklin D. Roosevelt's campaign song, but a prediction of things to come.

Midnight Mary was originally intended to be more socially conscious, but to what extent is hard to determine. The first writer to take a crack at it was veteran Anita Loos, who had a script ready in November 1932 entitled "Nora," featuring a prologue in "socialist" Vienna, where the state takes care of tenement children like Nora (Mary's original name). (Actually, Vienna was never socialist, although after World War I, socialists briefly dominated the Austrian National Assembly. Radicals were in their element, but their fervor was dampened when Engelbert Dollfuss became chancellor.) The prologue was not intended as a critique of capitalism, but as an example of a humane way of dealing with parentless children. In 1933, Gene Markey and Kathryn Scola took over; the title was still "Nora," but it was minus the Vienna prologue, and opened, as the film does, with Nora on trial. Whoever was responsible for the change of title realized "Midnight Nora" has as much appeal as flat beer. *Midnight Mary*, apart from being alliterative, could raise eyebrows and revenues. It did both.

The film was a triumph not only for Loretta but also for the other Warner loan outs, William Wellman and James Van Trees, who photographed Loretta so strikingly in *Life Begins*, *They Call It Sin*, *Taxi!*, and *Heroes for Sale* (not to mention Barbara Stanwyck in *Baby Face*). Although Mary was Loretta's most mature characterization to date, the film ultimately became Wellman's. Wellman worked out the flashbacks so that when the camera panned the dates on the court records, left to right, the action would return to the present by complementary horizontal wipes, proceeding from right to left—with the present emerging, as the past recedes. Usually, in a wipe, one is aware of a line moving horizontally, vertically, or diagonally across the screen, with one shot ending as the other begins. But here, it is as if the past exits to the left, as the present enters from the right. It is still a horizontal wipe, but done so artfully that it seems that past and present were once conjoined like Siamese twins and have now been separated. Although Loretta gave a performance worthy of an Oscar nomination, she did not get one. That year, the nominees were May Robson (*Lady for a Day*), Diana Wynyard (*Cavalcade*), and the eventual winner, Katharine Hepburn (*Morning Glory*).

Twenty-year-old actresses were rarely given such fulfilling roles as Trina and Mary. During the studio years, even the icons were stuck with parts they knew were beneath them, but which they were contractually obliged to accept. Warner's was perhaps the least sensitive to the entitlements of stardom, dismissing the idea that if one good turn deserves another, so should one good film lead to another. Bette Davis, for one, languished in a limbo of unmemorable films in the early 1930s, until out of desperation she moved over to RKO to give an indelible performance as the self-destructive waitress in *Of Human Bondage* (1934). Warner's punished Davis by ignoring her when Oscar nomination time came around. It was only a groundswell of support that resulted in her name being placed on the ballot. Many thought Davis would win, but dark horses have been known to reach the finish line before the odds-on favorite, and Claudette Colbert won that year for *It Happened One Night*. Davis had to fight for better roles, even though the Academy gave her a consolation prize for her performance in the potboiler, *Dangerous*, the following year. Then more of the same, until other leading roles resulted, but she never experienced one artistic triumph after another. Garbo fared better, but she was at MGM, where she was revered, with her films sufficiently spaced so that audiences were not given a surfeit of Garbo. Davis, by comparison, was at the Warner factory, where the merchandise varied from *Jezebel* (1938), for which Davis received a second Oscar, to the disastrous *Beyond the Forest* (1949), a transmogrification of Davis's art that reduced her to a gargoyle. Freelancing was the solution, as it later became for Loretta.

CHAPTER 6

Last Days at Warner's

After *Platinum Blonde*, *Man's Castle*, and *Midnight Mary*, which together required her to play three different types of women at two other studios, Loretta felt more secure about her art. The reviews bolstered her confidence, and she knew it was only a matter of time before she would be moving on. But where?

In November 1932, Jesse Lasky announced his intention to become an independent producer at the Fox Film Corporation, with *Zoo in Budapest* and *Berkeley Square* as his first productions. Loretta was well aware of Famous Players-Lasky, the studio resulting from the Famous Players-Lasky Feature Plays merger in 1916, with Adolph Zukor as president, and Lasky as vice president for production. It was there that Loretta's film career was launched in 1917. The company underwent various name changes, the most significant being the addition of "Paramount" in 1927. Paramount-Famous Players-Lasky was not the corporate name for long. Zukor was obsessed with creating a vertically integrated empire, with its own theatre chain, Publix. To prevent friction between the studio and its theater circuit, Lasky stepped aside. The new name was Paramount-Publix, eventually becoming just plain Paramount.

Lasky wanted Loretta for his first independent film, *Zoo in Budapest* (1933), with Gene Raymond as her costar. Raymond gave a bravura performance as Zanni, an animal trainer orphaned at an early age and raised by the director of the Budapest Zoo, where he grew into a combination of noble savage and animal activist, stealing fur stoles and burning them. Loretta also played an orphan, Eve, who is not as fortunate as Zanni. Eve lives in an orphanage, where a holiday is a trip to the zoo, and a chaperone or "keeper" is dependent on a guidebook to describe the attractions. Zanni locks eyes with Eve, beckoning to her to come with him. Another orphan, eager to cooperate, diverts the group's attention by diving into a lake, making it possible for Eve to escape and join Zanni's world, where humans bond with animals.

For those who only know Raymond as Jeanette MacDonald's husband, his Zanni is a revelation. It is a strikingly athletic performance, requiring Raymond to jump over partitions, and in the terrifying climax, to hop on the back of an elephant with a young boy he has rescued. He must then grab on to a rope to hoist the boy and himself to safety—but not before a tiger leaps up and takes a piece out of Zanni's leg. Regardless, Zanni survives, his gait no less springy, and both he and Eve are rewarded by the boy's father, who makes it possible for Eve to leave the orphanage, marry Zani, and live in a cottage on his estate. In the last scene—which is more like the finale of an operetta—the couple arrives at their new home, radiantly happy and unperturbed about the future.

Loretta had relatively little to do in the film. The real stars were Raymond and director Rowland V. Lee, who kept a fragile script from splintering. Raymond fancied himself the successor to Douglas Fairbanks; however, it was Errol Flynn and then Douglas Fairbanks, Jr., who buckled the swash and wielded a mean rapier. Still, Raymond's performance was admirable. He did not need a double; like Burt Lancaster, he did his own climbing and swinging, in addition to exuding the kind of machismo that won over audiences. Raymond was probably one of the leading men Loretta developed a crush on, not knowing at the time that he was bisexual, more homosexually than heterosexually inclined. In fact, when he married Jeanette MacDonald in 1937, she was still in love with Nelson Eddy, her first and only love. Raymond's lover at the time was Mary Pickford's husband, Buddy Rogers. On their honeymoon cruise to Hawaii, Jeanette and Raymond had a cabin next to Rogers and Pickford, then an incurable alcoholic: "There was a honeymoon going on—but the ones sleeping together were Gene Raymond and Buddy Rogers." But at the time *Zoo in Budapest* was filmed, Raymond had not met MacDonald, and only a few kindred spirits knew his sexual preferences. As for Loretta, the crush ended when the shoot was over, and then it was on to another leading man and another crush.

Except for *Heroes for Sale*, her last films for Warner's were as unmemorable as the first, requiring only that she have the stamina of a gymnast. For *The Hatchet Man*, she had to sit patiently in the makeup chair while she was turned into a mannequin and her face into a mask. Her best work was in the loan outs, which are now recognized as outstanding examples of pre-code filmmaking.

In addition to Wellman, the other director of note with whom she worked during her last year at Warner's was the German-born Wilhelm, later, William, Dieterle, with whom she made two films. They would team up again in 1948, but at another studio, Paramount, for *The Accused*. Dieterle, with his white gloves and riding crop, tended to single out one of the featured players, generally a novice, for criticism bordering on harassment. He steered clear of the stars, either because they were seasoned performers or because he knew they would not tolerate such behavior.

The Devil's in Love (1933) is more revelatory of Dieterle's ability as a director than Loretta's as an actress. If the misleading title attracted moviegoers expecting a steamy love story, they saw instead an imaginatively made film set in North Africa, where a French doctor, André Morand (Victor Jory), selflessly tends to the wounded, including a sadistic major who belittles his subordinates, including Salazar (J. Carrol Naish, Hollywood's ethnic specialist). When Morand is falsely accused of the major's murder, he escapes with the help of his boyhood friend, Jean Fabien (David Manners), to a port city, where he practices medicine under an assumed name, favoring the needy over the privileged. A friar prevails upon Morand, who, in another age would have belonged to "Doctors without Borders," to volunteer at his mission, where he meets and falls in love with Margot (Loretta), the friar's niece and Jean's fiancée. For the trio to become a duo, one of the men has to die. *The Devil's in Love* could end either way, particularly since Manners exudes more sex appeal than Jory, the better actor. Appearances are deceiving, and the ending does not disappoint. Truth triumphs, Salazar confesses to the murder, and Jean dies in battle, freeing Margot for Morand.

There have been better desert dramas than *The Devil's In Love*, such as *Under Two Flags, Beau Geste,* and *Gunga Din*. But the chief reasons the film is worth viewing are Dieterle's direction and Hal Mohr's poetic photography. Because Dieterle understood German expressionism, he was able to modify it for American consumption, purging it of its excesses and leaving in its place a monochrome palette, with subtle gradations of black and white. Photographed in the evening, Loretta did not so much look backlit as moonlit. The nighttime insurgency, with a disproportionate distribution of light and shadow—the only light sources being torches, the moon, and the natives' white robes—and the rebels on horseback, streaming over the sand as if they were riding the waves, was so breathtaking that one ceases to care whether Morand will be exonerated and marry Margot. Dieterle knew audiences expected the insurgency to be crushed, as indeed it was. But in the movies defeat can be ignominious or glorious. Here, the rebels do not so much die as make a graceful exit into another realm. A director can only achieve such visual poetry with the help of a sympathetic cinematographer, like Mohr, who also seems to have heard the siren call of the desert and to have responded with as much mystery as the budget allowed—which was enough to make the dark of the moon more romantic than ominous.

Dieterle's *Grand Slam* (1933) was a "triumph of the underdog" movie, set in the world of contract bridge, portrayed as if it had replaced baseball as the national pastime. One could get that impression from the tournament headlines that blazed across the screen, as families huddled around the radio to hear whether Stanislavky (Paul Lucas) would beat Van Dorn (Ferdinand Gottschalk) to regain his title as bridge champion. Since both share a lower middle class background, they would seem to have come up the hard way. The difference is that Stanislavky never denied his origins, while Van Dorn buried his. When Stanislavky publishes a book on contract bridge (which was ghost written), he proves, with his wife Marcia (Loretta) as partner, that his book can bring bridge-playing couples closer together. However, a cross-country tour creates such friction between the two of them that the Stanislavsky method seems to be a failure. The marriage is on the verge of deteriorating after the press learns the truth about Stanislavsky's bestseller. Determined to challenge Van Dorn one last time, Stanislavsky is losing until Marcia sweeps into the room and becomes his partner. Naturally, he wins, the marriage remains intact, the couple give up bridge, and Stanislavsky does what he always wanted to do: He writes political treatises.

Although Lucas was the star, turning on enough continental charm to air out Stanislavsky's stuffiness, Loretta played Marcia as if she were an experienced bridge player, and she looked enticing in her pre-code décolletage. Capra might have found a heart somewhere in the manipulative script, but Dieterle knew enough about plot templates to follow the rubrics.

Loretta's last Warner Bros. film, *She Had to Say Yes* (1933), had her playing a "working girl," Florence, a garment district secretary, expected to entertain buyers by dining and clubbing with them but shopping short of one-night stands, although that caveat was never enforced, as long as the buyer signed the contract. Loretta's costars were two competent but uncharismatic actors: Regis Toomey, as her supervisor and would-be fiancé, and Lyle Talbot, never intended to be a leading man, as a buyer, who respects Florence until he mistakenly concludes that she is damaged goods and therefore available. A near rape in a darkened bedroom, with the only light coming from a moonlit window, is averted when the buyer realizes that Florence is not playing hard to get, but only preserving whatever remains of the dignity she has had to sacrifice to entertain buyers without making herself part of the entertainment. Although the role did not call for an elaborate wardrobe, Loretta looked her beatific self, as if she were slouching toward sainthood, needing only a nimbus to encircle her head upon arrival.

Loretta was not sorry to leave Warner's. Like Coriolanus, she believed there was a world elsewhere, with better roles awaiting her. There were, but not as many as she had hoped.

CHAPTER 7

Darryl Zanuck's Costume Queen

In 1933, the worst year of the Great Depression, Darryl F. Zanuck resigned as production head at Warner's. The previous year, the studio had suffered a net loss of over $14 million, twice that of the 1931 deficit. Warner's was not alone; RKO reported a loss of almost $4.4 million, and Paramount declared bankruptcy. The studios knew that the only way to survive was to adopt a policy of temporary salary cuts. Although opposed to the decision, Zanuck voluntarily went on half salary. Even after Price Waterhouse and the Academy of Motion Picture Arts and Sciences agreed that salary reductions were no longer necessary, Harry Warner continued enforcing the policy. As president, Harry held the purse strings. Rather than renege on his promise that everyone's salary would return to what it had been, Zanuck left. It was time, anyway. Zanuck was meant to give orders, not take them.

If any of the 15 million unemployed Americans learned that, on 15 April 1933, a movie executive left his $5,000-a-week job at one studio to move to another that had just started up, he or she would have wondered if Zanuck were living in a utopia where there were no bank runs, foreclosures, breadlines, rioting farmers, store windows smashed in frustration, lootings, school closings, and suspension or curtailment of garbage collections. Didn't he have faith in the new president, Franklin D. Roosevelt, who had been inaugurated less than a month earlier? Zanuck had faith in himself. In terms of religion he was atypical of the movie moguls. He was not born in eastern or central Europe, or even New York, but in Wahoo, Nebraska, to parents with Swiss and British roots. Zanuck was a Christian in an industry founded by Jewish immigrants or their sons. When he formed Twentieth Century-Fox in 1935, the amalgamation of the Fox Film Corporation and Twentieth Century, it was nicknamed the "Goy Studio."

Zanuck had no dearth of offers after leaving Warner's. Columbia beckoned, but he would be facing the same problem he just left: two brothers, Jack Cohn in the New York office, and Harry in Los Angeles. And then there was the location: Gower Street, in the shadow of Poverty Row. Jack Cohn would have been easier to deal with than Harry Warner, but Harry Cohn could not brook a superior; he was president and production head. Exactly what Zanuck's title would have been is another matter. Executive producer, perhaps. Titles would not have mattered to Harry; he ran the show.

By now, Zanuck had changed jobs more often than some countries changed boundaries. At seven he was a movie extra; at fourteen, an underage army recruit; then a writer for the pulps; a gag writer for Charlie Chaplin; a short story writer; and a screenwriter who did not think it was beneath his dignity to write for Lassie's predecessor, the canine star Rin-Tin-Tin. In 1933, Zanuck knew he was one of the haves and would not suffer the fate of the have-nots. When MGM's production head, Louis Mayer, wanted to find a place for his son-in-law, William Goetz, later a distinguished producer (but not as famous as Mayer's other son-in-law, David Selznick), Mayer and Joseph Schenck of United Artists joined forces to create a new studio, Twentieth Century, with Goetz owning one-third of the stock, and Zanuck serving as vice president for production.

Zanuck needed talent. Even then, he was thinking of his own studio, not Twentieth Century, even though Joe Schenck was an improvement over the brothers Warner. He wanted contract players, recognizable names. Zanuck was well aware of Loretta. As one familiar with stars both in their ascendancy and their decline, he knew Loretta was destined for the firmament. Any producer would have been impressed by her work in *Platinum Blonde, Man's Castle,* and *Midnight Mary.* Zanuck also knew she was studio-shopping and therefore available. What Loretta did not know is that Zanuck thought of her as an actress who could shuttle between the ordinary and the exotic—a course she had run for the past five years. At Twentieth Century, it was more of the same, but the schedule was less hectic, the productions costlier, the costumes more elaborate, and the scripts, for the most part, more literate—as one might expect from Zanuck, a published author and occasional pseudonymous screenwriter. The problem was the leading men, many of whom (e.g., Clark Gable, Tyrone Power, even Don Ameche) stole the spotlight from her.

Her first year at Twentieth Century seemed no different from her last year at Warner's, except that instead of nine movies in one year, she only made five, none of which tarnished or enhanced her reputation.

Zanuck—hoping to cash in on the popularity of the "tough dame" movie (e.g., the Barbara Stanwyck films, *Ten Cents a Dance, Ladies of Leisure,* and *Baby Face*), and perhaps inspired by the offbeat casting of Loretta in *Midnight Mary*—thought she would be a natural for the lead in *Born to Be Bad* (1934). Loretta's character, Letty Strong, was an unwed mother with an incorrigible son she is raising to be a survivor like herself, even if it means conning, finagling, and stealing. Despite the presence of Cary Grant who, compared to Loretta, was a newcomer (he made his first movie in 1932), *Born to be Bad* was the kind of film in which "bad" was applicable to both Letty and the film. Loretta was mired in an impossible role, in which the character alternates between neurotic possessiveness and motherly gush. The problem is the bratty son, who should have been sent to reform school, so his mother could ply her trade, flirting and teasing to get her way—and steering the script in another direction. But smother love wins out over promiscuity, and the son's fate becomes more important than Letty's, even though, dramatically, it is of little interest.

When the boy is slightly injured by a dairy truck, Letty, with the help of a wily lawyer, turns the incident into a major accident that has impaired his ability to think and walk. When the defendant company provides evidence that the boy is mobile enough to jump down steps, Letty is judged morally unqualified to raise her son, who is then sent to an orphanage. At this point, the script turns sappy: Grant proposes to adopt the boy because he and his wife cannot have children, offering him a dream life that the boy sneeringly rejects. Letty, the professional mother, still wants him back and even crashes a party, dragging Grant onto the dance floor and pressing against him so tightly that they seem to be lovers.

What happens next makes verisimilitude seem like an academic artifact. Letty spends the night with Grant, who then confesses his infidelity to his wife. For no apparent reason; other than to resolve the plot, Letty has a change of heart and leaves the couple to patch up their tattered marriage, while she returns to her old job in a book store—and presumably begins a new life. Even at Warner's, Loretta was never saddled with such a script. Except when she turned shrill at any attempt to separate Letty from her son, Loretta knew exactly how to play the role: coy, when required; seductive, when necessary; and maternal, when warranted. In the early scenes, she looks as if she were "on the town"—glamorous, inviting, and available. But Letty is also a tough dame, who uses her classy wardrobe as bait for unsuspecting males so she can provide a comfortable life for her son. The problem was that the son does not deserve it.

But that did not prevent Loretta from playing the role as if he merited the moon. Lowell Sherman, who directed the Mae West classic *She Done Him Wrong* (1933), also costarring Grant, could do nothing with *Born to be Bad*, except shoot it. The film was atypical of what Loretta would be offered at Twentieth Century. Her other films received more elaborate productions, but never measured up to what she had expected. Understandably, her tenure at Fox would be brief, lasting from 1934 to 1939, with three return engagements.

The most interesting of Loretta's 1934 films was not *The House of Rothschild*, but *Bulldog Drummond Strikes Back*, in which she plays the proverbial damsel in distress to the true star, Ronald Colman, as the former British army officer turned adventurer and amateur sleuth. Hugh "Bulldog" Drummond first appeared in 1920 as a series character in the novels of "Sapper" (H. C. McNeile), which inspired a similar series of films, lasting from 1922 to 1971. There were various movie Drummonds (Ray Milland, John Howard, Ron Randell, and even Walter Pidgeon and Ralph Richardson), but the actor who captured the suavity and worldliness of Sapper's Drummond was Ronald Colman. His devilish urbanity was even reflected in his eyes, which looked amused by all the plot twists, never mocking them but simply treating the preposterous goings on as a parlor—or rather, drawing room—game.

Bulldog Drummond Strikes Back opens in fogbound London, exquisitely photographed by J. Peverell Marley, with enough cones of light filtered through the gloom to spotlight Lola (Loretta), who emerges out of the swirling mist. She seems disoriented, and after speaking incoherently to Drummond, disappears into the night. Explanations are eventually forthcoming, if not always plausible. Lola is the niece of the man whose body Drummond finds in a spectacularly appointed mansion, the home of an Asian prince (Warner Oland, a popular Charlie Chan of the 1930s), who has disposed of the body and plays dumb when Drummond and the Bobbies arrive. This is the kind of film whose plot points were recycled in the "nobody believes me" movie, wherein husbands try to drive their wives mad (*Gaslight, Sleep, My Love*), and avengers make the innocent suffer for another's actions (*The Secret Fury, A Woman's Vengeance*).

The McGuffin, as Hitchcock would say, is an encoded radiogram confirming that the furs the Prince is importing are infected with cholera, and that they could, if unloaded, precipitate an epidemic. Drummond not only trumps Scotland Yard but gets Lola, while his sidekick, Archie (Charles Butterworth), has to defer consummating his own marriage to be Drummond's best man. The film, which declared itself a "Darryl F.

Zanuck Production," did not stint on sets; the prince's mansion was a museum piece that looked as if it belonged to an eccentric millionaire. Although Loretta's wardrobe was properly British, prim and unglamorous, it does not stop Drummond from proposing to her once he discovers that Lola shares his fondness for hollyhocks. Loretta's British accent had improved considerably since *The Devil to Pay*. But she still hoped for one more chance to show her dream lover that she was a worthy costar. She did a year later, and again in the next decade—but then it was on radio.

Zanuck had nothing to do with *Caravan* (1934), which ranks high among Hollywood's misconceived films as Fox's disastrous foray into operetta, a genre best left to MGM with its resident warblers, Jeanette MacDonald and Nelson Eddy. *Caravan's* director was the German-born Erik Charell, whose signature scrolls across the screen before the title appears, heralding his authorial status. Although few in the industry knew who he was, Charell was hired because he had been a successful director of European operetta, particularly in Berlin; his knowledge of film, however, was rudimentary. Ernst Lubitsch might have turned *Caravan* into inexpensive champagne that at least had some fizz; in Charell's hands, *Caravan* was *vin ordinaire*.

Caravan was a clone of Sigmund Romberg's *The Student Prince*, the paradigm of the prince and the commoner romance that is doomed from the start because of the disparity in the lovers' classes. In *Caravan*, the sexes are reversed. A frivolous Hungarian countess (Loretta) discovers that she can only inherit the ancestral estate, with its profitable vineyards, if she marries before her twenty-first birthday. Forced to find a husband within a day, she balks at marrying a lieutenant from a prominent family, preferring a gypsy (Charles Boyer), solely because of his music—especially one song that begins as a violin solo and then swells into a chorus of gypsies, lip synching badly and acting like last-minute recruits from a road show. In his attempt to establish himself as a Hollywood director, Charrel resorted to elaborate tracking shots, with the camera pulling back from rows of gypsies with artificial smiles. Not knowing how to deal with a script that, without music, would have been a seventy-minute feature, Charell threw in production numbers, drawing on original music and snippets of familiar classics—for example, one of Listz's Hungarian Rhapsodies, which, instead of relieving the tedium, increased it.

The countess embraces the gypsy life, even exchanging her imperial wardrobe for a peasant blouse and skirt. Soon she realizes that she and her gypsy lover are from two different worlds and that her best bet is the lieutenant. From the way Boyer was made up, with a hairstyle that was a combination of Julius Caesar's and Napoleon's, one would never know that he would inherit Valentino's title, the Great Lover. That would not happen until *The Garden of Allah* and, especially, *Algiers*.

Perhaps a better director might have helped Loretta reveal the various stages of the countess's maturation, as she comes to realize that she can only marry within her class. But there was no character development, only a last-minute epiphany that writers resort to when they have driven the plot into a dead end from which it needs to be towed.

Loretta's most prestigious film during her first year at Fox was *The House of Rothschild* (1934), although it has never been associated with her, but with the great stage and screen actor, George Arliss, who played both Mayer Rothschild and his son, Nathan. Arliss had a magisterial voice that lent credence, at least vocally, to the historical figures he was so adept at portraying: Alexander Hamilton, Voltaire, Disraeli, and now the dual role of the founder of an international banking empire and his most successful son. In many ways, it was a daring film, addressing the subject of anti-Semitism, which became increasingly prevalent after Hitler's rise to power in 1933. In that same year, Jews were dismissed from universities, and anyone with Jewish grandparents was denied employment. Book burnings replaced bonfires; works by Thomas Mann and Arnold Zweig were tossed into the flames. The rise of German anti-Semitism, fruitlessly denounced by the League of Nations, was too controversial a topic for the major studios, whose heads (MGM's Louis Mayer, the brothers Warner, Universal's Carl Laemmle, Columbia's Harry Cohn, Paramount's Adolf Zukor) were Jews. They feared a backlash, particularly in view of the growing popularity of the "radio priest," Rev. Charles Coughlin, whose broadcasts grew more anti-Semitic as the persecution of German Jews intensified.

Zanuck, on the other hand, did not shy away from controversy, tackling postwar anti-Semitism (*Gentleman's Agreement* [1947]), racism (*Pinky* [1949], *No Way Out* [1950]), and mental illness (*The Snake Pit* [1948]); he even demythologized 7 December 1941, the "day that will live in infamy," in *Tora! Tora! Tora!* (1970). Zanuck was not, to quote the subtitle of Neal Gabler's *An Empire of Their Own*, one of "the Jews who invented Hollywood," men who, despite their extraordinary inventiveness, preferred to downplay their Judaism. They wished to avoid antagonizing Christian audiences who preferred their clergymen to be white and either Catholic or Protestant, and Jews who wished to remain as anonymous as possible—as was apparent even in a movie like Columbia's *The*

Jolson Story (1946), in which little is made of Al Jolson's religion, with his parents behaving like a comedy team doing ethnic shtick.

At Warner's, Zanuck produced two major films in which the main characters were Jews: *The Jazz Singer* (1927) with Al Jolson and *Disraeli* (1929) with George Arliss. Zanuck had no qualms about making *The House of Rothschild*. The film premiered in March 1934. Since Twentieth Century Films was still a year away from merging with Fox, it was distributed by United Artists; it also proved a critical and commercial success. As a historical film, *The House of Rothschild* was better documented than the typical Hollywood product depicting a straight Cole Porter in *Night and Day* (1946) and a straight Larry Hart in *Words and Music* (1948), or a Woodrow Wilson (*Wilson* [1944]) promoting his long cherished dream of a League of Nations in a film that makes no mention of the fact that the United States did not join the organization.

The House of Rothschild opens with Frankfurt Jews being herded into "Jew Street" (actually, *Judenstadt*, "*Stadt*" suggesting a city, or, in this case, a ghetto) before curfew. Among the residents of the *Judenstadt* are the Rothschilds: Mayer with his wife Gudula (the great character actress, Helen Westley, who played a memorable wife and mother without resorting to caricature), and their five sons, of whom Nathan becomes the most prominent. Perhaps if there had been a stronger Jewish creative presence behind the film it might have seemed more authentic. The writer, Nunnally Johnson, director Alfred Werker, producer Darryl Zanuck, and star George Arliss were all Christians, as were some of the supporting cast, including Boris Karloff, Loretta, Robert Young, C. Aubrey Smith, and Florence Arliss. Someone might have suggested that Arliss not play Mayer as if he were Shylock in a touring production of *The Merchant of Venice*, appearing before an audience that considered Jews a colorful but alien race. Mayer's groveling before the tax collector is understandable in view of the latter's patent contempt for Jews, but there is a way to bow before authority and at the same time keep one's dignity. Before Mayer dies, he instructs his sons to establish five branches of the Rothschild dynasty, with each son staking out a city: London, Paris, Vienna, Frankfurt, and Naples (which turned out to be short-lived). Since Arliss would also play Nathan, the London branch becomes the most significant in terms of plot.

Loretta, in a blonde coif with curls, was part of the subplot. Johnson knew that audiences expected a love interest, not the kind between Mayer and Gudula, or Nathan and Hannah (well played by Florence

Arliss, George's wife), but between a nubile young woman and her suitor: Loretta as Nathan's daughter, called Julie in the film, and another Young, Robert, as the historical Captain Henry Fitzroy, a Christian. The difference in their religions left audiences wondering, "Will they or won't they marry?" They will, but at the end.

Historical films, like historical novels, collapse time, simplify genealogies, and romanticize the past, as if it were a myth needing to be recreated rather than an aggregate of facts awaiting fresh interpretation. To Johnson's credit, history, for the most part, is not upended, even though three decades—roughly 1783 to 1815—are subjected to year-jumping, which is not always that easy in an eighty-eight-minute movie. Loretta's character's name, Julie, contrasts sharply with the preponderance of Jewish names, such as Mayer, Nathan, Gudula, Solomon, and Amschel. Nathan Rothschild's daughter was Hannah, not Julie. Since Hannah was also the name of Nathan's wife, Johnson probably decided that two Hannahs in one film could be confusing. Although Julie refers to herself as a "Jewess," Loretta does not come across as one. "Julie," a name without any ethnic or religious associations, would suit Loretta Young better than "Hannah." Also, the historical Hannah was born in 1815. Since Loretta was almost twenty-one (but could pass for eighteen) when she was making *The House of Rothschild*, Julie must have been born at the end of the eighteenth century.

No matter. Loretta had virtually nothing do in the film, although she did appear in the final sequence, shot in Technicolor, in which Nathan is honored for averting a financial crisis in Britain. Color added nothing to the film. Zanuck probably wanted to test the new three-strip Technicolor process, a vast improvement over two-strip Technicolor, before introducing it in *Ramona* (1936), Fox's first color feature film, with Loretta in the title role. The finale is anticlimactic; *The House of Rothschild* reaches its peak in the penultimate scene, with Nathan at the London Exchange. Since Napoleon's victory over Wellington seems inevitable, "Sell!" becomes the buzzword. When Nathan, who has his own way of obtaining information (via carrier pigeon), learns that Wellington has actually defeated Napoleon at Waterloo, he immediately countermands with "Buy!" Apparently, there was a rumor spread by the anti-Rothschild faction that Nathan knew in advance about Wellington's defeat, but withheld the information to fill his own coffers. The rumor has now been discredited; even if Johnson believed it, which is doubtful, adding it the screenplay would have marred his loving portrait of the Rothschilds. Still, it was the climax, not the coda, that audiences took home with them.

The historical Nathan Rothschild was an enigmatic figure, who behaved as if he had grown a carapace over his skin to deflect the slings and arrows of bigots and competitors. Arliss portrayed that aspect of Nathan's character brilliantly. From Arliss's strikingly angular face, one could easily see that Nathan was a man who did not wear his heart on his sleeve for daws to peck at. Rather, he cultivated an inscrutable look that discouraged those expecting a bear hug and a warm handshake and challenged others who just wanted a deal without feigning bonhomie. The latter he understood; the former, he held at arm's length.

The House of Rothschild was a film in which Loretta was third billed, after Arliss and Boris Karloff, who plays Nathan's nemesis, Baron Ledrantz, and is eventually brought to his knees. If Americans responded to the film—and they did—it was not because of Loretta, but because the plot of *The House of Rothschild* epitomized the American dream: Start small, suffer persecution, triumph over your oppressors, and relax in the gilded cocoon of financial independence.

The House of Rothschild established Loretta as Twentieth Century's costume queen. One of her better costume dramas was *Clive of India* (1935), which chronicled the life of the so-called "conqueror of India," who had subjugated southern, then northern India when he was twenty-six. By the time he was thirty-four, he was Lord Clive, lauded for bringing the subcontinent under British rule. As in most biopics, time is collapsed, details omitted, and historical figures reduced to walk-ons (Burgoyne) or references (George III). But most of the film was credible even when it turned hagiographic. Both Clive (Ronald Colman) and his wife Margaret (Loretta) had real character arcs to trace, Colman especially. At first, Clive is a romantic, a combination of Lord Byron and Werther. Suffering from *Weltschmertz*, which was probably clinical depression, he attempts suicide (a prefiguration of his manner of death, only hinted at in the film), but the pistol fails to discharge. All Clive has to see is a picture of his friend's sister, Margaret, before he declares that she will be his wife. Romeo and Juliet were not the only ones whose eye contact set a plot in motion. Similarly, Margaret takes one look at Clive and succumbs. Since Colman was one of Loretta's first crushes, she had no problem playing the love-stricken lady—even though her first scene required her to bathe a dog, which seemed like an inauspicious beginning. But Loretta, again in a blonde wig, was game, acting as if she had been bathing dogs since she was a child.

Once Clive arrives in India, he realizes that his mission in life is to add India to the British Empire, even if it means defeating one warlord by wooing another and forging an admiral's signature. The Clives undergo the usual adversities, including losing their first child. And Loretta has some poignant moments once they have settled in London, when she tells Clive what a trial India was for her and how grateful she is to be back on British soil. The corrupt East India Company officials, whom Clive fired, return to London and proceed to sully his reputation, costing him his seat in Parliament. Clive has no other choice but to return to India to work for the company again. Visually, his return results in the most impressive sequence in the film: an attack during a monsoon in which elephants trample their victims or sweep them up in their trunks. Clive's speech in Parliament to justify his actions is historically accurate; neither the real nor the cinematic Clive lost his fortune. Husband and wife have grown wise through suffering, each showing it in a different way: Colman by lowering his commanding voice during the brief speech and concealing the pain he feels with slow, measured speech; Loretta by adopting an air of determination, inflexible yet touchingly feminine, when she refuses to accompany her husband to India even though he has become a pariah in Britain. Audiences to whom Clive of India was a history book figure like Christopher Columbus or Marco Polo would have had no idea how Robert Clive died—and the writers intended it that way, offering the knowledgeable enough clues by portraying Clive as being plagued by headaches that drove him to stab himself at forty-one. The writers could only hope that some moviegoers would understand their tragically flawed hero; for the others, what mattered was that Robert Clive was not financially ruined, thereby escaping the fate of so many less fortunate Americans in the Great Depression.

 Twentieth Century Pictures was just on the verge of becoming Twentieth Century-Fox. Thus *Clive of India* was advertised as a Twentieth Century film, and also—in equally imposing type—"a Darryl F. Zanuck Production." Like the other Twentieth Century features, it was released by United Artists. *Clive of India* was also Loretta's last film with Colman. Zanuck had found another leading man for her, Tyrone Power.

 Paramount was going through an exotic phase in the early thirties, with such films as *Morocco* (1930), *Shanghai Express* (1932), *The Sign of the Cross* (1932), *Madame Butterfly* (1932), *White Woman* (1933,) and *Cleopatra* (1934). When it came time for the studio to cast *Shanghai* (1935), a Walter Wanger Production, the studio was hard pressed to come up with any contract players to portray Barbara Holland, an American socialite, or Dimitri Koslov, the Eurasian who falls in love with her. Thus, Loretta was loaned out to play Holland, and since Charles Boyer was under contract to Wanger, he was cast as Koslov.

Shanghai might have fared better under Zanuck; at least he would have encouraged the writers to look for a way in which the couple could transcend the boundaries of race. The 1934 version of the production code forbade miscegenation, defined as "sex relationships between the black and white races." Theoretically, the code did not apply to Boyer's character, since Koslov was not black; he was the son of a Russian father and a Manchurian mother. Still, if Koslov and Barbara Holland married, they would be an interracial couple, which would not set well with moviegoers who believed in strict separation of the races. Like love affairs between a prince or princess and a commoner, theirs was doomed from the start.

Koslov discovered the ideal way to triumph over prejudicial whites: He founded a financial empire in Shanghai. When the Chinese ambassador (Warner Oland, in another Asian role) warns Koslov that he must tell Barbara about his mother, he finally agrees. At a costume party, he pays tribute to the two women responsible for his success: Barbara and his mother, a Manchurian princess, whose portrait hangs on the wall. Shocked, the guests leave one by one. Just when it seems Barbara might remain, she puts down her drink and exits. Since Wanger suspected that moviegoers might behave similarly, *Shanghai* ends with a chastened Barbara and a resigned Koslov admitting that, if they married, they would encounter the same prejudice that Koslov's parents did, prejudice so strong that it drove his mother to suicide. In his closing speech, Koslov yearns for the day when people are not judged by the color of their skin—which is ironic, since Boyer looked no different in *Shanghai* than he did in Wanger's other 1935 film, *Private Worlds*.

Nineteen thirty-five was a benchmark year for both Zanuck and Loretta. For Zanuck, it was the year that he achieved his goal: At thirty-three, he would be production head of his own studio, Twentieth Century-Fox. In the early 1930s, the founder of the Fox Film Corporation, the Hungarian born William Fox, realized his empire was crumbling. In 1932, Fox reported a loss of nearly $17 million. In 1935, Twentieth Century was valued at $4 million, as opposed to Fox's $1.8 million. A merger was proposed in the form of an exchange of stock, and Twentieth Century-Fox became Hollywood's newest studio. For Loretta, 1935 was the year of her "mortal sin." Early that year, she learned that she was pregnant. Her relationship with her *Call of the Wild* costar did not result in one of her usual crushes. This time it was not a romantic fantasy, or *grand amour* à la Hollywood, where the camera tracks back from the passionate couple, followed by a slow fade out. It was rather like a "one indiscretion, one conception" movie on the order of *The Old Maid* (1938), *To Each His Own* (1946), *Letter from an Unknown Woman* (1948), and *Not Wanted* (1949). If Loretta went through with the pregnancy, the child's father would be one of Hollywood's best-known actors who, in February 1935, won his only Oscar for *It Happened One Night*. Ironically, the Academy Awards ceremony coincided with Loretta's discovering she was pregnant. Clark Gable was no dream lover. He was the genuine article.

CHAPTER 8

The Men in Her Life

"I have been in love fifty times," Loretta admitted to an interviewer in 1933. "If I didn't fall a little bit in love with the men I play opposite, I could not do love scenes with them. " This was not the boast of a starlet, eager to graduate to siren, or at least love goddess, status. Loretta was a star; she was also speaking truthfully. Her adolescence was spent in the movie business. While other girls her age went off with their boy friends to the local soda fountain and sipped ice cream sodas through two straws—the era's idea of safe sex—Loretta was constantly in transit, spinning through Warner's revolving door, with an occasional break. Few other actresses could claim to have appeared in fifty-five films by the time they were twenty.

Not every actor made the cut. Walter Huston, who played Loretta's racketeer father in *The Ruling Voice* (1931), giving the only memorable performance in a less-than-classic crime film, was too avuncular for fantasy. Besides, Huston was twenty-nine years her senior, and Loretta had been cast as his daughter. When Loretta spoke of falling in love, she was talking about a transferable infatuation generated by her imagination that enabled her to perform credibly on the screen. Whether she knew it or not, she was talking about the art of acting, an art so elusive that, once experienced, it can only be described, not defined. Even in her early thirties, Loretta sounded like a child of fancy. Quoting a limerick that ends, "I like men," she cited some of her favorite screen lovers: Douglas Fairbanks, Jr., Don Ameche, Richard Barthelmess, Ronald Colman, Charles Boyer, Gary Cooper, Tyrone Power, and Alan Ladd. When she mentioned Clark Gable, it was only to record, like a school teacher, that knowing how she felt about swearing, he observed decorum on the set, even when something went wrong and justified a bit of profanity.

Anyone who knew what had happened when they were making *The Call of the Wild* would have been amused that while Gable curbed his language, he did not do the same to his libido.

When Loretta was sixteen, and making *The Second Floor Mystery* (1930), she fell in love with her leading man, Grant Withers. This time, it was not love filtered through the lens of the imagination, but an emotional attachment that may have been love. But how would Loretta know? She was so used to fantasy that, if she ever experienced the real thing, she might not have known the difference. Loretta was always attracted to older men. Withers, born in 1904, was nine years her senior. They seemed to have much in common: both were born in January, Withers on the sixteenth in Colorado, the state in which Loretta's sister, Sally Blane, was born; Loretta on the sixth in Utah. Before becoming an actor, he loaded freight at the Santa Fe railroad yards, reported on the crime scene for a Los Angeles newspaper, and drove a riot squad car for the LAPD. Loretta responded immediately to his rough-edged masculinity. She had no idea that he had been married before, but soon learned when his ex-wife, Inez, filed for alimony the first week of February 1930, shortly after Loretta and Withers were married. That January, Loretta thought she had found her future husband and was even willing to ignore the mandates of the Church and elope with him. "When love comes so strong, / There is no right or wrong. / Your love is your life," Anita sings to Maria in Leonard Bernstein's *West Side Story*. Loretta felt similarly. However, when she experienced that love, short-lived as it was, she was sixteen, which was not a marriageable age in California. Once Withers learned that a woman could be married in Arizona at seventeen, they waited until Loretta had reached her seventeenth birthday.

On Sunday, 26 January, Loretta and Withers boarded an early morning flight to Yuma, Arizona, where they were married. When the couple returned, a furious Gladys Belzer met them at the airport, threatening to have the marriage annulled, until she learned it was legal. Gladys was savvy enough to know that the press would make fodder of the three of them. She withdrew the annulment suit, and Loretta informed the press that she would remain married to Withers and that her mother had accepted her decision. The situation changed on 8 February, when Loretta received a subpoena to testify in an alimony suit brought by the first Mrs. Withers against her ex-husband, whom she had married in 1925, and with whom she had a child. If Loretta was devastated by the news, she did not show it. There was a front to maintain and a press to contend with. Still, at the end of June, Loretta, who knew how to make her life into a movie, informed reporters that she and Withers were taking a delayed honeymoon in Denver, as if, "God's in his heaven and all's right with the world." But it wasn't. God ruled otherwise, and in early July, Loretta initiated divorce proceedings.

But she still carried a torch. As she confessed to Gladys Hall in 1933, in an interview that never saw print, "I never, I know, felt that way about any man again. I was in love with him. I shall always be in love with him." The torch burned out the following year when she made *Man's Castle* with Spencer Tracy. *Modern Screen* (December 1933) reported that Tracy and Loretta were often seen lunching together and going out dancing in the evening. Ironically, both were Catholics, and Tracy was married but estranged from his wife. The Tracys never divorced; as Catholics, they remained faithful to their marriage vows, even though their marriage was foundering. Loretta was also a Catholic, yet she thought nothing about clubbing with a married man. Perhaps it was her youth or just the desire to enjoy the nonthreatening company of a man who respected her. There was no "affair." At the time, Loretta had a rainbow-colored notion of love: it was passion viewed through a kaleidoscope, a swirl of colors, with kissing and petting in place of sex. Loretta's idea of love was a precoital paradise. Still, she should have realized that, as a single Catholic, she was consorting with a married man whose marriage, the press implied, was imperiled because of her. But from her standpoint, it was not adultery; she was merely enjoying the companionship of a man who was secure in his masculinity and could be her "cleft in the rock of the world." Tracy was the male companion and surrogate father that she desperately sought, and Loretta was the soul mate that Tracy's wife could never be. "Soul mate" is apt. If Tracy harbored any physical desire for Loretta, her virtue-emblazoned face would have inhibited him—although it did not stop Clark Gable two years later.

In early 1934, Loretta and Tracy knew they had to address the subject of their "romance" and put their fans at ease. Loretta stated unequivocally that marriage was out of the question: "I would never marry outside my church. Nor will I. Consequently, Spencer and I might as well part company now as later." Yet she did acknowledge her debt to him: "He has given me gentleness, thoughtfulness, and consideration such as I have never known in any other man," adding, "[H]e has a rare masculine quality—a refined mind." In November 1934, the Tracys separated but never divorced. Tracy told Gladys Hall that, although he was in love with Loretta, she "had nothing whatever to do with our separating, Mrs. Tracy's and mine. Nothing whatever to do with it."

Loretta found other male admirers, and Tracy found Katharine Hepburn, who implied that they were lovers, although Tracy was too guilt-ridden for adultery. "I tried to save him from drink," Loretta told celebrity biographer Donald Spoto when he visited her Sunset Boulevard mansion to do a piece for *Architectural Digest*. Hepburn couldn't save him, either. Tracy had his own desert places that others could not visit. Apart from chronic alcoholism and a marriage gone sour, there were unconfirmed tales about male prostitutes who allegedly serviced him in a bungalow on George Cukor's estate, where he spent his final years.

There was no happy ending for Grant Withers, either. He married three more times, and his career, which was never meteoric, spiraled downward. In 1959, his landlord discovered Withers's body in his apartment, a suicide note in one hand and a telephone receiver in the other. It's tempting to think that he might have been trying to call Loretta.

If Loretta pined over Tracy, no one would know it. There were other men—several, in fact. When David Niven arrived in Los Angeles in 1933, he stayed at the home where Loretta, her mother, and sisters lived until he found a place of his own. An unreconstructed (and unapologetic) ladies' man, Niven was immediately attracted to Loretta and escorted her to nightclubs. According to his biographer, he and Loretta were "never lovers, certainly not at first." On the other hand, it was "common knowledge that he had practically every star in Hollywood." If that's the case, perhaps Niven could not distinguish between his successful conquests and his failures.

In 1939, Loretta set her sights on James Stewart. Supposedly, she was too forward for Stewart, whose shyness challenged her femininity and put it in overdrive. At that stage in his life, Stewart was "fearful of, a bit confused by, and more than a little tinged with guilt about her strong sexual advances." What Stewart misinterpreted as sexual advances, strong or weak, was flirtatiousness. If Loretta was more aggressive than usual, it was because she had encountered a man who resisted her platonic notion of eros, preferring the reality to the dream. Stewart did not marry until 1949, when he was forty-one. In 1949, Loretta was thirty-six and had been married twice.

It would have been impossible for Loretta not to have been smitten by Tyrone Power, who, as Jeanine Basinger phrased it, was not handsome, but "beautiful." As a Fox contract player, Power was a natural partner for the studio's resident beauty queen, with whom he made six films. The press declared them an "item." To Zanuck, Loretta and Power were an investment, which he had no intention of losing to marriage. Zanuck discouraged any further relationship with Loretta by setting up a romance between Power and his latest discovery, Olympic medalist Sonja Henie, whose talent lay in her spectacular skating, not her acting. With Henie, there was no hope of real romance, nor would anyone think of her and Power as an "item." With this arrangement, Zanuck could keep his beauties at his studio. Power and Henie made one movie together, *Thin Ice* (1937), after which, one would like to think, Zanuck decreed that Power deserved better scripts and better costars. One movie with Henie was punishment enough.

Henie was no beauty, and Loretta was off limits, both by fiat and by choice. Loretta had no problem with Zanuck's ultimatum. But she was always salary conscious. When she discovered that Zanuck found Power a greater asset to the studio than herself, she confronted him, complaining that in all the years she had been at Fox, she had never received a raise, unlike Power, who had received two. Worse, Zanuck committed the unpardonable sin of never sending her flowers. Power was the bigger star, and Zanuck knew his name meant more at the box office than Loretta's. Besides, she received $4,000 a week for *Suet* (1938), her last picture with Power—not bad for a film in which she was eclipsed by Power and the newest addition to Fox's talent roster, Annabella, who got the best notices of any of them. Annabella was Power's kind of woman—temporarily, at least—and they soon married. He and Loretta remained friends. With Loretta, it was simple: One romance ends, another begins. When Power died in 1958, Loretta, now a television star, made a dramatic entrance at his funeral at Hollywood Memorial Park, coming straight from the set of her series, *The Loretta Young Show*. The episode being filmed that day required her to play an Asian. Since Loretta did not change her costume, she created a photo op, even upstaging the deceased.

One would think that she would have had a crush on Cary Grant, with whom she made two films: *Born to Be Bad*, which she "thought . . . was perfectly terrible," and *The Bishop's Wife*, which really belonged to Grant and the great character actors Monty Woolley, Elsa Lanchester, James Gleason, and Gladys Cooper. Grant paid little attention to Loretta, spending what she considered an inordinate amount of time "dissecting" his scenes with the director, Henry Koster. Finally, she confronted him: "I don't mind your doing this because I know you're trying to get a better film, but please don't do it around me." A true gentleman, he never did it again.

Loretta's oddest relationship was with director Edward Sutherland, the oldest man (eighteen years her senior) she ever dated. He was not only a father figure; he was old enough to be her father. Since never appeared in any of his films, the most famous of which were W. C. Fields vehicles (*International House, Poppy, Mississippi*), they must have met on some social occasion. For a staunch Catholic like Loretta, going out with Sutherland was even more problematic than it was with Tracy. Sutherland was now on his fourth marriage; his second wife had been the enigmatic Louise Brooks. Like Tracy, Sutherland was what Loretta was seeking: He was paternal, erudite, sophisticated (London-born, he still had an accent), and good for a night on the town. Although Sutherland imbibed, Loretta never felt that she had to save him from drink. What Loretta sought in Sutherland was a combination father-friend. What Sutherland sought was a woman who could give him what none of his wives could: fulfillment, sexual and otherwise—a love that heats the blood and cools the mind.

Sutherland's understanding of Loretta was so accurate that he seemed to have had access to her unconscious: "Loretta idealizes, and she is rebuffed by the slightest intimacy. A platonic love would suit her, I think. I hope she marries again. When real love comes along, perhaps she won't be so finicky." To which Loretta replied: "I don't blame him. He was and is a perfectly darling man, but I just didn't want to get married. I wasn't especially in love with him. I was in love with love."

"I was in love with love." She was in love with a word and all it conjured up. And the word became flesh in the person of Clark Gable.

CHAPTER 9

Heeding the Call of the Wild

When Loretta learned she would be costarring with Clark Cable in *The Call of the Wild* (1935) and working for the fourth time with William Wellman, she was elated. She was prepared to have a crush on her leading man, salving her Catholic conscience by limiting her crushes to fantasies more romantic than erotic. But that was before she went on location at Lake Chelan in Washington—although it would have been the same if she and Gable were in Nevada as originally scheduled. But a change of climate required a change of plan, and the state of Washington was a logical stand in for the Yukon at the turn of the twentieth century. Wellman was in his element with *The Call of the Wild*. The more masculine the milieu, the more legible the Wellman signature. From the opening scene—with men slugging it out in the mud, bars thronged with hard-drinking prospectors, and poker players at their tables too absorbed in their game to ogle the chorines who languidly went through their routines—there was no doubt that *The Call of the Wild* was a William Wellman film, the only one in which a dog upstaged the stars.

Anyone who read Jack London's *The Call of the Wild* never forgot Buck, the combination Saint Bernard and Scotch shepherd, as London describes him, from whose point of view the story is told. Buck is indisputably the main character. London's empathetic prose makes the reader wince every time Buck is mistreated by his sadistic owner or forced to contend with emaciated sled dogs so crazed by the smell of food that they attack each other. His point of view informs the novella, making it impossible to think of any of the other characters as real people, but only as obstacles that Buck must overcome in his Darwinian struggle for survival. To the fiercely socialist London, Buck was "the dominant primordial beast," relegated to the underclass in a world that exploits laborers, even depriving them of their identity. Buck does not even qualify as a wage slave, since he is not paid for his services. He is simply a beast of burden, serving the dominant class but giving it a run for its money. Docile, Buck is not.

The film is so radically different that it is practically an original screenplay inspired by the novella. Virtually all of London's characters have been eliminated except Buck. In the novella, he heeds the call of the wild and joins a wolf pack, becoming the head and protector of his brood, staking out his domain, which mortals enter at their peril. The only other character that made the transition from novella to film was John Thornton (Gable, called Jack in the film), who is killed in the original, a fate that would not be visited upon the star. A host of other characters were added, including a female costar (Loretta) and a male sidekick (Jack Oakie). If the film were made a decade later during the Lassie craze, a more faithful re-creation of the novella might have been possible. But screenwriter Gene Fowler heeded his own call of the wild (as did Gable and Loretta) and concentrated on the Gold Rush, and the extremes of rugged individualism and murderous greed that it generated.

When "Shorty" Houlihan (Jack Oakie), one of many invented characters, learns about an unclaimed gold mine, he enlists the support of another adventurer, Jack Thornton. Guided only by a map that Shorty has sketched from memory, the two make their way into a world as awesomely beautiful as it is dangerous, not knowing that the real heirs to the mine, John Blake and his wife Claire (Loretta)—created as a plot complication, with Claire as the love interest—have also set out to claim it. A storm sends Blake in search of help, leaving his wife to contend with the elements, especially the wolves. When Thornton and Shorty find her, she insists on joining them, unaware of their own plans. Claire—and, for that matter, Loretta—was indifferent to Thornton/Gable at first, but few women could resist Gable's penetrating eyes. When he looked at Loretta bundled in fur, it was as if he could see through all the insulation. Four years later, his eyes still had their disrobing power. The first time we see Rhett Butler (Gable) in *Gone with the Wind*, he is standing at the foot of the staircase, looking up at Scarlett (Vivien Leigh) so knowingly that Scarlett remarks, "He knows what I look like without my shimmy."

During the making of the film, Loretta was having her first real affair, the others being romantic interludes re-enacted in dreams and reveries. But Gable was no fantasy. Neither of them suspected that the fate of their characters would, in part, be theirs. When John Blake, who was presumed dead, turns up, Claire's relationship with Thornton comes to an end. This was the age of the new morality, spearheaded by the reinforced production code and the increasingly powerful National Legion of Decency. The writers (chiefly Gene Fowler) could have had someone discover Blake's body, so that true love could triumph. But who would object to a romance that could not continue once the missing spouse reappears? The costars paid no heed to that aspect of their characters' fate and continued their affair during a projected six-week shoot that dragged on for three months because of the weather. Gable and Loretta were two professionals who knew there is a time to work and a time to make love, the latter in private. Perhaps the weather contributed.

Claire challenged Loretta only in the sense that she was on location and had to rough it, wading through water, catching duffle bags as they were thrown to her, and going down the river in a makeshift raft. As far as characterization went, there was hardly any—only the transition from indifference to devotion, with a bit of ocular foreplay. That Loretta could easily manage. Wellman had no interest in her character; his was a world of men, fearless and resilient (e.g., *Wings, The Ox-Bow Incident, Yellow Sky, The Story of G.I. Joe*) and occasionally tough dames (*Midnight Mary, Roxy Hart*). As a "What price, Hollywood?" film, *A Star Is Born* (1937) may seem atypical of Wellman, but the main characters are a fading star who commits suicide, and his widow who displays incredible strength when she makes her first public appearance after his death.

The star of *Wild* was Gable, and his costar was Buck, who, in a more faithful adaptation, might have been billed above the title. Buck's emotional range (menacing, dangerous, affectionate, and, at one point, poignantly selfless) makes it possible for Thornton to win a $1,000 bet if Buck pulls a staggering load a hundred yards. Buck was a real actor; Lassie (or rather, the myriad of Lassies) was only a personality.

Although by contemporary standards it is hard to believe that *The Call of the Wild* incurred censorship problems, it did. After a hue and cry over films with women who were braless, promiscuous, or both; couples cohabiting outside of wedlock; unmarried mothers; hard drinkers of both sexes; charismatic gangsters; and Mae West, whose films were seasoned with double entendres, the National Legion of Decency was formed in April 1934. Two months later, the Production Code Administration came into existence, with Joseph Ignatius Breen as production code administrator. After a decade of salutary neglect, which Breen considered far too salutary, the production code would be rigorously enforced. Breen took a dim view of sex, marital or otherwise, animal or human. The film posed two problems: Claire and Thornton must not engage in a "sex affair," and scenes with Buck and his "lady friend" (Breen's euphemism for a female wolf) should not carry any "unpleasant connotations"—meaning that there must be no indication that they copulate. Breen was truly catholic when it came to sex: He regarded human and animal intercourse with similar contempt, believing only that the sacrament of matrimony justified the former, but never on screen; the same was true of animals who could not even sniff each other, even though they may be on the verge of a "sex affair."

Once they became lovers, Loretta and Gable knew they had to be discreet, even though their off screen behavior during the shoot reflected more than two actors rehearsing their scenes or discussing their roles. Studio contracts contained a morals clause, typified by the one MGM's Irving Thalberg drew up for Clark Gable in 1931:

> The artist agrees to conduct himself with due regard to public conventions and morals, and agrees that he will not do or commit any act that will degrade him in society, or bring him into public hatred, contempt, scorn, ridicule—or [any act] that will shock, insult, offend the community or ridicule public morals or decency, or prejudice the Motion Picture industry in general.

Golden Age Hollywood was a closed community, where powerful studio heads and their publicists operated under the radar to keep indiscretions from exploding into national headlines. George Cukor's homosexuality was common knowledge—but not to the general public. MGM's Howard Strickling kept Cukor's indiscretions out of the press, which considered him to be a "woman's director" and nothing more. When producer Anderson Lawler mistook an undercover cop for a male prostitute to whom he offered cocaine, Zanuck intervened, and the charges were dropped. Sometimes, when either a murder or a bizarre death was involved, even Zanuck was powerless. Nineteen twenty-two was not Hollywood's glorious year. The still unsolved William Desmond Taylor murder case adversely affected the career of Mabel Normand, supposedly the last to see him alive. Fatty Arbuckle's wild San Francisco weekend that resulted in the gruesome death of starlet Virginia Rappe turned the beloved comic into a pariah. Hollywood would behave similarly if the unmarried Loretta gave birth to Gable's child. No one in Wilkes-Barre or Oshkosh cared about Cukor's gay escapades. Only movie buffs would even know who he was. But Loretta was a household name. As Hollywood's preeminent Catholic, she would have been excoriated by the religious right and the National Legion of Decency. Her mortal sin would have occasioned "wages of sin" sermons. She would have become as unemployable as the blacklistees of the late 1940s and 1950s. Perhaps she could have found work at a Poverty Row studio like Monogram, Republic, or later, PRC. She could have worked in theatre, except that she knew she could never excel on the stage. Her media were film, radio, and finally, television.

In the Gospel according to John, Jesus saved an adulteress from death by stoning when he revealed the sins of her persecutors through symbols that he sketched on the ground which, in some way, they understood. He then challenged them: "Let him who is without sin cast the first stone" (John 8:7). To rid herself of guilt, Loretta might have recalled Jesus's final words to the woman: "Has no one condemned you?" he asked. "No one, sir," she replied. "Neither do I condemn you. Go and sin no more." But Loretta's guilt had become so all-consuming that even Jesus's words, cited chapter and verse, would have had no effect. First century Jerusalem was another time, another place. In 1935, it was not a question of absolution, but of survival. No one could rescue her except her mother, her doctor, and particularly Zanuck—but only if they worked out a credible scenario. Abortion was anathema, leaving her no choice but to bear the child others would have called a mistake, but which she termed a mortal sin. As a Catholic, she knew about the sacrament of penance and no doubt confessed what she had done. But whatever penance she was given was not enough. Loretta imposed her own penance, which lasted until the end of her life.

Loretta was an actress in an industry where image was all, and hers could be irreparably sullied. Since neither murder nor drugs—unpardonable sins in neo-right wing Hollywood (even though the latter never vanished from the movie scene)—were involved, all Loretta needed was the celluloid wall of silence, buttressed by the Church. Rumors and conjectures were inevitable, but the public had to remain ignorant of the facts, notably that the child had been placed in an orphanage and later adopted by Loretta, portrayed in the press as a woman eager to embrace motherhood, however vicariously. Would it work? Loretta was an excellent actress. She would make it work.

In March 1935, Loretta's immediate problem was fulfilling her next assignment. She had been loaned out to Paramount to star in Cecil B. DeMille's *The Crusades* (1936). Such was the price of being the costume queen. She was scheduled to report to the studio on 30 January. By 8 February, she still had not arrived. DeMille grew impatient; to him, she was replaceable. He considered Sylvia Sidney, whose screen test convinced him she was not medieval enough. Next, he turned to Elissa Landi, one of the stars of his hugely successful *Sign of the Cross* (1932). Landi was unavailable. DeMille had no choice but to go with Loretta, shooting around her until she was able to join the production. Doing so was not that difficult, since Henry Wilcoxon as Richard I (Richard the Lionheart) had the bigger part, but not the billing. Loretta suspected she was pregnant in late January 1935; by February, she knew she was. When Gable was informed, he was sympathetic but bewildered: "I thought she knew how to take care of herself. After all, she had been a married woman," he confided to Gladys. Married, yes. A consummated marriage? Loretta was probably not ready for sex when she eloped with Grant Withers. Once she learned a week after their wedding that Withers's ex-wife was suing him for alimony, she must have been even more inhibited, frightened at the idea of any intimacy that could result in conception. Elopement was bad enough, but with a divorced man? Loretta's first sexual encounter must have been with Gable. Everything else was amateur night.

Sometime in March, Loretta made her first appearance on the set of *The Crusades*. Supposedly, she was the main character. She was billed first, but under the title—she had been upstaged by the producer-director, who was giving moviegoers another Cecil B. DeMille production. By the mid 1930s, DeMille was known for his ability to integrate sex, religion, and history into a pseudo-spectacle that looked like Joseph's multicolored coat. Occasionally (e.g., *Cleopatra, The Sign of the Cross*), he at least worked within a historical canvas on which he lavished his own color. "Directed by Cecil B. DeMille" was his calling card, inviting audiences, particularly those with a limited knowledge of history, to learn a paucity of facts and experience a wealth of invention.

Loretta may have thought she was the star of DeMille's homage to the Third Crusade, but she was overshadowed by Wilcoxon, who gave the same kind of high testosterone performance he gave when he played Antony to Claudette Colbert's Cleopatra. At least in *Cleopatra*, Colbert was the main attraction; in *The Crusades*, Loretta was not. Dressed in costumes that trailed down her body and would have concealed the slightest bulge—if there were any (not yet, fortunately)—Loretta was Berengaria, the Navarrese princess whom Richard reluctantly weds but, in a typical movie turnaround, eventually grows to love. Historically, theirs was a marriage of expediency. The DeMille version, scripted by Dudley Nichols and others, has Richard join the crusade—not because Jerusalem has fallen to the Muslims, who toppled crosses, burned bibles, and enslaved Christian women (as vividly depicted at the beginning of the film)—but to avoid an arranged marriage with the French princess Alice, the mistress of his father, Henry II, a fact that was not commonly known.

Richard deserved his sobriquet, "Lionheart." He was a pragmatist who marries Bergenaria because his men are starving, and the king of Navarre can provide them with grain and beef.

The most problematic historical figure in *The Crusades* is Saladin (Ian Keith), the Muslim leader and Sultan of Egypt, whom Dante (*Inferno*, Canto 4), believing that Saladin's sense of justice and forgiveness has exempted him from eternal punishment, places in limbo. DeMille's Saladin is an amalgam of fact and myth. He is correctly portrayed as a benign ruler, ruthless when necessary but generous to his captives. As an example of his magnanimity, the writers devised a subplot in which Berengaria is captured by Saladin's soldiers. Earlier in the film, Berengaria flirted innocently with Saladin. Since Loretta specialized in playing the coy maiden, the scene works splendidly, with Loretta and Keith letting their eyes do the courting. Saladin falls in love with Berengaria, who agrees to become his wife if he will spare Richard. Her selfless offer is pure invention: Berengaria was never captured, and Richard achieved a significant victory at Acre, portrayed in the most impressively photographed sequence in the film, with exploding fireballs, bodies tumbling into the moat, and boiling oil poured from the ramparts.

Although it is true that Richard failed to take Jerusalem, he succeeded in negotiating a treaty with Saladin that gave pilgrims access to the holy city. In the film, Saladin, realizing that Berengaria loves Richard, frees the Christian captives, one of whom is she. There is no treaty; instead, Saladin forbids Richard to enter Jerusalem. In a moment of superhuman strength, Richard breaks his sword in half, giving the cruciform hilt to Berengaria to place on the tomb of Christ, which seems to be in a cathedral. Again, the writers have taken extravagant liberties. In Mark 15:42, the tomb is described as hewn out of rock, its entrance closed by a large stone. Also, the four evangelists agree that the tomb was empty when two (Matthew), three (Mark), or several (Luke) women, or one (John) arrive on the climactic third day and discover that the stone had been rolled back. Biblical scholars might care, but what mattered was the exquisitely photographed scene at the tomb, wherever it was. Loretta strikes a beatific pose, looking as if she were about to take the veil. Richard, too, becomes a believer. "Oh, merciful God," he exclaims, as he watches the Christians wend their way toward Jerusalem. From their enraptured faces, one almost expected the couple to embrace the contemplative life—Berengaria in a convent, and Richard in a monastery.

Of all of DeMille's re-creations of the past, *The Crusades* was the least successful, finding favor with neither the public nor the critics. But to

DeMille, the film was a labor of love that eventually cost $11.9 million. He set a cap of $100,000 for costumes, and, to save money, had the scimitars and helmets made in the machine shop. A specialist was hired from New York's Metropolitan Museum of Art to authenticate the crossbows and armor. DeMille insisted that Richard's and Saladin's horses look majestic, yet different in appearance. Trifles upset him: The crosses on the knights' coats of mail were too small; perspiration seeped through Wilcoxon's costumes.

When filming ended in May, Loretta's pregnancy was still not noticeable. But she could not undertake another film that year. By the time *The Crusades* premiered on 25 October, she was less than two weeks away from having Clark Gable's child. Earlier, in June, Gladys decided that Loretta should take a sabbatical from Hollywood. They would travel to Europe for a much needed vacation. She would inform the press that her daughter's dizzying schedule had caused a host of health problems, exhaustion being one. Rest, relaxation, and a change of pace were the answer. It was impossible for someone of Loretta's reputation to travel unnoticed. She arrived in London in early July, when tennis star Fred Perry was Wimbledon's main attraction. Soon rumors began circulating that she and Perry were romantically involved. In loose-fitting but appealingly feminine dresses, Loretta had not lost her ability to attract men; nor men, their fascination with women who can be provocative without being a tease. Loretta denied the rumors with her usual finesse, no doubt disappointing reporters looking for a story.

The real story, however, was that Loretta was beginning to show. She could not give birth in London or anywhere but California. Gladys decided it was time to return home and weave the final strands in the web of deception. Mother and daughter arrived in Los Angeles on 21 August, with Gladys acting as spokesperson: "Loretta has been in ill health for some time and lost considerable weight recently." The truth was just the opposite, but Gladys knew not only how to decorate a house, but also how to conceal a pregnancy approaching the end of the second trimester. Just a few more months to go—two and a half, to be exact.

CHAPTER TEN

The Great Lie

Loretta was a regular on *Lux Radio Theatre*, which aired on Monday evenings from 9:00 p.m. to 10:00 p.m. and featured radio versions of recent and, sometimes, older films, often with their original casts. The radio dramatization scheduled for 2 March 1942 was *The Great Lie* (1941), with Loretta as Maggie in the part created by Bette Davis. Her costars, George Brent and Mary Astor, reprised their original roles. Although it is seems hard to imagine Loretta in a Davis vehicle, she did remarkably well, modeling her interpretation on Davis's. Davis gave a subdued performance, devoid of the mannerisms and histrionics that became her trademark and here would have been out of character. Maggie, who lives on a Maryland plantation, is too genteel to play the diva; her fate is to suffer in silence without loss of dignity. Loretta gave a similar reading, using a voice that was subtly Southern and bore little resemblance to her own. Maggie is the fiancée of a reckless flyer (Brent) who goes off and marries her friend, Sandra, a concert pianist (flamboyantly played by Astor), not realizing that Sandra's divorce is not final and that the marriage is invalid. The flyer then returns to Maggie, who agrees to marry him. But in a woman's film, nothing ever ends, until THE END appears on the screen. Meanwhile, the women undergo a series of trials until the writers declare a moratorium. Sandra discovers she is pregnant, the flyer is reported missing somewhere in Brazil, and Maggie programs herself into sacrificial mode, offering to adopt the child. The women retreat to the Arizona desert, where the baby is born.

As often happens in the "missing husband/wife" film (e.g., *My Favorite Wife, Too Many Husbands*), the flyer turns up. Will the baby go to Maggie or Sandra? Sandra, who was never a poster mother, realizes that the child belongs with Maggie and the flyer. "The child goes with the mother," she announces, pounding away at the piano, her one and only love.

Loretta must have sensed some parallels between Sandra's situation and her own back in fall 1935. Loretta was more fortunate than Sandra; thanks to her mother's foresight, she was spared the ordeal of giving birth in the wilds of Arizona. By 1935, Loretta knew about plot construction, as did Gladys and Dr. Walter Holleran (Loretta's physician, well known in Hollywood for his valuable connections with the Los Angeles Archdiocese, connections which proved beneficial to many stars, particularly Loretta). Holleran could lend credibility to the great lie and defuse the rumors circulating about Loretta's "illness" before they exploded in searing headlines, leaving her career in ashes. Gladys, who looked upon real estate as an investment, and encouraged Loretta to think similarly, had purchased a house in Venice in western Los Angeles, known in 1935 for its easy living and sandy beaches (It was not yet Los Angeles' Greenwich Village). It was the perfect hideout.

Since Loretta was neither a murder suspect nor a drug addict, it was not that difficult for Zanuck to prevent her from becoming a Hollywood outcast. Loretta had committed a sin only in the eyes of the Church. And if moviegoers in Wilkes-Barre or Oshkosh heard rumors about their idol, they would have dismissed them as Hollywood gossip, no more believable than "eat what you like" weight loss programs and beauty creams promising to restore the bloom of youth by eradicating lines and wrinkles. Although Zanuck and Loretta had no love for each other, he was astute enough to realize he could not incur the wrath of the National Legion of Decency by having a star on his roster who had violated the morals clause in her contract. Others had done the same, but they were not in Loretta's virginal league. Image is all, and hers had to be maintained.

The birth was the easiest part. Venice, at the time, was somewhat seedy, the last place a nosy reporter would think of as a movie star's getaway. On 6 November 1935, Loretta gave birth to a baby girl, whom she called Judith. Exactly why Loretta chose that name is unknown. Perhaps she was thinking of the biblical Judith, whom the Church regarded as a prefiguration of the Virgin Mary. Judith saved her people from the Assyrians by cutting off the head of their general, Holofernes, and Mary was portrayed as the new Judith, crushing the head of the serpent, Satan's avatar. As an observant Catholic, Loretta would have attended Mass on 15 August, the feast of the Assumption and a holyday of obligation, where the epistle in the liturgy with which she grew up was from the *Book of Judith* (13:22–25, 15:10). The last verse (15:10) was added to associate Mary with her predecessor: "You are the glory of Jerusalem, you are the joy of Israel, you are the honor of our people."

Loretta's Judith would need a different kind of courage to slough off the taunts of Hollywood brats who learned the details of her birth from their parents or know-it-all friends. Children can be unconscionably cruel when they discover another's secret. Judith inherited Gable's floppy ears; "Judy's got elephant ears," the children chanted as they giggled, making her even more determined to learn the truth about her parents. William Wellman's response did not help the situation: "All I know is Loretta disappeared when [*The Call of the Wild*] was finished and showed up with a daughter with big ears."

Dr. Holleran was not the only Catholic conspirator. Judy's baptismal certificate was a fabrication. She was identified as Mary Judith Clark (an interesting juxtaposition of the Virgin and her prototype), whose parents were William and Margaret Clark. The surname "Clark" was her birth father's first name; "William" was the first name of Gable's father. Her godparents were Mr. and Mrs. R. C. Troeger. "R. C." was a common abbreviation for "Roman Catholic." Was that the case? How "Troeger" originated is a mystery. "Troeger" is German, derived from Trogen, a place name shared by both Bavaria and the German-speaking part of Switzerland. The 1930 census listed 240 Troegers in Los Angeles, including a Roy C. Troeger. Were Roy and Mattilda Troeger the phantom couple? If so, who knew them and under what circumstances?

In fall 1935, all that mattered was Judy's receding into the background, then moving ever so slightly into the spotlight until it was time to introduce her to the Hollywood community, most of whom knew or suspected the truth, but realized that divulging it would backfire. Loretta was an asset; as such, she was protected. All that mattered was that Mary Judith Clark, later to be known as Judy Lewis after her mother married Tom Lewis in 1940, was legitimate, the possessor of a baptismal certificate as well as a birth certificate that identified her more accurately as Judith Young, whose father was "unknown." One truth, one lie. Regardless, Judy Lewis had proof of birth.

The first two acts of "The Great Lie" (clandestine birth, semi-falsified documents) had come off smoothly. The celluloid wall of silence did not preclude whispers, but better whispers than tabloid headlines. Now, how to pass off Judy as Loretta's daughter? Holleran's connections with the church hierarchy made it possible. In early July 1936, the eight-month-old Judy was brought to St. Elizabeth's, a combination children's hospital/orphanage and home for unwed mothers, in San Francisco. For the time being, Judy was an orphan.

The plight of the unwed mother became one of Loretta's causes. She was a four-time president of St. Anne's Foundation in San Francisco, which supports St. Anne's Maternity Hospital for Unmarried Mothers and St. Anne's Adoption Agency. Her "swear box" was prominently displayed on the set of every film. Whenever a profanity—or worse, an obscenity—was uttered, the offender was charged proportionately: twenty-five cents for "hell," fifty cents for "goddamn" and "Jesus Christ." The proceeds went to St. Anne's

By July 1937, the epilogue had been written. The ever-maternal Loretta would be adopting a child, possibly two children. The exact number had not been determined, but it was good press as well as bait for fans who cherish every detail of a star's life. For them, there is no such thing as trivia. On 4 July, the *Los Angeles Examiner* reported that Loretta had adopted two girls: June, three, and Judy, twenty-three-and-one-half months. Who June was is unknown. At least Judy's age was correct. As an actress, Loretta was familiar with the situation-complication-resolution screenplay model. She may have been thinking of adopting two children—or was it a matter of tying another knot in the narrative cord to slow down its unraveling? There is no drama in a single adoption; but a double adoption requiring the adoptive parent to give up one of the children commands greater attention. Which will it be? June was most likely a plot point, introduced to create a dilemma for Loretta.

Loretta played the adoptive mother as if she were the heroine of a woman's film. "I am the happiest girl in the world," she gushed. "Until [the children] came here, I just haven't known what I've been missing." She had the perfect answer when asked how she found them: "I can't tell . . . . That is a secret I hope I never have to reveal." That part was true. But then the mother of one of the girls supposedly had pangs of remorse. And so, the magnanimous Loretta, no stranger to sacrifice, had to make a wrenching decision. Which child has to be returned to the mother? Loretta had an answer to that question, too: She was too conflicted to "bring herself to disclose . . . which of the youngsters she must give up . . . declaring that she realized that she must keep that in confidence and must bow to the natural love of the mother." The resolution did not have the combination of pity and fear that haunted the Holocaust survivor in William Styron's *Sophie's Choice*, nor was it in the tradition of the weepie that left behind a sudsy residue. There would be a partially happy ending: One child is better than none.

The press added to the apocrypha. In one version, Loretta gave up the older child, June (if that was her name) because her aunt (a relative in another version) wanted her back. Then there was the story that Loretta discovered the girls at a Catholic orphanage in Los Angeles when she was there to decorate a Christmas tree. In that account there was no June, but a James, age three, and Judy, twenty-three months. When Pontius Pilate asked Jesus, "What is truth? (John 38)," Jesus did not reply. Neither did Loretta.

The most powerful gossip columnist in America was Louella Parsons. To secure her friendship, such as it was, you had to play by the rules—her rules. Parsons understood the nature of patronage from personal experience: Her patron was newspaper tycoon William Randolph Hearst, the model for Charles Foster Kane in Orson Welles's *Citizen Kane* (1941). Hearst made it possible for an Illinois society page writer to become the voice of Hollywood, with a syndicated column that could lavish or withhold praise. Whether the individual was praiseworthy or not was irrelevant. Parsons wanted obeisance, and Loretta willingly gave it. If anyone could deliver the official Hollywood line, it was "Lolly" Parsons. And if there were still rumors about Loretta's adopted daughter, Parsons would quell them. Two weeks before the other papers picked up the adoption story, Parsons had one of her "first exclusives," as she called them. She reported that Loretta had adopted two "babies." When Parsons requested a picture, Loretta graciously declined: "I don't want them to be photographed—not yet. They're so little and they shouldn't have a lot of publicity while they are just babies."

Loretta and Parsons shared the same religion, although Parsons' Catholicism did not even approximate Loretta's. What they really had it common was irresponsible husbands and children who needed more than either could offer. Louella's first husband abandoned her for another woman when she was pregnant with her first and only child, Harriet, who in 1931 called off her wedding because she realized she was a lesbian. Loretta knew all about skirt-chasing men and women with dark pasts. Louella and Loretta were "sisters under the mink," as Gloria Grahame said about herself and Jeanette Nolan in Fritz Lang's *The Big Heat* (1953). Parsons proved a powerful ally. Although she knew about the so-called adoption, she understood Loretta's predicament. All Loretta had to do is pay homage to her benefactor, which included appearing on Parsons's radio show, *Hollywood Hotel*, which premiered in October 1934. Guests could either receive the munificent sum of $18.00 but no publicity, or forego the fee and promote their latest movie, perhaps even perform a scene from it.

One fanzine writer actually did see the children—or rather Judy and one other child. The writer was Liza Wilson, who was not the voice of Hollywood but who could qualify as one of its oracles. She had become so popular that she only used her first name. A story signed "Liza" carried credibility. The day that Liza called at Loretta's Bel-Air home, Judy and June were on display. Who June was, and where she came from (an orphanage, a casting agent) did not matter. June was a protatic character, needed for one scene and then written out of a script that had one star and one newcomer, who in a movie would have received a separate credit: "Introducing Judith Young." The adoption script now had the imprimatur of Parsons and Liza, Hollywood's equivalent of the *Good Housekeeping* Seal of Approval.

Loretta always remained loyal to Parsons. The end of *Hollywood Hotel* did not silence Parsons's voice. She returned to the air in 1946, more powerful than ever with her own interview show, sponsored by Woodbury Soap. Loretta was one of her favorite guests. The show was carefully scripted, with Louella and her guests engaging in shamelessly insincere banter that set the fans swooning. If a woman felt inferior about her looks, Loretta could help her, explaining that glamour comes from within, a combination of wardrobe, makeup, and—above all— integrity. Wardrobe and makeup are really accoutrements, but from the sound of Loretta's comforting voice, they seemed more like nature's embellishments. But the supreme paradox was Loretta's argument that glamour is achieved by being unselfish:

> PARSONS. So you think being glamorous is being unselfish?
> YOUNG. Yes, I do, Louella. It's hard work to be glamorous. It takes a lot of thought. You have to deliberately put other people's happiness and their likes and dislikes before your own. And between you and me, I think being glamorous is every woman's duty.
> PARSONS. Do you actually believe that every woman can be glamorous?
> YOUNG. I know she can, if she'll work at it. Glamour is more than skin deep. It comes from within. It creates a sort of glow. It's understanding of yourself and other people. It's integrity. It's pride but not false pride.

The 21 March 1948 program must have been an ordeal for Loretta. The theme was the recent Academy Awards, for which Loretta won best actress for *The Farmer's Daughter,* and Darryl Zanuck had won for Fox's

Gentleman's Agreement, which was voted best picture. Most of the program was devoted to Loretta, who left Fox in 1939 largely because of Zanuck. At the end, Zanuck made a brief appearance. He said a perfunctory "hello" to Loretta and then suffered through Parsons's gush about *Gentleman's Agreement*. Parsons praised Zanuck for making a film about "intolerance," avoiding the term "anti-Semitism," the film's theme. Parsons had no intention of alienating any anti-Semites who might be listening.

On 13 December 1985, thirteen years after Parsons' death, Loretta received the Louella Parsons Award at the Golden Apple luncheon. It was now time to repay Parsons for her discretion: "Louella never wrote one word about me that wasn't a fact, which she had checked and double checked. Not only with me, but with everyone who had anything whatsoever to do with the story." There must have been some at the luncheon who knew the truth about Parsons's fact checking and smiled. But the myth had to be preserved, and Loretta was now the keeper of the book. A speech by Loretta would have been incomplete without a benediction: "God bless you all, keep you well, and happy and safe."

Once the adoption was no longer an issue, all the scenario needed was a bluebird ending, with Loretta acquiring a husband and Judy a father. Even if a knowledgeable writer decided to weave the details of the adoption into a real screenplay, no studio would have green lighted it. In Hollywood, it would have been a *film à clef*; to women, it would have been another example of the circuitous route one of their sex was forced to take because of an irresponsible male; to the critics, it would have just been implausible. Some might even have quoted the final line of Ibsen's *Hedda Gabler:* "People don't do things like that." Little did they know. In a sense there was no need to film "My Mortal Sin." It had already been done live and on location.

Loretta was never a good judge of men. In 1938, she had another short-lived romance, this time with Wall Street broker and playboy William P. Buckner, Jr., who was six years her senior—for Loretta, something of a record. He too failed to be her cleft in the rock of the world. Buckner's gimmick was Philippine railway bonds that would guarantee a 20 percent profit on $2 million. The investors he envisioned were not members of his own circle, many of whom were familiar with his scams and steered clear of him. Rather, the target was movie stars, obscenely wealthy with money to invest in any enterprise that promised a healthy yield. Whether he included Loretta in his pool of suckers is unclear. He preferred to negotiate with male actors (e.g., Ronald Colman, Herbert Marshall, Frank Morgan, Bing Crosby) through intermediaries, such as a retired British army officer, J. Stuart Hyde, and a former Wall Street acquaintance, C. Westley Turner.

Buckner may have fancied himself in love with Loretta or thought of her as a way of acquiring credibility in Hollywood. Even at twenty-five, Loretta was an amateur in the game of love. Buckner had charm; he was a well-traveled bon vivant who knew how to woo the impressionable Loretta. She must have been surprised when, on 1 December 1938, he returned from England on the Queen Mary and was promptly arrested for mail fraud. Buckner claimed he was innocent and was en route to Los Angeles to marry Loretta! But the next day, Buckner told a different story: "It would be nice to be able to say that I am engaged to Loretta Young . . . but it is not so." Still, Buckner protested his innocence: "I have the fullest expectation of being able to show that I am wholly innocent of the charges." On 12 January 1939, Loretta told federal agents that she never invested with Bruckner, but she evaded their question about a possible marriage: "Am I going to marry him? I don't care to make any statement." She was now an expert at dealing with the press. On 5 July 1939, Buckner was fined $2500 and sentenced to two years in prison.

On 31 July 1940, Loretta became a bride. This time, there was a church wedding. Naturally, the groom was an older man—eleven years older, to be exact. And he was from advertising, not from the movies, like Grant Withers. Even more important, Tom Lewis was a Catholic, who took a more rational approach to his faith than Loretta, whose Catholicism was rooted in convent school notions of sin and guilt, tinged with emotion but not always buttressed by reason. She often behaved irrationally, particularly in her determination never to miss Sunday mass for fear of committing a mortal sin.

Lewis met Loretta in January 1939 when Young and Rubicam sent him to the West Coast to handle programming for *Screen Guild Theatre*, which debuted on CBS radio in 1938 and, like *Lux Radio Theatre*, featured stars in adaptations of films, sometimes re-creating their screen roles. Lewis wanted Loretta for his first show, and she agreed. Unmarried, Lewis, the quintessential Catholic layperson, was immediately attracted to her. When Lewis scheduled a Sunday 9:00 a.m. rehearsal, Loretta's agent at William Morris called him, explaining that his client would be at a party the night before and would be attending 11:00 a.m. mass. Lewis countered that he, too, would be at a party and planned to attend the 8:00 a.m. service. There was no compromise: Lewis accompanied Loretta to the 11:00 a.m. mass at Blessed Sacrament, a Jesuit parish on Sunset Boulevard. There, they encountered Loretta's first grade teacher,

Sister Marina, who instinctively knew the couple was destined to be together and promised to make a novena for them. Loretta, who had gone through the "right man" phase before, grew apprehensive, wondering if the nun's premature optimism could land the two of them "in a spot." Did Loretta imagine another romance headed toward marriage, only to be derailed by scandal? Or did she think that the nun's prediction was a jinx?

This time, everything worked out—at least it did so for almost two decades. On Wednesday, 31 July 1940, the feast of St. Ignatius of Loyola, Loretta and Lewis were married at the Church of St. Paul in Westwood. The service had been scheduled for noon, but crowds started gathering much earlier, and by the time the bride and groom arrived, 2,000 spectators had assembled. Loretta looked ravishing in an "iridescent water-lily blue tulle dress." Loretta insisted on a simple ceremony. Accordingly, there were no bridesmaids, only a maid of honor, her half sister Georgiana, and a best man, Lewis's brother Charles. Since Loretta's father had disappeared twenty years earlier, her brother John gave her away. The ceremony was restricted to family and friends, much to the disappointment of the fans. But at least they saw Loretta step into a limo amid a shower of rice, through a path that had been cleared by five police officers.

Judy now had a stepfather. Henceforth, she would be Judy Lewis. By 1945, she had two half brothers: Peter Charles, born in 1944, and Christopher Paul, born in 1945. It seemed a perfect ending to a scenario that shifted back and forth between hope and disillusionment. For Judy, it was also a happy ending—but not for very long.

CHAPTER 11

Return from the Ashes

By January 1936, it was time for Loretta to go back to work. Like the phoenix, she had risen from the ashes of unwed motherhood—the stigma expunged, the evidence temporarily concealed, and the future brighter than it had been the previous fall. Although Loretta had convinced herself that she had committed a mortal sin, she at least had the satisfaction of knowing that it was not as serious as abortion.

Loretta might have enjoyed some peace of mind if she sought out a liberal priest, accustomed to hearing actors' confessions, who would have given her a penance of five Hail Marys and told her to get on with her life. Loretta did, in her own way. She returned to her Bel-Air home with Gladys, while a trustworthy nurse remained in Venice to take care of Judy, whom Loretta visited periodically. But the subterfuge could not continue indefinitely. Loretta and Dr. Holleran were fleshing out the plot points in the adoption scenario, which would be finished in six months, with Judy being placed at St. Elizabeth's. Loretta was still a working actress, slated for four films in 1936, and four more in 1937. Professional obligations had to take precedence over the joys of motherhood.

The orphan adoption scenario was worthy of Dickens, who used a similar one in *Bleak House*, in which Lady Dedlock's affair with an army captain involved a more elaborate subterfuge, as one would expect in an eight-hundred-page novel that allows for considerably more subplots than a ninety-minute film. Since the reconciliation between Loretta and her daughter had not yet occurred when *Uncommon Knowledge* was published, but instead happened a short time before Loretta's death, only Judy Lewis can reconstruct that moment of truth. It was probably never as theatrical as Lady Dedlock's disclosure to her daughter, Esther, when, dropping to her knees, Lady Dedlock implores, "Oh, my child, my child, I am your wicked and unhappy mother! Oh, try to forgive me." That would have been a great scene for any actress—including Loretta, if Hollywood had decided to film the novel. But Zanuck had other plans for his star.

When Loretta checked in at Fox that January, she discovered that Zanuck had loaned her out to MGM again. Because *Midnight Mary* proved so successful, MGM wanted to reunite Loretta and Franchot Tone in *The Unguarded Hour* (1936), an adaptation of a British melodrama with Tone as Lord Dearden, a leading barrister, and Loretta as his wife. Loretta's voice was now sufficiently cultivated that she did not have to affect a British accent, as she was forced to do in *The Devil to Pay*. Instead, she injected a melodic lilt into her speech, as if she were playing drawing room comedy, which was enough to suggest the character belonged to a world of peerage. Tone's, on the other hand, was faux British but adequate for a film where intricacy of plot was more important than authenticity of accent.

There is always a villain in melodrama, and in *The Unguarded Hour* it is Hugh Lewis (the lethally suave Henry Daniell, London-born and sounding it). Lewis informs Lady Dearden that his wife has incriminating letters from her husband, dating back to the time when they were lovers, which, if published, will derail Dearden's political career. Rather than jeopardize her husband's future, Lady Dearden offers to buy them, unaware of the consequences, which include a fall from a Dover cliff, a murder, a false confession from Lord Dearden, and his unmasking of the real killer, who, of course, is Lewis. Like *Dial M for Murder*, *Sleuth*, and *Deathtrap*, *The Unguarded Hour* is the kind of film with enough plot twists to hold the viewer's attention until the narrative cord can bear no further knotting and slackens, buoyed up one last time for an unexpected but not implausible denouement.

The Unguarded Hour's significance lies in its director, the estimable Sam Wood, who preferred directing films based on novels (e.g., *Goodbye, Mr. Chips*, *Kitty Foyle*, *Kings Row*, and *For Whom the Bell Tolls*) to those based on plays. Yet he did well with stage adaptations, which require careful pacing to hide their theatrical origins. Wood learned the importance of pacing and rhythm in the silent era; he had directed thirty-two silents before he made his first talkie, *So This Is College* (1929), with two actors from Broadway, Elliot Nugent and Robert Montgomery. By 1935,he displayed his ability to hold a fractious narrative together in the Marx Brothers classic *A Night at the Opera*, a magnificent example of controlled anarchy. By 1936, a creaky melodrama like *The Unguarded Hour* posed no problem; he knew how to keep the film from splitting into narrative fragments, preserving its theatricality by using a fade out to mark the end of a scene, like the lowering of a curtain. Wood's best stage adaptations are *Our Town* (1940) and *Command Decision* (1949). Despite Wood's sensitive direction and Aaron Copland's evocative score, *Our Town* lacked the original's uncompromisingly bleak ending. In the film, Emily's death in childbirth and her return to earth to relive one day, moving among the living who cannot see her, turns out to be a dream—except to those who knew Thornton Wilder's play.

Janet Gaynor headed the cast of Loretta's next film, *Ladies in Love* (1936), but was not the star. No one was; it was not a question of stardom, but of empathy. Although the leading roles are evenly distributed, the script was structured in such a way that audiences could root for their favorite lady. But if their sympathies lay anywhere, it was with Loretta. Gaynor was costarred with Loretta and Constance Bennett, as three young women from the provinces who set out for Budapest in search of wealthy husbands—only to discover that a Cinderella can meet her Prince Charming, have a fling with him, and then stand by while he marries someone from his own class. Since Gaynor was an Oscar winner (few could forget her performance in *Seventh Heaven* [1929]), and highly respected by the industry and the public, she received top billing, followed by Loretta and Constance Bennett. When Tyrone Power (then Tyrone Power Jr.), looking preternaturally beautiful as a Hungarian count, spots Loretta working as a chorine in a nightclub, their interlocked gaze, etherealized by front lighting, suggests that the lady of the chorus has met her royal deliverer, and that a fairytale ending is in the offing. But it was not to be; theirs was the only kind of dalliance that royalty have with commoners. As a result, *Ladies in* Love became a sobering study in the disappointments of working class women who set their sights on upper class men.

Some moviegoers might have sensed a similarity between *Ladies in Love* and *The Greeks Had a Word for Them* (1932), a Samuel Goldwyn production. And theatergoers would have known that Goldwyn's film was based on a play by Zoë Akins (at the time America's leading female dramatist) called *The Greeks Had a Word for It*, which opened on Broadway in September 1930 and enjoyed a run of 253 performances. Goldwyn, an avid follower of the New York theatre scene, bought the rights, expecting little, if any, opposition from the Hays office. Will Hays, Warren Harding's postmaster general, had been relatively tolerant about film content during the early years of the sound era, but in this case he did not object to the subject matter (husband hunters) so much as to the title, which he suspected the self-righteous would consider prurient. "It" could be interpreted as a euphemism for what Annie Oakley in Irving Berlin's *Annie Get Your Gun* calls "doin' what comes naturally." And so, *The Greeks Had Word for It* became *The Greeks Had a Word for Them,* as if "them" was less suggestive than "it." Regardless, the film was not one of 1932's major attractions. It might even have been a noble failure if Sidney Howard (a fine playwright, toiling in Hollywood) had retained Akins's denouement, in which the trio continued to ply their trade. Instead, Howard has one of them succeed in finding a husband.

Two years later, Loretta found herself in the *Ladies in Love* remake, *Three Blind Mice* (1938), which resurrected—and not for the last time—the trio of husband hunters, who, like the women in Akins's play, decide that to trap a millionaire, they must pretend to be millionaires so they can move in the right circles. Akins did not even receive a "Suggested by" credit; rather, the source listed was a play by Stephen Powys, the author of *Walk with Music.* But Powys's play did not premiere until 1940; when it was written, when Fox bought it, and if it opened in its original form remains unknown. *Three Blind Mice* was so radically different from Akins's play that Fox felt there was no reason to acknowledge the playwright, even though there would not have been a *Ladies in Love* or a *Three Blind Mice* without her.

The "three blind mice" were three sisters—played by Loretta, Pauline Moore, and Marjorie Weaver—who use their inheritance to leave Kansas and try their luck in Santa Barbara. Loretta is romanced by the two male leads, Joel McCrea and David Niven, while all Weaver can attract is the buffoonish Stuart Erwin, who turns out to be her ideal mate, without the baggage that weighs down the wealthy. Loretta has the more difficult choice. In an early scene, when McCrea and Loretta are lolling around in their bathing suits on a stretch of sand, a clueless Niven does everything but bless their union. The scene has an understated sexuality about it; neither McCrea nor Loretta seemed shy about lying together in such close proximity. In fact, they look as if they enjoyed it and probably did. They seem headed to the altar until McCrea confesses he has no money. Will Loretta choose love or money? McCrea never gave a sexually charged performance; his were always subtly calibrated. Sexuality was regulated, like a thermostat that was never raised beyond the comfort level. Loretta knew how to raise the temperature to cozy warm, and when she did, McCrea responded effortlessly. McCrea was exactly the kind of actor to whom she could give herself—in fantasy terms only—because both understood the difference between propriety and passion: the former meant for the camera, the latter for later.

If all three sisters were to pair off with their respective husbands, Moore seemed to be the odd sister out. The only possible pairing was the provincial Moore and the worldly Niven. Strangely, this worked: Niven plays a rancher with cattle and chickens, and Moore plays a girl who grew up on a chicken farm, giving them at least poultry in common. Three sisters, three husbands, only one of whom, Niven, is a bona fide millionaire.

Three Blind Mice did not mark the end of the gold diggers movie; two years later, the theme resurfaced in the Fox musical, *Moon over Miami* (1940), and again in 1946, in *Three Little Girls in Blue*. With the advent of CinemaScope, Fox remade it again, this time with Lauren Bacall, Betty Grable, and Marilyn Monroe as the trio in *How to Marry a Millionaire* (1953). But the theme goes back even earlier, to Anita Loos's novel *Gentlemen Prefer Blondes* (1925), in which Lorelei Lee and her sidekick do not need a third party to achieve their goal.

Loretta gave a less satisfying performance in *Three Blind Mice* than she did in *Ladies in Love*, which at least proved that attempting to ensnare a rich husband (which may occasion temporary euphoria) usually ends in disillusionment. *Three Blind Mice* insisted that the three sisters, unlike Chekhov's, found their mates, however circuitously. Loretta was more effective in a fairy tale that went sour than in one that was cloyingly sweet.

Less than a year after Judy's birth, Loretta was a mother again—on screen. She looked unusually radiant, perhaps because the adoption scenario was finished, and in a few months Judy would be ensconced in a San Francisco orphanage. Loretta no longer had to visit the house in Venice on the sly. Gladys could return to decorating the homes of the famous, and Loretta to the only profession she knew. It was picture-hopping time, and Loretta made four in 1936, five in 1937, four in 1938, and three in 1939, her last year at Fox. For Loretta, a mother's place was before the camera.

Private Number was released in early June 1936, a month before Judy's removal to St. Elizabeth's. Insiders must have exchanged smiles, or smirks, when Patsy Kelly described Robert Taylor, Loretta's leading man in the film, as being "as handsome as Gable." Loretta laughed knowingly, but innocently, and replied: "I'll say so." It was not exactly an apt comparison. The young Taylor, like the young Power, had a masculine beauty that complemented Loretta's shimmering femininity. Gable was the opposite; he was all high testosterone and devilish eyes that could seduce without exerting the slightest effort.

By 1936, audiences had become accustomed to the class distinction film—either rich boy/poor girl, or vice versa—a plot template common to both serious drama and screwball comedy. *Private Number* was a woman's film, with Loretta triumphing over falsehoods and perjured testimony that would have felled an ordinary mortal, which her character was not. She was Ellen, a maid in an affluent household, ruled by a demonically creepy butler (Basil Rathbone). When he sees Ellen, he is taken with her beauty, suggesting that he can help her "advance," which she does without having to lose her virtue. The son (Taylor) is also smitten with her, so much so that class barriers dissolve and they secretly marry. But other barriers arise. *Private Number* would not be a woman's film without Ellen undergoing a series of trials that would have broken the spirits of an ordinary mortal. The rebuffed butler dredges up her past, including a prison stint. When Ellen becomes pregnant, her in-laws threaten to have the marriage annulled. The courtroom sequence is a free-for-all, with false testimony, histrionics, and the climactic arrival of Taylor, who vindicates his wife and embraces fatherhood.

The one scene Loretta has with her newborn is done with uncommon tenderness. Judy was about three months old when *Private Number* started production. Loretta transferred the affection that she could not lavish on Judy to the infant in the film. In that one scene, Loretta displays the kind of maternalism that transcends mere acting. Or was the unfeigned love that she lavished on the infant in the basinet her last act of motherhood before she consigned Judy to St. Elizabeth's?

Loretta's return to Fox did not result in better roles. But there were no great roles for any actress at the studio. Zanuck was only interested in promoting the careers of those whose names would guarantee an audience: namely Shirley Temple, Sonja Henie, and perhaps the up and coming Tyrone Power. Temple and Henie had gifts that had little to do with acting, at which neither excelled. Temple became an industry, with coloring books, cutouts, and even a non-alcoholic cocktail named after her. She was also an extraordinary child star, whose deficiencies as an actress became evident when she moved into her teens. There was a sad ordinariness about her work in her last films (e.g., *Adventure in Baltimore, The Story of Seabiscuit,* and *A Kiss For Corliss*), which revealed a young woman no different from the generic brand that had been banished to B movie limbo. But there had never been a skater in film like Henie, whose bubbly personality and spectacular feats on the ice (a sound stage at Fox was converted into a rink just for her) ensured her popularity for a decade, after which she began appearing in icecapades, lavishly staged with Broadway-worthy choreography. Temple and Henie were flavor-of-the month stars, with careers that lasted sixteen and twelve years, respectively. Temple's could easily have ended in 1942, ten years after she made her screen debut, since her roles from 1944 to 1949 could have been played by others. Similarly, Henie could have left Hollywood after *Iceland* (1942), rather than following the now forgotten *Countess of Monte Cristo* (1948). Loretta's career, on the other hand, spanned more than three decades. She might have consoled herself with the realization that, for the time being, Zanuck was not turning out Oscar-winning or Oscar-nominated films. Between 1936 and 1939, the studio could only boast of two Oscars, both in the supporting category: Alice Brady for *In Old Chicago* and Walter Brennan for *Kentucky* (both 1938). None of Loretta's films were even Oscar material.

But Loretta was useful to Zanuck. When he decided to make *Ramona* (1936), Fox's first full-length Technicolor feature, he knew he had no other actress for the title role. If anyone could photograph well in color, it was Loretta. The director was Fox's specialist in Americana, Henry King, ideally suited to re-create 1870s Southern California. The studio publicists concocted a story that must have given every wannabe hope. On the basis of "exhaustive tests . . . made of practically every feminine star and some hundred-unknowns," Loretta was chosen to play the convent-educated heroine of Helen Hunt Jackson's 1886 novel, whose strongest appeal was to young women. The "exhaustive tests" bit was pure hype. Zanuck already had his Ramona.

Since Loretta was cast as the daughter of an interracial union (white mother, Indian father), she was given an exotic look, with burnished cheekbones tinged with red, and long black hair, parted in the middle and cascading down her shoulders in folds. The wig and makeup were in keeping with the character, who, once she learned about her origins, considered herself an Indian. Jackson never describes Ramona in detail, writing only that her protagonist had a "sunny face" and a "joyous voice" and extended a friendly greeting to everyone. The nuns at her convent school referred to her as the "blessed child." Screenwriter Lamar Trotti did not have a problem with the racial aspects of the plot; he merely followed Jackson's lead and had Ramona become romantically involved with another Indian, Alessandro (Don Ameche). Although by contemporary standards Ameche looked like a racial stereotype, with a feather sticking out of his headband, he was the film's sole revelation, creating a genuinely moving—and ultimately tragic—figure. Ameche divested himself of his sometimes-oily smugness and connected empathetically with his character, as did Loretta with hers.

King was in his element, reveling in slow tracking shots and the opportunity to embellish what he probably thought was a hokey melodrama by supplying local color and detail, including sheep-shearing and a fiesta, in which Loretta danced so authentically that some moviegoers might have wondered what she would have been like in a musical, a genre that she never attempted. Melodramatic as *Ramona* is, there are scenes that generate real tension, especially when the newly married Ramona and Alessandro discover that the whites whom they had befriended and fed have returned to practice their own version of manifest destiny by taking over their property, the property of mere Indians. Another near tragedy occurs when their newborn child becomes gravely ill. Alessandro locates a doctor, who is too busy to travel and can only give him the medicine. One of the whites, to whom the couple was so generous, shoots Alessandro for commandeering his horse after his own became lame.

These scenes elevate *Ramona* from the level of storybook romance to tragedy, in which Indians suffer at the hands of rapacious whites. The film ends with a shot of Ramona after Alessandro's funeral, greeted by Felipe (Kent Taylor), who was always in love with her. Ramona sighs ecstatically, "Don Felipe." Fade out, The End. *Ramona* discreetly skirted the implications of another interracial union—this time between a white man (Felipe) and a woman of mixed blood. The novel, however, does not end ambiguously. Ramona and Felipe relocate in Mexico, where she and her daughter, also named Ramona, can live without prejudice. We read that the couple had a large family, "but the most beautiful of them all and . . . the most beloved by both father and mother, was the eldest one, the one who bore the mother's name . . . Ramona, daughter of Alessandro the Indian." If the film version had included Jackson's epilogue, Zanuck would have been hailed (and in some circles, denounced) as a champion of civil rights. In the post World War II era, Zanuck would tackle such controversial themes as anti-Semitism and racism. But to quote Cole Porter, 1938 Hollywood was "the wrong time" and "the wrong place."

One would think from the movies of the 1930s that heiresses merited front-page headlines, however frivolous their actions. In *It Happened One Night*, Claudette Colbert can dive off her father's yacht and embark on a series of escapades that capture the attention of the nation during one of the worst years of the Great Depression. It is as if *It Happened One* Night, classic that it is, were taking place in a world antipodal to the real one—a world where wealthy runaways and scoop-hungry reporters dispelled the grim present and offered the public a Neverland where all that matters is that boy gets girl, regardless of class distinctions and compatibility. If they embrace at the fadeout or, as in *It Happened One Night*, when the blanket barrier between their beds falls to the floor, the audience exits, believing that happiness is right around the corner.

When *Love Is News* was released in March 1937, the Spanish Civil War was in its second year, the Rhineland had been remilitarized, and the bloody Detroit steelworkers' strike that left ten dead and more than ninety wounded was over. But what did it matter if a brash reporter (Tyrone Power) was writing unflattering pieces about a fabulously rich young woman (Loretta), who retaliates by informing the press that they are engaged? All audiences wanted to know is how two people who hate each other could possibly fall out of enmity and into love. With Loretta and Power in the leads, the film could hardly have ended with the two going their separate ways.

Love Is News is purportedly about the newspaper world. The staccato dialogue and newsroom ambience invite comparisons with the prototype, *The Front Page* (1931), directed by Lewis Milestone, who put his stars (Adolphe Menjou as the editor, and Pat O'Brien as his star reporter) through their paces, so that the scenes had the rhythm of a professional typist, hitting the keys at 120 words per minute. *Love Is News* is not in the same league as *The Front Page*—either the play by Charles MacArthur and Ben Hecht or Milestone's film. Three years later, it was eclipsed by the definitive newspaper film, Howard Hawks's radical makeover of *The Front Page, His Girl Friday* (1940). *His Girl Friday* featured Cary Grant as the editor, playing the role with the kind of serpentine charm that tempted Eve in the Garden of Eden, and Rosalind Russell as the reporter, who did not mind taking a bite of the apple and typed away as if she had printers' ink in her veins.

Tay Garnett was a perfectly competent director, best remembered for *The Postman Always Rings Twice* (1946). *Love Is News* is lesser Garnett. His problem was not with Power and Loretta, who knew that the more improbable the plot, the more convincing they had to be. And they were convincing, in addition to looking as if they were made for each other. But the early scenes in the newsroom, the fiefdom of the managing editor (Don Ameche), could have taken place in some corporation. There is no ebb and flow of language, no dialogue delivered with the propulsive rhythm of a drill.

What made *It Happened One Night* a classic and *Love Is News* just another flick is not just running time: seventy-two minutes (*Love*) versus 106 (*Night*). Even if *Love Is News* ran close to two hours, monotony would have set in; the plot would have either stalled or chugged along until the writers recharged the narrative. The beauty of *It Happened One Night* is that, in addition to being screwball (and romantic) comedy, it is also a road movie, with the characters learning enough about each other to constitute a courtship, even though they assume they are just traveling east. In *Love Is News*, one must assume that the couple will find whatever they have in common off screen; all Loretta and Power had to do was convince the audience that they would. If Loretta, then twenty-three, was having more mature crushes on her leading men, she could not have done better than Power. Zanuck had declared them a team. The press and the public concurred. And if Power was unavailable, there was Ameche.

Because she wore clothes so elegantly, Loretta was cast as an heiress again in *Café Metropole* (1937), a frothy romance that appeared two months after *Love Is News* and that might have had more buoyancy if it had been directed by Ernst Lubitsch instead of Edward H. Griffith. Screenwriter Jacques Deval devised a pretzel-like plot with enough twists to hold an audience's attention and a denouement involving a phony check. The café owner (Adolphe Menjou) is amoral, but as played by Menjou, who gives the most satisfying performance in the film, he deceives with such silken charm that any attempt to expose him would be a violation of good taste. When a Princeton-educated playboy (Tyrone Power) cannot pay his gambling debts, Menjou has him impersonate a Russian prince and woo a millionaire's daughter (Loretta). Despite his inconsistent accent, Loretta is so taken with Power (as she was in real life) that she goes along with the deception. Who could resist Power, who never looked so good as he did in the 1930s?

But if Cinderellas have their midnight, so do bogus princes. Loretta even resorts to having her father falsely arrested to keep Power out of prison for passing a bad check. And since the two of them complement each other—looking as if they had been sprinkled with Peter Pan's fairy dust—neither prison nor parental opposition will stand in their way. Power's accent is supposed to be "on and off," and with just a quizzical look, Loretta lets the audience know that she is not deceived. She had also fallen in love with the imposter, gazing at him as if she were moonstruck and flirting her way into his affections. Loretta was now more adept at comedy of manners; at least she had dialogue that was sufficiently literate to pass for wit, delivering the lines as if they were lyrics set to the music of her voice. Loretta would appear in other romantic comedies, but few that allowed her to treat the dialogue like bonbons—delicious but unsubstantial.

Zanuck did not want to spend much money on *Café Metropole*. He only cared about 1937 releases that would yield a profit: the Shirley Temple movies *Heidi* and *Wee Willie Winkie*; the *Seventh Heaven* remake with James Stewart and Simone Simon; and the Dick Powell–Alice Faye musical, *On the Avenue*, with a score by Irving Berlin. He pared down the budget; insisted that *Café Metropole* be made in thirty days; demanded that at least twelve pages (he preferred fifteen) be cut from the script; and vetoed the tracking shot that would open the film, showing patrons entering the café. Just use a dissolve to move from the exterior to the interior; it's cheaper.

Loretta's weakest film with Don Ameche was *Love Under Fire* (1937), supposedly set during the Spanish Civil War, a conflict that Hollywood avoided until World War II erupted in 1939, the same year the Spanish Civil War ended; or, as some would say, the year the dress rehearsal in Spain for World War II did. By 1939, it was clear that the Spanish Civil War was the prologue to a global tragedy. But as far as Hollywood was concerned, World War II provided such a wealth of screen material that the prologue could be detached from the tragedy and, if not performed separately—as it was in *For Whom the Bell Tolls* (1943)—become part of a character's past (e.g., Humphrey Bogart in *Casablanca*, Orson Welles in *The Lady from Shanghai*, John Garfield in *The Fallen Sparrow*, Ray Milland in *Arise, My Love*). But even *For Whom the Bell Tolls* seemed like a World War II movie, in which the Spanish partisans, mostly Communists, were part of an anti-fascist resistance—which they were, in a sense.

Hollywood was uneasy about the Spanish Civil War (1936–39) not because the United States was neutral during the conflict, but because of the identities of the two battling factions and their allies. There were the Loyalists, who were fighting to maintain Spain as the duly elected republic the popular vote mandated, and there were Franco's Nationalists, who wanted a Catholic Spain under the control of the Church and the military, as it had been in the past. The Catholic Church naturally supported the Nationalists, and radicals (socialists, communists, and anomalous left-wingers) passed the plate for the Loyalists, staging fund-raisers and benefits for the cause. The war produced its own idealists. Unlike the First World War, it was not a war to end wars, but one to prevent the one that a prescient minority sensed would occur within a few years and might be averted by the extirpation of fascism. The American Left's finest hour came when 3,100 Americans joined the Abraham Lincoln and the George Washington battalions of the Fourteenth International Brigade. At long last the Left had a cause—to many, a noble cause. But the cause was perverted once outside forces intervened. Fascist Italy, sensing an ally in Franco, supported the Nationalist cause even if it meant bombing Spanish cities like Madrid and Guernica. Since the battalions were dominated by socialists and communists, the Soviet Union posed as their ally, while secretly subverting the noble gesture with the goal of turning what would have been a socialist utopia into communism's newest convert—with Spain as the first communist country in Western Europe.

Zanuck hoped to release the first movie that dealt, at least peripherally, with the war. Walter Hackett had written an unproduced play, *The Fugitives*, in which the Nationalists were portrayed trying to keep valuable jewelry from falling into the hands of the Loyalists. It was a boilerplate plot, with enough intrigue, romance, and politics to sustain audience interest. In October 1936, three months after the war began, Kathryn Scola and Darrell Ware had an adaptation ready for Zanuck's scrutiny. The script was a skein of contradictions; the characters were so chameleon-like with their shifting allegiances that if the Scola-Ware script were ever filmed, it would have only reflected many moviegoers' own ambivalence about the war. Defenders of a democratic form of government might have been thrilled that the Spanish people voted to make Spain a republic, but they might have balked when they realized it would be a socialist one. Those with fascist sympathies might have hoped for a Nationalist victory, but they were uneasy about Franco's contempt for the democratic process. And when it was known that both sides were guilty of atrocities, some might have wondered if either side was worth supporting.

Zanuck finally realized that he could never make the kind of film he envisioned and issued an ultimatum: "Eliminate all references to 'loyalists' and 'traitors', etc. Refer to all other sides as General so-and-so and his forces." The title went from *The Fugitives* to *Fandango* and ended up as *Love under Fire*, with new screenwriters: no longer Scola and Ware, but Gene Fowler, Allen Rivkin, and Ernest Pascal. All that remained of Hackett's original plot were the jewels, reduced to a pearl necklace that Loretta's character supposedly stole. Once a Scotland Yard inspector (Ameche) learns she is not a thief, they can fall in love and leave Madrid, which is under bombardment for reasons that would not have interested most of isolationist America. And those who decided to see *Love under Fire* were more interested in "love" than in "fire," knowing that with Loretta and Ameche in the leads, the lovers could enter the fiery furnace and not get singed.

Power and Loretta were teamed for the penultimate time in *Second Honeymoon* (1937), which had potential. But the paradigmatic comedy of remarriage, Leo McCarey's *The Awful Truth*, was released the same year, relegating *Second Honeymoon* to the oubliette for runners up. The writers, Kathryn Scola and Darrel Ware, imagined a retread of Noël Coward's *Private Lives*, filmed in 1931, in which a couple divorce, remarry, and discover that all the parties involved are spending their honeymoons at the same hotel. Eventually the original couple shed the new spouses and reunite. In *Second Honeymoon*, Loretta and Power do not meet cute; they run into each other in Palm Beach, impeccably dressed—Loretta in chiffon that streams down her frame, and Power with glistening hair and a figure-flattering tuxedo, usurping the moonlight for no other reason than to make love to his ex-wife.

In *The Awful Truth*, the divorced couple (Cary Grant and Irene Dunne) has not remarried, giving each partner the opportunity to undermine the other's marital prospects. In *Second Honeymoon*, Power has to woo Loretta away from her stolid husband (Lyle Talbot), which is not that difficult. With Power's piercingly compassionate eyes, promising dream fulfillment, and Loretta's knowing smile and coy body language, how else could the film end? *Second Honeymoon's* main problem is its uneasy juxtaposition of high and low comedy. The latter involves carry-overs from *Three Blind Mice*: Stuart Erwin as Power's valet and the lively Marjorie Weaver as his fiancée. Although intended as comic relief, they emerge as the only real characters in a world where the problems of the idle rich alone matter. Neither Loretta nor Power was at his and her best. When they quarrel, Loretta is gratingly shrill; by way of comparison, in *Private Lives*, the couple literally comes to blows, but the dialogue remains on the same urbane plane. Loretta and Power engage in a shouting match that is totally out of character. Although *Second Honeymoon* aspired to be an amalgamation of screwball and comedy of remarriage, it was so only in theory.

For the third time in one year, Loretta was cast as a woman of privilege. In *Wife, Doctor, and Nurse* (1937), she was a socialite, married to a doctor (Warner Baxter) who suspects that her husband's nurse (Virginia

Bruce, in the film's best performance) is her rival. Properly handled, the film could have qualified as respectable screwball comedy, but the plot turned out to be just another triangular template without the wit of *My Favorite Wife* and *Too Many Husbands*. The nurse is an atypical "other woman": She is neither a gold digger nor a home wrecker, but merely a victim of unrequited love. Her refusal to join the ranks of rebuffed women by seducing the husband or feeding the wife's suspicions gives her a stature that Loretta's character lacks. Because she is one of the upper East Side ladies who lunch, Loretta invites the nurse to a classy restaurant where she plans to confront her, discovering instead that the nurse does not even realize that she is in love with the doctor until Loretta brings it up. Privilege allows the privileged to play psychiatrist, getting the unsuspecting "patient" to reveal unconscious motives and desires. Satisfied, the wife returns to her Park Avenue apartment, unappreciative of the nurse's integrity. The nurse is a professional, not a rival. The wife does not even have to reclaim her husband, who never cheated on her. If there was ever a film to dispel the myth of woman's intuition, this was it.

The role made no demands on Loretta, whose name preceded Baxter's in the credits only because she was a bigger star than he. Baxter was never A list; it was only when he starred in the "Crime Doctor" series at Columbia in the 1940s that he found a new audience, less discriminating than those he once knew, who could accept his workmanlike performance. To his credit, Baxter could register intensity and menace, but when it came to romance, it was hard to envision him as a lover. Loretta had to work doubly hard to convince the audience that she was attracted to him. Bette Davis had a similar problem with George Brent in *Dark Victory*. Actress that she was, Davis convinced audiences that Brent was her great love, even though he, too, was not the most charismatic of actors.

There was no "working actress" job description during the studio years. If one had existed, it would state that a working actress is one who works, despite the quality of the material handed to her. And if she balks at the assignment, she goes on suspension, switches studios, or freelances, as Loretta began doing when she left Fox in 1939. She must have sensed that in the coming decade the roles would be fewer or not worth accepting, unless money or ego were the sole considerations.

At the end of 1937, Loretta knew it was only a matter of time before her days at Fox were over. The previous year, she refused to do *Lloyds of London* (1936), claiming that the role she was offered, which went to Madeleine Carroll, was too small. "Loretta Young Walks Out In Huff Over

Film Role," a *Los Angeles Times* headline (6 September 1936) announced. It was true: Loretta flew to San Francisco and took a boat to Honolulu. She was developing a reputation for being difficult. Zanuck did not know how difficult she could be. Loretta had not yet begun to fight.

CHAPTER 12

Addio, Darryl

Zanuck was so pleased with the box office receipts for *Wife, Doctor and Nurse* that Loretta and Warner Baxter were teamed again in *Wife, Husband and Friend*, adapted from James M. Cain's novella, *Career in C Major* (1936). By 1936, Cain's bestseller, *The Postman Always Rings Twice* (1934), had already established him as a novelist who transcended the gaudy prose of the pulps. By the time *Wife, Husband and Friend* was released, he had published another novel, the controversial *Serenade*, fraught with racial stereotyping and homophobia, none of which appeared in the 1956 movie version with Mario Lanza as an operatic tenor caught between two women. Opera was not alien to Cain. Although he was an acknowledged master of hardboiled fiction, he aspired to be an opera singer but soon discovered that his forte was language; however, he never lost his love of opera, which resonates throughout *Career in C Major*, in which a contractor discovers he is a natural baritone, as opposed to his untalented wife, who aspires to be a concert artist. *Career* is a first-person narrative, told almost exclusively from the point of view of the contractor, Leonard Boland, in a style hardly befitting an opera singer. It mixes streetwise vernacular, tangy and colorful, with the kind of metaphors (a conductor's demeanor is "as cheerful as cold gravy with grease caked on the egg") that became the hallmark of Dashiell Hammett, Raymond Chandler, and James Ellroy.

The specter of the Great Depression broods over Cain's novella. Leonard's business is suffering, although his socialite wife, Doris, is oblivious to the country's economic woes and focuses solely on her concert debut, which proves a disaster. When Cecil Carver, a concert and opera star, accidentally hears Leonard sing, she experiences the "star is born" syndrome and immediately grooms him for a singing career, introducing him to the rituals of the concert and operatic stage. Leonard is an overnight sensation, and Cain allows his narrator to describe his initiation into an alien world as he dissects the plots of *La Bohème* and *Rigoletto* in a refreshingly muscular style, lacking in highbrow pretentiousness. But Cain knows enough not to have Leonard triumph at his wife's expense. After a catastrophic *Rigoletto*, Leonard realizes he is out of his element. Then, in an eleventh-hour reprieve, an offer comes through to build a bridge in Alabama. And *Career* ends with the Bolands en route to the Deep South as they sing, off key, the duet, "Là ci darem la mano " from *Don Giovanni*.

Wife, Husband and Friend follows the broad outlines of the novella, with Loretta and Baxter as the Bolands, and Binnie Barnes as Cecil Carver. In the film, Leonard's operatic debut is a singer's nightmare. A grotesque costume that looks like a fat suit, a stringy beard, and a floppy hairpiece all conspire against him. Leonard storms off stage, now able to understand how Doris felt when she read her hostile notices. Nunnally Johnson wrote an engaging script, which Gregory Ratoff directed capably, but without much flair. Still, the film featured a number of good performances, particularly from Loretta and Barnes, who played Cecil as if she were as serious about making Leonard into an artist as she was about netting him for herself—thus adding another dimension to the "other woman" type. The character actors did their usual scene stealing: the blustery, gravel-voiced Eugene Pallette as the owner of the construction company, and the imperious Helen Westley as Doris's mother.

Ten years later, Fox remade *Wife, Husband and Friend* as *Everybody Does It* (1949), and in this case the remake was superior to the original. But it used the same basic plot, with Cecil (Linda Darnell) becoming Leonard's (Paul Douglas) muse, determined to launch his career and steal him from his wife (Celeste Holm). The production values were much higher in the remake, and Douglas, looking burlier and more befuddled than Baxter, was a more suitable quarry for the predatory Darnell. To coincide with the remake, New American Library published a Signet paperback with the same title, *Everybody Does It*, noting that the novella was originally published as *Career in C Major*.

There was a powerfully acted scene in the original that did not appear in the remake, perhaps because either the writer (Johnson again) or director (Edmund Goulding) thought it would not work with Holm and Douglas as the Bolands. In *Wife, Husband and Friend*, when Doris discovers the truth about Leonard's supposed business trips, she lashes out at him, pelting him with blows and landing both of them on the floor. Loretta played the scene so realistically that her slim, 105-pound body must have sustained more than a few bruises. The sight of Douglas—looking like a construction worker getting pummeled by the petite Holm—would have produced guffaws. In the original, Loretta acted the scene so convincingly that it can still make one feel uncomfortable.

Four Men and a Prayer (1938) was Loretta's first and only experience working with John Ford. Despite the title, Loretta's character—a globe-trotting socialite who, in a different film, would have been a screwball heroine—is the movie's catalyst; without her, the plot could not have been resolved. Although Ford dismissed the film ("I just didn't like the story, or anything else about it, so it was a job of work"), a few scenes bear his signature. One such scene is a barroom brawl set to an Irish jig coming from a player piano and Barry Fitzgerald feinting like a boxer without any opponents. Ford's fondness for Irish shtick could derail a film, as it almost did in *She Wore a Yellow Ribbon* (1949), where Victor McLaglen's high jinx left a smudge on one Ford's most poetic works.

There was no poetry in *Four Men and a Prayer*, in which the four sons of a disgraced colonel (C. Aubrey Smith) vow to restore the reputation of their father, who was murdered before he could prove his innocence. For lack of evidence, his death is classified as a suicide. The sons know otherwise and set out for India and South America, where they discover that their father was a victim of an arms cartel that had no qualms about selling weapons to both insurgents and their oppressors. The film includes an uncommonly violent scene, in which Loretta watches in horror as soldiers gun down the rebels, leaving the steps on which they have assembled strewn with bodies. One cannot help but think of the massacre on the Odessa Steps in Eisenstein's *Potemkin*. The romantic idyll that the socialite envisioned has brought her into the midst of a struggle for self-determination, where men and women are willing to sacrifice their lives for a cause. Once Loretta learns that her father is the president of the cartel, she confronts him, not acting as if she were morally superior, but simply wanting to right a wrong—particularly after having fallen in love with one of the sons (Richard Greene). The father explains that artillery is not the company's sole export and henceforth will cease weapons production. Developing a conscience or activating one that has been dormant is not usually that sudden, but the film had to come in under ninety minutes (it ran eighty-five), so the conversion process was reduced to an epiphany. The colonel's killer is unmasked, the sons see their father honored posthumously, and Loretta becomes part of the family.

Loretta's character is integral to the plot. The socialite moves in international circles, attracting the attention of shady characters like war profiteers and making it possible for the brothers to learn their identity. Although Ford expressed disinterest in the script, Loretta—her stylish wardrobe not withstanding—gave the film whatever degree of credibility it had. The brothers' two-continent manhunt is the stuff of espionage and detective fiction, and their way of piecing information together is a variation on connecting the dots, with Loretta doing some of the connecting. Loretta's character is achingly real. A child of privilege, indulged by a multimillionaire father, she witnesses the dark side of colonialism. She may have grown up hearing the familiar jungle movie line, "The natives are restless," but she never saw the extent of that restlessness until she was caught in the crossfire of a rebellion. Her revulsion at the sight of innocent men, women, and children gunned down in cold blood may have been required by the script, but her face, drained of its beauty by shock and anguish, suggests that she was reacting to the scene on a more personal level. Loretta had never before been in a film in which violence erupted with such frightening immediacy that horror was the only possible reaction. Politically, *Four Men and a Prayer* was liberal and mildly anti-capitalist—except when politics took a back seat to high adventure, with the action shifting from India to England, then back to India and Argentina, and finally to England. Moviegoers who sensed that the film was ambivalent about imperialism were in the minority. This was 1938, when honor, reputation, and romance were more important than self-determination. For the prescient few, *Four Men and a Prayer* offered a glimpse into the future, when liberation movements became more widespread after the European superpowers divested themselves of their colonies.

Suez (1938) was Loretta's last film with Power, who received first billing—as one would expect in a biopic about Ferdinand de Lesseps (Power) and his dream of building the Suez Canal. Philip Dunne and his collaborator, Julien Josephson, devised a script involving an ill-starred romance between de Lesseps and the Countess Eugenie de Montijo (Loretta), who must choose between Louis Napoleon (Leon Ames), later known as Napoleon III, and de Lesseps. She is not influenced by Louis's looks. Ames was a fine actor, but no match for Power's dark beauty. Power and Loretta had already become such a romantic team that audiences expected a combination of love story and spectacle. But history, when passed through the Hollywood prism, separates into a spectrum of fact and fancy. True, there was a Ferdinand de Lesseps who, physically, would never have been mistaken for Tyrone Power; however, Napoleon III was every bit as dictatorial as he is portrayed in the film, dissolving the legislative assembly and imprisoning dissidents. Since the historical Eugenie was reputedly a beauty, who else but Loretta could play her? Loretta could turn costumes into period attire and wigs into authentic coiffure. You could almost hear the rustle of silk when she walked—or rather glided—across a room. But Eugenie, unlike de Lesseps, is royalty, and in mid-nineteenth century Europe, a countess does not marry a diplomat obsessed with creating a waterway connecting the Mediterranean with the Red Sea. The film's omission that Eugenie's mother was the niece of de Lesseps's mother, making Eugenie and de Lesseps cousins, is more significant. The historical de Lesseps married his first wife in 1837, thirteen years before the time of the main action. No matter; unrequited love plays better than domestic drama.

Although *Suez* was directed by the venerable Allan Dwan, it owes much to the second unit director, Otto Brower, who knew how to stage action in the desert, as he proved in *Under Two Flags*. A landslide that dislodges a mass of rock and earth was the work of Brower and the great special effects artist, Fred Sersen; so was the cyclone that sucks Toni (Annabella), the army brat who worships deLesseps, into it and disgorges her body on the sand. These are the scenes that linger in the memory.

Annabella, who received better notices than Power or Loretta, became the first of Power's three wives a year after the film's release. The marriage was short-lived, ending in divorce seven years later. Power's second marriage, to Linda Christian, also lasted for seven years. His third marriage, to Debbie Ann Minardos, was tragically brief; six months after they were wed, Power suffered a heart attack and died on 15 November 1958 at the age of forty-four. His son was born two months later.

Loretta might well have been Power's first wife. Once she learned that Power was Catholic (probably one in need of a refresher course), he was no longer an adolescent crush, but a desirable costar and potential mate. Whether Power felt similarly about Loretta is a matter of conjecture. The press felt they were made for each other, and the public did, too—but not Zanuck. To him, they were good copy—fan food, like hors d'oeuvres, not the main course. If they married, Zanuck feared he would lose his investment, and he had no intention of taking such a loss. It would be better if Power were seen with someone much plainer, another Fox contract player without a definable persona or the promise of a major career. In other words, Sonja Henie. Loretta continued to harbor some affection for Power, even though she was demoralized, as she later told Zanuck, when she learned that after Power's first year at Fox, his salary was raised twice, and hers was not. At Power's funeral, she arrived in costume after filming an episode for her television show, in which she played an Asian. Loretta claimed she had no time to change, but flashbulbs popped, and her appearance was the highlight of the occasion. Photo op or farewell? Probably both.

The last of Loretta's 1938 films was *Kentucky*, released just before the end of the year to qualify for the Oscars. It was nominated in one category: Best Supporting Actor. The winner was Walter Brennan as a Yankee-hating son of the Confederacy, whose bias is explained in the 1861 prologue, when his character, Peter Goodwin, appears as a boy. Although Kentucky remained in the Union during the war, there were families, like the slave-holding Goodwins, that sympathized with the Confederate cause. To the Unionists, such families were rebels. When a Union official, John Dillon, arrives at the Goodwin plantation with an order to confiscate the livestock, Peter's father, Thad Goodwin, becomes so enraged that he draws his pistol, but he is shot before he can fire. Peter witnesses the killing; unable to avenge his father's death, he harbors a deep hatred for Dillon's descendants.

The prologue had more potential for drama than the film proper, which cannot make up its mind if it is a domestic tragedy, a romantic melodrama, or a horse-as-hero movie on the order of Capra's *Broadway Bill* (1933). Seventy-five years go by, and the main action takes place in 1938. Thad Goodwin Jr. has a daughter, Sally (Loretta), who is also Peter's niece, and John Dillon Jr. has a son, also named John (Richard Greene). Even though Sally is a Goodwin, and John a Dillon, we are only in feuding family, not Montague-Capulet, country—which does not mean that the course of true love will run smoothly. Sally eventually gets John Dillon III, even though the audience is denied the usual kissing couple fadeout—perhaps because the romantic subplot is secondary to what is implied by the title. No matter how the credits read, the star is Kentucky, the costar is Walter Brennan, and the supporting cast is headed by a horse, followed by Loretta and Greene.

Any movie entitled *Kentucky* would have to highlight the Derby, which is cleverly worked into the plot so that the climax can take place at Churchill Downs. A horse joins the cast: Bluegrass, the proverbial dark horse that everyone hopes will come in first. And if Bluegrass does, will he suffer the same fate as Broadway Bill, the horse that gallops triumphantly through the finish line and then collapses in death? Bluegrass is a bona fide character; he may be a horse, but he stands in for anyone who has been pegged a loser and confounds the skeptics by doing a star turn. We know Loretta and Greene will resolve their problems and go into a clinch, on or off the screen. It will be much easier with the death of Peter, who is adamantly opposed to his niece's involvement with a Dillon. Once Bluegrass wins the cup, it is Peter whose heart gives out from excitement, and it is Peter who posthumously gets the last scene when John Dillon Jr. delivers the eulogy at his funeral, reminding the mourners that, with Peter's demise, "We are burying a way of life."

Some moviegoers might have felt that Peter's was a way of life that should be buried, based, as it was, on false ideals and festering hatred—not to mention racism, which is also reflected in the film's portrayal of the Southern black as illiterate darkie, a stereotype that Hollywood perpetuated over the years and that many whites accepted as fact. Although the Goodwins treated their slaves and later their servants humanely, they did so condescendingly, as if, as Christians, they were expected to be tolerant of inferiors. And for all the accolades heaped on Walter Brennan for his portrayal of Peter, he gave a performance in one key, in a voice so petulant that he would have been a prime candidate for anger management classes if they had existed in 1938.

This was Loretta's second color feature. She was given a wardrobe with soft colors: white, yellow, pink, and pale blue. Although an equestrian like Sally Goodwin would have been comfortable in jodhpurs, they did little for Loretta except call attention to her backside. Her makeup was also a problem. Her face lacked its usual translucence and delicately sculpted cheekbones. Instead, it looked like an alabaster mask with rouge-tinged cheeks that seemed stained. Neither her makeup nor Greene's was consistent. At times, Greene looked as if he were not so much made up as painted. When Loretta's makeup was applied less extravagantly, the old aura returned. But black-and-white truly did her justice, and it was not until 1949, when she was thirty-six, that she appeared in another color film. Zanuck was pleased with the final script, requesting only minor changes. But the film did nothing for Loretta, who was eclipsed by a state, a horse, a race, and Walter Brennan, who for some reason endeared himself to the public.

The Story of Alexander Graham Bell (1939), Loretta's last film at Fox, was not hers; both the title and the credits confirmed as much. Don Ameche in the title role headed the cast, followed by Loretta and Henry Fonda as Bell's assistant, Thomas Watson, the recipient of the world's first phone call: "Mr. Watson, come here. I want to see you." Bell was Ameche's most memorable role, which he played with an ardor that reduced everyone else to supporting cast status, despite their billing. Like Loretta, Fonda learned that at Fox, contract players were the equivalent of repertory actors: a lead today and a supporting role tomorrow. The year that *The Story of Alexander Graham Bell* was released also saw the release of one of Fonda's best-remembered films, John Ford's *Young Mr. Lincoln*, in which Fonda played the title role. Only a movie buff would associate Fonda with *The Story of Alexander Graham Bell*, which was Ameche's film, and his alone. Everyone else was relegated to the wings until needed on stage.

Loretta was not needed that often. When she was, she looked ravishing—particularly when Bell proposes marriage on the staircase, both of them using an encoded language that might seem too decorous for ordinary mortals, but not for the angelic Loretta or her character, Myrtle Hubbard, who is propriety incarnate. Myrtle is also deaf; it is Bell's reputation as a teacher of the hearing-impaired (who performs scientific experiments in his spare time) that results in his meeting Myrtle, who has mastered the art of lip reading. Since the historical Myrtle Hubbard was deaf, the screenwriter, the invaluable Lamar Trotti, acknowledged her condition and then consigned it to plot point limbo, the repository of once used and then discarded information, so Loretta would not be burdened with the dual task of looking beautiful and reading lips. Once the film takes a romantic turn, Myrtle's deafness becomes irrelevant; Loretta plays her scenes with Ameche as she would with any leading man with whom she is supposed to fall in love.

The Story of Alexander Graham Bell is one of Fox's more accurate biopics; certainly there is less embroidering of the facts than there was in *Suez*, even though the latter is cinematically more impressive with its disaster scenes and special effects. But there is some massaging of facts. The historical Myrtle was not enthusiastic about her husband's experiments with the telephone; her father, one of Bell's chief financial backers, preferred that he concentrate on the telegraph. Trotti's Myrtle, in contrast, is the perfect inventor's wife: She simply tells her husband to continue with the telegraph, while he secretly works on the telephone.

The film was handsomely mounted and well acted, but with little sense of urgency or drama. Essentially, it was an information retrieval movie. Since everyone knows the outcome, there is no suspense. Trotti realized he could not make the world's first phone call the climax. For those who did not know that Bell might have become a historical footnote, and that the invention of the telephone could have been attributed to Western Union, Trotti devised as dramatic a conclusion as the facts would allow. Bell initiates a law suit that generates little heat. Myrtle, now pregnant, is in the courtroom; she is also in possession of a letter proving that Bell succeeded in transmitting sound through a wire. When she goes into labor, Bell uses his invention to contact the hospital. Bell wins his suit, and the film ends as he describes his dream of air transportation.

For Loretta, *The Story of Alexander Graham Bell* had a personal significance. It was the only time she and her three sisters appeared in the same film. The three played Myrtle's sisters: Gertrude (Sally Blane), Grace (Polly Ann Young), and Berta (Georgiana Belzer). Sally's resemblance to Loretta is so striking that seeing them together is like the charm of recognition that comes from leafing through the family album on a rainy afternoon. Perhaps in any year other than 1939 Ameche might at least have garnered an Oscar nomination. But 1939 was the year of *Mr. Smith Goes to Washington, The Wizard of Oz, Stagecoach, Destry Rides Again, Ninotchka, Wuthering Heights, Dark Victory, Goodbye, Mr. Chips, The Women,* and the one and only *Gone with the Wind.* Who cared about an invention that in 1939 was taken for granted?

Loretta had mustered enough courage to say her own farewell to Zanuck, not knowing that she would be back for three more films. In 1939, she felt that the cord had been severed. At a meeting with Zanuck and Joseph Schenck, then president, she voiced her disillusionment: "Darryl, I won't work with you . . . . In all the years I've been here, you never once sent me flowers or given me a bonus or even a raise . . . . I went back for 'Mother Was (sic) a Freshman' and 'Come to the Stable' And boy, Fox paid!" Zanuck felt the same about Loretta, going to whatever lengths he could to see that she paid for her ingratitude. Hollywood buzzed with "Loretta will never eat lunch in this town again" rumors. But Loretta was always able to find a protector, at least temporarily. And she found champions now in Walter Wanger and Harry Cohn.

CHAPTER 13

The Price of Freedom

Loretta could have continued indefinitely at Fox, but if she stayed beyond 1939, there would have been nothing for her except more of the same. She must have known that Zanuck had his favorites: the more bankable talent, the bigger box office draws such as Betty Grable, Alice Faye, Maureen O'Hara, and Loretta's replacement, the sylphlike Gene Tierney, the perfect mirror image for Tyrone Power, who still had his looks, but without the androgynous glow. Loretta was no longer one of the inner circle.

While Loretta was shimmery and angelic, a beam from the moon's bright side, the exotic Tierney seemed to emanate from both the light and the dark. She could play the daughter of Hecate or Diana. Put Tierney in a rowboat, with sunglasses shielding her eyes from the sight of her drowning disabled nephew (a fate that she diabolically engineered in *Leave Her to Heaven* [1945]), and she is even deadlier than Regina in *The Little Foxes* (1941), who makes no effort to retrieve her husband's medicine when he is having a heart attack. Loretta could never have played Ellen in *Leave Her to Heaven*. Nor was there any likelihood that, when Zanuck decided to remake *Love Is News* as *That Wonderful Urge* (1948), he would have had Loretta reprise the role she had originated. Once Zanuck saw Tierney on the stage in *The Male* Animal (1940), he knew he had found Loretta's successor. Tierney was not long for Broadway; she was off to Hollywood that same year, making her movie debut in Fox's *The Return of Frank James* (1940). Zanuck had no problem with Power—ten years older and now merely handsome rather than beautiful—re-creating his role in the *Love Is News* remake. But Power needed a younger and fresher talent, and Tierney could easily step into Loretta's shoes. Like Loretta, Tierney could also play Asians (*China Girl*). She was the new Loretta, even as Jeanne Crain was the ingénue and budding dramatic actress that Loretta once was.

Zanuck was also going through his blonde period. At first he touted Alice Faye, holding Betty Grable in reserve. But Grable gradually came into her own, supplanting Faye as Fox's musical queen. Longevity was a major concern of Zanuck's. As Grable was nearing thirty, he began grooming the younger June Haver, a superb dancer but no match for the World War II pinup in a white bathing suit. Haver was "the girl next door," not the kind that GIs taped inside their locker doors. Perhaps out of gratitude, Zanuck threw Grable a few crumbs, even costarring her with her successor, Marilyn Monroe, in *How to Marry a Millionaire* (1953). Since Monroe was only a passable dancer, he tapped Sheree North, whose dancing was the highlight of the Broadway musical *Hazel Flagg*. But the Fox musical had seen better days, and Marilyn was too bedeviled by the demons of insecurity to be reliable. Still obsessed with blondes, he found a Marilyn clone in Jayne Mansfield, a comically gifted actress with a sense of self-parody she revealed in the Broadway play *Will Success Spoil Rock Hunter?* Mansfield re-created her role in the 1957 movie version that bore the same title but little resemblance to the original, a mordantly clever Faustian take on the extent to which some will go to achieve fame in a medium where "integrity" is not in anyone's lexicon. Mansfield's tenure at Fox was brief, as was her career, which ended with a fatal car crash in 1967.

Fox in the 1940s and 1950s was no place for Loretta Young. Loretta insisted on claiming that Zanuck had her "blacklisted" for walking out on him. She did not know what it was like to be blacklisted. The writers and actors who were persecuted by the House Committee on Un-American Activities (HUAC) in the late 1940s and 1950s for their politics knew. Loretta was a blacklistee who continued to work. Zanuck had no choice but to express outrage at Loretta's decision, although whether or not he felt it was another matter. It was a variation on the "Nobody leaves a star" syndrome: Nobody leaves Zanuck until he decides it's time.

Zanuck probably was relieved. He had essentially written Loretta off. Her expectations did not coincide with his perception of her as a competent but essentially decorative performer, whose idea of passionate love was convent school foreplay. Loretta could never be a femme fatale like Linda Darnell, or a mysterious beauty like Gene Tierney, who seemed too well bred for passion, but whose veiled look could make a viewer curious about the difference between Tierney veiled and unveiled. Loretta was already a star. Now she could fend for herself, while Zanuck added newer celestial bodies to the Fox firmament.

Unlike a typical blacklistee, Loretta had no gaps in her filmography. Both 1939 and 1940 were accounted for: three films in 1939, two in 1940. Walter Wanger's production, *Eternally Yours*—released in November 1939, seven months after *The Story of Alexander Graham Bell*—marked the beginning of Loretta's post-Fox period. Although she would return to the studio for two films in 1949 and one in 1951, she was now a freelancer. *Eternally Yours* was a bauble, not a fresh water pearl. In that *annus mirabilis*, 1939, Garbo had *Ninotchka*; Rosalind Russell, *The Women*; Bette Davis, *Dark Victory*; Marlene Dietrich, *Destry Rides Again*; Judy Garland, *The Wizard of Oz*; Merle Oberon, *Wuthering Heights*; and Vivien Leigh, *Gone with the Wind*. And what did Loretta have? A film in which she played a bishop's granddaughter, who falls for a magician. But at least she was in a film produced by one of the industry's premier independent producers.

Dartmouth-educated Walter Wanger was not so much an independent, as a semi-independent producer, who could supply a studio with product that was distinctive but still had audience appeal. Wanger would provide most of the financial backing, minimizing the studio's contribution, which was at times non-existent. He sought real autonomy, not the relative kind that that came from being dependent on a studio's largesse. Unlike Hal Wallis, who, after leaving Warner Bros. encamped at Paramount for thirteen years before heading for Universal where he ended his filmmaking career, Wanger preferred to studio hop, cutting deals that worked to his advantage. At Columbia, Wanger produced, among other films, Frank Capra's *The Bitter Tea of General Yen* (1933) and at MGM, Gregory LaCava's *Gabriel over the White House* (1933), in which the Deity allows a president to survive a supposedly fatal car accident by assuming the persona of a dictator, who cures the ills of the Great Depression. More impressive was Wanger's sumptuous MGM production of Rouben Mamoulian's *Queen Christina* (1934), with Garbo at her peak. His first Paramount production was William Wellman's phantasmagoric *The President Vanishes* (1935), a strangely allegorical film in which an isolationist president, fearing he has lost popular support for refusing to embroil his country in a European war, allows himself to be kidnapped by right-wing extremists. After he is rescued, the president returns to office, where he continues to advocate non-intervention, espousing George Washington's admonition in his Farewell Address to "steer clear of permanent alliances, with any portion of the foreign world." Wanger did not shrink from controversy, although he knew he had to sweeten the brew: The president proposes to force the nations of Europe to sign a disarmament treaty and to establish an oxymoronic "dictatorial democracy" that will eliminate unemployment and crime. *The President Vanishes* neither embraced fascism nor advocated the suspension of civil liberties, but instead argued for a program that combined both—for the good of the American people, of course.

In 1937, United Artists gave Wanger a five-year contract at $2,000 a week and "complete control of all production matters." It was there that Wanger produced his most famous films: Frank Borzage's *History Is Made at Night* (1937); William Dieterle's *Blockade* (1938); John Ford's *Stagecoach* (1939) and *The Long Voyage Home* (1940); Hitchcock's *Foreign Correspondent* (1940); and Henry Hathaway's *Sundown* (1941). *Eternally Yours* was not in their league; it was Wanger in down time. Wanger's dream was a repertory company on the order of the one John Ford was assembling. He started recruiting talent like Sylvia Sidney, Madeleine Carroll, Charles Boyer, and Joan Bennett, none of whom wanted to be bound by the standard seven-year studio contract. When a studio beckoned, they might sign on for a film or two, but generally they preferred a multi-picture arrangement. Wanger's stock company eventually consisted of two stalwarts, Susan Hayward and Joan Bennett, each of whom starred in five of his productions. Of the two, Hayward fared better, gaining an Oscar nomination for *Smash-Up—The Story of a Woman* (1947) and the coveted statuette for *I Want to Live!* (1958). Bennett was actually more than one of Wanger's stars; she married him in 1940, continuing as his wife in name only after he shot her lover—wounding, but not killing, him in 1951. At first, Bennett stood by Wanger, as he made his way through the Hollywood labyrinth, stopping off at one studio, then another, creating production companies under various names, and adding to his legacy a parcel of films that are now taken seriously. By 1965, Wanger's producing days were over; Bennett, tired of his infidelities, demanded a divorce. Wanger enjoyed three more years of life, dying of heart failure in 1968.

Back in 1939, Wanger never thought of Loretta as one of his company, knowing that she would not be making long-term commitments. But he also was aware of her less-than-amicable departure from Fox. That did not faze Wanger, nor did Zanuck's blacklist—if it ever existed. Wanger knew there was no place for him at Fox, where one testosterone-driven producer was enough.

Loretta was useful to Wanger; she had appeared in his production of *Shanghai* and still had the gossamer femininity that he needed in *Eternally Yours*, in which she literally fell under the spell of a magician-mesmerist

(David Niven). Exactly how that happens is left to the imagination. Anita (Loretta) attends a performance by the Great Arturo (Niven), who during a Q-and-A session makes ocular contact with her. What follows is a scene without any dialogue, in which Arturo/Tony is shown conversing with Anita, citing incidents from her past that only she would have known. He is so successful that she becomes his assistant and eventually his wife. When "the other woman" (Virginia Field) threatens their marriage, Anita sues for divorce, and Arturo/Tony resorts to mesmerism to win her back. Loretta worked well with Niven; she could turn coy and kittenish when he behaved like a proper Brit. When he relaxed, shedding stuffiness for urbanity and sexual indifference for sexual attraction, Loretta was transported into the realm of Eros, Hollywood style, radiating the glow that comes from fantasy recollected in tranquility.

Loretta would make one more film for Wanger, but meanwhile it was off to Columbia, where Harry Cohn offered her a multi-picture deal but not at the salary that her agent had requested: $75,000 a picture. Cohn drew the line at $50,000. Loretta agreed, and stayed on to do five pictures for him between 1940 and 1943, then one more in 1952, the year before she quit the big screen. Cohn respected Loretta, who had appeared in two of Columbia's best films of the 1930s, *Platinum Blonde* and *Man's Castle*. He was an unusual studio boss, serving as both Columbia's president and production head (under ordinary circumstances, an atypical combination, but understandable in the egomaniacal and insecure). He was notorious for his gleaming white office, with a desk on a riser that made him seem taller. Behind the desk were shelves stocked with expensive perfumes and nylon stockings for services rendered. There was also a white couch, smaller than a love seat but able to accommodate Cohn's needs—which, if short term, were often satisfied with fellatio. Otherwise, it was a courtship, aggressive but amorous, the kind he resorted to when he wooed—or rather, pursued—Joan Perry, a Columbia contract player. He knew Perry could never be a star, but she could be his wife. Joan Perry became the second Mrs. Harry Cohn in 1941 and provided him with two male heirs.

Cohn knew all about Loretta, the devout Catholic, who suffered a moral relapse at which Hollywood winked—as if to say, "Yes, we know, but why should the public?" And the public didn't. Cohn also distinguished between ladies and broads; Loretta belonged to the former category. He treated her with respect, as he did her close friend and fellow Catholic, Rosalind Russell. Both were indebted to him—Russell, for giving her some excellent comedic roles in the 1940s, especially her Oscar-nominated *My Sister Eileen* (1942); and Loretta, for providing her with a temporary haven as she learned to negotiate the slippery slope of free lancing.

Loretta was in better pictures than Columbia's *The Doctor Takes a Wife* (1940), a romantic comedy with a dash of screwball, but not enough of either genre to make it distinctive. Director Alexander Hall was the perfect match for Rosalind Russell during her decade at Columbia, eliciting performances from her in *This Thing Called Love* (1941), *My Sister Eileen* (1942), and *She Wouldn't Say Yes* (1945) that confirmed her extraordinary gift for comedy. He could not do the same for Loretta. *The Doctor Takes a Wife* had potential: A feminist writer (Loretta), whose espousal of the single life has made her the idol of spinsters, cadges a ride to New York with a neurology instructor (Ray Milland). A simple trip becomes a cause célèbre when the press assumes they are married. Complications abound, affecting each party. With Loretta behind the wheel of a souped-up plot, only the happiest of endings is possible: Loretta sabotages Milland's engagement to a ditzy socialite (Gail Patrick, out of her sophisticated element), but also gets him promoted. Academics, take note. Once the couple makes it legal, the dean, who only doles out full professorships to married faculty, promotes Milland from instructor to full professor without his even going through the assistant and associate professor ranks—not to mention peer review. In 1940 few moviegoers would question such largesse; if any academics caught the film, they would attribute the premature promotion to Hollywood's ignorance of higher education—unless perhaps they were unmarried and wondered if there were colleges where the sole qualification for a full professorship was a wedding band.

Although *The Doctor Takes a Wife* is far from vintage Loretta, it illustrates the difficulty studios had pairing her with a compatible costar. In *Easy Living* (1937), Milland enjoyed a genuine rapport with Jean Arthur, looking as if he were amused by her wackiness. But it was not the same with Loretta. Once it is time to press the love button, Loretta's eyes turned limpid, as if they were the windows not so much of the soul as of the psyche. She began moving sinuously, provocatively with an erotic rhythm that was always genteel, but also sexy—as if she were having one of her fantasies, in which the only sighs were her own. You could not imagine Milland making any sound, except perhaps a groan because he was stuck with a script that gave him no control of the narrative. When Milland was in control, he was superb—but rarely in comedy. His best work was in drama: Mitch Leisen's *Arise, My Love* (1940), Fritz Lang's

Ministry of Fear (1944), and especially Wilder's *The Lost Weekend*, (1945), for which he won an Oscar playing an alcoholic writer. Milland may have looked as if he were meant for the drawing room, but he could also stagger, unshaven, up Third Avenue in search of a liquor store and experience the DTs in a dingy apartment.

Loretta had a slightly better vehicle in Columbia's *He Stayed for Breakfast* (1940), a Lubitsch-like film without the Lubitsch touch. *He Stayed for Breakfast* was Columbia's response to MGM's *Ninotchka* (1939), in which Melvyn Douglas converted Greta Garbo as an extraordinary Soviet envoy, to the joys of capitalism, inducing her to shed regulation attire for evening gowns and negligees. In *He Stayed for Breakfast*, the roles are reversed. Douglas is the Communist spouting the party line to Loretta, an ardent capitalist (who looks it). Communism comes in for a good deal of ribbing, which is understandable in an industry where capitalism reigned unchallenged, and communism was regarded with a combination of fear and loathing. There were also lingering memories of the 1919 Palmer Raids and the infamous and soon-to-be ignored nonaggression pact between the Soviet Union and Nazi Germany, signed on 23 August 1940, one week before *The Doctor Takes a Wife o*pened at New York's Roxy. Under the circumstances, there was no doubt who would win this ideological battle. *The Doctor Takes a Wife* did not require a suspension of disbelief; it inspired disbelief that was too pervasive to be suspended.

He Stayed for Breakfast is so deliciously improbable that one accepts it on the level of *Märchen* or fairy tale, a pleasant diversion that cannot subvert verisimilitude because there isn't any. The Paris depicted in *Ninotchka* did not seem like a soundstage creation, although it obviously was. The sets looked too authentic to be questioned in *He Stayed for Breakfast*, in which much of the action takes place in Marianna and Maurice Duval's (Loretta and Eugene Pallette) opulent apartment; a sense of place is totally lacking. But since *Ninotchka* was set in Paris, so must *He Stayed for Breakfast*. Melvyn Douglas looked and sounded no more like a French Stalinist than Eugene Pallette seemed a French banker. Both were French in name only. But perhaps the greatest test of credibility is the marriage between Loretta and Pallette, who specialized in playing blustery and blubbery characters. Pallette was a Dickensian figure, with a waistline reminiscent of Mr. Pickwick's in Dickens's *The Pickwick Papers*, where it is described as the product of "time and feeding [which] had expanded that once romantic form."

What could have attracted Marianna to Maurice except his wealth? At the beginning of the film she is preparing to divorce him because of the unbearable loneliness that she has felt since the first day of their marriage. Paul Boliet (Douglas) is so revolted by the effete (read "capitalist") way Duval holds his coffee cup that he shoots the cup out of Duval's hand, nicking him in the finger. Boilet is now the proverbial man on the run. Disguised as a policeman, he takes refuge in the Duvals' apartment, much to the delight of Marianna, who considers being his prisoner a divertissement. It is also an opportunity for Loretta to model some classy outfits, such as billowy negligees with diaphanous sleeves, and an art deco lamé gown with a metallic sheen. This was clearly Loretta's film; it is Marianna who guides the trajectory of the plot, convincing Boliet that there are only two classes of people: not capitalists and communists, but men and women. And when she succeeds, her face registers the resplendent look of victory.

Boliet goes before the his party's executive committee, and in a scene that would have garnered applause in some quarters, denounces communism for its insistence on unswerving loyalty to Marxism and its subordination of the individual to the collective. Marianna, who has also become disgusted at the way Duval extends his index finger, whips out a pistol and shoots him in the finger. Now that she and Boilet are fugitives, they have no other choice but to emigrate to America, where they plan to settle in—of all places—Maine, where Boilet hopes to be a lobster fisherman! Whether they have money or passports is irrelevant; a fairy tale cannot be subjected to logical analysis. All audiences wanted was for Boilet to leave the party and Marianna to leave her husband so the two could settle in the land of the free and home of the brave.

If Douglas looked exasperated and, at times, lost, it was because the script placed Loretta in the driver's seat, with Douglas behind her. He did not undergo the gradual conversion to capitalism that Garbo experienced so convincingly in *Ninotchka*. Although director Alexander Hall was not Ernst Lubitsch, the fault lay more with the script than with either Douglas or Hall. Paul Boliet was a cardboard character, whose only purpose was to illustrate the folly of communism and make audiences feel grateful that they were living in a country where the unit of currency was not the ruble.

Loretta discovered dance when she was a teenager. Dancing became one of her passions; she even studied dance with Marge Champion's father, Ernest Belcher. But to play a circus performer, whom an impresario (Conrad Veidt) transforms into a world-famous ballerina in Columbia's *The Men in Her Life* (1941), Loretta had to learn the rudiments of ballet. Although a stand-in was used for the long shots, audiences expected some proof that the versatile Loretta could stand en pointe, as she did in several scenes—and quite convincingly. It was difficult for a woman in her late twenties to master such technique, but Loretta, ever the perfectionist, did. She also looked like a ballerina.

The screenplay was another matter; it was a generic starmaker scenario, in which a successful actor/director/producer/agent turns an unknown into an icon. In *The Red Shoes* (1948), the impresario (Anton Walbrook) fails to convince his prima ballerina (Moira Shearer) to forgo marriage to a composer and remain his protégée. In *The Men in Her Life*, the ballerina (Loretta) marries the impresario, who expects her to give up her career. When he suddenly dies, the ballerina can either continue dancing or remarry. Career or remarriage? Remarriage, with a daughter and the resumption of career, perhaps? But this outcome would not set well with audiences. Instead, the ballerina remarries and returns to the world of dance. Once she realizes that her performing days are over, she decides to live vicariously through her daughter by preparing her for a career of her own.

The Men in Her Life opened at Radio City Music Hall, then known as "The Showcase of the Nation," on 11 December 1941, four days after the Japanese bombing of Pearl Harbor—when a ballerina's love life was not uppermost in audiences' minds. The *New York Times* critic, Bosley Crowther, panned *The Men in Her Life*, even implying that Loretta was not much of an actress. It was a mean-spirited review, but at least Music Hall audiences, seeking refuge from the bleak headlines, could settle into their seats, watch a movie about selflessness, and get a stage show as a bonus. As for Loretta's performance: How many actresses could stand on point, look like a prima ballerina, marry a domineering male, remarry after his death, temporarily abandon her daughter, and then monitor the girl's career? Even Bette Davis never ran such a gamut at Warner Bros. But Columbia was not Warner's, and Harry Cohn was grateful that his film made it to the Music Hall.

The best of Loretta's Columbia films of the 1940s was *Bedtime Story* (1941), her third with Alexander Hall. Loretta had now adjusted to Hall's approach to domestic comedy, which required an airiness that kept the action afloat, gradually bringing it down to earth for the denouement. The idea was to convince viewers that they were being served a soufflé that may have sagged a bit, but had not collapsed. *Bedtime Story* ranks as one of the unheralded films about remarriage, which owes a great deal to *The Awful Truth* (1937) and *His Girl Friday* (1940). Loretta and Fredric March play a married actress and playwright— like Alfred Lunt and Lynn

Fontanne—who, in true Hollywood tradition, have never had a flop. Still, after seven years of eight performances a week, Loretta yearns to retire to a farm in Connecticut. March agrees, but continues writing a play that will give her the greatest role of her career. Loretta, however, is so determined to retire that she divorces March, who goes on writing his masterpiece, while she becomes the wife of a banker (Allyn Joslyn).

Robert Flournoy's clever script adds a new complication to the traditional comedy of remarriage plot: the wife's second marriage turns out to be legally questionable. There are other plot divagations, all of which are beautifully integrated, including a credit card receipt from a California motel (then called an auto court) that invalidates the wife's required residency in Reno, the nation's divorce capital. But, as expected, Loretta returns to March and appears in his play, which is a hit as well as a personal triumph for her. Loretta was surprisingly convincing as a Broadway star. She had never performed on stage, although she was not averse to doing live radio drama, like *Lux Radio Theatre*, where she was a regular. She was also at ease on the lecture circuit. Apparently, the theatre held little interest for her. Yet she understood the way a stage diva moved and spoke, perhaps because she assumed that stars from all media behaved similarly. For *Bedtime Story*, she had the walk, grace, and technique to execute a flawless cross from one side of the stage to the other and then swivel around. She knew enough about stage acting to re-create it. Perhaps Hall, a former stage director, helped her; more likely, Loretta just tapped into those hidden resources that actors possess and found the stage diva within the movie star—the only difference being that, in the theatre, an actor has to master the entire script, while in the movies, learning several pages a day is standard.

Despite top billing, Fredric March fared less well. March was a fine dramatic actor, but without much of a flair for comedy. The script required the playwright to woo his wife back to the stage, and when she remarries, to cause as much mayhem as he can to return her to both the theatre and himself. Thus, March behaves no differently than the ex-husbands in *The Awful Truth* and *His Girl Friday*, who resort to whatever means they can to bring their ex-wives to their senses. March has nothing to do but orchestrate the chaos; he does not have to participate in it. Loretta, however, has to delve into her character's unconscious, as Rosalind Russell did in *His Girl Friday*, in which Hildy Johnson (Russell) has no desire to wed her dullard fiancé (Ralph Bellamy) and settle down in Albany, hoping instead that her ex (Cary Grant) will deliver her from the boredom awaiting her. Similarly, Loretta secretly hopes March will rescue her. He does, and one assumes Broadway will be the better for it.

Loretta's next picture to fulfill her Columbia commitment was her least memorable: *A Night to Remember* (1943), not to be confused with the harrowing 1958 British film of the same name about the sinking of the Titanic. This was not a memorable occasion for any of the cast, which included some of Hollywood's finest character actors: Jeff Donnell, Sidney Toler (minus his Charlie Chan makeup), Gale Sondergaard, Lee Patrick, and Blanche Yurka. It was a species of screwball mystery, inspired by *The Thin Man* series, in which amateur sleuths solve murders, as they do in *The Gracie Allen Murder Case* and *It's a Wonderful World* (both 1939). *The Thin Man* (1934) is really faux screwball. Pure screwball does not center on a married couple, but rather a man and a woman who come from totally different backgrounds (e.g., *It Happened One Night, Easy Living, Nothing Sacred, Bringing Up Baby*). Loretta could do romantic comedy with screwball overtones, but playing the "dizzy dame" was not in her repertoire. She was not the sort who could release her madcap self, probably because, unlike Jean Arthur, Claudette Colbert, Carole Lombard, and Katharine Hepburn, she did not have one. Nor did her costar, Brian Aherne. Aherne's best Columbia films were the two he did with Rosalind Russell, *My Sister Eileen* (1942) and *What a Woman!* (1943), where his urbanity complemented Russell's cool sophistication.

In *A Night to Remember*, Loretta, the wife of a mystery writer (Aherne), rents the basement apartment of a Greenwich Village brownstone, hoping that he will give up thrillers in favor of romantic fiction. She could not have a picked a worse address. *A Night to Remember* is a variation of the old, dark house movie—with an emphasis on "dark." The film looks as if each frame had been dipped in stygian waters. It was not so much film noir as noir film. There were times when the screen grew so dark that it was impossible to see what was going on, or who was doing what to whom. No one in the brownstone is what he or she seems; even Jeff Donnell is not her usual perky self, because, as we discover, she is being blackmailed by someone who knows she fled the scene of a notorious penthouse murder. Practically everyone in the building is the victim of the same blackmailer. Eventually Aherne does what the police cannot, unmasking the blackmailer—with little help from Loretta who is swooning when she isn't screaming. This is the kind of film in which doors lock mysteriously, rooms are suddenly plunged into darkness, a horseshoe disappears from the garden and ends up in the living room, a roving turtle is mistaken for a monster, and a body falls out of a closet. With different leads (e.g., Jean Arthur and Ray Milland), more subtle direction, and better low-key lighting instead of inky darkness, *A Night to Remember* might have been a respectable addition to a sub-genre: screwball mystery, which was far from overcrowded. Bosley Crowther's skimpy two-paragraph review in the *New York Times* (1 January 1943) summed it all up: "a hairbrained [sic] excursion with a couple of frightened stars" and "a thoroughly adequate" company, trapped in a "tedious and involved plot," resulting in "a succession of looming shadows, conversations and mediocre gags."

Perhaps *A Night to Remember* was Harry Cohn's revenge on Loretta for inflating the cost of her *Bedtime Story* wardrobe. Loretta found a gown at a department store that she preferred to the one Irene had designed for her. It cost $155, but the price rose to $400 after the fastidious Loretta requested extensive alterations. Knowing that Irene would have charged anywhere between $600 and $800 for the same gown, she submitted a bill for $700. Harry retaliated by giving March top billing. Loretta was not one to take defeat lightly; when Cohn ordered a new outfit for her, Loretta had the wardrobe department change it so radically that it ended up costing the studio considerably more than $700. Eventually, Loretta and Cohn reconciled after she sought forgiveness. But she did not return to Columbia until her movie career was drawing to a close. She gave the studio one more film, *Paula* (1952), and left the screen the following year.

The Men in Her Life had no sooner opened than Loretta was ready for another film: Universal's *The Lady from Cheyenne*, which started production the first week of January 1941. As a freelancer, Loretta could honor her five-picture commitment to Columbia and still check into another studio for a movie or two. *The Lady from Cheyenne* was the first of a two-picture arrangement with Universal. She was intrigued by the idea of doing a western, a genre she had never attempted. Trekking off to the Mojave Desert for exteriors appealed to her sense of adventure. It would not be like *The Call of the Wild* shoot—there was no Gable, and she was now a married woman. Loretta welcomed the challenge. If she could play a homeless waif, a stage diva, a hearing-impaired wife, and a ballerina—among other types—she could also play a schoolmarm in the Wild West.

The *Daily Committee Meeting* reports reveal a relatively uneventful, six-week shoot that came in under budget: $535,000, as opposed to the estimated $622,000. The title was a misnomer; Annie (Loretta) hailed from Philadelphia and headed west with her inheritance, planning to educate settlers' children. Loretta played Annie like a crusading optimist, believing that no hurdle was insurmountable, and that reason would prevail over partisanship and chauvinism. She was not prepared for a robber baron (Edward Arnold), determined to acquire her water rights. When Annie refuses, he dispatches his goon squad to burn down the schoolhouse. Annie still does not give up, despite initial opposition from Arnold's stooge lawyer (Robert Preston). She stops at nothing, even pitting Republicans against Democrats to get a suffrage bill passed in the state legislature.

The Lady from Cheyenne, set in the late eighteen sixties, is accurate in its depiction of suffrage. Women were given the right to vote in 1869, but not in national elections. That did not come to pass until 1920 with the passage of the Nineteenth Amendment. For the time being, women had to be content with voting in local elections, which was all the film claimed. Still, for Annie and her cohorts it was a triumph. What prevented *The Lady from Cheyenne* from becoming a milestone in feminist cinema is the ending, intended to satisfy women who were too insecure to assert their independence, and men who wanted women kept in their place. Preston's attempts to bring Arnold to justice—which was only delivered with the formation of an all-female jury after the men refused to sit in judgment on one of their own—should have spelled the end of their relationship. Since Preston was Loretta's leading man, the script had her doing an about face in the fade out and promising to be his forever, darning his socks, making his meals, and bearing his kids. Greater love than this hath no woman, sacrificing her selfhood for her husband—something Loretta Young never did.

The Lady from Cheyenne was Loretta's introduction to the conventions of the Hollywood western, a male-centered genre in which women existed primarily to ensure a happy ending. The western was not a genre in which Loretta was comfortable. She did one more, *Along Came Jones* (1945), which was actually a send-up of the traditional western and gave her a much less passive role. In *Jones*, her character proves that she can handle a rifle as well as any man.

The Lady from Cheyenne was released in spring 1941. But after 7 December, the film was swept into the dustbin of forgotten cinema, rarely resurrected and remembered, if at all, as a historical curio.

CHAPTER 14

Loretta Goes to War

In 1943, as a freelancer cutting multi-picture deals, Loretta realized that, without a home base, she would be leading a nomadic existence, while her peers, ensconced at their own studios, would be starring in more prestigious films: MGM's Greer Garson, a recent Academy Award winner for *Mrs. Miniver* (1942), in *Madame Curie* (1943), which brought her an Oscar nomination; Warner's Bette Davis in *Old Acquaintance* and *Watch on the Rhine* (1943); Fox's Gene Tierney in *Heaven Can Wait* (1943); and Jennifer Jones in *The Song of Bernadette* (1943). The last was a role that Loretta could have played, as if Bernadette had already been beatified, awaiting canonization. Loretta may have been six years older than Jones, but at thirty, she looked just as youthful as Jones did at twenty-four.

Loretta knew that the parts she was offered were not choice; freelancing may have brought independence, but not necessarily the kind that leads to Oscars or Oscar nominations. Loretta surprised Hollywood when she won an Oscar for *The Farmer's Daughter* (1947), a Samuel Goldwyn production (she was not Goldwyn's first choice). A final nomination, ironically, came for a picture that she made upon her return to Fox after a ten-year absence, *Come to the Stable* (1949).

When Loretta committed to four pictures at Paramount, she was not exactly a stranger on the lot. She had been there a decade earlier in *The Crusades*. But this was a different Paramount, headed by Buddy De Sylva, who did not have any new female dramatic stars. Claudette Colbert had been with Paramount since 1929; other actresses, such as Paulette Goddard and Veronica Lake, were primarily decorative. The Paramount contract player in the ascendant was a male: Alan Ladd, whose portrayal of the cold-blooded Raven in *This Gun for Hire* (1941) heralded the arrival of a star, but one whose career needed nurturing so that he would avoid the pitfalls of stereotyping. Instead, Paramount capitalized on Ladd's banked anger, knowing that audiences sensed it was only a matter of time before the lid popped.

With America's entry into World War II, a new type of character became popular: the apolitical American, usually male, who undergoes a transformation from detachment to commitment—and, in some cases, commitment with a vengeance. The classic type is the "I stick my neck out for no man" Rick Blaine (Humphrey Bogart) in *Casablanca* (1942) who, once he comes over to the other side, sticks his neck out for everyone, going so far as to join the Free French at the end of the film. That same year, Paramount released *Lucky Jordan*, in which Alan Ladd became a son of Uncle Sam after an elderly woman (memorably played by Mabel Paige), who posed as his mother to prevent his being drafted, was brutalized by Nazi thugs. That does it: "Nazi is another way to spell cockroach," he declares, becoming, as existentialists would say, *engagé*.

In *China* (1943), the first of Loretta's four Paramount films, Ladd was cast opposite her as a similar type: an employee of a petroleum export company, one of whose clients is Japan. The time is shortly before Pearl Harbor; the place is China, where anti-Japanese sentiment is strong after Japan's ruthless attempts to reduce China to a satellite. Although Loretta had top billing, Ladd was the real star. Loretta knew that the plot did not require a fashionable wardrobe, even though the costume designer was the legendary Edith Head. Loretta played Carolyn Grant, an American teacher determined to bring her female students to their university, using her powers of persuasion to get Ladd to transport them. Throughout the film, there are veiled references to Nanking, which the Japanese invaded in 1937, precipitating what is now called "The Rape of Nanking," during which 20,000 women were sexually assaulted within a month. The specter of rape hovers over the film, and when it happens, even though off-screen, it is the single unforgettable scene in a movie that is part flag-waver, part tribute to our Chinese allies and their leader, General Chiang Kai-shek.

When one of the students decides to return to her parents' village, Loretta prevails upon Ladd to bring her back. In an earlier scene, the student has just arrived when a Japanese motorcade pulls up. Soldiers disembark and kill the parents. As the soldiers eye the student, one of them grins malevolently, as the glare of the sun blinds him to the young woman's premature sense of shame when she realizes the inevitable. In 1943, it was impossible to show a female being gang raped; forty-five years later, she could be seen to be raped, even on a pool table (*The Accused* [1988]). In *China*, the rape is still in progress when Ladd and

Loretta arrive. Director John Farrow composed the shot in such a way that when the two enter the house, we can see clear across the frame to the bedroom. The door is ajar, and the girl is writhing on the bed in agony. Three soldiers emerge; once they see Ladd with his machine gun, they try to be conciliatory. At that moment, Loretta rushes into the bedroom, stripping off her raincoat and throwing it over the student. Ladd, now thoroughly committed, kills the soldiers, referring to them as "flies in a manure heap."

The student's death from the ordeal provides Loretta with an opportunity to give a moving reading of the Twenty-Third Psalm. At the end of the film, Ladd and some Chinese partisans prepare to dynamite a ravine, causing an avalanche to block the passage of a Japanese convoy. To buy time, Ladd makes small talk with one of the soldiers, who spouts the familiar expository line to explain his command of English: "I have studied in your country." When the soldier boasts that Japan has just bombed Pearl Harbor, Ladd launches into a speech about freedom; the solder, incensed, shoots him, and the rocks come tumbling down. Loretta did what she could with the role, which was far from a stretch. The script implied that her character would awaken Ladd's dormant conscience, but it was the rape that did so. He was once again "Lucky Jordan," the avenger of women who suffered at the hands of America's enemies. High fashion was also out of the question, since the script required Carolyn to wear the same outfit for the entire film. At least Loretta had the luxury of starting at 9:00 a.m. and ending at 6:00 p.m.

China was one of Loretta's two contributions to the war effort at a time when Hollywood's leading ladies were expected to appear in films designed to convince audiences that America would not fall victim to the Axis. Claudette Colbert, Veronica Lake, and Paulette Goddard were Red Cross nurses on Bataan in Paramount's *So Proudly We Hail* (1943). Greer Garson played a British wife and mother who encounters a Nazi in her garden in *Mrs. Miniver*. Bette Davis was the wife of a freedom fighter in *Watch on the Rhine* (1943). Gene Tierney played a Eurasian teacher in Fox's *China Girl* (1942). Ginger Rogers kept the home fires burning while her husband, never to return, was at war in RKO's *Tender Comrade* (1943). Ann Sheridan was a Norwegian resistance fighter in Warner's *Edge of Darkness* (1943). Joan Crawford outwitted the Nazis in MGM's *Reunion in France* (1942) and engaged in espionage in MGM's *Above Suspicion* (1943). Loretta was in good company, and in a reasonably good film—although not as memorable as *So Proudly We Hail*, which had greater appeal. The problem was that she was upstaged by Ladd, Paramount's golden boy, who was being groomed for stardom that was to prove short-lived. Loretta, on the other hand, was not a Paramount regular; she encamped at whatever studio offered her the better deal. Ladd was not quite ready to freelance.

In 1943, Loretta also demonstrated her patriotism by traveling to the East Coast for a bond drive. When she returned to Los Angeles, she was welcomed by the Monterey Park Girls Drum and Bugle Corps and given a military escort to Pershing Square, where she was so persuasive that a man bought $1,500 worth of war savings bonds from her. Earlier that year, she flew to Washington to celebrate President Roosevelt's birthday and visit her husband, who was then a lieutenant colonel stationed in D.C. Again, she was formally greeted on her return, this time by two Chinese children who presented her with a bouquet of gladioli. Unlike Bob Hope, Marlene Dietrich, Martha Raye, and Frances Langford, Loretta did not travel to Western Europe or the Pacific to entertain the GIs; nor was she a regular at the Hollywood Canteen like Bette Davis. Still, she did her part—and of course, a little publicity did not hurt. Loretta was never shy about speaking in public, particularly if it was for a good cause and meant press coverage.

Loretta owed Universal a second picture, which turned out to be another Walter Wanger production. Wanger was then based at Universal, which offered him $2,500 a week and creative control, except for the choice of director and cast—and the right of final cut, which the studio reserved for itself. One of the reasons Wanger became a semi-independent producer was his desire to build up his own stock company, so that he would not necessarily be saddled with a studio's contract players. That plan did not always work out. When Wanger arrived at Universal in 1941, he discovered that he had to draw, for the most part, on the studio's regulars: e.g., Jon Hall, Maria Montez, Lois Collier, June Vincent, Evelyn Ankers, Anne Gwynne, Yvonne De Carlo, and David Bruce—all of whom were familiar to B movie aficionados. Wanger had no illusions about the quality of the Universal product: horror films, Abbott and Costello comedies, Deanna Durbin musicals, Donald O'Connor and Peggy Ryan teenage romps, and sand and sex adventures. But he was shrewd enough to know that, with the advent of World War II, a producer could not go wrong with flag-wavers. Since Wanger sensed that the army, navy, marines, and air force would receive enough exposure on the screen, he convinced Universal to buy the script and the footage that had already been shot for *Eagle Squadron,* a tribute to the American pilots who offered their services to the Royal Air Force (RAF) during the Blitz, after United Artists passed on the project. At the same time that Wanger was working on *Eagle Squadron* (1942), he was making the hokey but entertaining *Arabian Nights* (1942), with Universal's own Jon Hall, Maria Montez, Turhan Bey, and Sabu.

Eagle Squadron was a respectable film, but *We've Never Been Licked* (1943) was one of the most blatantly anti-Japanese movies of the decade. The film portrays Japanese students at Texas A&M who hope to learn how they can "apply the best of American civilization" to their country—while at the same time justifying Japan's conquest of China in animal imagery: "Sometimes, it is necessary to choke the dog to give it medicine for the dog's own good."

Wanger's fourth Universal film was slightly better, but not enough to make it eligible for inclusion among the great World War II films such as *Mrs. Miniver, Bataan, So Proudly We Hail, They Were Expendable,* and *Pride of the Marines*. Wanger had found an even less familiar subject than Americans in the RAF: the Women's Auxiliary Ferrying Squadron (WAFS), founded in 1942 and a year later combined with the Women's Flying Training Detachment (WFTD) to form the Women Air Force Service Pilots (WASPS). After various title changes, including "When Ladies Fly," the film became *Ladies Courageous* (1944). Wanger did not have to be reminded that women made up more than half of the movie going population during World War II. Nor did Hollywood, releasing such films as *Cry Havoc* and *So Proudly We Hail* (both 1943), which dramatized the plight of the nurses abandoned on Bataan. Home front fare like *The Sullivans* (1944), in which the mother of five sons who enlisted in the Navy is informed that all are dead, and *Since You Went Away* (1944), in which a wife and mother waits for news about her missing husband, as countless women did at the time, also appeared on movie screens.

For *Ladies Courageous* to succeed, Wanger needed a star. Loretta was never a real Wanger actress, like Joan Bennett and Susan Hayward. She was rather like a passenger on a boat that sailed from port to port. But Wanger had to keep the film afloat, and Loretta had a commitment to Universal. She may have balked at the supporting cast that included Universal stalwarts such as David Bruce, Anne Gwynne, Lois Collier, June Vincent and Evelyn Ankers, all of whom acquitted themselves well. Not quite as prestigious as Loretta was Geraldine Fitzgerald, a fine actress on loan from Warner Bros. Loretta and Geraldine played sisters who ran a California school for training pilots—which itself may have proved a revelation to 1944 audiences. Unlike *The Lady From Cheyenne*, which opened at New York's Roxy, "the cathedral of movie palaces," *Ladies Courageous* was booked into the Criterion, a less prestigious venue. The *New York Times* (16 March 1944) was highly critical of the film, not on aesthetic grounds, but for its depiction of the WAFS, implying that Wanger, who had served in the Signal Corps in World War I, should have known better than to make a movie about the WAFS that was just a melodrama involving infidelity, suicide, enlistment for publicity purposes, reckless endangerment, and an MIA husband. The *Times* critic seemed to want a documentary rather than a feature film. If such a documentary were ever made, it would not have been made by Wanger, who knew that it would only be shown in newsreel theaters, such as the one that used to be located in Grand Central Station.

If Hollywood was able to grind out so many war-related films in the 1940s, it was partially because screenwriters had concocted a workable formula: Take an event, a battle, or a branch of the armed services and weave a plot around it. In *Ladies Courageous*, based on a novel by Virginia Spencer Cowles, the same principle was applied to the WAFS. The movie did not downplay the tension between the male and female pilots (the latter originally intended merely to ferry planes to military bases, freeing the men for combat). Although the men are clearly sexist and sneer at the "lady pilots," the WAFS are not exactly a community of saints. Among them is a wife (Lois Collier), who commits suicide by crashing her plane because her philandering husband has taken up with another WAF (Diana Barrymore), and a reckless celebrity (Geraldine Fitzgerald), who only enlists for publicity and is so irresponsible that she almost costs another WAF her life. Loretta is the exception: a faithful wife with an MIA husband. Will he return for the fade out? He does, the movie ends, and *Ladies Courageous* goes into a tailspin, landing in the sea of forgotten films.

In case feminists wondered whether Wanger could have used the same plot points for a movie about male pilots, for the most part, he—or anyone—could have. Only suicide posed a problem, although at the end of *Bombardier* (1943), Randolph Scott sacrifices himself so that Colonel Doolittle's raid on Tokyo would succeed. Generally, the suicides in World War II films were women. Veronica Lake, as a Red Cross nurse in *So Proudly We Hail*, conceals a grenade in her shirt, raises her hands as a sign of surrender, and blows herself up—along with the Japanese soldiers encircling her, thus enabling the other nurses to escape the proverbial fate worse than death. Rosalind Russell, as an Amelia Earhart type pilot, runs out of fuel in *Flight for Freedom* (1942) and chooses to remain airborne, knowing that her plane will eventually plunge into the Pacific—but better a watery grave than landing on a Japanese-held island where an unknown fate awaits her.

A male version of *Ladies Courageous* would have been atypical and unpopular. Men in the 1940s combat film could be competitive, particularly in the "two men-in-love-with-the-same-woman" movie (*Thunder Birds* [1942], *Bombardier* [1943], *They Were Expendable* [1945]), but the loser never resorted to suicide. Men have their fears (*Thunder Birds*) and could be prickly, pugnacious, and smart-alecky (*Action in the North Atlantic, Air Force* [both 1943]), but not reckless to the point of endangering another GI's life. According to Hollywood, men apparently bond better than women (*Wake Island* [1942], *Corregidor* [1943]); divergent opinions (*Bombardier*) and generational conflicts (*Destroyer* [1943]) exist but are eventually resolved. Hollywood's GIs were uncommonly religious (*Destination Tokyo* and *Guadalcanal Diary* [both 1943]). This is the image of the fighting man that the films of the war years have bequeathed to subsequent generations. World War II veterans would know better, but Hollywood's version was meant for mass consumption.

The *Ladies Courageous* plot points, *sans* suicide, could have been recycled for a similar screenplay about men, except that no studio would have produced it. Any studio would have realized that such a film could never be shown on army bases, and that women would have wondered how America could ever win the war if such men were representative of our armed forces. *Ladies Courageous* at least acknowledged that there were women's divisions other than the well-known WACS and the WAVES, and moviegoers, who knew nothing about the WAFS, at least learned the acronym. But Loretta's fans just wanted a movie with enough suspense to justify the price of admission. That they received, but no upgrades.

CHAPTER 15

"Age cannot wither" (but Hollywood Can)

At thirty-one Loretta looked as porcelain-skinned as ever. When she endorsed a beauty soap, like Lux, it was as if she had bestowed beauty upon the product, not vice versa. But to remain a star, rather than a working actress who once knew stardom and was now reduced to playing leads in minor films (Virginia Bruce, Kay Francis), or who was relegated to supporting cast status (Fay Wray, Anna Lee, Mae Clark), a dewy complexion was not enough. Loretta had not yet been nominated for an Oscar, although she should have been for *Man's Castle* and *Midnight Mary*. The situation would change in 1947, six years before she left Hollywood, where an Oscar nomination, or even an Oscar, is just an annual honorific that is often forgotten the next year. "You're only as good as your last picture" was the mantra. Loretta was always good, even though some of her pictures were only adequate.

Billing varied with her costars. In *China*, Loretta was billed first, Alan Ladd, second. In her next and last film with Ladd, the billing was reversed; now it was Alan Ladd and Loretta—Paramount's pride and a freelancer in the second of her four-film contract with Paramount—starring in *And Now Tomorrow* (1944). With a script by Frank Partos and Raymond Chandler adapted from Rachel Field's novel, *And Now Tomorrow* should have been an outstanding film. Partos was a respected screenwriter (*Jennie Gerhardt*, *Thirty Day Princess*, *Cradle Song*), although his script for *A Night to Remember* might have fared better with actors who could don a bit of the motley (Jean Arthur and Fred MacMurray, or Jean Arthur and Joel McCrea, instead of Loretta and Brian Aherne). Chandler's reputation rested on novels that are paradigms of detective fiction: *The Big Sleep*, *Farewell, My Lovely*, and *The Lady in the Lake*. But he was a novice screenwriter, whose other 1944 script was *Double Indemnity*, coauthored with writer-director Billy Wilder, who admired Chandler's fiction, but deplored his inability to grasp the differences between writing a novel and writing a film script. Chandler, who found working with Wilder an "agonizing experience," at least acknowledged Wilder's "genius" as a director. Chandler's voice is heard intermittently in *And Now Tomorrow*, a "woman's film" about a deaf heroine (Loretta) cured by a street-smart surgeon (Alan Ladd).

Loretta played Emily Blair of Blairstown, where the railroad tracks were the line of demarcation between the haves and the have-nots. The surgeon, Merek Vance (Ladd), revels in coming from the "wrong side of the tracks," known as "Shantytown," and delights in baiting Emily. The two no sooner meet than they start sparring, each trying to outdo the other in put-downs and behaving like people who do not know they are in love, until they realize they have armed themselves with verbal ammunition to keep from declaring it. Ladd and Loretta play these scenes as if they were veterans of the mating game—Ladd talking tough and Loretta unflappably genteel. It is in these scenes that Chandler's voice comes through, as it did in *Double Indemnity*, when Barbara Stanwyck and Fred MacMurray meet for the first time and launch into sexually encoded dialogue.

In *And Now Tomorrow*, Chandler's voice is discernible in Merek's opening line. Emily is returning to Blairstown from Boston, where she has learned that her deafness, brought on by meningitis, is incurable. While waiting for the train, she stops at a coffee shop. Vance enters, sitting near, but not alongside her at the counter. His order comes straight from the pulps—hardboiled, terse, clipped: "Coffee. Hot, strong, and made this year." Chandler was probably the one who punched up Vance's dialogue, which Ladd delivered with the self-assurance of a man who worked his way to the top without ever having to say "thank you." Vance may be a noted otologist, but he is still blue collar to the core.

Alan Ladd was the main draw; it was he who contributed to the film's financial success, despite hostile reviews. Loretta gave the more demanding performance, always remaining in character. Edith Head's wardrobe was a different matter. It looked as if it came out of Emily's 1944 closet, not from 1937, the year in which the film is set. The cast does not even remotely look 1930s. Such mismatches, however, did occur. MGM's *The Postman Always Rings Twice* (1946), based on James Cain's 1934 novel, seems to be set in the 1930s, but one would never know it from Lana Turner's costumes. Another Turner vehicle, *Johnny Eager* (1942), also evokes the 1930s, although Turner does not. In *And Now Tomorrow*, it was not the costumes but Loretta's performance that was memorable—beautifully nuanced, faithful to the script and the character. Before Emily learns sign language, she fixes her gaze on her fiancé (Barry Sullivan); frustrated that she cannot understand what he is saying, she hovers over him as he writes out his answers to her questions. Even after Emily learned to read lips, she always focuses on the speaker, as if she were trying to see if there was a discrepancy between the words and the facial expression.

More demanding was Emily's transformation from a creature of privilege to the wife of a doctor, who has not forgotten his commitment to the class from which he came. When Emily accompanies Vance to "Shantytown," one could easily imagine her devoting one day a week to serving its residents. In its own way, *And Now Tomorrow* succeeds as an amalgamation of melodrama (Emily's sister, a wickedly cunning Susan Hayward, has designs on the fiancé) and social consciousness (Vance saves the life of a Shantytown child). Audiences had no problem with Ladd's cockiness and Loretta's initial coolness—particularly after Loretta sheds the mantle of privilege when she finds herself dependent on Vance. Ladd's tough guy persona had been forged in *This Gun for Hire* (1941); from then on, he used the same mask in different settings: Asia (*China, Calcutta* [1947], *Saigon* [1948]); Los Angeles (*The Blue Dahlia* [1946], Raymond Chandler's only original screenplay); the Old West (*Whispering Smith* [1948], *Streets of Laredo* [1949]), and even as Jay Gatsby of West Egg in the much maligned movie version of F. Scott Fitzgerald's *The Great Gatsby* (1949), in which Ladd played the perfect nouveau riche with a past and an attitude. In *And Now Tomorrow*, Ladd may not have played the kind of specialist moviegoers ordinarily consult—except those who don't mind a surgeon whose rough edges will never be planed down.

There are two exquisite touches by director Irving Pichel that merit attention. The first is a flashback in which Emily, returning to Blairstown, looks out of the train window as the rain beats against it. A slow dissolve begins, as the present yields to the past, and the train window fades out as the window of Emily's bedroom fades in, revealing the day she awakened and discovered that she was hearing-impaired. She could see the rain-streaked window but hear no sound. The second occurs after Emily has completed the treatment prescribed by Vance. This time she awakens to the sound of sleet and a crackling fire. Knowing that she can hear, Emily claps with childlike glee. It was a poignant moment in a film that was by no means the disaster that some critics claimed.

Loretta would return to Paramount, but not immediately. *Ladies Courageous* fulfilled her two-picture commitment to Universal. She was now at liberty, and so was William Goetz, Louis Mayer's son-in-law by his marriage to Mayer's daughter, Edith. Goetz was eager to start his own studio. Although he could never compete with Mayer's other son-in-law, David Selznick, who married Mayer's daughter Irene (later a major stage producer), Goetz had the same goal: independent production. Realizing he needed a distributor, Goetz turned to Leo Spitz, RKO's corporate president from 1935 to 1938; together they formed International Pictures in 1944, with RKO as distributor.

Goetz was eager to recruit name talent, not necessarily luminaries, but actors of sufficient luminescence to attract audiences. International's first release, *Casanova Brown* (1944), with Oscar winners Gary Cooper and Teresa Wright, opened at New York's Radio City Music Hall. But the others bearing the RKO trademark—*The Woman in the Window* (1944), *Belle of the Yukon* (1944), *It's a Pleasure* (1945), *Along Came Jones* (1945), *Tomorrow Is Forever*, and *The Stranger* (both 1946)—did not live up to Goetz and Spitz's expectations. Ironically, Fritz Lang's *The Woman in the Window* is now enshrined in the film noir canon; Orson Welles's *The Stranger* is not *Citizen Kane*, but still brilliant moviemaking, if for no other reason than the mounting suspense that culminates in the clock tower scene.

When RKO no longer wanted to distribute International's product, British movie magnate J. Arthur Rank, Universal's biggest shareholder, brokered a merger with Universal, resulting in the formation of Universal-International in 1946, which released International's last film, *Temptation* (1946). What made International especially attractive to Rank was its talent, in particular Gary Cooper, Edward G. Robinson, Orson Welles, and Loretta, who costarred in two International films, *Along Came Jones* (1945) and *The Stranger* (1946), opposite Gary Cooper and Orson Welles, respectively.

Along Came Jones is a western satire, produced by Gary Cooper himself, who wanted to spoof the misleading image the public had of him as an innocent making his way through the world of experience. Anyone who saw his extraordinary performances in *The Plainsman* (1936), *Sergeant York* (1941), and *For Whom the Bell Tolls* (1943), knew that he was a multidimensional actor. But comics and commentators stamped him with a signature phrase, "Yup," as they did Cary Grant ("Judy"), Greta Garbo ("I want to be alone") and Bette Davis ("Peter"), to such an extent that Grant and Davis impressionists felt obliged to reproduce the stars' eccentric pronunciation ("Jeudy,""Petah"). As Melody Jones, Cooper succeeds in mocking the public's misconception of him as a hayseed by laughing both at himself and, in a sense, at the audience for its naïveté. Nunnally Johnson's screenplay revolves around a case of mistaken identity, in which Melody is mistaken for Monte Jarrad (Dan Duryea), an outlaw with the same initials. When Melody spots Cherry (Loretta), Cooper reacts with his eyes, as if wondering how the West could ever have produced a woman of such otherworldly beauty. But Loretta is very much at home on the range: She can drive a carriage, ride horseback, and at the climax, handles a rifle better than Melody or the other men. She and Melody share a sexuality that simmers, never boiling over into passion. In a wonderfully erotic moment, Cherry rolls a cigarette for Melody. Loretta handles the paper and tobacco as if she were preparing an aphrodisiac, doing it properly but also provocatively. The ending might have inspired the climactic moment of another—and more famous—Cooper film, *High Noon* (1952), for which he won his second Oscar. In *Along Came Jones*, just when it seems that Jarrad will kill Melody, he is struck by a bullet from a rifle—Cherry's. In *High Noon* there is a similar scene, in which Cooper's wife (Grace Kelly) does the same to save her husband, even though she is a Quaker. In each case, it is a woman who saves a man's life. Coincidence or influence?

One might ask the same about the bell tower climax in Hitchcock's *Vertigo* (1958), which bears a resemblance to a similar one in *The Stranger*. *The Stranger* was Loretta's last film for International, although she would return to the new Universal-International (UI) for two films, including her last. Goetz and Spitz were fortunate to find a producer in "S.P. Eagle," soon to be known as Sam Spiegel, who adopted the alias to avoid deportation because of his criminal record. Eagle's identity was common knowledge in Hollywood, and with the backing of powerful friends, he managed to become an American citizen after World War II—just at the time that the place of his birth, Galicia, was about to become part of what was then the Soviet Union. If he had been deported during the Cold War, it would have meant death or the gulag.

By 1954, he felt confident enough to identify himself as Sam Spiegel, the producer of *On the Waterfront*, occasioning one of *Variety*'s cleverest headlines: "The Eagle Folds Its Wings." But even in the mid-forties, Spiegel knew how to gain access to the studio's coffers, using a combination of charm, business savvy, and clever networking, even though, as director William Wyler's wife, Talli, put it: "He operated on the edge of a financial precipice better than anybody I ever saw." That may have been true, but if he fell over it, there was always a safety net: a bank, a financier, a friend, or backers who were repaid not with a check but with an invitation to one of his legendary parties.

As a Jew who knew that there were still war criminals at large after World War II ended, Spiegel was attracted to the script of *The Stranger*, in which an ex-Nazi assumes a new identity and takes up residence in Connecticut. It was Spiegel who put the package together and helped Goetz and Spitz sell it to RKO, on the basis of both the script and the A-list cast: Edward G. Robinson, Loretta, and Orson Welles. It was Spiegel who entrusted the screenplay to Anthony Veiller and John Huston (uncredited), with Huston scheduled to direct. Spiegel changed his mind, once he learned that Welles would not appear in *The Stranger* if he could not direct it. Huston went on to better films (*The Treasure of the Sierra Madre* and *The Asphalt Jungle*), and Welles came on board, promising to behave and bring the film in as budgeted. Welles would never behave. Put him behind a camera and he was like a kid in a toy store. When Welles wanted the script changed so that the Nazi hunter would be a woman, played by his friend and Mercury Theatre alumna Agnes Moorehead, RKO wisely refused, as Spiegel expected. Moorehead was a fine character actress but not a star. Welles agreed to all the terms, but for him, making *The Stranger* was a joyless experience. The billing in *The Stranger* was deceptive: Edward G. Robinson as Wilson, the Nazi hunter, who tracks down Franz Kindler (Orson Welles), a former top-ranking Nazi masquerading as Charles Rankin, a history instructor at a Connecticut prep school. Second billed was Loretta, as Mary, Rankin's wife. Welles may have been third, but his presence, both as actor and director, permeated the film. Welles, also uncredited for his contribution to the screenplay, was the kind of director who imposed his signature on anything with which he was involved, even projects he disliked.

Visually, *The Stranger* bears Welles's signature: chiaroscuro lighting; spectral faces; silhouettes, menacing and otherwise; high and low angle shots; and long takes (but not as long as those in *Touch of Evil*). There are other Wellesian touches. Exactly who decided that Rankin's first name would be Charles is unknown, but one cannot help but think of Charles Foster Kane, who dominated his second wife, Susan Alexander, just as Rankin does Mary. The scene in which Mary, still dubious about her husband's Nazi background, is asked to look at newsreel footage of the death camps that ends abruptly with the film flapping off the reel recalls the News on the March sequence in *Citizen Kane*, at the end of which the projector sputters, as if exhausted from the ordeal of compressing seventy years of a life into seven or eight minutes. Mary is also a Supreme Court justice's daughter; Kane's first wife, Emily, was a president's niece. Clearly, Welles was more than the film's costar and director; he was its auteur, courtesy of Veiller and Huston.

When Rankin discovers that Mary's brother has learned his identity, and then, that Mary has, Loretta is forced to play the imperiled wife/avenger, which she does well—although audiences were only interested in how Rankin would meet his fate. Perhaps Veiller, Huston, and/or Welles brainstormed and recalled the way Uncle Charlie (Welles alumnus Joseph Cotten) in Hitchcock's *Shadow of a Doubt* (1943) planned to get rid of his niece (Teresa Wright), who has figured out that he is the Merry Widow murderer. He weakens a step on the outdoor staircase, which, if his niece loses her balance, could result in a broken neck.

Rankin asks Mary to join him at the church tower, where he is working on the clock, whose biblical figures—one of which is a spear-wielding angel—revolve on a track when the bell tolls. Rankin saws off a rung of the ladder leading to the tower, which he then glues together. Mary, however, has asked her brother Noah (Richard Long) to go in her place;, fearing that her housekeeper has had a heart attack, she stays behind. Noah brings Wilson with him; when Wilson nearly falls to his death, he realizes what Rankin had done.

Knowing what her husband had in store for her, Mary sets out for the tower, where Rankin has taken refuge and where she intends to kill him. Wilson arrives, and the gun goes off, activating the mechanism that starts the statues circling around the belfry. Rankin is skewered on the angel's spear. Clasping the figure, now the avenging angel, the two come crashing down. How could Loretta compete with such a *coup de théâtre* or with Orson Welles, arguably the greatest showman in American film? Her work, as usual, was respectable, but she was in an Orson Welles production, in which the auteur hogged the spotlight, leaving everyone else, except Robinson, in shadow. Still, she endured the shoot, despite occasional bouts of illness and a schedule that wreaked havoc with her five-o'clock-quitting-time policy. At least twice, on 18 October and 1 November, respectively, she worked from 4:30 p.m. to 10:50 p.m., and again from 6:00 p.m. to 2:40 a.m.

Loretta's last day was 30 November 1945, after which it was back to Paramount for two pictures for Hal Wallis, two for Sam Goldwyn, and three for the man for whom, she once said, she would never work again, Darryl F. Zanuck. But how could Loretta pass on playing a college student, a nun, and a somnambulist?

Mother and daughters. Left to right: Elizabeth Jane (Sally Blane), Polly Ann, Mother Gladys, and Loretta. Academy of Motion Picture Arts and Sciences.

Loretta and Gladys. Academy of Motion Picture Arts and Sciences.

Loretta with her children: Christopher, Peter, Judy. Academy of Motion Picture Arts and Sciences.

Loretta and godchild, Marlo Thomas. Academy of Motion Picture Arts and Sciences.

Loretta at prayer. Academy of Motion Picture Arts and Sciences.

Actor Grant Withers, with whom Loretta eloped at seventeen. Photofest.

Loretta and Tom Lewis on their wedding day, 31 July 1940. Photofest.

World-famous designer, Jean Louis, whom Loretta married at eighty. Photofest.

A teenage Loretta and Lon Chaney in *Laugh, Clown, Laugh* (1928). Academy of Motion Picture Arts and Sciences.

The eighteen-year-old Loretta and Robert Williams in Frank Capra's *Platinum Blonde* (1931). Photofest.

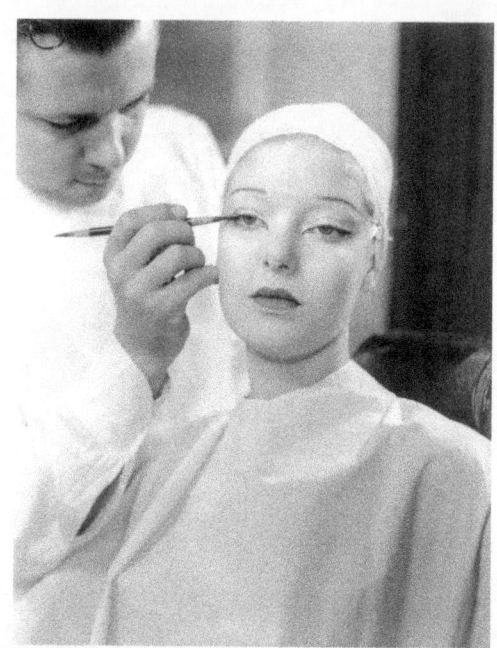

Loretta being made up to look Chinese in William Wellman's *The Hatchet Man* (1932). Academy of Motion Picture Arts and Sciences.

Loretta as the daughter of the title character. Academy of Motion Picture Arts and Sciences.

Loretta and Spenser Tracy, with whom she fell in love while making Frank Borzage's *Man's Castle* (1933). Photofest.

Loretta as the title character in *Midnight Mary* (1934). Academy of Motion Picture Arts and Sciences.

Costars and lovers: Loretta and Clark Gable in Wellman's *The Call of the Wild* (1935). Academy of Motion Picture Arts and Sciences.

Costars as ex-lovers: Loretta and Gable in *The Key to the City* (1950). Academy of Motion Picture Arts and Sciences.

Loretta, now pregnant, in Cecil B. DeMille's *The Crusades* (1936). Academy of Motion Picture Arts and Sciences.

Loretta as Eugenie in *Suez* (1938). Academy of Motion Picture Arts and Sciences.

Loretta as Katie in the Oscar-winning *The Farmer's Daughter* (1947). Photofest.

Loretta and Celeste Holm as nuns paying a visit to artist Elsa Lanchester in *Come to the Stable* (1949). Academy of Motion Picture Arts and Sciences.

The Last Picture Show: Loretta and John Forsythe in *It Happens Every Thursday* (1953). Academy of Motion Picture Arts and Sciences.

Tyrone Power and Loretta in *Suez* (1938). Academy of Motion Picture Arts and Sciences.

Alan Ladd and Loretta in *China* (1943). Photofest.

Loretta and Gary Cooper in a western satire with serious overtones, *Along Came Jones* (1945). Academy of Motion Picture Arts and Sciences.

Loretta on CBS's *Lux Radio Theatre*.
Academy of Motion Picture Arts
and Sciences.

The living room opening of
NBC's *The Loretta Young Show*.
Academy of Motion Picture
Arts and Sciences.

Loretta authentically costumed in "I Remember the Rani" (*The Loretta Young Show*, 1 May 1955). Academy of Motion Picture Arts and Sciences.

Loretta as a terminally ill wife and Joseph Cuby as the hitchhiker who persuades her to visit Lourdes in "The Road" (NBC, 20 September 1959). Photofest.

Trevor Howard (left), Arthur Hill, and Loretta in the Emmy-winning *Christmas Eve* (NBC, 22 December 1986). Academy of Motion Picture Arts and Sciences.

Fredric March presenting Loretta with her Oscar, 28 March 1948. Photofest.

The 1956 Emmy-winning Youngs for best continuing performance as actress and actor in a dramatic series: Loretta for *The Loretta Young Show* and Robert for *Father Knows Best*. Photofest.

Loretta and best director Oscar-winner Warren Beatty for *Reds* (1981), 29 March 1982. Photofest.

CHAPTER 16

Thrice Blessed
A Reunion, a Replacement, and an Oscar

Loretta owed Paramount two more pictures, which turned out to be Hal Wallis productions. As production head at Warner Bros. from 1930 to 1944, with credits ranging from *Little Caesar* (1930) and *The Adventures of Robin Hood* (1938) to *The Life of Emile Zola* (1937) and the forever fabulous *Casablanca* (1942), Wallis could have remained at the studio indefinitely. Instead, he chose to leave in 1944 after Jack Warner's hubris brought their once amicable relationship to an end on Oscar night, 2 March 1944. When director Sidney Franklin opened the envelope and announced that the Academy's choice of best picture was, not surprisingly, *Casablanca*, Wallis immediately rose from his seat to accept the award. It was he who monitored the transformation of an unproduced play into a classic film bearing a title that he personally gave it. But Warner, assuming that *Casablanca* was the studio's film—and, therefore, his—beat him to the stage and accepted an Oscar for a movie to which he had contributed nothing.

Tired of playing the crown prince to the clown king, Wallis moved to Paramount, where he set up his own production company with Joseph Hazen, a lawyer friend from his Warner Bros. days. With the formation of Wallis-Hazen, Inc., which by 1952 would be Hal Wallis Productions, and with backing from Paramount, Wallis began recruiting talent that would form the basis of a repertory company. He fancied himself a "starmaker," the title he gave his highly selective autobiography. But his stars could not equal the Warner galaxy that he once had at his disposal. Wallis discovered some promising newcomers, such as Lizabeth Scott, Wendell Corey, Kristine Miller, and Douglas Dick. But, with few exceptions, he failed to find starmaking vehicles for them, even though Dick and Corey delivered standout performances—Dick in *The Searching Wind*

(1946) and *The Accused* (1948), and Corey in *The File on Thelma Jordan* (1949) and *The Furies* (1950). Three of his discoveries—Kirk Douglas, Burt Lancaster, and Charlton Heston—appeared in a few Wallis productions, but defected once they achieved stardom. The films for which they will be remembered—*The Bad and the Beautiful, Paths of Glory, Lust for Life* (Douglas); *Sweet Smell of Success, Elmer Gantry, Birdman of Alcatraz* (Lancaster); *The Greatest Show on Earth, Touch of Evil, Ben Hur* (Heston)—were not Wallis's. It was not until 1949, when Wallis discovered Dean Martin and Jerry Lewis, and later Elvis Presley, that he could truly claim to be a starmaker. Most of the others were stars in the making who never made it to the firmament.

Wallis was a regular theatergoer, who found Lancaster and Douglas in short-lived Broadway plays that revealed a talent that could be transferred to the screen. Significantly, some of Wallis's best films were stage adaptations: *Tovarich, Jezebel, The Male Animal, Watch on the Rhine, The Searching Wind, Come Back, Little Sheba, The Rose Tattoo, Summer and Smoke,* and *Becket*. Naturally, quality mattered, but even if the play were not a masterpiece, Wallis would option it if he thought it could work as a film. Samson Raphaelson's *The Perfect Marriage*, costarring Miriam Hopkins and Victor Jory, had a respectable, but not impressive run during the 1944–45 season. The play had a promising premise, involving a couple on the verge of divorce after ten years of marriage. Wallis thought *The Perfect Marriage* (1946) might be another *Skylark* (1941), which was also based on a Raphaelson comedy about an imperiled marriage. When it came to casting the film, Wallis decided that none of his discoveries had the style for the leads—but Loretta Young and David Niven did.

Wallis knew that Loretta could handle repartee, and Niven could exude a sophistication that moviegoers would not find snobbish. Wallis and Loretta were also not strangers; their relationship had been forged at Warner's, where Wallis witnessed Loretta's versatility and later acknowledged her as not just a "star" but also a "friend." In 1946, Loretta was not a prima donna, nor would she ever be; but she had reached a stage in her career when she could insist, as she did when she signed on for *China*, on a 9:00 a.m.–6:00 p.m. (sometimes 5:00 p.m.) schedule. She had to make an exception for Orson Welles when she did *The Stranger*. Loretta's policy was meant for mortals, not for Welles. She accepted his erratic shooting schedule, even if it meant working past midnight. She had often done so during her apprentice years and now found herself marching to the beat of a drummer whose tempo was like no other's. Although Loretta gave her usual professional performance, she could not compete with the boy wonder of Hollywood, who was no longer a boy but would always be a wonder. *The Perfect Marriage* contracts imply that Niven was the bigger draw (compare his $150,000 for ten weeks, and $15,000 per week thereafter to Loretta's $100,000 for the same period and $10,000 per week thereafter). The reason, however, was that Niven was under contract to Goldwyn, who determined salary when he loaned the actor out to Paramount. *The Perfect Marriage* turned out to be a twelve-week shoot beginning on 2 January 1946, with Niven and Loretta receiving an additional amount ($30,000 and $20,000, respectively) for additional filming.

Loretta had a genuine flair for sophisticated comedy—as opposed to a flair for comedy as a genre, a characteristic shared by Jean Arthur, Carole Lombard, and Claudette Colbert, all of whom were especially adept comediennes. But if Loretta had lines that were elegantly crafted, without sounding sententious or pompous, she could toss them off with aplomb. She was at her best with dialogue that was more parlor than drawing room, more town house than penthouse. Samson Raphaelson was not Philip Barry, but he could write dialogue that, if it did not conjure up the image of cut glass, at least suggested a 60-watt chandelier.

Skylark was a better play than *The Perfect Marriage* and enjoyed a longer run. Leonard Spiegelgass adapted *The Perfect Marriage*, opening up the single-set play in the interest of realism and moving the action toward a believable conclusion, in which the couple's fathers, each of whom disliked his child's choice of spouse, became co-conspirators, pooling their wiles to save the marriage. Wallis assembled an excellent supporting cast: Virginia Field, the "other woman" angling to become Niven's second wife; Eddie Albert, who has similar designs on Loretta and is already planning to send her ten-year-old daughter to boarding school; and Zazu Pitts, as the maid whose pixilated expression got a laugh with every entrance.

Loretta made one more film for Wallis, *The Accused* (1948), which tested her ability as a serious actress in a way that no other film had. *The Accused* begins with a shot of a car at the edge of desolate cliff, overlooking the Pacific. A woman emerges in a trench coat, clutching a briefcase. She heads for the Freeway, shielding her face from the glare of the headlights. She finally accepts a ride from a truck driver, who drops her at a bus stop. The woman is Dr. Wilma Tuttle, a Los Angeles psychology professor, who has just killed one of her students. In a flashback, the cliff is revealed as the murder scene, the car, as the student's, and the motive as self-defense. The flashback also explains why Wilma was with a troubled student at such a lonely place.

Ketti Frings's screenplay is a model of criminal detection, until the denouement. Academics might quibble about Wilma's way of dealing with Bill Perry (menacingly played by Douglas Dick), a brilliant but disturbed student who studies her in class, mimicking her mannerisms. Although Perry makes Wilma uneasy, she has no qualms about accepting a ride, as well as a dinner invitation, from him in her naïve belief that she can rehabilitate him. Or is the coolly dispassionate professor intrigued by Perry's penetrating stare, as if he can see through her emotionally calcified exterior to the unfulfilled woman within? Loretta played Wilma with startling ambivalence, as if dinner with Perry was as much of an adventure as a form of therapy. Perry, however, has other plans. He drives her to the fatal cliff and changes into a tight-fitting bathing suit. Although Wilma is fascinated by the swirling water below and perhaps by the buff Perry, she also suspects his intentions. Loretta now makes it clear that Wilma is alternately attracted to, and repelled by, the libidinous Perry, who pins her down on the back seat of the car, kissing her passionately. The kiss restores the professional virgin to her senses; realizing what comes next, she reaches for the steel bar on the seat and clobbers Perry to death. Anyone hoping Wilma would get away with ridding herself of a creepy kid had more plot to contend with. Perry's guardian, Warren Ford (Robert Cummings), a San Francisco lawyer, comes looking for his ward but falls for Wilma instead. Police detective Ted Dorgen (Wendell Corey) starts building a case, at first suspecting a lovesick student (Suzanne Dalbert), but finally settling on Wilma, who eventually confesses.

The plot twists and counter twists keep the action from flagging until the courtroom ending, when Ford delivers an impassioned but morally flawed speech to the jury, admitting that Wilma was guilty of concealing evidence out of fear but not of committing homicide. Cummings sounds so persuasive, that, although the film ends before the verdict comes in, audiences assumed that Wilma would not do time for defending herself against a rapist.

Edith Head designed a wardrobe for Loretta that was faithful to her character. At the beginning, she looks like a typical unmarried professor, with hair piled high, sexless suits, and an austerity that keeps her from enjoying the give-and-take of the classroom. To avoid being recognized as the woman on the freeway, Wilma abandons the academic look, morphing into an ultra feminine, even alluring, woman, with hair framing her face and a wardrobe that few academics could afford. The transformation from uptight professor to woman in love is even reflected in her relaxed classroom manner.

The director, William Dieterle, who with his white hat and gloves behaved like a Prussian general, was known for his habit of subjecting one member of the cast (never a star) to withering criticism, whether it was merited or not. In *The Accused*, the scapegoat was Suzanne Dalbert, and according to Douglas Dick and Wallis's publicity director, Walter Seltzer, Dieterle almost succeeded in breaking her spirit. Loretta had no problem with Dieterle. Wallis was another matter. She now insisted on not working after 5:00 p.m. and even refused to do an over-the-shoulder shot favoring her. She and Wallis also disagreed on a variety of issues: stills ("old fashioned"), close-ups, and even the soundtrack. Wallis was unsympathetic, accusing her of taking an "arbitrary stand"; when she persisted, he reminded her in no uncertain terms that there were "legal steps" he could take if she continued to be uncooperative. Loretta understood; she was in no position to challenge Wallis. All Loretta wanted was to be recognized as a serious actress, as if that was necessary. But Hollywood has a short memory; in 1948, few remembered her extraordinary performances in *Life Begins, Man's Castle, Platinum Blonde*, and *Midnight Mary*.

Loretta was also briefly reunited with Samuel Goldwyn, for whom she had last worked in 1930, when she replaced Constance Cummings in *The Devil to Pay*, which was not a happy experience for either party. At seventeen, Loretta had been out of her element, unable to master a British accent and still in awe of the star, Ronald Colman, who had been one of her fantasy lovers. Since Goldwyn disliked both *The Devil to Pay* and Loretta's performance, he had no intention of rehiring her, even though he must have known that she had improved considerably since 1930. Goldwyn desperately wanted Teresa Wright for *The Bishop's Wife* (1947). He had a great affection for Wright, whom he considered one of his protégées. Wright made her film debut in his production of Lillian Hellman's *The Little Foxes* (1941), for which she received a best supporting actress nomination. The following year she was nominated again—but as best actress—for another Goldwyn film, *Pride of the Yankees* (1942). However, the movie that brought Wright an Oscar was not one of Goldwyn's; it was MGM's *Mrs. Miniver* (1942), for which she was voted best supporting actress. In 1946, Wright appeared in one of Hollywood's most time-honored films, Goldwyn's *The Best Years of Our Lives*, which received eight Oscars, including best picture, actor (Fredric March), supporting actor (Harold Russell), director (William Wyler), and screenplay (Robert E.

Sherwood). Teresa Wright was Goldwyn's first—and, in 1947—his only choice for the title character.

Just before filming began, Wright, then married to author Niven Bush, discovered that she was pregnant. Goldwyn had to find a replacement—and quickly. He needed a "name" who looked as if she could be the wife of an Episcopal bishop. And who could better fill the bill than Loretta? David Niven and Cary Grant had already been cast as the bishop and an angel, respectively. Goldwyn recalled that Loretta and Niven worked well together in *Eternally Yours*. When he read that they would be re-teamed in *The Perfect Marriage*, which began filming during the first week of January 1946, he assumed that, once it was finished, Loretta would be available. She was, but not immediately. She had signed on for *The Farmer's Daughter* at RKO, having no idea that it would result in her one and only Oscar.

Later, when Goldwyn finally met Niven Bush, he berated him for making Wright a mother: "When you were fucking Teresa, you were fucking me." Actually, *The Bishop's Wife*, despite its title, would have done nothing for Wright's career. After two forgettable 1947 Paramount films (*The Trouble with Women* and *The Imperfect Lady*), Wright returned to the Goldwyn fold, giving an eloquent performance in *Enchantment* (1948), opposite Niven. At least they costarred once.

Loretta was wasted as Julia Brougham, whose husband's dream of building a new cathedral could only happen through some form of divine intervention. *The Bishop's Wife* is one of several post–World War II films suggesting that America was in need of spiritual renewal—if not from the clergy, then from above. In 1946, two films were released with angels in major roles: *A Matter of Life and Death* (also known as *Stairway to Heaven*), and the most famous of all heavenly messenger films, *It's a Wonderful Life*. The following year, *Here Comes Mr. Jordan* (1941) was remade as *Down to Earth* (1947), a Rita Hayworth musical in which an angel (Edward Everett Horton) and the muse Terpsichore (Hayworth) turned a troubled Broadway show into a hit. There were other films that were intensely spiritual without invoking an angelic presence. Henry Fonda played a priest who risked his life to minister to Mexicans during a time of religious persecution in *The Fugitive* (1947), John's Ford dark and brooding version of Graham Greene's *The Power and the Glory*. Frank Sinatra donned a Roman collar for *The Miracle of the Bells* (1948). In *Winter Meeting* (1948), a naval hero (Jim Davis) confesses to a lonely poet (Bette Davis), with whom he has fallen in love, that their relationship must end because he has decided to become a priest. And in *Joan of Arc* (1948),

Ingrid Bergman hears heavenly voices, urging her to help the dauphin, Charles VII, reclaim his throne.

Hollywood got religion when the times required it. The religion boom continued once writers discovered the Cold War, with Communists replacing Nazis and Japanese imperialists. God took to the airwaves in *The Next Voice You Hear* (1950); angels turned the Pittsburgh Pirates into a winning team in *Angels in the Outfield* (1951); and the communist son of staunch Catholic parents recanted too late in *My Son John* (1952). Since the nuclear age conjured up the specter of a nuclear war, the Deity alone could save the planet. A spate of doomsday films (*Five* [1951], *When Worlds Collide* [1951], *War of the Worlds* [1953]) stressed the need for belief. In their sermons, priests often emphasized the significance of the dates of America's official entry into World War II (December 8, the feast of the Immaculate Conception) and V-J Day (August 14, the eve of the feast of the Assumption of the Virgin Mary), implying that a country so ill prepared to enter a global war was granted a miracle. Perhaps another was needed to prevent World War III. Historians, naturally, would argue otherwise. Yet many Catholics, and perhaps others as well, did not discount the possibility of some form of divine assistance, the same way moviegoers hoped for a deus ex machina in the form of a last-minute reprieve for an innocent prisoner on death row, or the arrival of the cavalry when the fort under Indian attack seemed doomed.

The Bishop's Wife combines both the need for faith and for miracles. An angel, Dudley (Cary Grant), is dispatched to assist Bishop Brougham (David Niven) achieve his goal. As played by Grant, Dudley is the most sophisticated angel who ever came down to earth. His clothes are impeccably tailored, he plays the harp exquisitely, and he is an accomplished figure skater. But his emotions (one must assume angels have them, once they take on human form) surface when he meets Julia. Loretta's best scenes are those with Grant, especially the scene in which they turn skating into a courtship ritual. Their growing rapport is even apparent in another scene that would ordinarily have no romantic connotations: the one in which Dudley helps Julia choose a hat, behaving more like a beau or a husband than an angel. A happy ending is inevitable, as one would expect of a film that ends on Christmas Eve with the conversion of an agnostic (Monty Woolley) and Dudley's winning over the wealthy Mrs. Hamilton (Gladys Cooper), who had previously opposed the construction of the cathedral. When one thinks of *The Bishop's Wife*, Loretta's is the last name that comes to mind. It was Grant's film. Loretta had nothing to equal Niven's climactic Christmas Eve sermon, nor could she compete with the outstanding supporting cast (Monty Woolley, James Gleason, Gladys Cooper, and especially Elsa Lanchester).

Loretta's two 1947 films—*The Farmer's Daughter*, released in March, and *The Bishop's Wife*, released in December—were never intended for her. Ingrid Bergman was producer David Selznick's preference for the former; Teresa Wright, Goldwyn's choice for the latter. In the mid 1940s, Selznick came upon an obscure play, *Hulga for Parliament*, by a Finnish playwright writing under the pseudonym Juhni Tervataa. Hulga was a politically astute woman from a Swedish farming community who succeeded in getting elected to parliament. After buying the rights, Selznick assigned the adaptation to Laura Kerr and Allen Rivkin, with instructions to Americanize the plot. They entitled their first draft "Katie for Congress," in which a young Swedish woman from Minnesota runs for Congress and wins, despite an unsuccessful attempt to defame her. "Katie for Congress" underwent a name change, becoming *The Farmer's Daughter*, designed as a vehicle for the Swedish-born Ingrid Bergman—the title change presumably a way of attracting audiences familiar with risqué jokes about the farmer's daughter that were a staple of every burlesque comic's repertoire. Bergman, now an Oscar winner for her performance as the terrorized wife in *Gaslight* (1944), passed on it, claiming that she could do more than act with her accent, especially after it had become a plot point in *The Bells of St. Mary's* (1945).

Once Bergman bowed out, Selznick lost interest in the project and sold the rights to RKO, where Dory Schary had just become production head. Schary was eager to produce the film, but as compensation for losing Bergman, Selznick wanted to maintain a measure of control by loaning out two of his other stars: Joseph Cotten, who played Congressman Glen Morley, and Ethel Barrymore, who appeared as his influential mother, thereby maintaining a presence in a film that was no longer his. Selznick also tried to cajole Schary into hiring Sonja Henie for the lead, believing that the Norwegian Henie could pass for a Swede. Schary, refusing to be cowed by Selznick, insisted on Loretta: "I honestly feel with deep conviction that Loretta Young could approximate much more of what we want."

Schary was familiar with *Along Came Jones* and *The Stranger*, which were released by RKO. Obviously he knew of Loretta's other work as well, but it was the RKO connection that made her a perfect candidate for the role. In addition, Loretta was a good friend of the Scharys and a regular at their parties, despite political differences. Schary was an impassioned liberal (but not a radical); to Loretta, the only politics that mattered were studio politics. Once Loretta signed on, she "plunged into the role," mastering the Swedish accent and settling for clothes that Katie, not Loretta, would wear. Her efforts paid off, and the Oscar that Schary predicted came to pass.

Schary entrusted the direction to H.C. Potter, who was equally at home in the theatre, where he directed such notable Broadway plays as *A Bell for Adano*, *Anne of the Thousand Days*, and *Sabrina Fair*. Potter took a stage director's approach to film, using occasional long takes to minimize cutting, and composing shots so that—at least for a minute or so—they looked as they would on the stage, with the action framed within the proscenium. Then Potter would cut, but at least for those few moments, audiences experienced the wholeness of theatre. Potter also understood that, in film, a shot from above or below should match the character's perspective. Thus when Clancy, the gruff but kind-hearted butler (Charles Bickford), observes activity in the parlor from the second story, the shot matches his angle of vision. The script required a skating scene between Cotten and Loretta. Both of them appeared to be passable skaters, but when it was time to waltz on the ice, Potter cut to a long shot, with doubles dressed like the principals but capable of doing what they could not. There is no way of knowing whether Potter or the writers were aware of a similar skating scene in *The Bishop's Wife*, in which Henry Koster used a double when Cary Grant's character did some fancy figure skating. But in each film, skating seemed more like a mating dance than a spin on the ice.

As Katie Holstram, Loretta sounded like an authentic Swede. Sent from her parents' farm to work as a domestic for the Marleys, Katie revels in being part of a household that throws cocktail parties for politicians and journalists, eventually becoming brave enough to attend a political rally in support of Anders Finley (Art Baker), for whom she has no respect. During Q & A, Katie innocently asks Finley, "Why are you running for Congress?" Once the hecklers are silenced, she summarizes his shoddy record during the Great Depression: practicing nepotism, complaining that bread lines were too costly, and requiring apple sellers to have a license. Mocked at first, Katie garners so much popular support that she is on the verge of winning the nomination, when the opposition mounts a smear campaign that almost destroys her self-confidence.

Encouraged by her father, Katie reenters the fray; in a montage straight out of Capra's *Mr. Smith Goes to Washington*, with newspaper headlines dissolving into each other, Katie wins both the election and Morley. What the film leaves unresolved is the question of how two members of Congress with different agendas can have a successful marriage. But moviegoers who prefer the ending of their dream scenario to the film's would not even have raised the question. To them, Katie is so strong-willed that whatever political disagreements arise, it is clear Morley will come around to her way of thinking.

The Farmer's Daughter was the first time Loretta worked with Joseph Cotten; the second was in a less worthy vehicle, *Half Angel* (1951). Cotten, the courtly Virginian and connoisseur of beauty and talent, was awed by Loretta: "Her knowledge of her own technique as well as the offstage mechanics of movie makeup, is enormous. She can never be unglamorous, and her beautiful eyes are as innocent today as ever." That technique paid off in 1948 when Loretta received her first Oscar nomination, not for *The Bishop's Wife*, but for *The Farmer's Daughter*. Also nominated that year were Joan Crawford (*Possessed*), Susan Hayward (*Smash-Up, The Story of a Woman*), Dorothy McGuire (*Gentleman's Agreement*), and Rosalind Russell (*Mourning Becomes Electra*). Although Loretta was thrilled with the nomination, she was convinced she did not stand a chance after the trades had all but awarded the Oscar to Russell.

When RKO agreed to co-produce Dudley Nichols's scrupulously faithful version of Eugene O'Neill's *Mourning Becomes Electra* with the Theatre Guild, the studio knew it would only be a prestige film that needed some incentive (an Oscar nomination or preferably an Oscar) to build an audience. As it happened, *Mourning Becomes Electra* found favor with neither the public nor the critics. The subject matter, Aeschylus's *Oresteia* as it might have unfolded in post-bellum New England, became a lexicon of neuroses: a brother and sister are in the advanced stages of the Oedipus and Electra complexes; an adulterous wife poisons her husband and commits suicide after her son avenges his father's murder by killing his mother's lover and later himself; the daughter makes a Freudian slip, calling her suitor by the name of her mother's lover and then admitting that he had been her lover, too. If the wildly operatic plot seems like a retrospective of a daytime soap, O'Neill's trilogy has the power to draw audiences into the mind's dark places, holding them there for the duration (four hours for the play, three for the film) and leaving them exhausted but purged.

Mourning Becomes Electra was not so much a movie as an event. It opened at the Golden, a legitimate playhouse on West 45th St. in New York, which during World War II was home to the long-running (1,293 performances) *Angel Street*. *Mourning* was a road show engagement, with two performances daily, and three on Sunday. By 1947 standards, the tickets cost about the same as most stage plays: $2.40 (orchestra and mezzanine) and $1.80 (balcony) in the evenings; $1.80 (orchestra and mezzanine), $1.20 (balcony) at the matinees. *The Farmer's Daughter*, on the other hand, opened in New York at the "showcase of the nation," the egalitarian Radio City Music Hall, where the price of a ticket included a movie and an elaborate stage show featuring the world-famous Rockettes. *Mourning* was tough going for the uninitiated; *Daughter* was pure mass entertainment.

On 28 March 1948, the Academy Awards ceremony took place at the Shrine Auditorium in Los Angeles. When Fredric March opened the envelope to announce the name of the best actress of 1947, he looked shocked. Meanwhile, a confident Russell, sitting in the rear, was about to rise, until she heard March say, "Loretta Young for *The Farmer's Daughter.*" To avoid embarrassment, Russell made it seem that she had risen to lead an ovation for her friend. A euphoric Loretta, in a green silk taffeta dress, her neck encircled by a diamond necklace, swept down the aisle. She graciously acknowledged the other nominees but could not resist adding, as she kissed the statuette, "And as for you, at long last."

It was not surprising that Loretta won. *The Farmer's Daughter* was an American Dream movie: You, too, can run for Congress and win—despite your background. In fact, your background can work for you, freeing you from hangers-on and smarmy campaign managers and imbuing you with courage even in the face of defeat. *Mourning Becomes Electra* was marketed as cinema: highbrow entertainment for the elite, caviar for the masses. Since *The Farmer's Daughter* was movie rather than cinema, more Academy members saw—and enjoyed—it, contrasting its ninety-seven-minute running time with the three-hour *Mourning Becomes Electra*. Imagine students given a choice between writing a paper on either "The Aeschylean Background of *Mourning Becomes Electra*" or "*The Farmer's Daughter* as a Reflection of the American Dream." Most would have chosen the latter; the Academy certainly did.

Three months later, another event occurred that received as much publicity as Loretta's Oscar. Shortly after 6 June, Loretta received a brief note from her maternal grandmother informing her that her father, John Earle Young, died of a stroke. Loretta reacted unemotionally; to her, he was the man who abandoned them when she was four. "He may have been my father," she told the *Los Angeles Times* (14 June 1948) about the man who died under the name of John V. Earle. She went on to explain that, on the advice of her parish priest, she sent her father monthly checks, even though he made no effort to see her. Polly Ann and Sally

Blane attended the funeral; Loretta did not—or would not, claiming that she was making a film. John Earle Young was buried in Woodlawn Cemetery in Santa Monica. On the day of his burial, there was no headstone to mark his grave, although there were baskets of flowers without cards to identify the senders. To Loretta, 1948 meant her Oscar, not her father's death.

Like other Oscar winners, Loretta found that the statuette was a blessing and a curse. Judy Holliday was also a dark horse in 1951, when most insiders expected the 1950 Best Actress Oscar to go to either Gloria Swanson for her spectacular comeback in *Sunset Boulevard* or to Bette Davis for *All About* Eve, which resurrected her career—but not to Judy Holliday for reprising the role that made her a Broadway star, Billie Dawn in *Born Yesterday*. Yet Holliday won, and probably for the same reason that Loretta did: *Born Yesterday* was accessible. Holliday's Billie was a refreshing alternative to the gothic bravura of Swanson's Norma Desmond and the epigrammatic egomania of Davis's Margo Channing. Billie Dawn was a recognizable human being, the mistress of a loutish junk dealer, resorting to self-deprecating humor to hide her vulnerability. Billie needs—and gets—a deliverer (William Holden), who convinces her of her potential, equipping her with enough of an education so that she can leave her overbearing lover. More Academy members could identify with Billie than with Norma or Margo; like Katie, Billie was palpably real.

But the public wanted Holliday, the dizzy dame, not the educated woman; sadly, her subsequent films were a footnote to *Born Yesterday*, and her great potential was never realized once she was diagnosed with breast cancer, which brought her life to an end at the age of forty-two. Swanson's movie career dead-ended after *Sunset Boulevard*, and Davis did not have another film that clicked with the public until the ghoulish *Whatever Happened to Baby Jane?* (1962), which at least brought her a Best Actress nomination.

Loretta was also not inundated with quality scripts after her Oscar; few winners are. But those that she chose to do were respectable, even when the material was tissue-thin. At least her next and last RKO film, *Rachel and the Stranger* (1948), was anything but flimsy.

When Loretta's sister, Sally Blane, married Norman Foster in 1935 after his divorce from Claudette Colbert, Loretta never thought that, a decade later, her brother-in-law would direct her in a film. Loretta first met Foster when he was an actor, costarring with him in *Play-Girl* and *Weekend Marriage* (both 1932). In the mid 1930s, Foster discovered his true calling: directing. He revealed a knack for avoiding racial stereotypes in the Mr. Motto series about a Japanese amateur sleuth played by Peter Lorre. Foster directed and coauthored six of the eight Mr. Moto films. Before Orson Welles began *Citizen Kane* (1941), he screened a number of films, including the Mr. Motos. Welles was particularly taken with Foster's ability to evoke a menacing environment through the manipulation of light and shade. His subtle use of chiaroscuro was exactly what Welles wanted for *Citizen Kane*. When Welles realized he could not edit *The Magnificent Ambersons* (1942) and direct *Journey into Fear* (1942) at the same time, he entrusted the latter to Foster. Sadly, RKO had its own ideas about *Ambersons*, and Welles's masterpiece underwent radical surgery. But even in its truncated form, it remains a testimony to Welles's genius.

Nineteen forty-eight saw dramatic changes in the film industry. The boom year of 1946, Hollywood's *annus mirabilis*, when paid attendance was at an all-time high, was followed by a period of budget cutting and the curtailment of unnecessarily lavish productions. As RKO's new production head, Schary sought a mix of the prestigious but financially unsuccessful (*Mourning Becomes Electra* [1947], *Joan of Arc* [1948]), and the popular (John Ford's *Fort Apache* and *Rachel and the Stranger*, which reaped profits of $445,000 and $395,000, respectively). Schary expected *Rachel and the Stranger* to have great popular appeal, which it did. Since Norman Foster was a known quantity at RKO, Schary entrusted him with the film, which was based on Howard Fast's short story, "Rachel," with a screenplay by Waldo Salt. Knowing that Loretta was not bound to any studio and had time before starting *The Accused*, Foster cast his sister-in-law in the lead. Her costars were William Holden, on loan from Paramount, and RKO contract player Robert Mitchum.

Anyone who expected a movie with an anti-capitalist subtext was disappointed, even though Fast and Salt had both been members of the Communist party. Fast served three months in prison in 1950 for refusing to cooperate with the House Committee on Un-American Activities (HUAC). In 1956 he severed his connections with the Party after learning that Joscf Stalin, the avuncular "Uncle Joe," was nothing more than a genocidal dictator. Salt had been subpoenaed by HUAC in fall 1947 to testify to the preposterous charge of Communist subversion of the movie industry. Eleven were called, the last being German playwright Berthold Brecht, then residing in Los Angeles, who denied being a Communist and immediately returned to East Berlin. If the hearings had not been temporarily suspended, Salt would have been next. But, as an unfriendly witness, Salt was soon blacklisted, working only intermittently and under pseudonyms. He was finally vindicated when his adaptation of James Leo Herlihy's *Midnight Cowboy* (1969) was awarded an Oscar, followed by a second one for 1978's best original screenplay, *Coming Home*.

Rachel and the Stranger, however, is apolitical. Loretta was cast as a bondswoman in the 1820s, bought by widower David Harvey (Holden) to run his household and educate his young son. Until the end of the film, Rachel is a wife in name only, a combination servant-housekeeper. Loretta was the perfect frontierswoman, in her high-necked dress that made her look austere but could not conceal her body's natural curves—actually, the dress emphasized them. The high neck worked to the character's advantage, forcing her to hold her head high, despite the treatment she received from her husband. A specially created makeup gave Loretta's face an earthen glow, the opposite of the lustrous look she had in romantic comedies.

Of all her mother's films, *Rachel and the Stranger* is Judy Lewis's favorite. It is certainly one of Loretta's best. To see her churning butter is to watch an actress inhabit a character that was completely at odds with her persona. Yet when Loretta had to play women from society's lower echelon (e.g., *Life Begins*, *Man's Castle*, *Taxi!*, *Midnight Ma*ry), she gave them a sense of dignity that steeled those women against life's injustices and men's callousness. Loretta played Rachel as a woman so inured to a hard-knock life that she would never break down. Like Cherry in *Along Came Jones*, Rachel can handle a rifle. During a Shawnee attack, Rachel kills one of the Indians, her face registering the pain she feels about taking a life as she presses herself against a wall.

Robert Mitchum gave an unusually sympathetic performance as Harvey's itinerant friend, Jim Fairways, who falls under Rachel's spell. Knowing that Harvey regards Rachel as little more than a hired hand, Fairways makes a bid for her, as if she were up for auction. Here, perhaps, is a vestige of Salt's leftism: two men vying for a woman as if she were chattel—at least from the woman's point of view. After the Indian attack interrupts what would have been a violent confrontation between the men, Fairways realizes that, from the way Rachel rallied to protect a family that was not even hers, she is meant for Harvey. And the film ends with a close up of Harvey kissing Rachel, who emerges as morally superior to both her husband and her suitor.

Expecting a stream of obscenities from Mitchum, whose maverick ways and public brawls always made the papers (he was jailed for marijuana possession in 1948, the same year *Rachel* came out), Loretta arrived on the set with her swear box. When Mitchum learned what each bit of profanity or blasphemy cost, he asked within Loretta's hearing distance, "How much does Miss Young charge for a 'fuck'?" He then stuffed a $5.00 bill into the box and indulged himself with his favorite expletive. Loretta's response is unknown. In her profession she must have heard the national obscenity before, but she probably referred to it as the "f word."

CHAPTER 17

The Return to Fox—and Zanuck

In 1939 Loretta told Zanuck she would never work for him again (which, in effect, meant never working at Fox), but the passage of time, an Oscar, and a three-picture contract—including one in which she would play a nun—prompted Loretta to think differently about the studio where she had spent five years, making twenty-two films. However, only one of three that Zanuck offered her, *Come to the Stable* (1949), was significant. If the other two, *Mother Is a Freshman* (1949) and *Half Angel* (1951), had never reached the screen, audiences would have been spared two more mediocre movies.

A college administrator should have been hired as technical advisor for *Mother Is a Freshman*, which gleefully flaunted academic protocol. It was filmed in Technicolor, never the ideal medium for Loretta, whose sculpted cheekbones were suffused with red, making her face look flushed. Anyone planning to send a child, particularly a female, to college might have thought twice after seeing the movie. Loretta played Abigail Fortitude Abbott, a widow with a spendthrift daughter, who finds herself in financial straits—although one would never know it from Abigail's elaborate wardrobe and Park Avenue apartment. When Abigail remembers that her grandmother had established a scholarship at her daughter's college for anyone with the name of Abigail Fortitude (Abigail's unmarried name), she decides to apply, even though she and her daughter Susan (Betty Lynn) would be attending the same school and perhaps taking some of the same classes.

Loretta's costar was Van Johnson, five years younger than the thirty-six-year-old Loretta, and still looking like the boy next door. We must take it on faith that he is not only an English professor, but has also become so attracted to Abigail that he pressures her into coming for tutoring to his house, where he has prepared a candlelit dinner. Although he has also invited his parents, he makes sure that Abigail arrives early. We are also asked to believe that the professor and Abigail's lawyer (Rudy Vallee) were contemporaries at Yale, even though Vallee was seventeen years older than Johnson—and looked it. "That's Hollywood for you," as columnist Sidney Skolsky used to say.

Complications arise when Susan develops a crush on the professor. Once she learns that he is her mother's prom date, she invites the lawyer to attend as Abigail's escort, pitting the two men against each other. Any veteran moviegoer could predict the ending: Abigail will continue working toward her degree—but in the dual role of student and professor's wife—and Susan will discover someone her own age. Although Loretta did not disappoint her fans, who wanted their fashion plate in Christian Dior's "new look," *Mother Is a Freshman* is more of an ellipsis than a footnote in her career.

Loretta was in her element in her next Fox film, *Come to the Stable* (1949), as Sister Margaret of the Holy Endeavor, humble but wily enough to use her charm and powers of persuasion to achieve her goal. She was a Catholic child's ideal grade school nun: not the knuckle-rapper, but the kind who would enter a classroom with a gentle rustle of her habit as it trailed along the floor and the jingle of the fifteen-decade rosary suspended from her belt, heralding her arrival as she approached the desk. The habit was only the exterior; beneath it lay a determined educator and, in Sister Margaret's case, an entrepreneur. Loretta would play nuns again, but not on the big screen. Loretta looked as if she were to the habit born. There have been other authentic movie nuns (Ingrid Bergman in *The Bells of St. Mary's*, Gladys Cooper and Jennifer Jones in *The Song of Bernadette*, Audrey Hepburn in *The Nun's Story*, Rosalind Russell in *The Trouble with Angels*, Claudette Colbert in *Thunder on the Hill*, Donna Reed in *Green Dolphin Stree*t), and actress-nuns for whom the habit was just a costume (Greer Garson in *The Singing Nun*, Maggie Smith in *Class Act*). Loretta was the genuine article.

Come to the Stable was one of Fox's top-grossing films of 1949, nominated for seven Oscars: Best Actress (Loretta), Supporting Actress (Celeste Holm and Elsa Lanchester), original story (Claire Boothe Luce), original song ("Through a Long and Sleepless Night"), set direction, and black-and-white photography (Joseph LaShelle). It did not matter to Zanuck that *Come to the Stable* failed to win a single award. He was happy with the gross and thrilled that Dean Jagger was voted Best Supporting Actor for Fox's *Twelve O'Clock High*, Zanuck's personal favorite that year. If some of the others made money, all the better.

Although *Come to the Stable* was not Zanuck's kind of film, he took it more seriously than one might expect. Loretta was his only choice to star as Sister Margaret, even though Luce envisioned Irene Dunne in the role. Zanuck wanted "a great Catholic," which to him meant Loretta, and a "great Catholic" required a "great script." Zanuck made sure the great Catholic got it. Dorothy Parker and John B. Mahin collaborated on one, but it was not great enough. By mid November 1948, Sally Benson came on board and managed to write, with some assistance, a script that conformed to Zanuck's requirements: "a comedy about faith that is not preachy or religious." *Come to the Stable* is a comedy in the classical sense: a work with a happy ending, despite what transpires earlier.

Come to the Stable was inspired by the visit of Catholic convert and playwright Clare Boothe Luce (*The Women, Margin for Error, Kiss the Boys Goodbye*) to what was then the Priory of Regina Laudis in Bethlehem, Connecticut. Luce believed that the priory's backstory was movie material and proceeded to write a screenplay, "From a French Battlefield to the Connecticut Hills"—not exactly the sort of title that would attract moviegoers. Luce was eventually given story credit, but the screenplay was primarily the work of Sally Benson, known for injecting a shot of humanity into scripts, particularly those about families (*Meet Me in St. Louis* [1944], *Junior Miss* [1945], *Joy in the Morning* [1965]). Benson had read Luce's script, which catalogued the frustrations a Benedictine nun, Mother Benedict, experienced in her efforts to build Regina Laudis, which later became the Abbey of Regina Laudis. Benson also realized that certain changes had to be made. In the film, the nuns bury a medal of St. Jude at the top of the hill that marked the Abbey's future site. Actually, it was a St. Benedict medal, as one would expect from Benedictine nuns. But Benson knew that more moviegoers were familiar with St. Jude, the patron saint of the impossible, than with St. Benedict.

Zanuck ignored Luce's casting suggestions: Irene Dunne in the lead, Cary Grant as the composer, Zazu Pitts as the artist, and Monty Woolley as the owner of the property that the nuns desire. Irene Dunne, like Loretta, was a Hollywood Catholic, but while she succeeded in getting a king to honor his promise to give her a house (*Anna and the King of Siam* [1946], also coauthored by Benson), she was not Zanuck's idea of the Chicago-born Sister Margaret: stationed in France during World War II, where she made a bargain with God that if her children's hospital were spared, she would establish a similar one in the United States, named after St. Jude. Prayers are usually answered in movies, and Sister Margaret's was no exception. Inspired by a postcard reproduction of *Come to the*

Stable, and believing it was providential that the artist, Amelia Potts (the ever delightful Elsa Lanchester) lives in Bethlehem, Connecticut, Sister Margaret and her companion, Sister Scholastica (Celeste Holm, sporting a flawless French accent) set out for the American Bethlehem.

Although Holm was not a scene-stealer, she had a way of deflecting attention from others—except Loretta, who held her own. But unlike Loretta, who had to speak some French, but with an American accent, Holm had to sound like a native, which she did, even though she was born in New York. Holm also had to compete in a tennis match to raise the money the nuns need for their hospital. The intercutting of close-ups, medium shots, and long shots indicated that Holm had a double for some of the scenes, which were so skillfully edited that the audience assumed Holm was also a tennis pro. She was not, but Sister Scholastica had been. Still, Holm could work the court until it was time for a double. How many actresses could play tennis in a nun's habit, as Holm did? Celeste Holm deserved the Oscar nomination she received. She did not win (Mercedes McCambridge did for *All the King's Men*), although she had won the previous year for *Gentleman's Agreement* (1947), which was more of a Zanuck production than *Come to the Stable*.

Although Sister Scholastica lost the match, the screenplay adhered to the setback-success model à la *Going My Way* (1944) and *The Bells of St. Mary's* (1945), in which a church is rebuilt and a school is saved from the wrecking ball. The nuns also realize their dream after overcoming such obstacles as an initially dubious but eventually persuaded bishop, a shady businessman (charmingly played by Thomas Gomez), and a composer of popular music (Hugh Marlowe), who has no intention of having nuns as neighbors—until he discovers that the "original" song he composed derived from a chorale he heard the nuns sing when he was serving in France during the second world war.

Benson was not the sole screenwriter; she shared credit with Oscar Millard, who early in 1948 submitted a brief to Zanuck, identifying Loretta's character as the historical Mother Benedict Duss, "an American raised since early childhood in France." The London-born Millard had only turned to screenwriting in 1945, after having been a journalist, novelist, and short story writer. He may have been hired because he had worked for French and Belgian publications and could write the kind of English that Sister Scholastica would speak—the words carefully chosen, precise and unambiguous, as might be expected of a woman whose native language was French. Millard's brief supplied the facts. The St. Benedict medal that the nuns buried was on a forty-five-acre property on the outskirts of Bethlehem. Determined to build the priory on that site, Mother Benedict contacted Lauren Ford, the artist whose painting inspired the trip to America, and who provided a home for her and her companion. On the site was a vacant factory, whose owner agreed to sell if the nuns could pay off the mortgage. To raise the money, other Benedictine nuns and a German priest come over to sell their handicrafts and ceramics, but the profits only amounted to a down payment. In the same file with Millard's brief is a treatment that adds an important plot point: the owner agrees to give the nuns the property if the body of his son, who was killed during World War II, is buried there. The father (Thomas Gomez) makes a similar bargain in the film, but it's for a stained glass window commemorating his son. Eager to get papal recognition, the historical Mother Benedict and her companion, Mother Mary Aline, with the aid of a contessa, fly to Rome where they have an audience with the pope, who gives them his blessing but nothing more.

With the officially designated "Holy Year" coming up in 1950, the year after the film's release, an apathetic pope, who could only have been Pius XII, would not have set well with Catholics. Naturally, neither the contessa nor the papal audience even reached the script stage. But the composer did, religion unspecified. In an early draft he was a Jew, Tony Marx, who is at first opposed to the nuns' founding a priory on the property adjacent to his, but soon does a spiritual turnaround and composes a Christmas symphony. In the film, the religion-neutral composer (Hugh Marlowe) writes pop music, but has unconsciously appropriated the melody of his latest song from a medieval chorale. Benson and Millard did not make the composer a Jew, who decides to convert to Christianity after being exposed to the nuns' transcendent faith. A Jewish convert in a film about Catholics might have proved edifying to some, but anti-Semitic to others. Zanuck wanted a moneymaker that incorporated religion in a plot about overcoming setbacks, convincing moviegoers that they, too, could realize their dream with the right combination of grit, luck, and divine assistance.

Antoinette Bosco's *Mother Benedict: Foundress of the Abbey of Regina Laudis* provides the historical context for *Come to the Stable*, inspired by the true story of the Pittsburgh-born Vera Duss, who spent much of her early years in France pursuing a degree in medicine until she discovered her true calling. Vera was the daughter of a controlling mother and a father whose gentle ways were misinterpreted as lack of ambition. Since Vera's mother, Elizabeth Duss, had converted to Catholicism, divorce was out of the question; instead, Elizabeth left for Paris, her father's home, with her (almost) two-year-old son and three-year-old Vera. They arrived at the outbreak of World War I, which they survived. Since Elizabeth returned periodically to America, Vera was raised for the most part by her grandmother. Although a Catholic education attracted Vera to the religious life, she preferred to study medicine at the Sorbonne before making her decision. By graduation time, she was ready to enter the Benedictine abbey at Jouarre, first as a postulant, then as a novice with the name of Sister Benedict, and finally a nun, known for the rest of her life as Mother Benedict. Mother Benedict believed it was her mission to establish a Benedictine presence in the United States. When World War II erupted in 1939, and France fell to the Nazis the following year, Mother Benedict, technically an American, was in danger of being imprisoned or perhaps sent to an internment or, worse, a concentration, camp. When the Nazis began checking the papers of Americans living in France, members of the Resistance furnished Mother Benedict with a new identity card and name.

If *Come to the Stable* seems like a boilerplate "triumph in the face of adversity" film, the true story, with its supporters and skeptics, is not that dissimilar. The difference is that the actual supporters were a heterogeneous group that included Major General George S. Patton, the future Pope John XXIII (then papal nuncio, Archbishop Angelo Roncalli), President Truman's personal representative to the Vatican, Myron Taylor, philosopher Jacques Maritain, and Monsignor Giovanni Montini, the Vatican Undersecretary of State and future Pope Paul VI.

Once Mother Benedict and Mother Mary Aline (*Come to the Stable*'s Sisters Margaret and Scholastica) learned that they could stay with painter Frances Delehanty (who shared her Bethlehem home with another artist, Lauren Ford, like her a devout Catholic), they sailed from Le Havre on 20 August 1946, arriving in New York eleven days later. Like their film counterparts, the two nuns ran a similar obstacle course, including an encounter with an indifferent bishop. Their savior is a wealthy donor, who wants his property used as a place of worship. By 1947, a converted factory became the Priory of Regina Laudis, then and three decades later The Abbey of Regina Laudis. Mother Benedict's life was far more complex than the simplified version in *Come to the Stable*. In 1949, the true story could never have succeeded on the big screen—any more than it could today, despite the intriguing plot points: a troubled marriage; a three-year-old expatriate child; a woman with a medical degree subjected to the rigors of convent life; endangerment during an enemy occupation; and the realization of a goal born of belief, courage, and unstinting effort. Rather, Mother Benedict is the perfect subject of a TV documentary, for among the nuns at the Abbey is Mother Dolores Hart, currently Mother Abbess.

In 1963, Dolores Hart—a Broadway (*The Pleasure of His Company*) and movie (the Elvis Presley films *Loving You* and *King Creole*, and others including *Wild Is the Wind* and *Where the Boys Are*) star—made a decision that shocked Hollywood: She gave up an acting career to become a postulant at Regina Laudis, which she had visited earlier, hoping to find the longed-for peace that passes understanding. That she found it there resulted in a commitment that lay beyond the powers of ordinary mortals. But then, Regina Laudis is not a community of ordinary women. Despite some unfavorable press, the Abbey has survived, attracting visitors from the entertainment world such as Maria Cooper Janis (Gary Cooper's daughter and pianist Byron Janis's wife), and actresses Patricia Neal, Gloria DeHaven, Celeste Holm, and Martha Hyer Wallis, all of whom have benefited from exposure to an environment that comes close to offering what T.S. Eliot in *Ash Wednesday* calls "the still point of the turning world." Strangely, perhaps, Loretta never visited.

Half Angel completed Loretta's three-picture agreement with Fox. Although Julian Blaustein was nominally the producer, Zanuck, as production head, gave the film his imprimatur, considering it a minor addition to Fox's 1951 slate of releases that was rather thin in terms of quality. The best of the lot were *People Will Talk* and *Decision before Dawn*. That *Half Angel*'s running time was a mere seventy-eight minutes was an indication of the studio's lack of faith in its drawing power. Critics and audiences felt similarly, and *Half Angel* disappeared shortly after it opened in 1951.

Zanuck had no reason to make *Half Angel*, except to provide Loretta with a third film. Story analyst Michael Abel wrote a two-and-a-half page critique of a draft, then entitled "Half an Angel," dismissing it as "unreal and imaginary," with a "contrived and artificial" plot. Abel was also disturbed that the heroine's alter ego was a "crude and self-centered tart, with her dangling cigarette, undulating hips, and a general emphasis on sex." By 1950's standards, the script seemed to be—to use the vernacular of the period—"hot stuff."

Abel was not the only one offended by the script. Joseph Breen found the material "totally unacceptable," chiding Fox's director of publicity for submitting a script to the Production Code Administration in which marriage was treated shabbily and "without dignity." He was also concerned about the heroine's less angelic self, insisting that "breasts should be completely covered" and "the subconscious conduct herself" in good taste—as if a film with Loretta could be otherwise.

Amazingly, Robert Riskin, Capra's best screenwriter (*American Madness, Platinum Blonde, It Happened One Night, Mr. Deeds Goes to Town*) was responsible for the screenplay. Riskin was in his early fifties, with his best work behind him. However, since he had to adapt George Carleton Brown's story, he treated it as just another assignment. Possibly, he exaggerated the pervasive sexuality of the scenes depicting the heroine's other self to emphasize the disparity between the daytime woman and the nighttime seductress. The sexed-up scenes could also have been the inspiration of the original director, Jules Dassin, whose forte was certainly not romantic whimsy. He was a specialist in the dark side (*Brute Force* [1947], *The Naked City* [1948], *Thieves Highway* [1949], and especially *Night and the City* [1950]) and assumed that even a repressed nurse had hers. When *Half Angel* was at the story conference stage, Dassin was still involved. But Dassin was also a Communist, who decided to return to his native France, knowing that it was only a matter of time before he would be blacklisted. It was a wise move; on 23 April 1951, director Edward Dmytryk one of the original Hollywood Ten, realizing that unlike writers he could not work under a pseudonym, cooperated with HUAC, naming Dassin along with five others.

The title is misleading; *Half Angel* is a comic variation on the dual personality film that could have been called "The Two Faces of Nora." Loretta played Nora Gilpin, a nurse by day, who has relegated her infatuation with a prominent lawyer, John Raymond (Joseph Cotten), to the depths of her unconscious, only to find it surfacing at night. Like her mother, Nora is a sleepwalker who, at night, becomes the woman she imagines herself to be. Once Nora the vamp—slinky, provocatively dressed, and coquettish—takes over, she literally stalks Raymond, who is fascinated by the fey creature who has entered his life. The problem is the discrepancy between Nora the vamp and Nora the nurse. Loretta gravitated to the former, reveling in her low cut aquamarine dressing gown that revealed the lacy edge of her petticoat, which she had no qualms about displaying as she assumed an enticingly recumbent position. Neither she nor director Richard Sale, Dassin's replacement, seemed to have any interest in the daytime Nora, whose troubled psyche eluded both of them. When day breaks, all Loretta can manage is a reversion to Nora's dull professional self, much to Raymond's confusion. The film can stand only so much role reversal. The ending is a variation on the "flight from the altar" movie (*It Happened One Night, Cover Girl, It Had to be You,*

The Runaway Bride): The sleepwalker ends up marrying Raymond, then upon wakening, she realizes there is a man in the next bed, who indeed is Raymond. (Twin beds were the norm then.) Nora also awakens on the day of her wedding to dull Timothy McCarey (John Ridgley), which Raymond interrupts, causing Nora to faint and the film to expire.

If Capra had made *Half Angel* in the 1930s with a screenplay by Riskin, it would have been a model screwball comedy, a genre that was never Loretta's forte. Ideally, it needed an actress like Jean Arthur or Claudette Colbert, who could slip in and out of Nora's two selves more effortlessly than Loretta, who could handle the sexy, but not the sexless self. What *Half Angel* became in 1951 was a depressingly unsophisticated and humorless movie, unworthy of Riskin, Cotten, or Loretta. If Riskin had ever planned to enrich the script with the same wit and humanity that he brought to his Capra films, it would have been impossible after 27 December 1950, when he suffered a major stroke, leading to his death five years later. The Riskin touches are few: a father-daughter relationship in which "father knows best"; an interrupted wedding (*It Happened One Night*); a trial in which Raymond is discredited (*Mr. Deeds Goes to Town*) until his marriage to Nora is authenticated. But Riskin, always one to tie up loose—not to mention dangling—ends, could not do so after his stroke. And so, what should have been an important plot point is never resolved: Raymond ignores his opportunity to plead a case before the U.S. Supreme Court to pursue the nocturnal Nora. If any lawyers saw the film, they would have been disgusted at such indifference to an occasion that could have been a milestone in his career. But the moviegoers who saw it—and could remember it a few weeks later—went for the stars. And those, who saw it in June 1951 at New York's Roxy, "the cathedral of movie palaces," were at least treated to a stage show that included the Andrews Sisters—perhaps not as popular as they were during the World War II years, but still able to draw an audience.

Sadly, Zanuck felt the film had potential, and he expressed his views in an eight-page summary of a May 1950 story conference with Blaustein, Dassin, then set to direct, and Riskin, seven months away from his debilitating stroke. All Zanuck seemed to want from the script was more humor: "My only worry about this story now is—is the last act funny enough?" He should have asked the same question about the first two. The only moviegoers who found *Half Angel* humorous were those who were amused by the idea of a plain Jane by day morphing into a sex symbol at night. Loretta did not play the role for its humor because she did not find any in it. Actually, there wasn't.

CHAPTER 18

Slow Fade to Small Screen

It was probably Dore Schary's idea to reunite Clark Gable and Loretta in MGM's *Key to the City* (1950). In July 1948, Schary, realizing he could never work with RKO's new owner, Howard Hughes, left the studio and accepted Louis Mayer's offer to become MGM's vice president in charge of production. Schary does not mention *Key to the City* in his autobiography, although he includes it in his filmography as one of the movies made under his "executive supervision." The credited producer was Z. Wayne Griffin, whose chief function was dealing with logistics (schedule, budget, daily reports). George Sidney, the versatile director who was equally at home with musicals (*The Harvey Girls, Annie Get Your Gun, Show Boat*), costume dramas (*The Three Musketeers, Scaramouche, Young Bess*), and comedies (*Who Was That Lady?, A Ticklish Affair*) was more than competent to handle the creative end of the production. Reuniting *The Call of the Wild* stars could only have been the inspiration of MGM's new production head.

Gable was still an MGM contract player, but he would leave the studio four years later. Loretta was freelancing, interested only in two or three picture commitments. She could have declined, but she owed much to Schary for her Oscar. Although she knew *Key to the City* would win no awards (she was right), she was intrigued about a reunion with the actor who changed her life in 1935.

The film itself is a sporadically witty comedy about two small town mayors: Steve Fisk (Gable), an ex-longshoreman from California, and Clarissa Standish (Loretta), a Harvard Law School alumna from Maine, who meet at a convention in San Francisco. For budgetary reasons, San Francisco's unique ambience was only suggested. *Key to the City* did not require on-location filming; whatever significance it has lies in its contrast with *The Call of the Wild* shoot on Mount Baker in 1935, when Loretta costarred with a man who could not just provide her with romantic fantasies, but with the real thing and all its trappings. That was her first encounter with raw masculinity, not the madras silk kind that colored her dreams. But in 1950, Loretta was the mother of three children, two of whom she acknowledged as her own. History would not repeat itself.

In *Key to the City*, Loretta is at first the paragon of propriety—a by-the-books conventioneer, committed to agendas and parliamentary procedure and chastising those like Fisk, who do not adhere to them. Irene's costumes, influenced by Christian Dior's "new look" (tailored jackets, full-length skirts with tapered waists) reflected Loretta's character, suggesting that Clarissa's libido had disappeared into the fabric. Loretta played Clarissa as if clothes were her personal armor, easily removable under the right circumstances. When Fisk suggests a night on the town, Clarissa demurs: "I only want to uphold my title of honorable mayor," to which Fisk replies—as only Gable could—with a skeptical smirk and mischief in his eyes: "How honorable can you get?" The battle of the sexes is on, and Fisk frees Clarissa's libido from the folds of her skirt, returning it to its proper location. Watching Gable break down Loretta's virginal façade (forget the characters' names for a moment), knowledgeable viewers—and there were enough in Hollywood—could make the connection with *The Call of the Wild*, except that this time, Loretta, who would atone for her "mortal sin" until the end of her life, did what only a true artist can: She summoned up the emotions needed for the scene, however personal they may be. When Gable presses his lips against the back of Loretta's neck, then her ears, and finally her face, the foreplay becomes a replay of the earlier event, with the eroticism intact. Nineteen fifty dissolves into 1935, as the witchcraft in Gable's eyes overlaps with the willingness in Loretta's.

However, the foreplay in *Key to the City* does not lead to consummation. Fisk holds off kissing Clarissa on the mouth, expecting her to ask him. She does, indicating that she is ready for what comes next. "I respect you," Fisk admits guiltily. "I don't want to be respected," Clarissa answers defiantly. As they kiss in silhouette, the camera slowly tracks back, and the audience can assume what it wants. The professionalism that Gable and Loretta brought to the seduction (or would-be seduction) scene that evoked their short-lived affair is a tribute to their ability to re-enact so convincingly the collision between a highly sexed male and a sexually unemancipated female.

Although Loretta did not owe MGM another film after *Key to the City*, Tom Lewis, sensing that his wife's Hollywood days were nearing the end, decided to try his hand at producing. He found an original story based on a radio play by Larry Marcus about a wife whose husband, convinced that she and his doctor are lovers and plotting his death, sends a letter to the district attorney implicating both of them. Lewis hired Mel Dinelli to write the screenplay, which became *Cause for Alarm!* (MGM, 1951). In selling the package to MGM, Lewis insisted on co-screenplay and producer credit in addition to copyright ownership.

Lewis may not have known that most of Dore Schary's productions were under his "executive supervision" even when Schary's name did not appear in the credits, which was often the case. It was the same with *Cause for Alarm!* Exactly whom Lewis envisioned for the wife is unknown, but it was not Loretta, perhaps because he knew that she was more knowledgeable about moviemaking than he and could usurp his authority. Schary felt otherwise, and cast Loretta, who gave a riveting performance—one of her best, in fact, though unappreciated at the time.

There is no way of knowing what Lewis contributed to the script, particularly since Dorothy Kingsley, an accomplished screenwriter (*Neptune's Daughter, Seven Brides for Seven Brothers, Pal Joey*, etc.) did a rewrite. The imperiled heroine script was a Dinelli specialty (*The Spiral Staircase; Beware, My Lovely*, which he adapted from his play, *The Man; Jeopardy*) Despite Lewis's co-screenplay credit, *Cause for Alarm!* is classic Dinelli. Auteurists, on the other hand, would call it a Tay Garnett film. Garnett worked in various genres, including romantic comedies like *Eternally Yours*, his first film with Loretta. He was especially good at building suspense in films where dashed hopes result in either deliverance or death (*Bataan, The Cross of Lorraine, Mrs. Parkington, The Postman Always Rings Twice*). Lewis brokered the deal with MGM and probably helped shape the screenplay, but *Cause for Alarm!* is a Dinelli-Garnett film, acted by a first-rate cast.

Loretta, looking like a typical 1950s homemaker, is married to a mentally unstable man (Barry Sullivan) with a heart condition. The husband, convinced his wife and doctor are planning to murder him, devises a diabolical scheme to trap them. He deliberately spills some of his heart medication, making it difficult for the prescription to be renewed, and making it look as if he is being overmedicated. The husband then writes an incriminating letter to the district attorney, which his unsuspecting wife gives to the mail carrier. Growing increasingly irrational, the husband boasts about the letter, attempting to shoot his wife but collapsing before he can pull the trigger. Except for a flashback showing how the couple met, *Cause for Alarm!* unfolds in real time. The film was a tour de force for Loretta who, in order to retrieve the letter, must deal with a skeptical mail carrier, his sympathetic supervisor, her husband's nosy aunt, a curious notary, and an intrusive child. Everything leads up to the denouement in which the mail carrier informs the wife that the letter has to be returned because of insufficient postage. The tension that had been building up in her erupts in hysterical elation, which Loretta conveys convincingly, sounding almost inarticulate as she gropes for words to express her relief.

Schary had little faith in *Cause for Alarm!*, which clocked in at a mere seventy-four minutes. The 1951 films that he was championing were *The Red Badge of Courage* (which failed miserably at the box office), *The Great Caruso*, *Quo Vadis*, *Show Boat*, and *An American in Paris*. *Cause for Alarm!* was a low-budget movie that generated enough suspense to sustain audience interest and enough money to justify its being made. Except for *Paula* (1952), *Cause for Alarm!* was the last film that made demands on Loretta. The other two were cut from an old, now frayed, fabric.

After Loretta and Harry Cohn reconciled, she returned to Columbia for the first of her final three films. Larry Marcus, who wrote the original story that became *Cause for Alarm!*, came up with another that James Poe and William Sacheim turned into *Paula* (1952). Dismissed at the time as a three-hankie flick, *Paula* is as engrossing as it is morally disturbing. In her haste to attend a reception for her husband (Kent Smith), Paula (Loretta) accidentally runs down a young boy (Tommy Rettig). The accident is not a typical hit and run; Paula pulls up, rushing over to find the boy conscious but aphasic. Despite his condition, the boy notices Paula's necklace, which becomes an important plot point. A truck driver stops and assumes the worst: drunk driving. He orders Paula to follow him to the hospital where he is taking the boy. Too many traffic problems intervene, and the driver informs the police that the boy was a hit and run victim of a drunk driver. The script is crafted in such a way that audiences know it is only a matter of time before Paula will be found out. Instead of turning herself in, Paula atones for what she has done by teaching the boy to regain his speech. Naturally, at some point, Paula will wear the incriminating necklace, causing their relationship, originally based on trust, to deteriorate, as the boy grows sullen and fearful.

Paula is a twist-counter twist film. First, Paula encourages the boy to resume his lessons, with the understanding that once he can speak, he can disclose her identity. Then the truck driver (venerable character actor Raymond Bascom in a frighteningly self-righteous performance) reappears. But just when it seems that Paula is doomed, the boy, now able to speak in rudimentary English, addresses Paula as friend, and then as mother. The detective, who thought he had nabbed Paula, relents, reminding her that she will get the DA's sympathy. Obviously, Loretta would not be going to jail.

In case anyone felt that Paula should have been prosecuted for leaving the scene of an accident, the writers covered themselves by showing that she would have followed the driver to the hospital if she had not encountered a series of delays. There is a moral issue here, the kind that might be debated in an ethics class: namely, her refusal to identify herself as the driver. Paula, however, chooses retribution over confession, and the boy's magnanimity suggests that even a child is capable of forgiveness. Naturally Paula should have come forward, but that would have resulted in a different kind of film: a courtroom melodrama, in which the boy, who had now progressed to grandiloquence, would deliver an impassioned speech in Paula' s defense. The film's ending is as believable as *The Accused*, in which Loretta got away with homicide, thanks to Robert Cummings's powers of persuasion.

Paula was one of Loretta's better, if unheralded, late-career performances. Especially impressive was the maternalism she lavished on the boy (sensitively played by Tommy Rettig). When Loretta prepared him for his bath and taught him the rudiments of speech, she did more than just play a mother surrogate; she was the dream mother, the kind to whom any child would gravitate. Loretta may not have been that way to Judy, but one would like to think she was to Christopher and Peter.

As Loretta approached 40, she found herself, like other stars in the same or an older age bracket (e.g., Rosalind Russell, Claudette Colbert, Joan Crawford) playing opposite younger actors. She committed herself to two pictures for Universal-International (UI): *Because of You* (1952) and *It Happens Every Thursday* (1953). *Because of You* was a low budget production that cost $625,690 and filmed over a five-week period (21 April–26 May 1952). Loretta received $75,000, and Norman Brokaw, her agent at William Morris, arranged for a 9:00 a.m.–6:00 p.m. time clause in her contract. *Because of You* was a shamelessly manipulative woman's film with a victimized heroine and a target audience of female moviegoers who had suffered at the hands of unscrupulous (played in the film by Alex Nicol) or unforgiving (played in the film by Jeff Chandler) men. Chandler was thirty-four, but his prematurely gray hair made him seem older and at the same time enhanced his sex appeal. Nicol was thirty-three, but his character's brand of sleaze is ageless. Fortunately, Loretta's still milky complexion only needed some carefully applied makeup and subtle lighting to place her character, Christine, in her twenties. Loretta took care of the rest, which, for a thirty-nine-year-old actress, was no easy feat. In the opening scene, as the camera tilts up her back while she is dancing with Nicol, it seems to be ogling her every curve. Loretta is wearing a form fitting dress and sporting an obvious platinum blonde wig. Breathy and clueless, she appears to be channeling her inner Marilyn Monroe. Christine is the mistress of drug dealer Nicol, who sets her up for a prison sentence when he gives her incriminating evidence for safekeeping. In jail, her hair returns to its original—and natural—color. She also acquires a marketable skill that she can use on the outside: She trains as a nurse's aide. Once she gives Chandler a rubdown, which she performs with a soothing eroticism, he is smitten. They marry, have a daughter, and are enjoying domestic bliss until Nicol crops up. So much for happily-ever-after, at least for the moment.

The screenwriter, Ketti Frings, must have seen *Eternally Yours*, in which Loretta became a magician's assistant. In fact, the working title of *Because of You* was "Magic Lady." Once Chandler dumps her and takes their child, Loretta masters a repertoire of magic acts that she performs at children's birthday parties, one of which happens to be her own daughter's. Since her former husband is now engaged, she runs off to Oregon, and works on a farm (shades of *The Farmer's Daughter*). A repentant Chandler tracks her down, scoops her up in his arms, and the reunited couple go bounding through the field—an idyllic ending to a film that may have convinced Loretta that her movie career was coming to an end, which it did the following year. It was not that Loretta gave a bad performance, only that *Because of You* was a 1930s-type movie that should have been made around the same time as *Midnight Mary*. A twenty-year-old Loretta would not have had to work as hard playing a woman in her twenties as Loretta did when she was pushing forty.

Her Hollywood swan song was somewhat better. At least it didn't occasion disbelief like Irene Dunne's envoi, *It Grows on Trees* (1952), in which the "it" was real paper money sprouting on Irene's trees; Joan Crawford's in *Trog* (1970), in which the star was upstaged by a gorilla; or Bette Davis's cameo witch in *Wicked Stepmother* (1989). Like an augur, Loretta could read the signs. *It Happens Every Thursday*, which ran a mere eighty minutes, a little longer than *Cause for Alarm!*, and looked distinctly low budget, was filmed over twenty-five days (5 January–3 February 1953) at a cost of $617,085. Loretta received her usual $75,000, but despite the time clause, the *Daily Production Reports* show that for half of the shoot, she started at 8:00 a.m. and finished at 4:30 p.m., which still gave her time to recoup for the next day. UI considered the film a potboiler that might attract Loretta's aging fan base—but certainly not that of her costar, John Forsythe who achieved stardom in another medium, television. While Forsythe went on to *Bachelor Father* and *Dynasty*, and had his own show for a season, Loretta also found her niche on the tube where, for eight years, she attracted the biggest audience of her career.

The "it" in *It Happens Every Thursday* is a local paper, *The Eden Archives*, that a journalist (Forsythe) and his wife, pregnant with their second child (Loretta) take over. Loretta plays the dutiful wife, using her ebullience to increase circulation, until Eden suffers a serious drought. Forsythe does some research and finds a scientific way of ending the drought, but before he can, nature intervenes and delivers five days of rain. The once rain-hungry populace turns on the couple, demanding compensation for their losses. In this deceptively feminist film, Loretta saves the day by bringing in a meteorologist, who explains that nature alone was responsible for both ending the drought and causing the excessive rain. In Capraesque fashion, the formerly vindictive citizens rally around their editor and his wife, as small town pettiness evaporates in the presence of a husband and wife without an ounce of guile.

It Happens Every Thursday may not have been Loretta's shining hour, but it was far from embarrassing. Loretta was totally credible as a homemaker, believing so strongly in her character that she gave the wife a blazing integrity that put her husband to shame—particularly since he could not bring about the resolution that audiences expected. Loretta could at least claim that her last film portrayed a woman who may have been her husband's intellectual inferior, but who could do for him what he could not do for himself: restore the people's confidence, and from the audience's standpoint, guarantee a happy ending.

CHAPTER 19

Radio Days

When Loretta closed the book on her film career, she could say with justifiable pride that for someone who started in pictures at four and stopped at forty, she had left behind an impressive gallery of characters. Her beauty made her difficult to cast; it was obvious that she was neither a femme fatale nor a musical comedy diva. In fact, Loretta never made a musical; the closest she came was the vaudeville bit she did with her sister in *The Show of Shows*. She was not a character actress as such, but an actress able to grow into her characters, and, for the most part, fit into their skin, whether they were tight rope walkers, orphans, champion bridge players, ballerinas, academics, criminals, socialites, waitresses, royalty, actresses, reporters, authors, politicians, aviators, homemakers, or nuns. She could be white, Asian, or mixed race.

Loretta was at her best when she was playing either a reflection of her real self (iron butterflies like Katie and Sister Margaret), or her anti-self, women at the other extreme (waifs, shop girls, molls)—the kind she might have encountered if, at four, she had never been exposed to the world of make believe on Catalina Island. But when she had to play someone in that intermediate zone, the no man's land between those selves (a middle-aged college freshman, a sleep walker, a screwball sleuth), she found herself caught between knowing how the role should be played and being unable to play it convincingly. At least none of her films was an embarrassment, unlike *The Iron Petticoat* (1956), which featured the unlikely team of Katharine Hepburn and Bob Hope, with Hepburn as a Soviet commissar with an Russian accent that sounded like a Muscovite's idea of Bryn Mawr English; or *Beyond the Forest* (1949), in which the forty-year-old Bette Davis, vampire-like in a black fright wig, tried to pass for a woman in her late twenties.

Loretta was always looking for ways to expand her repertoire. Her growing fame as a movie star paralleled the rise of live radio drama. Arguably, the best and most popular of the dramatic shows—at least for moviegoers—was *Lux Radio Theatre*, which aired on CBS from 1934 to 1955. Until June 1936, the show was broadcast from New York, after which it moved to Hollywood, where it originated from the Music Box Theatre on Hollywood Boulevard, and then from the Vine Street Playhouse. Tickets were always at a premium. Movie lovers, both Angelenos and tourists, relished the opportunity to see their favorite stars in front of a microphone either re-creating one of his or her own roles or taking on another's. The program allowed for both; availability was the key. If the original actor had a prior commitment, usually a film, another substituted who could play the part—if not as well, at least believably. When Loretta was unavailable for the 17 December 1949 broadcast of T*he Bishop's Wife*, Jane Greer filled in. Similarly, Loretta assumed Claudette Colbert's role in *Arise, My Love* (18 June 1942). The replacements were at least adequate, and occasionally better than the originators. Sometimes, an actor missed the point of the script, which was the case in the 12 April 1948 broadcast of *The Perfect Marriage*. Loretta knew how to play a stage actress without overdoing the histrionics. Lizabeth Scott, of the darkly sensuous voice, alternately throaty and husky, did not. Scott was the perfect standby for Tallulah Bankhead in *The Skin of Our* Teeth on Broadway, but not for Loretta in *The Perfect Marriage*. Scott, a good enough actress, was unable to locate the fine line between theatricality and flamboyance and aimed for the latter.

Although Loretta appeared on other radio shows, *Lux* was special: It was the one on which she performed more often than anyone else—twenty-six performances, followed by Fred MacMurray (twenty-five) and Claudette Colbert (twenty-four). Live radio, unlike theatre, made it relatively easy for a working actress. For *Lux,* there was a read-through on Thursday afternoon, a noon rehearsal on Friday, and another on Saturday. Two dress rehearsals were scheduled for Monday: the first at 10:00 a.m., the second, ninety minutes before airtime. Salaries varied: Established stars received $5,000 a week, except for Clark Gable, who received $5,001. The director Cecil B. DeMille was the program's host from 1936 to 1945, followed by another director with a sonorous voice, William Keighley, from 1945 until the show went off the air ten years later.

Loretta joined the program the year after *Lux* premiered, making her last appearance in 1952. She re-created some of her roles (*Man's Castle, Bedtime Story, The Lady from Cheyenne, China, And Now Tomorrow, Mother Is a Freshman*, and, of course, *The Farmer's Daughter* and *Come to the Stable*). But more often, she appeared in roles originated by others. Her first *Lux* appearance was in *The Patsy* (16 June 1935) in the Marion Davies part. She also took on another Davies role, the bareback rider in *Polly of the Circus* (30 November 1936).

But her greatest challenge was assuming roles made famous by others, especially Bette Davis and Katharine Hepburn. Loretta played four of Davis's parts. The first was Miriam Brady in *The Girl from Tenth Avenue* (16 May 1938), a sympathetic woman lacking in social grace who consoles an attorney jilted by his fiancée, marries him, and then discovers he is still infatuated with his ex until he learns to appreciate Miriam's decency. This was the kind of part Loretta could handle; it was lesser Davis, minus the mannerisms. But Loretta was only partially successful when she played Julie in *Jezebel* (25 November 1940), the role that brought Davis her second Oscar. Julie is kin to Scarlett O'Hara, a pampered Southern belle who flaunts convention and matures only after her lover marries another and is stricken with yellow fever. At the beginning Loretta's Southern accent was inconsistent, and her simpering was grating. But when Pres (Jeffrey Lynn in Henry Fonda's role) marries Amy, an Easterner, Julie grows in stature. After Pres becomes a plague victim, Julie begs Amy to allow her to become his caregiver and accompany him to that "desolate island, haunted by death," where the infected are quarantined. Loretta delivered her lines as if they were poetry—not like a woman with a martyr complex, but like one desperate to perform a selfless act to compensate for her selfish ways. Julie reminds Amy that she understands Creole, while Amy does not, and, therefore, can be of greater help. "Give me the right to be clean again, as you are clean," she implores Amy. At the end, Loretta is every bit as effective as Davis—so much so that one can forgive the unpromising beginning.

Two of the roles, both Bette Davis vehicles, must have struck a responsive chord in Loretta: *The Old Maid* (30 October 1939) and *The Great Lie* (2 March 1942). In the former, Loretta was Charlotte, who bears a child out of wedlock and is forced to live in her sister Delia's home, where her daughter grows up calling Delia "mother" and referring to Charlotte as her maiden aunt. *The Great Lie* was another woman's film, with its share of complications. Maggie (Loretta) raises her friend Sandra's child as if it were hers and her husband's. If Sandra's maternal instincts resurface, will she demand the child back? Yes. Good complication. Does Sandra succeed or does she perform a magnanimous gesture? *The Great Lie* was a two-, not a three-hankie movie.

Katharine Hepburn will always be the definitive Tracy Lord in Philip Barry's *The Philadelphia Story* (1940), a role that she created on the stage and repeated on the screen. Loretta offered a fresh take on Tracy in the *Lux* version (14 June 1943), making no attempt to duplicate Hepburn's mandarin line readings, but delivering the dialogue as if she were in a romantic comedy like *Love is News* or *Eternally Yours*. When she tells Mike Connor (Robert Young in the James Stewart role) that she has fallen in love with his short stories, she sounds as if she were having one of her romantic fantasies; her voice has a dreamy quality, as opposed to the yearning that Hepburn was so adept at expressing. There is an inside joke in the broadcast that was also in the film. When Tracy and Connor become slightly tipsy, they break into a boozy rendition of "Over the Rainbow" from *The Wizard of Oz*, which, like *The Philadelphia Story*, was an MGM film. It's a lovely moment that was probably intended to evoke memories of a movie that was never as popular in its day as it has become, and of a song that in 1943, the bleakest year of World War II, envisioned a place "where troubles melt like lemon drops" that just might turn out to be America.

While Loretta's flair for romantic comedy could easily transfer to *The Philadelphia Story*, nothing that she had done in film prepared her for screwball comedy on radio. Yet she did reasonably well in both *Theodora Goes Wild* and *True Confession* in roles created by two of the best exponents of the genre, Irene Dunne and Carole Lombard, respectively. In *True Confession* (13 May 1940), Loretta assumed the Lombard role of a writer who also happens to be an incorrigible liar, not one motivated by malice, but by her hyperactive imagination. She takes a job as secretary to a broker, but his wandering hands send her running to the nearest exit. When he is murdered, the writer is a suspect. Although innocent, she pleads guilty, thus giving her lawyer-husband (Fred MacMurray, in his original role) the chance to defend her. Acquittal follows, of course. *True Confessions* is respectable screwball, but not on a par with the best of the genre. Thus Loretta treated it like a bauble, not like a pearl of great price. The key to screwball is to keep it buoyant so that it does not sink into whimsy. This Loretta managed, playing the dizzy dame with the same kind of intelligence that Lombard brought to the role by wearing the motley—but not on her brain.

Theodora Goes Wild was another matter. This was classic screwball, aired not *on Lux*, but on *Campbell Playhouse* (14 January 1940). *Campbell Playhouse*, sponsored by Campbell's soup, premiered on CBS in 1939 under Orson Welles's supervision and was devoted to adaptations of well-known novels, plays, and films. *Theodora* represented a double challenge: doing vintage screwball and appearing opposite the formidable Welles (neither of them knew they would be playing husband and wife six years later in *The Stranger*). For Loretta, screwball on radio was easier than it would have been in film. Radio allowed her to play a madcap without having to become one for the camera. To Loretta, screwball—or at least, *Theodora Goes Wild*—was a romantic caper involving the title character, a respected citizen in small town America, who writes a steamy best seller under a pseudonym, and an illustrator (Welles, in the Melvyn Douglas part), who discovers Theodora's identity. Just as he is about to out her, Theodora discloses it herself through a publicity campaign. Theodora indeed went wild, and Loretta relished every bit of the comic mayhem. Realizing that the action has to move away from the illustrator and over to Theodora, Loretta took control of the script, not hijacking it out of ego but steering it in the direction of her character, as the plot required. Theodora is in love with the illustrator and can do for him what he cannot do for himself: bring his tottering marriage to a state of collapse. *Theodora Goes Wild* was Loretta's show, just as it had been Irene Dunne's movie, not Melvyn Douglas's. Welles would move on to far greater prominence the following year in his directorial debut, *Citizen Kane* (1941).

Loretta costarred with Welles again in the *Lux* broadcast of Charlotte Brontë's *Jane Eyre* (5 June 1944), with Welles as Rochester and Loretta as the title character. Unlike Joan Fontaine in the movie, released four months earlier with Welles as Rochester, Loretta gave Jane an armor-clad exterior that concealed her insecurity, as might be expected of a Victorian governess who came out of a school for "charity-children" and was treated accordingly. Loretta was not fluttery and breathy like Fontaine, who played servant to Rochester's master, never forgetting her origins. Loretta's Jane was closer to Brontë's; Her Jane traveled the same route from Lowood School to Thornfield, without losing the survival skills that she learned at Lowood. Loretta, strong-willed but respectful, gave Welles a run for his money; the novel was entitled *Jane Eyre*, not "The Master of Thornfield." It was Jane's story, of which Rochester was part. Unfortunately, the radio version did not include the novel's famous line, "Reader, I married him." If it did, listeners would have heard the voice of an exotic steel blue butterfly, with no intention of ending up in anyone's net, even one with silken meshes.

Casting Loretta in the *Lux* presentation of *Algiers* (14 December 1942) in the role that Hedy Lamarr originated was, to be charitable, casting against type. Loretta was not a world-weary siren like Lamarr, whose exotic looks made her seem an alien breed, unlike any of her Hollywood peers. But then, Hedy Lamarr had no peers; she was a gorgeous hieroglyph awaiting decipherment that never came. Loretta, in contrast, could be elusive but never Sphinx-like. Thus the writers wisely made Loretta the narrator recounting her short-lived affair with the gangster, Pepe Le Moko (Charles Boyer). Loretta could not dispel memories of Lamarr, who never lost the Viennese lilt in her voice that carried with it an air of mystery. Lamarr's Gaby was a woman of the world, always eager for a new adventure and, this time, finding it in the Casbah. Gaby was a creature of wanderlust; if a trip leads to an affair, so be it. It would always be short term. And if it ends in tragedy, as her trip to Algiers did, there's always a plane to another romantic place. Those who tuned in that Monday night were more interested in Boyer than Loretta. If the leads had been Boyer and Lamarr, the audience would have quadrupled to hear the Great Lover and the Love Goddess re-create their original roles. What Lamarr had, and Loretta lacked, was a world-weary, "been there, done that" voice. Loretta did not even attempt an accent—ersatz European or otherwise—but simply delivered the lines in a cultured voice reflecting the character's privileged background. It was Boyer's show, because it was Boyer's film. Whether or not Loretta realized it, she was a member of the supporting cast.

Loretta's best radio performances were in *Christmas Holiday* (*Lux*, 17 September 1946) and *Love Letters* (*Lux*, 22 April 1946), in roles created by Deanna Durbin and Jennifer Jones, respectively. Durbin had been Universal's resident soprano since 1936. In 1944, the studio thought it was time for her to change her image and go dramatic as a singer in a New Orleans dive married to a murderer (Gene Kelly, also cast against type). Durbin was surprisingly effective, but the studio was unimpressed and, except for the screwball mystery, *Lady on a Train* (1945), it was back to the same bland movies with porous plots for the next three years, until in 1948 Durbin had reached the stage of surfeit and left Hollywood for good.

In *Christmas Holiday*, a soldier (William Holden, right out of the army), whose plane has been grounded because of a rainstorm, drops into the club where Loretta is performing. They are instantly compatible, and she asks him to take her to Midnight Mass. That scene proved that Durbin could have been a serious actress. Whatever memories the church service evoked for her, Durbin alone knew; her barely audible but genuine weeping suggested someone in desperate need of spiritual guidance or even renewal. This was also the kind of scene to which Loretta could relate. Her weeping, also subtly controlled, was not that of an actress playing a scene calling for her to cry, but of a suffering wife forced to make her living singing for drunks and lotharios, while her husband (David Bruce in Kelly's role) is serving a life sentence. When he escapes and is shot, Loretta, like Durbin, undergoes another round of emotional release, again unfeigned and movingly heartfelt.

It is hard to imagine anyone improving on Jennifer Jones's performance as "Singleton" in *Love Letters* (1945), which brought her an Oscar nomination. Singleton, whose real name is Victoria Moreland, became an amnesiac after allegedly killing her husband Roger for destroying the love letters he had supposedly written to her. The plot, a neat blend of whodunit and psychological melodrama, was resolved without straining credulity. Roger did not write the letters; his buddy (Joseph Cotten, reprising his film role) did. Victoria did not kill Roger; her aunt did. Loretta's Singleton/Victoria was much like Jones's—poignantly sincere and guileless, a dweller in a self-inhabited world with no memory of the evening that changed her life. With Cotten functioning as both sleuth and therapist, Victoria is forced to confront her past and relive that fatal evening. The action builds to a climax in which the past is purged, and a woman's identity restored. Loretta played the climactic scene as if she were shedding every layer of emotional insulation that kept out the real world and drove her into her own. Her performance was so compelling that someone in the audience cried, "Bravo!" at the end. "Brava!" would have been more accurate, but the sentiment was the same.

Loretta looked on any radio show as a means of enhancing her popularity. *Lux Radio Theatre* was her favorite; it allowed her to showcase her versatility, which was not always apparent in her films. But "versatility" was not limited merely to re-creating one of her film roles or taking on someone else's. Loretta took advantage of any program, dramatic or otherwise, that provided an opportunity for self-promotion. It was not that she was leading a life of quiet desperation, obsessed with recycling her image in every available medium—although it is easy to come to that conclusion. She simply wanted as much exposure as she could get as compensation for her second-tier status in a business where the icons are enshrined, while the statues are relegated to dimly lit alcoves. An alcove was not what Loretta had in mind; if she had to be a statue, it would be at a dedicated side altar like those at New York's St. Patrick's Cathedral. Naturally, she preferred movies and radio; next, fan magazine articles; and finally, as a Hollywood beauty queen, endorsements of soaps, cleansing creams, and cosmetics. But it was movies that made her famous and radio that streamed her fame throughout the country.

"Noël Coward" was not a name ordinarily associated with Loretta, yet she often cited him among her favorite writers, perhaps because she aspired to the heady brand of sophistication his heroines possessed (Amanda in *Private Lives*, Elvira in *Blithe Spirit*, Gilda in *Design for Living*) and that she strove for in *Bedtime Story*, *Eternally Yours*, and *Love Is News*. Her determination to master the high style stemmed from her dissatisfaction with her performance as the socialite in *The Devil to Pay*, believing that if she had the wit and flair that the role required, she would have been the ideal costar for Ronald Colman. And yet what seventeen-year-old actress had such technique? It's hard to imagine Coward specialists such as Lynn Fontanne (*Design for Living*, *Quadrille*) and Gertrude Lawrence (*Private Lives*, *Tonight at 8:30*) possessing it at that age. Thus when Loretta had a chance to appear in Arch Obler's radio adaptation of Coward's *Blithe Spirit* on *Everything for the Boys*, she accepted immediately. *Everything for the Boys*—the inspiration of Loretta's husband, now Lieutenant Colonel Lewis, head of the Armed Forces Radio Service—was broadcast to members of the military during the height of World War II, from 18 January 1942 to 12 June 1944. The host and leading man was Ronald Colman, Loretta's adolescent crush, with whom she had costarred in three films. Convinced that she had now acquired a serviceable British accent, she joined the cast as Elvira, the spectral first wife of Charles Condomine (Colman), along with Mercedes McCambridge as Ruth, his second wife, and Edna Best as the medium Madame Arcati. After dying of a heart attack. Elvira returns as a ghost to disrupt Charles's household and sabotage his marriage to Ruth. The role required Loretta to be sexy, fey, and cunning—all the character traits that she had mastered over the years—in addition to sounding authentically British. She could toss off a line like, "I was playing backgammon with a sweet Oriental gentleman, and then that child paged me and the next thing I knew I was in this room," and make it seem the quintessence of wit. It got a laugh from the men and women stationed in New Guinea, the intended location of the broadcast. Each episode of *Everything for the Boys*, which consisted of half-hour versions mostly of outstanding plays (e.g., *The Petrified Forest*, *Quality Street*), was transmitted to a particular part of the globe where the war was being fought. It is difficult to determine the exact date of the *Blithe Spirit* transmission; most likely, it was either late 1943 or spring 1944, when Allied operations had neutralized the Japanese threat to New Guinea.

An invitation to appear on Louella Parsons's show, even though it only aired for fifteen minutes, was a command performance—particularly since the influential Parsons had given her imprimatur to the scenario Loretta had fabricated about Judy's adoption. Loretta owed Parsons, and when Parsons beckoned, Loretta obeyed. However, appearing on the show worked to Loretta's advantage. Parsons always promoted her guest's latest or forthcoming picture; it was payment for speaking silly, scripted lines that allowed the voice of Hollywood to gush over an actor, who would humbly accept the compliment in words that others had written.

Loretta's more discerning fans must have wondered why she agreed to be a guest on *The Burns and Allen Show* (23 November 1943). But Loretta was savvy enough to realize that not everyone was tuning in on Monday nights to *Lux Radio Theatre*; others preferred comedy shows that did not require an hour's investment of their time. The offbeat humor of George Burns and Gracie Allen—particularly Gracie's—was the main attraction of *The Burns and Allen Show*, which premiered on CBS in 1932, moving in 1950 to television, where it delighted audiences until 1958, when Gracie, whose heart condition had worsened, announced her retirement, dying that same year. But even in 1943, Burns and Allen were household names. Loretta would have been foolish to pass on a chance to appear on their show, especially since her movie career had shifted into low gear. In 1943, Gracie was at her zany peak, and Loretta knew that her sole purpose was to play "straight man" to Gracie, providing her with set-ups for the punch lines. Burns did likewise, knowing that he could not compete with Gracie's brand of humor, which belonged to a tangent universe, where everything is inverted, the lingua franca is the non sequitur, and illogic has displaced rational discourse. Sample:

> BOLINGBROKE (TO GRACIE). I have great news for you, dear lady! The Bolingbroke Little Theatre is about to open its winter theatrical season. I shall want you as the leading lady, naturally.
> GRACIE. Oh, naturally. Say, wouldn't it be wonderful if we could get Charles Boyer for my leading man?
> GEORGE. Oh, sure, sure. You could get him easy for around twenty-five thousand dollars.
> GRACIE. We wouldn't have to pay him a cent, George—he's Free French.

In the 23 November 1943 broadcast, Gracie's obsession with supplementing the family's income by writing lurid pieces for exposé magazines leads to a lawsuit when her article, "The Secret Love of Loretta Young," is published. Even more libelous was the accompanying question: "Does Her Son, Robert Young, Know About This?" The two Youngs were not related, although they ended up achieving greater fame on television than they did in film—Loretta, in her own show, which ran for eight years, and Robert in *Father Knows Best* (1954–63) and *Marcus Welby, M.D.* (1969–76). The loopy dialogue did not faze Loretta. When she slaps Gracie with a $50,000 libel suit, Gracie makes George the culprit, insisting that he is mad.

LORETTA. George always looked all right to me, mentally, of course.
GRACIE. Oh, you can't go by appearances, Loretta. Think of George as a chocolate. Yes, you can't tell by looking at him whether inside he's plain or nut.

Corny? Of course. But it got a laugh.

This was not Loretta's finest hour on radio, but at least announcer Bill Goodwin plugged her forthcoming movie: "Our guest tonight . . . is currently working in the Paramount Picture, 'And Now Tomorrow.'" It did not matter if Loretta's appearance on *Burns and Allen* sold more tickets to *And Now Tomorrow*. What mattered was that Loretta was a guest on a radio show that drew more listeners than *Lux Radio Theatre*. And when *Burns and Allen* became *The George Burns and Gracie Allen Show* (1950–58) on television, it lasted as long as *The Loretta Young Show* (1953–61), eight years.

If Loretta were asked to name the radio program that gave her the greatest satisfaction, she would not have answered *"Lux Radio Theatre"*—despite her record number of appearances on the program—but *Family Theatre*, the inspiration of Father Patrick Peyton. Loretta had great rapport with priests. Among her closest friends was Bishop Fulton J. Sheen, America's first television evangelist, whose CBS show, *Life Is Worth Living* (1952–57), became so popular that it caused defections from its only competition on Tuesday evenings, *The Milton Berle Show*. Bishop Sheen was the epitome of panache. He turned his monsignor's cape into a costume, as if he were an ecclesiastical Batman; he handled the blackboard, his essential prop, like a seasoned teacher, which he was (more or less).

Television, more than the pulpit, released the actor within whenever he had the opportunity to dramatize, as he did when he used as his text Shakespeare's *Macbeth*. A year after *Life Is Worth Living* went on the air, *The Loretta Young Show* debuted. Bishop Sheen's theatricality matched hers. But as television personalities, they were not competitive: He was on CBS on Tuesdays; she, on NBC on Sundays.

Loretta had known Bishop Sheen since the 1940s. In November 1944, she wrote to him, asking that he see "a friend . . . fearful of dignified persons," a rather quaint way of saying "celebrity-priest." Who the friend was is difficult to say. The letter is part of the Gladys Hall Collection, and the friend may have been the prolific magazine writer, Gladys Hall herself. Another Gladys, Loretta's mother, also sought his advice. "Do as you truthfully and honestly feel about it," was his oracular reply. When Loretta's first son arrived, he congratulated her on the "beautiful fruition of your mutual love," an equally quaint, if not euphemistic, way of attributing a birth to something more spiritual than physical. With Bishop Sheen, rhetoric was all; with Loretta, it was discretion.

Fr. Peyton was the antithesis of Bishop Sheen—a crusader with a mission, not a charismatic showman. Patrick Peyton was born in 1909 in "the bleak western part of County Mayo, Ireland." Having grown up with the ritual of the after-dinner family rosary, he was convinced that the nightly recitation of the rosary would produce harmony in the home and throughout the world. Naturally, his message was directed at Catholics, who were familiar with the rosary and understood its function as an instrument of prayer. The rosary is a five-decade string of beads that Catholics would finger while meditating on significant events in the Greek New Testament, such as: the Annunciation, in which the angel Gabriel appeared to Mary, informing her that she was chosen to be the mother of the Messiah; Mary's visit to her cousin Elizabeth; and Christ's birth, death, and resurrection. These events were divided into the Joyful, Sorrowful, and Glorious Mysteries, each of which commemorated five such incidents. Traditionally, Mondays and Wednesdays were devoted to the Joyful Mysteries (events preceding and following Christ's birth); Tuesdays and Fridays to the Sorrowful (details of Christ's Passion); and the Glorious (post-crucifixion events such as the Resurrection and Ascension). This was the sequence that Fr. Peyton, Loretta, and countless Catholics knew until 2004, when a slight change was introduced: the Joyful Mysteries were relegated to Mondays and Saturdays; the Glorious to Wednesdays and Sundays. The Sorrowful were unchanged, but a new category was created for Thursdays: the Luminous Mysteries, commemorating other important events such as the turning of water into wine at the marriage feast at Cana and the institution of the Eucharist.

Fr. Peyton and Loretta had much in common, not just the rosary. They were destined to meet. Patrick Peyton emigrated to America in 1928, intending to join the Congregation of the Holy Cross. His dream was deferred when he was stricken with life-threatening tuberculosis. On his sick bed, he vowed that if he lived, he would spread devotion to the Virgin Mary and the rosary. He recovered and was ordained in 1941. Determined to keep his promise, he learned that the Mutual Broadcasting System—a network made up of four stations, three from the Midwest (WGN in Chicago, WLW in Cincinnati, WXYZ in Detroit), and the best known, WOR in Newark, New Jersey—would offer him thirty minutes of air time if he could come up with a star-driven program that was not exclusively Catholic like NBC's *The Catholic Hour*. What Father Peyton envisioned was *Family Theatre*, a half-hour dramatic series consisting of original stories and literary adaptations, geared to the entire family and subtly promoting his Rosary Crusade.

Fr. Peyton knew he needed a Hollywood contact. A friend furnished him with a letter of introduction to Loretta's husband, still Lieutenant Colonel Tom Lewis, head of the Armed Forces Radio Service. After learning that Lewis was a devout Catholic, Fr. Peyton persuaded him to kneel and recite the *Memorare*, St. Bernard's prayer to the Virgin Mary, followed by the rosary. Lewis was speechless; he had never encountered anyone—not even Loretta—who was so devoted to the Virgin. Confident that Loretta would be similarly impressed with Fr. Peyton, Lewis put him in touch with her. However, Loretta had just given birth to their second son, Christopher Paul, on 1 August 1945. That did not deter Father Peyton. Not one for wasting time, he called on her three days later. Loretta could not say "no" to a priest, particularly one so committed to spreading devotion to Mary.

When Loretta was a child, Gladys advised her to turn to Mary, her only solace during the trying years of her marriage to John Earle Young. Mary also became an integral part of Loretta's spiritual life: No matter where she lived, a statue of the Virgin was prominently displayed in her bedroom. When her godchild, actress Marlo Thomas, was confirmed, Loretta presented her with a statue of the Virgin and the Christ Child on a jade base. On a visit to Mexico, she spotted a wayside shrine of the Virgin and instinctively dropped to her knees. Loretta traveled to Lourdes, where Mary's appearances to the fourteen-year-old Bernadette Soubirous, a day laborer's daughter, culminated in a spring gushing out of the earth, whose waters could cure the infirm and gravely ill who traveled there from all over the world. Loretta's visit to Lourdes inspired an episode on *The Loretta Young Show, The Road to Lourdes* (1959).

In 1981, Loretta read that the Virgin had appeared in the village of Medjugorje, in the former Yugoslavia. That was all she needed. Determined to go there, even though it was not the most accessible of places, Loretta persuaded her son Peter to accompany her. Loretta may well have had a vision there herself. Supposedly, she saw the sun change color and shape, until there was a communion wafer in its center. A foot injury, later diagnosed as a fracture, did not deter Loretta from ascending the hill where the Virgin appeared, even if she had to be transported on a stretcher. To Loretta, Mary was more than Christ's mother. She had mythologized the Virgin to the extent that Mary became the standard by which Loretta measured herself, knowing she could never achieve such perfection. But she was satisfied with the title that Mary used of herself when she consented to be the mother of the Messiah: "Behold I am the handmaid of the Lord. May it be done to me according to your word" (Luke: 1.28). Actually, Loretta was the handmaid of Mary.

"Medjugorje solidified everything." The solidification, by which Loretta meant the harmonious blending of the tensions that once polarized her life (career vs. family, actress vs. wife/mother, star vs. business woman, past indiscretion vs. saintly persona). It began in the mid 1940s when she became active in St. Anne's Foundation, noted for its support of St. Anne's Maternity Hospital for Unmarried Mothers. Loretta was a four-term president of the foundation, whose mission she championed. She was rewarded for her efforts in 1961, when the Board of Trustees staged a testimonial reception at which she was honored for "her Noble Contribution to the Unknown World of the Unwed Mother and Her Body for the past fifteen years." The citation was not entirely accurate; Loretta was quite knowledgeable about the world of the unwed mother. For a time she lived in it. But by 1961, the myth of Judy's origins had become part of Hollywood lore, neither provable nor deniable. For the time being, an exposé was out of the question. Loretta had been enshrined in her own niche, and no one had come forth to dislodge her from it. Not in 1961, anyway.

In 1947, anyone promoting devotion to Mary had Loretta's endorsement. It did not matter if she considered Fr. Peyton part of her ongoing penance for her mortal sin or a fellow Marian in need of her help. Probably the latter, although guilt has a way of coloring decisions. Whatever the case, in the mid 1940s, Fr. Peyton had become Loretta's latest cause. Knowing that he would be the guest celebrant at a Sunday mass at The Church of the Good Shepherd in Beverly Hills—the church most frequented by Hollywood Catholics, including herself—Loretta advised him, as a visitor, to defer to the pastor, who would invite the stars in the congregation to meet him after mass. "Then, when you get them one by one in the sacristy, close the sale." Loretta knew Church politics. As a visiting priest, Fr. Peyton must not steal the pastor's thunder. Such was the advice of a shrewd woman, who, in a less patriarchal era, could have been a CEO in the corporate sector or a studio head.

Loretta's advice paid off; stars, not just Catholics, signed on. Fr. Peyton, with Loretta's help, recruited Irene Dunne, James Stewart, Bing Crosby, Bob Hope, Ethel Barrymore, Pat O'Brien, Ruth Hussey, Ann Blyth, Maureen O'Sullivan, Ricardo Montalban, Vanessa Brown, and Rosalind Russell. Loretta was on board from the beginning. Loretta may have taught Fr. Peyton how to work the Hollywood circuit, but others were equally helpful. Ruth Hussey introduced him to her producer-husband, Robert Longenecker, who "proved an essential cog in the machine I was laboriously building." So did screenwriter Fred Niblo, who drew up contracts in which the actors agreed to donate their services. Tom Lewis was far from a bystander. He persuaded Al Scalpone, a copywriter at Young and Rubicam, to come up with sign-off maxims, the most famous being, "The family that prays together, stays together."

Mutual's fear of another Catholic program was allayed when Fr. Peyton presented the network with a slate of the stars and stories, many of which were adaptations of classics such as "The Necklace" (Jeanne Crain), *The Song of Roland* (Terry Moore and Jeff Chandler), *Evangeline* (Mona Freeman), *The Gold Bug* (Maureen O'Hara), *A Tale of Two Cities* (Robert Ryan), *Cyrano de Bergerac* (Robert Young), *Moby-Dick* (Dane Clark), *Work of a Lifetime* (Edward G. Robinson), *The Windbag* (Bing Crosby), *Ivanhoe* (Macdonald Carey), and *A Daddy for Christmas* (Shirley Temple). But Fr. Peyton often inserted a pitch for his Rosary Crusade, as if it were an encoded message that audiences had to decode. Apparently they did, since the crusade, to paraphrase one of the chapter titles of *All for Her*, girdled the earth. Like a film, *Family Theatre* was a cooperative venture, in which Loretta, along with others, played a role.

The inaugural program on 13 February 1947 costarred Loretta and Don Ameche in *Flight from Heaven*, hosted by James Stewart and written by True Boardman, whose specialty was Abbott and Costello comedies (*Keep 'Em Flying* [1941], *Pardon My Sarong* [1942], *Hit the Ice* [1943]). But there was no time for comedy on this occasion. Stewart's dedication of the program to families, reminding them that "all things are wrought by prayer," set the tone for both the play and the series. Ameche and Loretta played a married couple subjected to the ultimate test of faith: personal tragedy. When the husband is bypassed for the academic position he expected, he becomes an alcoholic, deserting his wife after she miscarries. Just as *Flight from Heaven* was turning into a sudsy melodrama, the plot veered off in a literary direction. The husband's favorite poem was Francis Thompson's "The Hound of Heaven," once part of the English curriculum in Catholic high schools. In this "dark night of the soul" poem, the speaker is fleeing a "Him" (capitalization is the key) "down the nights and down the days." When he finally confronts his pursuer, he discovers it is God: "I am the He whom thou seekest."

Loretta's best-remembered performance took place two years later on 21 December 1949, when she narrated *The Littlest Angel*, which proved so popular that it was repeated the following year, on 27 December 1950. It is the story of an angel eager to upgrade his status. Currently a cherub, he is also a klutz who sings off key, sniffles, arrives late for prayer, loses his halo, and bites his wing tips. Once the other angels hear about Christ's birth in a Bethlehem stable, they resolve to honor him. Having nothing to give the child, the littlest angel can only offer the box that he prized as a boy, to which he was adding at the time of his death. (How the angel still has his boyhood box in his noncorporeal state is not a question one should ask of a parable.) The box contains a butterfly, a blue egg, white stones, and a dog collar. The gifts find favor with God, who accepts them in honor of Christ. The littlest angel is promoted to the next category, whatever it is (perhaps "angel first class"), for those who have proved themselves worthy of advancement.

As narrator, Loretta turned her voice into an instrument, with the text as a score and the tempos marked. Her delivery was exquisitely cadenced, the voice rising and falling, as accented and unaccented syllables alternated. Her voice was not the creation of a coach or a speech therapist. Obviously, she had some professional training, but no instructor could have transformed the teenager's voice that she had at the beginning of her career into one the American Institute of Voice Teachers called "the finest feminine speaking voice." As she grew in her craft, so did her voice. Her true voice teacher was her profession, which required her to speak like her characters—whether she was playing molls, waitresses, actresses, clerks, authors, western heroines, farm workers, debutantes, queens, home makers, or nuns. When Loretta describes heaven in "The Littlest Angel," she colors the voice to convey the rapture that the narrator, and perhaps she herself, felt. For Loretta, painting a picture of heaven through voice alone was second nature.

As the 1940s were drawing to a close, so was Loretta's radio career—except for *Family Theatre*, which extended it into the 1950s. When the short-lived *Four-Star Playhouse* (3 July–11 September 1949) went on the air, Loretta, Fred MacMurray, Rosalind Russell, and Robert Cummings rotated in leading roles in adaptations of stories from *Cosmopolitan*. But audiences were indifferent, and Loretta returned to *Lux Radio Theatre* (24 March 1952) for the last time to reprise one of her favorite roles, Sister Margaret in *Come to the Stable*, opposite Hugh Marlowe, again as the composer. *Come to the Stable* was broadcast a year and a half before Loretta made her TV debut on 20 September 1953. As early as 1950, she sensed that television would be the new mass medium. "By 1949, a million [television sets] had been sold, and by 1951, ten million." Loretta had more portraits to hang in her gallery. The new ones would be displayed in an annex, called television.

CHAPTER 20

Another Medium, Another Conquest

Loretta never worked with Lucille Ball, although she knew who Ball was, and closely followed her growing fame in the medium that Loretta was planning to enter. Lucille Ball was star writ small. She appeared in some films—Dorothy Arzner's *Dance, Girl, Dance* (1940), Jules Dassin's *Two Smart People* (1946), Henry Hathaway's *The Dark Corner* (1946), Douglas Sirk's *Lured* (1947)—that have attracted film scholars, not because of her, but because of the directors. Ball's MGM career was erratic; she could have brought her own brand of zaniness to the MGM musical, except that the studio had its resident zany, Red Skeleton, with whom she costarred in *DuBarry Was a Lady* (1943). "Costarred" is not entirely correct—the only star was Skelton. Otherwise, she was upstaged by a musical comedy trouper (Nancy Walker in *Best Foot Forward* [1943]), or the MGM family (*Thousands Cheer* [1944]), or relegated to sidekick status (*Without Love* [1945], *Easy to Wed* [1946]). When Ball had a chance to release the scatterbrain within, using her body as a comic conduit, it was in a string of Columbia B movies—*Her Husband's Affairs* (1947), *Miss Grant Takes Richmond* (1949), and especially *The Fuller Brush Girl* (1950)—released the same year that she and her husband, Desi Arnaz, hit the road, offering audiences a prevue of the sitcom that made television history when it premiered in October 1951: *I Love Lucy.*

Although stars who defected to television were threatened with blacklisting, those whose movie careers had run their course were not alarmed. Television was small-screen film. Don Ameche, who made four movies with Loretta, entered television in 1950 as the Manager of *Holiday Hotel*, an ABC variety show. The same year, he emceed a quiz show, *Take a Chance*. Since Ameche was never a major movie star, threats—if he even heard them—did not matter. He had the next best thing in television, and Broadway as well. In April 1951, Claudette Colbert, who also knew her glory days were over, shocked Hollywood by appearing in a comedy sketch on *The Jack Benny Show* with one of film's masters of gravitas, Basil Rathbone (whose movie career petered out with the end of Universal's Sherlock Holmes series). Others had nothing to lose. Live television was another form of live theater for those who were as comfortable on the stage as they were on the screen (e.g., Madeleine Carroll, Melvyn Douglas, Zachary Scott, Jane Wyatt, William Lundigan, Diana Lynn, Lloyd Nolan, Margaret Wycherly, Claudette Colbert, Ethel Barrymore, and the venerable Lillian Gish, who knew that if she could make the transition from the silents to the talkies to the theatre, she could move on to television and work the tripartite circuit for the rest of her career). If live TV proved daunting, there was always filmed television, particularly sitcoms, such as *I Married Joan* with Joan Davis, *My Little Margie* with Gale Storm and Charles Farrell, and *The Donna Reed Show.*

Loretta had no fear of blacklisting. When Louis Mayer bluntly told her that if she defected to television, she would "never get another script—ever," Loretta replied that television was "the next, natural step" in entertainment. Mayer was wrong, but his death in 1957 precluded his realizing it. Loretta received movie offers over the years: for example, the part of the unmarried secretary vacationing in Venice in *Summertime*, which Katharine Hepburn inherited, along with an Oscar nomination. Producer Jerry Wald felt confident enough to inform the press that Loretta would costar with James Stewart in *Mr. Hobbs Takes a Vacation* (1962). She probably took one look at the script and realized that, despite costar billing, she would be in the supporting cast; the title made it clear who the main character was, and it wasn't Mrs. Hobbs. For an actress who was a natural nun, it was surprising that Loretta even passed on the role of the mother superior in *Lilies of the Field* (1963), in which an itinerant handy man (Sidney Poitier) helps a community of German nuns build a chapel. Just as Loretta would have been miscast in *Summertime*, she would have been eclipsed by Sidney Poitier in *Lilies of the Field*. Poitier deservedly won an Oscar for his performance, becoming the first African American actor to be so honored. The role of the mother superior, with whom Poitier spars, went to the Austrian actress Lilia Skala, who did not have to affect an accent and who was also rewarded with an Oscar nomination.

From the early fifties on, television was Loretta's only medium. She had Helen Ferguson present her to the public as an ex-movie star eager to embrace the new medium, not as a Hollywood diva slumming on the tube. Ferguson did not have to be told; she knew her job, even boasting, "I can give a better Loretta Young interview than Loretta herself. " Helen Ferguson Public Relations at 151 El Camino Drive in Beverly Hills was the address of Loretta's authorized image-maker, who wove together fact, conjecture, and myth so seamlessly that truth and fiction were indistinguishable. Ferguson represented other stars, such as Henry Fonda, Barbara Stanwyck, Maureen O'Hara, and Robert Taylor, but Loretta was special. For the others, Ferguson went the distance; for Loretta, she went beyond it, perhaps sensing that, despite her propulsive drive, Loretta could not banish the specter of failure that broods over any new venture. Not only was Loretta anxious about the show, she was also concerned about the way audiences would react to *her*. Being a star was no guarantee of success. Frank Sinatra disappointed his fans when *The Frank Sinatra Show* premiered in 1950, lasting for only two seasons. When the show was revived in 1957, it barely lasted the season, even though Sinatra was now an Oscar-winner for *From Here to Eternity* (1953). Television represented the greatest challenge Loretta had ever faced. She needed an image for the tube, a scaled-down version of her Hollywood persona. She had to be friendly and inviting, as if the audience were her guests and she their hostess. And that is exactly the image that she projected during all the years *The Loretta Young Show* was on the air.

Ferguson handled the packaging of Loretta carefully, portraying her as a convert to television, which was true. Equally true was Loretta's determination to perpetuate her image on the small screen. Since she had done film and radio, and had earlier ruled out the stage, television was the logical next move. Loretta may not have been a narcissist, but she refused to join the ranks of the forgotten when she had a public that remembered her. The Lewis household, as Ferguson described it, entered the television age in the early 1950s with the purchase of their first TV set. It was literally love at first sight. Loretta was delighted with such shows as *Hopalong Cassidy*, *The Kate Smith Evening Hour*, *The Ted Mack Family Hour*, and *Arthur Godfrey and Friends*, all good, wholesome entertainment—as if there was anything else at the time. "Loretta felt they were friends . . . . She loved everything about T.V." And soon TV would love her.

Loretta may actually have gotten the TV bug in 1950, when she was scheduled to speak at a Variety Club convention in Philadelphia hosted by Ken Murray, an ex-vaudevillian with a popular variety show, *The Ken Murray Show* (1950–53). When Murray heard that a baby girl had been abandoned in a local theater, he sensed a coup. Since his show that evening was a tribute to the Variety Club, he wanted to announce that the club would adopt the child. But Loretta upstaged him: She headed over to the hospital in street clothes and street makeup, and returned to the studio with the baby, knowing that there would be no studio lighting. At that moment, she was both a star and a mortal—a 75 percent star/25 percent mortal combination that would transfer to the small screen, when the time came. And two years later, the time came.

When Loretta informed the William Morris Agency that she was no longer available for movies, she was telling only a partial truth. Actually, Loretta was not being besieged with film offers. Although occasionally a few came her way, none of them would have been a comeback on the order of Gloria Swanson's in *Sunset Boulevard*. The same year that Loretta made her television debut, her last film, the enjoyable but inconsequential *It Happens Every Thursday*, was in release. And that was her Hollywood swan song. In 1952, even before *It Happens Every Thursday* began shooting, Loretta made up her mind: She was going to enter television. That year, the *Los Angeles Times* reported: "[Loretta Young] has succumbed to television [and] starts shooting in January on a series entitled 'Loretta Young and Your Life Story.'" The series would be produced for NBC by the Ruslew Corporation, the company's name a combination of the last names of its founders, Harry Ruskin, a screenwriter (*King of Jazz, Andy Hardy's Blonde Trouble, Between Two Women, Julia Misbehaves*, etc.) and Tom Lewis. Ruskin and Lewis acted as vice president and president, respectively.

At this stage, Loretta preferred to function simply as star. Her marriage was, as yet, not imperiled—although that would change once the series got underway. The cumbersome title was scrapped in favor of *Letter to Loretta*, but the basic concept—stories from Loretta's fan mail that would be dramatized, with Loretta appearing as herself in the prologue and epilogue and as the main character in the teleplay—remained the same until the middle of the second season, when the letter format was discarded.

Although Loretta never expressed any reservations about Ruslew, she obviously had some. A year later, Ruslew was supplanted by Lewislor, a combination of letters from Lewis's and Loretta's names (his full surname, and the initial three letters of her first name), probably an imitation of Desilu, Lucille Ball and Desi Arnaz's television corporation. At the time, Loretta did not question the order or the disparity. Lewis, after all, would be president and the accountant, Robert F. Shewalter, secretary-treasurer, with Loretta and Lewis splitting the stock and each transferring one-half, so that Shewalter would receive a munificent one percent.

In interviews, Loretta downplayed her role in Lewislor, insisting that her husband was executive producer and she the star: "I am not going to interfere with the production. I just like to act." But Loretta had no intention of separating production from performance, nor was she willing to relinquish the reins to her husband. Loretta was a micromanager before the term was even coined. When Loretta was displeased with the set for her television debut, she turned to her mother, Gladys Belzer, who had decorated the homes of Hollywood's A-list (John Wayne, Humphrey Bogart, Joan Crawford, Bob Hope). Within fifteen minutes, Gladys gave her daughter the right kind of set. Loretta was at a loss to describe her mother's magic act: "It's hard to explain just what happened but I know that mother had performed her usual miracle." Nothing could be left to chance, now that Loretta had sworn fidelity to television. The screen's dimensions did not matter; small screen was better than no screen. Television would be an extension of the portrait gallery to which she had been adding for thirty-five years in film and over fifteen in radio. In 1953, Loretta was only forty, and the gallery was far from complete.

When Loretta took a candid look at early 1950s television, she realized it lacked an essential element: glamour. She was determined to bring star quality to her program, which would not be the ongoing adventures of a series character, but rather anthology television, with a new story each week and disparate characters: a salesperson; a Muslim; a model; a gangster's moll; historical figures like Clara Schumann and Charlotte Brontë; a Japanese fisherman's wife; a maharani; an alcoholic; a nurse; a doctor; a deaf woman threatened by a murderer; and a television executive with a brain tumor. Regardless of what her character wore, Loretta would make her entrance breezing through a door, executing a perfect turn as she closed it, and sweeping into a living room where she would deliver a warmly effusive welcome. Her delivery was slightly theatrical and often too meticulously scripted, but on 1950s television, artifice was a sign of good diction. The pivoting about was not Loretta's idea. When her dress designer, the Polish-born Marusia, complained that viewers could not see the back of the dress, Loretta obliged by twirling around. At the end of the first season, Marusia was out, but the pivoting bit remained, embedding itself so deeply in audiences' memories that even those who cannot recall one episode have never forgotten the entrance.

The inspiration for the series came from radio drama, especially *Lux Radio Theatre* and Father Peyton's *Family Theatre*. On *Lux*, a different movie was dramatized each Monday, with the stars appearing at the end for a brief chat with the host. *Family Theatre* adhered to the same format, featuring a different story each week, an adaptation or an original—but always with a moral. Loretta imagined the visual equivalent of *Family Theatre*. Could it have been otherwise with an actress who fasted on bread and water two days a week "for spiritual reasons?" And *Lux* inspired the appearance of the star not just at the end, as was the case in the radio show, but at the beginning as well, so that viewers could see Loretta as both herself and her character.

On 20 September 1953 *Letter to Loretta* premiered, claiming to be based on letters that Loretta received from fans seeking advice about a problem or a dilemma. Movie magazine readers were familiar with advice columns, in which women (and occasionally men) sought answers to questions about conundrums ranging from romantic entanglements to the fast track to stardom. The letters were supposedly written by the viewers and the replies by the stars, although more likely a staff member was responsible for both. In fact, Loretta's letter motif may have derived from such columns. In the late 1940s, *Photoplay*, the leading fan magazine, featured a column by Claudette Colbert, "What Should I Do? Your Problems Answered By Claudette Colbert." Since Colbert was the embodiment of chic, her replies were carefully worded and unemotional. She was asked a variety of questions: Are teenagers "tops?" Answer: Yes, but not all. How should a widow deal with a man she loves but who is unable to commit to marriage? Answer: "End this affair." One of the most authentic-sounding letters simply inquired about the role of a movie producer. The answer, regardless of who composed it, is an accurate job description of a producer in the studio era: "A producer is to a motion picture exactly what a general manager is to a commercial concern. He selects or is assigned a story to turn into a picture; he selects or is assigned the personnel (stars, director, a technical crew). He is allowed a certain sum of money . . . and is also expected to complete a picture in a given length of time."

In 1945, *Movieland* had a similar column, "Your Problem and Mine," with Jane Wyman as problem solver. Wyman projected a down-to-earth, big sister image; hence the title, which suggested that the correspondent and Wyman were not just locked into the letter-reply format, but that they were sharing an experience, with Wyman as an empathetic respondent. These letters seemed more authentic that Colbert's. Wyman's came from, among others, an amputee who has lost her desire to live, and a woman whose fiancé, an army veteran, was in danger of becoming an alcoholic. Wyman at least gave practical advice, providing the amputee with information about another young woman who learned to use prostheses and could now even go out dancing, and telling the woman with the hard-drinking fiancé about organizations where service personnel and their families could go for help. Three years later, Joan Crawford took over the *Movieland* column, which had a new title that put the burden on the writer: "Can I Help You?" Crawford donned the mantle of oracle, delivering the same kind of ambiguous replies to rejected suitors, jilted lovers—and, in one case, a white woman in love with a Mexican. The last required careful wording. Deliberately avoiding any hint of racism, Crawford replied that the most successful marriages are between men and women with similar backgrounds, implying that theirs were not. But the time was 1948, when such unions were frowned upon. Although Ricardo Montalban, a Mexican, was married to Loretta's half sister, Georgiana, he was a movie star as well as the brother-in-law of one. The fanzine letters, regardless of who wrote them, rang true. There was an honesty about them, some even sounding heartfelt. The ones dramatized in *Letter to Loretta* (the title was wisely changed to *The Loretta Young Show* in February 1954), on the other hand, read more like segues into stories than requests for advice.

Anyone who turned on NBC at 10:00 p.m. on 20 September 1953 saw Loretta make her grand entrance into a soundstage living room that purported to be hers, and by extension, ours. She wafted her way from the living room door to a camera waiting to capture her greeting in close up. Loretta flashed a radiant smile with capped teeth looking like burnished ivory. In a honeyed voice, she delivered a greeting, "I've been looking for a special way to entertain you," as if she were offering something other than the usual fare. That much was true. Leafing through her mail so naturally that it seemed as if we were witnessing her daily routine, she came upon a letter written by Carol Brown, a "working girl" courted by a Philadelphia blueblood, who plans to introduce her to his Main Line family. When a spiteful rival hints that his mother expects her son to arrive with a trashy shop girl, Carol exchanges her conservative outfit for a polka dot dress, encircling her neck with a collar of costume jewelry, and clasping her wristwatch around her ankle. Not knowing that Carol had been misled, the family is scandalized. But the suitor (George Nader) is still enamored of her, even to the point of risking his inheritance. The writers were familiar with the classic screwball comedy *The Awful Truth* (1937), in which Irene Dunne, hoping to extricate her ex-husband (Cary Grant) from the clutches of an heiress and her suffocating family, masquerades as his flashy sister, leaving the family in a state of shock when she exits. Loretta's version was screwball for mass consumption, devoid of subtlety and double entendre. Regardless, the series slowly acquired a faithful audience, which was all that mattered.

Although Carol alienated her suitor's patrician mother, Loretta knew that Carol must make amends if she is to marry into a family that prides itself on decorum. In the epilogue, Loretta moved to the bookshelf and took down the Bible. Her text for the evening was from *Proverbs*: "A sensible wife is a gift from the Lord," implying that, to be worthy of that gift, Carol must explain her outrageous behavior and apologize. Father Peyton had done his job well. The revelation that evening was not Loretta, who had proved earlier that she could handle comedy that broadened into farce (e.g., *He Stayed for Breakfast, Half Angel*). It was the Paris-born director, Robert Florey, who directed all of the shows during the first season. Interestingly, his forte was not farce, but melodrama, florid and often macabre (*Murders in the Rue Morgue, The Face Behind the Mask, The Beast with Five Fingers*). Farce was not entirely alien to him (he co-directed the Marx Brothers' film debut, *Cocoanuts*), but it was never his strong suit. Fortunately, he only had to work with a half-hour script and a cast that knew it was not doing Restoration comedy. The formula was simple: democratize the script, raise the volume on the laugh track, and what would have been screwball morphs into farce.

Playing women facing a crisis or unmasking a murderer was second nature to Loretta, who had gone that route in such films as *Heroes for Sale, The Lady from Cheyenne, China, The Stranger, The Accused,* and *Cause for Alarm!* Handling a crisis was therefore a common theme in the series. In "Earthquake" (25 October 1953), a wife with a husband confined to an iron lung must operate the machine manually when an earthquake causes a power failure. This was the kind of script that Florey could easily direct, one in which most of the action takes place in the dark, enabling him to use low-key lighting, his favorite form, and alternate between semi-darkness and shadowy surfaces.

Florey was also in his element in "Lady Killer" (10 January 1954), with Loretta as a mystery novelist with a penchant for sleuthing. When an airline passenger, whose ticket she was using, is found dead, and the female detective investigating the case experiences a similar fate, the novelist connects the incriminating dots that point to her seatmate and his associate, the corrupt district attorney. Just when it seems that the novelist is the next in line, the police (whom she had alerted) break in. The moral was simple: men do not have a monopoly on the art of deduction.

When Florey had the opportunity to take the script to operatic heights, he indulged himself, as if he were back at Warner's. Everything was over the top in "The Clara Schumann Story" (21 March 1954), from the opening scene (Loretta as Robert Schumann's fluttery bride) to the end (Schumann's descent into madness). In between, Loretta moved from romantic to realist, as she came to terms with her husband's condition. Viewers, whose only exposure to Robert Schumann might have been MGM's glossy biopic, *Song of Love* (1947), were treated to an authentic— as authentic as a teleplay can be—portrait of a talent derailed and eventually silenced, an important aspect of the composer's life that the 1947 film ignored. Loretta's performance was the equivalent of opera without music, wildly gestural, with gradations of hysteria and pained resignation. It was a script that required little acting, only histrionics. "The Clara Schumann Story" was Florey's half hour, not Loretta's or George Nader's, whose Schumann came close to conveying the radical mood swings from which the composer suffered.

Claiming that she had received letters from young women dreaming of becoming movie stars, Loretta decided they should learn the truth, not in the *What Price Hollywood?* or *A Star Is Born* way, but rather in the form of a parable. In "Hollywood Story" (31 January 1954), an Iowan (Loretta), the star of her community theater, is convinced that she can conquer Hollywood. But the time was 1954, when the new mass medium was television. Television could have been the character's medium, too, except that a producer was honest enough to tell her that she must get more training, learn to put her career first, and, if she ever reaches the top, resort to any means to stay there. The manifesto was too much for a small-town girl who was never meant for the big time. Resigned to being a local celebrity, she rejoins the community theatre and marries her high school beau (refreshingly played by William Bishop). The parable was not dated; "Hollywood" still has a mystique as a synonym for America's entertainment capital. The television subplot was a canny move on the part of the writer, who downplayed film's cachet in favor of TV's broader appeal. "Hollywood Story" subtly justified Loretta's decision to enter the medium, while at the same time warning hopefuls that the odds of achieving her kind of stardom were slim. There was a significant difference: Loretta was already a star when she entered television, and she became a bigger one because of it. Loretta also had it much easier than her character. She became a movie star primarily because of her transformative art, which enabled her to play a wide range of characters. But stardom is not rooted solely in talent; in Loretta's case, there were other factors such as a family contact (her assistant-director uncle), mentors (Mae Murray, Colleen Moore), directors (Frank Capra, Frank

Borzage, William Wellman), and producers (Dore Schary, Hal Wallis), with whom she made some extraordinary films, and leading men from whom she learned that acting is the art of reacting (Lon Chaney, Robert Williams, Spencer Tracy, Clark Gable). Of course, physical beauty was not a deterrent, nor was an inner radiance born of faith. And starting at four gave Loretta a head start.

Of all the teleplays in the first season, "Forest Ranger" (18 April 1954) was the best. Loretta may have thought so, too. A stranger appears at the back door of a ranger's home, offering to chop wood in exchange for breakfast. The wife agrees, unaware that he is an escaped convict with an animus toward her husband. As the tension mounts, the wife succeeds in talking him out of his revenge. Some of Florey's compositions harked back to the tight framing of film noir. When the convict threatened the wife, Florey juxtaposed their faces: his menacing, hers apprehensive but not terrified. By flattening space, he created a depthless two-shot with the texture of a film still. Like so many teleplays in the first season, "Forest Ranger" undermined the myth of "woman's intuition" by showing that there are women who can handle crises and solve problems because they have something far superior to intuition: ingenuity.

Once the series was launched, Loretta grew more secure in her choice of script, selecting stories that reflected her beliefs, such as maintaining family unity, triumphing over adversity, subordinating self-interest to the needs of others, and accepting the divine will. She hired a story editor, Ruth Roberts, to commission teleplays embodying those themes. Roberts was invaluable to Loretta, so much so that by 1959 she had become associate producer as well as story editor. Roberts, who had been Ingrid Bergman's dialogue coach for *Arch of Triumph* (1948) and Hedy Lamarr's for *The Conspirators* (1944), was also "dialogue director" of one of Loretta's last films, *Because of You* (1952). Loretta sensed that Roberts understood the kind of material she wanted and could provide it—and Roberts did. Other members of the team included Harry Lubin, the music director until 1958; Norman Brodine, the cinematographer for most of the teleplays; and Frank Sylos, the art director, except for the first season. These were Loretta's people or, as she preferred to call them, her family.

Robert Florey did not return for the second season, which made up in human interest what it lacked in stylish direction. Nor did the second season see the return of Marusia, who was replaced by two other designers: (Daniel) Werlé, whose line was showcased in major department stores like Saks Fifth Avenue and I. Mangin; and Helga, who also dressed Ava Gardner, Lily Pons, and Mamie Eisenhower. Harry Keller, another addition to the team, directed most of the teleplays during the next two seasons. A former film editor turned director, first at Republic, then at Universal-International, where he was a regular from 1956 to 1968, Keller, unlike Florey, had no signature, only the ability to bring a script to the screen. All but two of Keller's films were distinctive: *The Unguarded Moment* (1956), a total about-face for ex-swimming star Esther Williams as a high school teacher terrorized by an emotionally disturbed student; and *Voice in the Mirror* (1958), an uncompromising look at alcoholism, with Richard Egan as an artist whose drinking problem has spiraled out of control. Given a script that made little or no demands—especially one about everyday problems—Keller could deliver a no-frills product. It was only when film directors who could personalize their work were behind the camera—for example, Loretta's brother-in-law, Norman Foster, who directed fifteen episodes; or Tay Garnett, who directed four; or Rudolph Maté, who directed sixteen—that an episode looked more like a film in miniature than a teleplay.

Once the letter opening was dropped, Loretta just introduced the play, typified by "The Lamp" (19 September 1954), with Loretta as a superstitious homemaker who believes that her husband's walking under a ladder cost him a promotion. When a package arrives with a present from her uncle, a lamp with the trademark "Aladdin," she instinctively rubs it, and immediately receives a designer dress from her grandmother. Then her husband gets a dream job in Arizona, but to her dismay the wife learns that "Aladdin" is the manufacturer's brand name. At message time, Loretta adopted a sober expression and reminded viewers that superstition is pseudo religion, and that its replacements are the virtues, faith and hope.

"Something about Love" (21 November 1954) could have been a gooey confection about two people with disabilities. Instead, it took an unsentimental approach to a relationship between a dancer, whose legs had been broken, and an embittered vet, once a promising architect, whose injured hands caused him to abandon his profession. Refusing to succumb to self-pity, the dancer reinvents herself as a singer, and her optimism inspires the vet to return to his trade. The conclusion is not a plot sweetener, but flows naturally from the action, in which one person's determination affects another. It may have been a bluebird ending, but there was no chirping.

By now, Loretta knew that crisis stories were ratings boosters, especially if they involved children. "The Flood" (9 January 1955) was formulaic: The dilemma of rising waters, life-threatening condition and delay of doctor, was resolved by the doctor's last-minute arrival and a successful surgery. A widowed nurse (Loretta), with a child in her care in need of an appendectomy, persuades a Korean vet, a former medic, to lay off the booze and help her perform the operation. Before they have a chance, the doctor arrives, the operation is a success, the vet embraces sobriety, and the nurse is on the verge of shedding her widow's weeds. This time, one could almost hear the bluebird warbling.

"The Case of Mrs. Bannister" (6 February 1955) was atypical. A child has a doll that she has named "Mrs. Bannister." When an actual Mrs. Bannister falls to her death from the terrace of the adjacent apartment, her death turns out to be the result of murder, not suicide. The child either had psychic powers or heard the name from conversations filtering in from the next apartment. For her adage of the evening, Loretta chose a quote from Seneca, more inspirational than apropos. A better one would have been "There are more things in heaven and earth, Horatio, / Than are dreamt of in your philosophy" (*Hamlet* 1.5)." Regardless, that was the point.

Loretta may have toyed with the idea of a television spin-off based on a character from her show. There were two possibilities: Inga, a farm worker; and Sister Ann, a hospital nun. In "Inga" (3 January 1954), Loretta appeared in the title role as a Norwegian woman who runs a farm almost single-handedly. Believing that farm work would be a way of rehabilitating convicts, Inga persuades a prison psychiatrist to release some inmates to her custody. This was the kind of Janus-faced scenario that could go in one direction (lustful convicts menace helpless woman) or another (convicts bond with Inga and become veteran farm hands). Having played her share of imperiled women, Loretta preferred something upbeat and sunny, like *The Farmer's Daughter*—clearly the inspiration for "Inga," which also allowed Loretta to revive her flawless Scandinavian accent.

Audiences reacted so favorably to "Inga" that Loretta brought her back for the second season ("Inga II," 20 March 1955). Although the rehabilitation (which the politically correct psychiatrist has termed "experimental retention") is successful, Inga runs into a problem when the son of a local real estate honcho totals one of her cars. The indomitable Inga persuades the father to have his pampered son pay off his debt by working on the farm. The son reluctantly agrees, then disappears, but redeems himself by saving the farm from foreclosure. Inga returned two more times in the third (8 January 1956) and fourth (18 November 1956) seasons, suggesting that the character's audience appeal might warrant a series of its own. An "Inga" series never materialized; if it had, it would have probably adhered to the timeworn crisis-resolution template, with either the convicts or Inga steering the narrative to a happy ending or a "to be continued" one. And how much drama could be extracted from a farm where the main concerns were crops and equipment? More to the point, Loretta was now in her early forties, not exactly the right age for a "farm girl."

A more likely series (which also never came off) would have been the one about Sister Ann, the head nurse and trainer of nurses at an urban hospital. The first episode was "Three and Two, Please" ("Sister Ann's Christmas," 16 December 1956), the title referring to the emergency code used to summon Sister Ann. Loretta had a great affinity for the character. The three "Sister Ann's"—the second and third being "Sister Ann" (11 January 1959) and "Faith, Hope and Mr. Flaherty" (8 May 1960)—revealed a different Loretta, an accomplished character actress who did not have to rely on makeup and wardrobe. "Sister Ann" was inspired by a nun, Sister Mary Rose, who was Loretta's nurse in 1955 during her four-month hospitalization at St. John's Hospital in Oxnard. The two became close friends. When Loretta's television career ended, they joined forces to establish a home for delinquent boys in Phoenix, Arizona. Loretta even went so far as to purchase a mansion and have her mother decorate it. But what began as an act of charity backfired when the neighbors vehemently objected to the presence of a rehabilitation center on their block. If her show were still on television, Loretta might have commissioned a teleplay, in which an act of benevolence, such as hers and Sister Mary Rose's, ran into opposition and triumphed over it. That was not the case in Phoenix, which was located in real life, not happy land. Still, Loretta and Sister Mary Rose remained close friends, and when Loretta last heard from the indomitable nun, she was running an orphanage in the former Yugoslavia.

If Sister Mary Rose were anything like St. Ann, it is no wonder that Loretta was attracted to her. In "Three and Two, Please," the best of the Sister Ann's, Loretta bustled about in her white habit, dealing with emergencies, consoling the sick, staging a Christmas pageant, arranging a wedding for a unmarried couple, and turning a curmudgeon into a humanitarian on whom she practices a bit of Christian trickery by cajoling him into paying for a bicycle that she bought as a Christmas present for a lonely young patient—and she accomplished everything in a single day. "I must be about my Father's business" is her mantra, as she solves one problem after another, interspersing her good works with a visit to the chapel. Bespectacled and wearing a costume that made her appear plumpish, she is the embodiment of benevolence, doing God's will in her own way—which often required a bit of fabrication, but for a good cause.

A "Sister Ann" series could have been effective. If it had come off, it would have been the precursor of *The Nurses*, which debuted in 1962. An urban hospital offered more possibilities for a series than a Minnesota farm. However, a predominately Catholic series would have had limited appeal. *Going My Way* (1944) won an Oscar for Bing Crosby as Father O'Malley who, like Sister Ann, knew how to convert crusty millionaires into church benefactors. The television series, with Gene Kelly as Father O'Malley, only lasted a season (1962–63), while the movie is a television staple, especially at Christmas time. NBC's *Sister Kate* fared somewhat better, airing from September 1989 to July 1990. But NBC could not find the right time slot for a series about a no-nonsense nun, moving it from Saturday to Sunday, and finally to Monday before it went off the air on 30 July. A Sister Ann, who was a sleuth like Father Dowling in the highly successful *Father Dowling Mysteries* (with Tom Bosley as the title character and the endearing Tracy Nelson as his sidekick-nun), might have worked. It certainly would have been a television "first." But Loretta had done her share of sleuthing in the forgettable *A Night to Remember* and would have balked at the suggestion of reducing Sister Ann to Miss Marple in a habit. Sister Ann remained just one of the characters in her vast repertory.

As important as it was for Loretta to integrate message and story, it was just as necessary for her to show Hollywood the range of types she could have played on the big screen if moguls like Zanuck and Mayer had believed in her potential. The greater the challenge the role posed, the more eagerly she embraced it. In the movies, Loretta had only played non-whites twice: in *The Hatchet Man*, with lacquered face and eyes elongated into slits, and, more naturally, in *Ramona*, where dark makeup and a wig did the trick. On television, Loretta was in her element when she played Asians. She understood their quiet demeanor, often interpreted as subservience. But she would not take a role that reduced a woman to an inferior status. She found the tranquility in the character, realizing that such women do not flare up in anger or display embarrassing emotion. In "I Remember the Rani" (1 May 1955), a British journalist recalls a proto-feminist maharini, who, when told about Queen Victoria, wonders why she herself couldn't be called "queen." Wiser than her male advisors, she knows that irrigation alone provides the solution to the lingering drought. Although the journalist and the maharani fall in love, an interracial marriage would have been unacceptable in India or on network TV. Instead, the maharani teaches him to say "I love you" so that it echoes through the palace halls. Unlike the lovers in *The King and I*, the two do not "kiss in a shadow," but in an echo chamber. At least the maharini achieves her goal: Irrigation, and with it, the arrival of the twentieth century. "I Remember the Rani" is almost a chamber piece in its orchestrated simplicity and avoidance of dissonance or sudden changes of tempo.

Loretta was a Muslim in "Incident in India" (25 January 1959). Then, casting white actors as nonwhites was not denounced as racist, although it certainly was. The time of "Incident" is shortly after India received its independence from Britain in 1947, followed by the separation of India from Pakistan. The sectarian violence is never mentioned. The show was feminist but apolitical—unless a clever Pakistani woman (Loretta) is considered a political tool. Hardly, in 1959. The woman succeeds in outwitting the Indian slave traders who captured her and her attendant. Loretta may have modernized the character, but she looked and acted authentically Muslim, showing a police officer how he can capture a notorious bandit in exchange for allowing her to return to her husband. Naturally, the woman succeeds, and at the end, Loretta dispenses her weekly bromide: "Where love is, there is no fear." It may have been an uplifting sentiment in 1959, but, in the twenty-first century, staying alive as a hostage in the Middle East requires much more than cleverness.

Her finest portrayal of an Asian was in "The Pearl" (13 February 1956), as the wife of a Japanese fisherman who finds a pearl in an oyster and begins fantasizing about what he can buy with it. To prevent him from squandering his money when he goes to Tokyo, the wife substitutes a stone. In his absence, she uses the pearl to purchase a boat, christening it "The Pearl," so he can have the latest model. Loretta found the core of the character, the still point within the wife that is unaffected by the turning world—her eyes bespeaking wisdom without sending up flares. It was her subtlest interpretation: minimalist, perhaps, but magnanimous in its expression of the inner tranquility that accompanies true wisdom. The moral: "Therefore, get wisdom, but with all the getting, get understanding." The wife had both.

As the series grew in popularity, ratings increased to the point that, by 1954, Loretta was honored with an Emmy for "Best Actress Starring in a Regular Series," which, of the thirty top TV programs, ranked twenty-eighth. (Interestingly, *The George Burns and Gracie Allen Show* was twenty-sixth.) Loretta was now a television celebrity, whose image graced the cover of *TV Guide* twelve times between 1953 and 1962. Two more Emmys followed in 1956 and 1958. Movie actors, whose careers were moribund, but whose names still carried weight (e.g., Virginia Bruce, Virginia Mayo, Merle Oberon, Jan Sterling, Teresa Wright, Phyllis Thaxter, John Hodiak, Robert Preston, and Herbert Marshall) signed up as guests. No longer a movie star, Loretta was honored for her work in television. For three consecutive years, 1957–59, she received the National Education Association's "School Bell" for "distinguished service in the interpretation of education"; for six consecutive years (1954–59), she was awarded the *TV-Radio Mirror* gold medal as "favorite dramatic actress on television." Organizations as diverse as the Boy Scouts, Girl Scouts, California Teacher's Association, Hollywood Women's Press Club, *Fame* magazine, Dell Publications, Radio and Television Women of Southern California, and the American Legion added to her laurels. Perhaps Loretta's proudest moment occurred in 1960 when *TV Guide*'s readers' poll voted her "the most popular female personality."

If such nationally recognized organizations as the Boy Scouts, Girl Scouts, and American Legion honored Loretta, it was because her show raised television to the level of edifying entertainment, going beyond anything that existed at the time. ABC tried an anthology series, *Summer Theatre*, from July to September 1953, when *The Adventures of Ozzie & Harriet* was off the air. *Summer Theatre* never found an audience, suggesting that the concept was not viable. *The Loretta Young Show* disproved that myth, raising the bar several notches higher than sitcom and providing viewers with a series that guaranteed a different story each Sunday evening with an Oscar-winning actress in the lead.

The Loretta Young Show debuted at the right time. In fall 1953, the Red Scare had become the latest American bogeyman with its supporting cast of nuclear spies, media-infiltrating subversives, and screenwriters accused of injecting communist propaganda into their scripts. This was the time of Reds and pinkos, denunciations of "godless, atheistic Communism" from church pulpits, informants, Fifth Amendment pleaders, sycophants, exiled writers working through fronts or pseudonyms, and unrepentant radicals. Dwight D. Eisenhower, a much-honored World War II hero, was in the White House. Richard Nixon and Senator Joseph McCarthy were attempting to combat the (non-existent) communist threat to America's internal security, shattering reputations in their zealotry. Tennessee Senator Estes Kefauver's televised hearings on organized crime garnered high ratings. Morality, with its concomitant self-righteousness, dictated the tenor of mass entertainment that, in 1953, meant television.

A few movies of the late forties and early fifties addressed social issues such as juvenile delinquency (*The Blackboard* Jungle [1955], *Rebel without a Cause* [1956]); blacks passing for white in segregated America (*Lost Boundaries* [1950]) and those who refused to pass (*Pinky* [1949]); suburban class-consciousness (*All The Heaven Allows* [1955]); the Ku Klux Klan (*Storm Warning* [1951]); and corruption on the docks (*On the Waterfront* [1954]). On the other hand, 1950s television offered an alternative: idealized families (*Father Knows Best*); model high schools (*Our Miss Brooks*); ditzy wives/ exasperated husbands (*I Love Lucy, The George Burns and Gracie Allen Show, I Married Joan, My Favorite Husband*); impish daughters and benevolent fathers (*My Little Margie*); and smart kids with a bellowing father (*Make Room for Daddy*). Such programs were evening entertainment for mass audiences who turned a deaf ear to McCarthyism. *The Loretta Young Show* never played politics; Loretta, who was probably apolitical, knew her target audience.

Bishop Fulton J. Sheen's *Life Is Worth Living*, which bore the same title as his popular television show, became a best seller in 1954, as did Norman Vincent Peale's *The Power of Positive Thinking* and the revised standard version of *The Holy Bible*. Song hits included "Little Things Mean a Lot" and "Young at Heart," both with lyrics that in an age of gangsta rap seem hopelessly square. Radio's best-loved soap, *Ma Perkins*, was still on the air, and would be until 1960. When *Letter to Loretta* premiered, *South Pacific, The King and I,* and *Guys and Dolls* were still on Broadway, and the new musicals—*Wonderful Town, Kismet,* and *The Pajama Game*—would pass muster as family entertainment. These were shows that seem, in retrospect, disarmingly innocent despite a few risqué moments that would have sailed over the heads of most tourists and even precocious adolescents. How many of them would have picked up on the interracial affair in *South Pacific* and the nurse's subtle transformation from racist to liberal? Concubinage in *The King and I*? The hooker with her calling cards in *Wonderful Town*? The aphrodisiac song in *Kismet*? Loretta entered the medium at the right time.

But *The Loretta Young Show* might not have continued as long as it did if the star had become as disillusioned as some of the characters in her series. Before the second season ended, Loretta was vacationing at her Ojai ranch when she experienced severe abdominal pains that seemed to signal an attack of appendicitis—but turned out to be more serious. On Easter Sunday, 10 April 1955, she was rushed to St. John's Hospital, where she was diagnosed with peritonitis. A four-hour surgery followed that supposedly was successful. The prognosis was good, and Loretta was expected to be discharged in three weeks. But doctors also discovered abdominal adhesions that required another operation, a hysterectomy—although the press was only told about the "abdominal adhesions." Still, there was speculation about the nature of the surgery, which increased when the hospital refused to divulge information about Loretta's condition or even accept phone calls. Questions were answered guardedly, suggesting knowledge of her condition but an unwillingness to reveal it. Three weeks dragged out to four months, and Loretta was finally discharged on 1 August.

Even when hospitalized, Loretta's primary concern was her show. Fortunately, she had assembled a staff as loyal to her as they were to the program and knew fellow actors who would pinch-hit until she could return for the third season, which she did in 1956. Until then, a number of outstanding guest hosts substituted (e.g., Joseph Cotten, Van Johnson, her brother-in-law, Ricardo Montalban, Rosalind Russell, Joan Fontaine, Irene Dunne, Claudette Colbert, and Barbara Stanwyck—who was so taken with the anthology concept that she used it for her own series, *The Barbara Stanwyck Show* (1960–61).

Loretta's confinement secretly delighted Tom Lewis, who, despite his executive producer title, believed that his wife's success relegated him to the wings, depriving him of the spotlight that shone on her. In her autobiography Judy Lewis, twenty at the time of her mother's hospitalization, writes about overhearing her stepfather boast to Helen Ferguson, "Finally, I have my little Gretchen back." Then Lewis started to behave more like a lover obsessed with reclaiming his lost love than a media professional committed to keeping a successful series on the air. Apparently, Lewis no longer thought of his wife as Loretta, but as Gretchen—as if he preferred the woman she might have been if she had never became a movie star. Lewis did not care about the series, either; it was Loretta's, not his. He only wanted his Gretchen back. Loretta Young was not his property; she belonged to the world. Lewis decided to take matters into his own hands and inform Norman Brokow, Loretta's agent at William Morris, that her present condition made it impossible for her to return to the show—in effect, canceling it. Once Loretta learned what he had done, she "called her own meeting" in her hospital room, announcing that *The Loretta Young Show* was hers, and assuring her sponsor, Proctor & Gamble, that, in her absence, high profile guests would substitute, as they did. Tom Lewis was a typical example of the "star wife" syndrome, dramatized so effectively in *A Star Is Born* (1937). In the film, Norman Maine, once one of Hollywood's leading men, is eclipsed by his wife, Vicki Lester, and is known to mail carriers as "Mr. Lester." Tom Lewis had become "Mr. Young." As Loretta told an interviewer in 1987, "It was awfully hard when there was no way of stopping a headwaiter from calling my husband Mr. Young."

Lewis may have been the original producer of *The Loretta Young Show*, but it was Loretta's protean repertoire that made television history, proving that there was an audience for an anthology series. *CBS's Four Star Playhouse* had debuted earlier in September 1952, but even with its four stars (Charles Boyer, Dick Powell, David Niven, and Ida Lupino), it only lasted until 1956. Loretta would double that record. None of the four stars had Loretta's cachet—not even Charles Boyer, who was no longer the Great Lover, except to the Broadway audiences that flocked to see him in person in *The Marriage-Go-Round* (1959–60) with Claudette Colbert. (Significantly, neither Boyer nor Colbert reprised their roles in the movie version, in which James Mason and Susan Hayward played the leads.) Anthology TV was Loretta's domain, which she intended to rule until she had to concede the throne. Nineteen fifties' television had never seen anything like *The Loretta Young Show*, in which one actress released the myriad women within her and brought them into the American living room.

If Lewis wanted a stay-at-home wife, he had completely misread Loretta. *The Loretta Young Show* was her property; if Lewis wished to continue as producer, he would play by her rules. Even at the beginning, he should have inferred from her weekly schedule that their lives had changed. The episodes were filmed each year from July to March, with rehearsals on Mondays and Tuesdays; filming, Wednesday-Fridays; Loretta's welcomes and au revoirs every other Thursday; and her quote of the week on alternating Sundays. Weekends were not that different: There were wig fittings; wardrobe shopping; scripts to be read; story, interview, cast, business, program, and rewrite conferences. For eight years, Loretta's life was not her own—and it was certainly not her husband's. The steel butterfly was afloat, and no one, particularly Lewis, would bring her down.

As of April 1956, the marriage was unofficially over. For the time being it was a separation. Divorce would not occur for thirteen more years, until Loretta finally realized that, like her mother, she too would be a divorcée. But there was no way that Loretta's ruptured marriage could be sutured, much less healed. On 11 May 1956, Lewis resigned as producer from *The Loretta Show*, at the instigation of Loretta and Robert Shewalter, Lewislor's secretary-treasurer and accountant, seeking control of Lewislor for themselves but knowing that the name would have to be changed. At first, Lewis seemed compliant. On 30 April 1956, he agreed to relinquish his role in the company, in return for which he was offered sole title to one of the apartment houses that he and Loretta owned on N. Flores Street, a house on Sweetzer Avenue, and the Ojai ranch. (There were actually two Flores Street apartment buildings; the final settlement, a decade later, allowed Loretta to chose the one she wanted, which, naturally, was the better one.)

By 13 March 1958, Lewis had second thoughts about his exclusion from Lewislor. He filed suit against Loretta and Shewalter, accusing them of treating him unfairly and depriving him of his rights as a shareholder; he also argued that, with his departure, Loretta and Shewalter doubled their salaries. Loretta countered with copies of their 30 April 1956 agreement, in which the couple divided their property, and Lewis disassociated himself from the company. The case dragged on until 1966, when it was finally dismissed by the appellate court. By that time, it was no longer front-page news. Nor was their divorce, which was granted on 20 August 1969, with Loretta receiving a dollar a year as token alimony.

The emotional toll that the litigation had taken on Loretta even caused her to question the career to which she devoted her life. Whether Loretta truly enjoyed acting or regarded it as a challenge that had to be met is problematical. Perhaps at the beginning, the excitement of stardom compensated for the grueling hours and often thankless parts. But when Judy announced that she wanted to be an actress, Loretta scoffed: "You're too nice.... You're going to have to be tough." Loretta learned toughness from a childhood characterized not by privation but by desertion, from a mother who refused to succumb to depression and self-pity when her adulterous husband walked out on his family and instead reinvented herself, first as a boarding house owner and then as one of Hollywood's leading interior decorators. A costar who impregnated her and turned her life into a scenario of fabrication, studios that exploited her, and a production head who failed to appreciate her range further seasoned her. At one point she even called acting a "dreadful profession." To Loretta, it had probably become that, creating a tension between her religion and her art. The polarity drove her to priests for guidance in resolving that tension or at least bringing the two opposing forces into a state of equilibrium. When that proved impossible, Loretta decided that she could do it herself with a television series that would both entertain and instruct—and with a sign off quote for the viewers' edification.

CHAPTER 21

The Road to Retirement

When Loretta initiated a separation from Lewis in spring 1956, she secretly hoped their marriage could be salvaged—not for personal reasons, but because she feared the stigma of divorce, a word that was anathema to devout Catholics. Her mother avoided the problem by not remarrying after her divorce from Belzer. Loretta's marriage to Lewis, on the other hand, was a media event, and a divorce would be a bigger one, particularly since it involved two exemplary Catholics. Thus, Loretta was careful to give the press the impression that she and Lewis were only separated, appearing together, if necessary, at important social functions. In 1962, Loretta and Lewis were invited to a fundraiser for Father Peyton. As close friends of the priest, they would be seated on the dais with him. It may not have been a command performance, but their absence would certainly have been noticed. It was one of those starry evenings with yesteryear's favorites (Dorothy Lamour, Rosalind Russell, Irene Dunne, Jack Haley, Dorothy Malone, etc.) processing into the Beverly Hilton to the sound of cheering fans, clicking cameras, and popping flashbulbs. If Loretta thought that her first public appearance with Lewis in four years would be interpreted as a sign of a possible reconciliation, she was mistaken. One reporter referred to Lewis as Loretta's "estranged husband," adding that, "[T]heir estrangement, never officially admitted, long has puzzled Hollywood." Although she and Lewis declined to be interviewed, some of the attendees expressed confidence that the couple would resolve their differences. Reconciliation, however, was highly unlikely, since they were embroiled in litigation, with charges of mismanagement, deception, and chicanery coming from both parties.

The future of their marriage, if there was one, rested with a higher authority. Loretta needed guidance, not just from a parish priest or her confessor, but from the highest possible source: the vicar of Christ on earth, Pope Pius XII. It doesn't seem likely that Loretta herself negotiated a private audience with the pontiff; she had powerful allies in Bishop Fulton J. Sheen and Claire Boothe Luce, who may have acted as intermediaries. Loretta's audience with Pius XII on 27 April 1957 was front-page news in Los Angeles. But Loretta was really on a pilgrimage, using her visit to Rome to meet those chosen few who had the stigmata—physical manifestations of the wounds that Christ sustained at the time of his crucifixion (impressions on the brow from the crown of thorns, the hands and feet from the nails, and the side from the centurion's lance). Loretta had become obsessed with the stigmata, believing that by consulting with those who had been blessed with it, she could better understand it and perhaps experience it vicariously.

While in Italy, she met the mystic and stigmatist, Padre Pio, who was canonized by Pope John Paul II in 2002. Although he purportedly understood only Latin and Italian, Padre Pio was said to be able to hear confessions in any language, as if, like the apostles after Pentecost, he were endowed with the gift of tongues. Then Loretta flew to Germany to meet Teresa Neuman who, since she was twenty-nine, reportedly never ingested anything but the Eucharist. She too was a stigmatist, speaking, when questioned, in Aramaic, Christ's dialect. After hearing Loretta's rapturous description of her spiritual odyssey, an interviewer noted in a cynical aside that Loretta "had assumed an aura of inspiration . . . as if she were in a state of mystical repose." Still, the interviewer could not conceal his respect for Loretta and her unshakable belief in experiences that would strike many as too bizarre to be credible.

But Loretta was a convent school product who never shed her fascination with stories about the saints, true or apocryphal— especially those about their miracles and martyrdoms. Taught by the nuns that "the blood of martyrs is the seed of Christians," Loretta learned that, according to tradition (a phrase rarely used in her day): St. Peter was crucified upside down; Cecilia was beheaded after she survived suffocation in her bath; Ignatius of Antioch was thrown to the lions; Agatha was dragged over burning coals; Lawrence was roasted to death; and Bartholomew was flayed alive. Loretta must have graduated from convent school convinced that Catholicism was a religion written in blood, which courses liberally through its liturgy, devotions, and feasts: meditations on the Seven Last Words of Christ on Good Friday, and commemorative feast days such as The Finding of the Holy Cross (3 May), The Precious Blood of Jesus (1 July), The Seven Sorrows of the Virgin Mary (15 November). Each month of the liturgical calendar has its share of martyrs and their special masses, for example: the beheading of John the Baptist (29 August), the Forty Holy Martyrs (10 March), and the Holy Four Crowned Martyrs (8 November). The nuns had transformed Gretchen Young into the layperson's equivalent of themselves.

Loretta Young, however, was not Gretchen Young. Gretchen was the private self that Loretta revealed episodically, like a serial: the devout Catholic, patron of unmarried mothers, the actress with the swear box, friend of the clergy. Gretchen never lost her childhood fascination with the miracles in *The Greek New Testament*, which expanded her imagination into a stage—soon, a sound stage for Loretta—where truth mingled freely, sometimes playfully, with illusion, legend with doctrine, and apocrypha with the canon. Loretta Young was Gretchen's public self, her persona: film, radio, and television star; glamour queen; Oscar, Golden Globe, and Emmy winner; the exquisite butterfly that men tried to net until they discovered her wings could cut; the canny business executive whose manicured nails could spout claws, if necessary. Gretchen's first encounter with narrative came from the Bible, which provided ballast for some of the sinkable films that Loretta kept afloat by convincing first herself, and then the audience, that the movie was worth their time. Was the real Loretta the miracle-believing devotee of the Virgin Mary, who had become the equivalent of her role model? Or was she the actress who bore Clark Gable's daughter out of wedlock and, with the help of her studio, a gossip columnist, and a loyal and well-connected physician, devised a cover-up worthy of a woman's film? Gretchen was the child who never outgrew convent school; Loretta was the actress, who, finally at seventy-four, revealed that Gretchen would always be a part of her.

She did so in the interview that she gave Gregory Speck in 1987, in which she rhapsodized about Pope Pius XII, Padre Pio, and Teresa Neuman. She also spoke with the utmost candor about sex. Loretta was forty-three when she separated from Lewis. She did not remarry until 1993, when she was eighty and Lewis had been dead for five years: "I must say that for the first ten years I thought I would go crazy. It was very difficult going without sex. And you never lose that need until you die." Loretta felt the same need, perhaps even more strongly, when she was in her early twenties and on location with Clark Gable for *The Call of the Wild*. Inevitably, Speck broached the subject of Gable, to which Loretta replied more honestly than she had ever done before: "One could very easily fall in love with him, and if we did it was nobody's business but ours and clearly nothing to discuss, for he was married. . . . I will confess I love the idea of Clark and me falling in love and having Judy. I have to admit it's really a charming idea, very romantic." It was more than an idea, as Judy revealed and as Loretta confirmed shortly before her death.

Speck had a much higher regard for Loretta at the end of the interview than he did at the beginning, when he was greeted by a woman in her early seventies, swathed in green silk to match her eyes, with a rope of beads dangling from her long neck—as if, like *Sunset Boulevard*'s Norma Desmond, she was ready for her close up. He left, realizing that what he saw was an eidolon, an image that emanated from the actress to the camera—or, in this case, to the interviewer. Although he did not share Loretta's religious convictions, he understood from the look on her transfigured face, that she believed every word she uttered about the pope, the stigmatists, and the miraculous. He heard Gretchen speaking through Loretta, the fervent believer in signs and wonders decked out like a movie queen.

The 1957 trip to Europe was one of Loretta's defining moments. Whatever transpired between Loretta and the pontiff, or Padre Pio and Teresa Neuman, was too private to divulge. But it is clear that Loretta was spiritually rejuvenated and ready to embark on a mission to prove that miracles come in various forms, including the spiritual kind that scientists would dismiss for lack of proof, because they have no access to another's inner self—much less to a divine plan.

The year 1958 marked the Lourdes centennial, commemorating the apparition of the Virgin to Bernadette Soubirous in the grotto of Massabielle near Lourdes in 1858. The waters that sprang forth from the earth formed a pool, where millions have come, hoping to be cured of chronic ailments or terminal illness. Unusual cures, perhaps even miraculous ones, have been reported. But the real drama, the human drama, did not lie in miracles, the equivalent of deus ex machina endings, but in non-miracles—or rather miracles of a different sort—the serenity that comes with the acceptance of the ultimate reality, particularly from someone who had treated mortality lightly until, quite by accident, she came to Lourdes.

This was the kind of script Loretta wanted: an hour-long teleplay, a first for her show, about a converted agnostic.

In summer 1959, Loretta and her television crew flew to France for on-location filming. Richard Morris had written the kind of script she requested: a philanderer's wife, aware of her husband's dalliances with secretaries, but choosing to ignore them, books a flight to Paris for a second opinion about her diagnosis of brain cancer, only to hear a French neurologist confirm that she has an inoperable tumor. When cognac and painkillers prove to be only stopgap measures, she rents a car and heads for Spain, meeting on route a boy, who persuades her to visit Lourdes. The Lourdes sequences are impressive in their documentary simplicity, with the infirm in wheel chairs, stretchers, and mobile beds, lined up in rows, waiting to be brought to the pool. Lourdes transforms the woman from a denier to a believer; she accepts the inevitable with a newly found serenity. The miracle of Lourdes is not that the character became cancer-free, but that she became free of cancer and the fear that it engendered, which she tried to banish with alcohol.

The Polish-born Rudolph Maté was Loretta's personal choice for director. He had directed an earlier woman-with-terminal cancer picture, *No Sad Songs for Me* (1950), with great sensitivity, which he also revealed in the one film he and Loretta made together, *Paula* (1952), in addition to a number of her television shows. Maté could also take material that another director would have reduced to treacle and treat it with respect, as he did in *Sally and St. Anne* (1952), in which Ann Blyth's devotion to the saint had a disarming sincerity about it. Shooting on location posed no problem for Maté, who had proven in *D.O.A.* (1950) that he could deal with a gritty urban landscape—specifically, the dark streets of Los Angeles and San Francisco—without prettifying it. Under his direction, Loretta gave an extraordinary performance, revealing each facet of the character: the wealthy wife of a cheating husband who hides her humiliation behind a stoic façade; the terminal cancer patient who confronts mortality by drinking her way into the safety zone of denial; the second opinion seeker who jets across the Atlantic to Paris, only to receive a confirmation of the original diagnosis; the doubter who turns believer after being sidetracked to Lourdes. The role allowed Loretta to shed the veils of self-deception in which the character had wrapped herself. One scene in particular attests to the subtlety of which she was capable (and which critics so often ignored). Drinking one cognac after another in a bistro, she piles the glasses on top of each other as she flirts with the non-English- speaking bartender across the glass façade that she has erected. Beckoning to him to join her, she at first seems to be taking advantage of his inability to understand English. But when she realizes that, from his point of view, there is no language barrier if all she wants is sex, she merely wags her finger, signaling that a drinking companion, not a one-night stand, is all she is seeking. Richard Morris's script enabled Loretta to trace a real character arc, as a skeptic gradually becomes a believer, achieving a spiritual transformation that she does not fully understand but that is visible in her face, which is finally at peace.

The show aired on 20 September 1959. Morris's script was nominated for an Emmy, but lost to *The Twilight Zone*'s Rod Sterling. Still, *The Road* was notable for its adherence to the terminal illness template, epitomized by *Dark Victory* (1939), in which Judith Traherne (Bette Davis), diagnosed with terminal brain cancer, learns to meet death "finely, beautifully," as if dying were somehow an art that could be mastered. In this kind of script, there can be no last-minute wonder drug or a misdiagnosis. The 1979 television update of *Dark Victory* with Elizabeth Montgomery and the film remake, *Stolen Hours* (1963), with Susan Hayward in the Bette Davis role adhered to the rubric, which resembles a Greek tragedy, with the protagonist's fate determined at the outset, and the audience waiting for the inevitable to occur. When it does, it brings with it the catharsis that comes from the portrayal of death faced "finely, beautifully." Other such films—*No Sad Songs for Me, The Miniver Story* (1950), *Terms of Endearment* (1983), and *My Life* (1993)—scrupulously observe the "no *deus ex machina*" rule. In view of Loretta's belief in miracles, it was to her credit that she asked for a spiritual, not a physical, cure for her character. Significantly, when Loretta was diagnosed with ovarian cancer, she behaved no differently than the wife she played in "The Road." Loretta had also experienced the miracle of faith that allowed her to maintain a beatific tranquility in the face of death, as if, like Judith and her successors, she had mastered the Stoic *ars moriendi*, the art of dying.

While she was in Lourdes, Loretta received an urgent call from her agent, Norman Brokow, telling her that Proctor & Gamble would not sponsor a show about a subject whose main appeal was to Catholics. Fortified by a "God will provide" philosophy, she went ahead with the shoot. Meanwhile, Brokow managed to come up with two new sponsors: Toni, the leading manufacturer of home beauty products, and the equally well-known mouthwash, Listerine. Loretta knew her mission would continue: What was the difference between detergents, home permanents, and oral antiseptics? To her, they were all part of God's plan. Proctor & Gamble may have regretted its decision when "The Road" proved so popular that it was repeated the following year on 10 April 1960. By then, Lewislor was history; the company had been renamed Toreto Enterprises.

The change of company and sponsor extended the run of *The Loretta Young Show* to 1961. But television was changing. Anthology series were no longer in vogue. *Alfred Hitchcock Presents*, which premiered in 1960, may have seemed like an anthology show with Hitchcock's familiar "things-are-not-what-they-seem" tales. But the teleplays—macabre, slyly cynical, and sometimes ghoulish—were not aimed primarily at a female audience. Hitchcock evidenced no favoritism; even seasoned moviegoers must have been surprised when a perpetrator seemed to get away with murder, only to hear Hitchcock appear at the end to explain that the character got his or her comeuppance—but using such a tongue-in-cheek delivery that only a self-righteous literalist would believe it. Loretta had her audience, and the Master had his. His show lasted longer.

Even with the end of *The Loretta Young Show*, Loretta had no intention of abandoning television. She was now approaching fifty; if she returned to movies, she would have been labeled over-the-hill, at best a character actress or a grotesque in neo-horror films like *Whatever Happened to Baby Jane?*, *Straight-Jacket* (1964), and *The Nanny* (1965). Television offered longevity, but Loretta needed a new format—not an anthology series but a sitcom. Loretta was not meant for a sitcom, much less one with herself as a widow with seven children. She must have believed in the concept, and some of the old team felt similarly. Producer John London, associate producer and story editor Ruth Roberts, and Toni stayed on. Loretta needed another sponsor and found one in Lever Brothers, a detergents and soap (Lifebuoy, Dove, Lever 2000) manufacturer. Loretta also acquired a new network, CBS, and a new day, Monday. The time slot remained the same: 10:00 p.m.–10:30 p.m.

Loretta was determined to make *The New Loretta Young Show* every bit as successful as her anthology series. Her character was a magazine writer, Christine Massey. Making Massey a widow with kids might have worked if Loretta had an antic side like Lucille Ball or a flair for screwball like Jean Arthur and Irene Dunne. The show should have been the flip side of *My Three Sons*, in which Fred MacMurray played a widower raising three boys by himself. That sitcom endeared itself to audiences and lasted a record twelve years, 1960–72. Part of the show's charm lay in MacMurray's ability to look befuddled, bemused, and even a bit pixilated at times—overwhelmed but never overcome by an ever-expanding household. *The New Loretta Young Show* needed a touch of the antic, but Loretta only seemed able to reveal her screwball self on radio; when she tried in film, notably in *A Night to Remember*, she simply seemed uncomfortable. Loretta wanted the show to appeal to children, particularly teenagers and their parents, but making five of Christine's children girls was hardly conducive to variety.

Perhaps the solution lay in the casting. The right child actors would give the show plausibility, freeing Loretta for episodes in which she would alternate between dealing with their problems and being courted by her editor, adding a romantic dimension and making the series more palatable to those who were put off by the star-as-widow concept. Thus Loretta was determined to get the perfect septet. All the children had excellent credentials. Portland Mason (Marnie), the daughter of James Mason and his then wife, Pamela, had done theatre and television. Beverly Washburn (Vickie) appeared in such movies as *Hans Christian Andersen* (1952) and *Shane* (1953), as well as on television's *Playhouse 90, General Electric Theatre,* and *Professional Father.* The sixteen-year-old Sandy Descher (Judy) started in the business when she was six and had built up an impressive résumé that included *The June Allyson Show, General Electric Theatre,* and *I Led Three Lives.* Carol Sykes (Binkie) appeared on major sitcoms such as *Father Knows Best, Leave It to Beaver,* and *The Donna Reed Show.* Tracy Stratford (Maria) made her acting debut in the film *The Miracle of the Bells* (1948) and went on to television, where she was featured in *The Twilight Zone, Kraft Mystery Theatre, Bonanza,* and *Ben Casey.* Either Loretta or her writers thought that having two twin sons—twins being a perennial source of humor in comedies about mistaken identity (Plautus's *Menaechmi,* Shakespeare's *The Comedy of Errors* and *Twelfth Night*)—would make *The New Loretta Young Show* different from the traditional sitcom. Finding twins who were teenage actors, was a tall order, which producer John London filled by casting two actual twins, Dirk and Dack Rambo, ranch hands with no acting experience, in the parts. Except for the Rambos, Loretta had assembled a cast of young professionals.

One of the actresses did not live up to Loretta's expectations; the actress's mother thought otherwise. Loretta should have anticipated problems from Portland Mason's mother, Pamela, formerly Pamela Kellino and the wife of the honey-voiced actor, James Mason. Portland was a child of privilege, the prototypical "daddy's little girl." Mason doted on his daughter, and stories circulated that she had her first designer gown at four, diamonds at six, and a mink at seven. Mason was convinced Portland could be an actress and had her cast in two of his films, *Bigger Than Life* (1956) and *Cry Terror* (1958). Just before *The New Loretta Young Show* was ready for filming, Mason walked out on his wife, which led to an ugly divorce in 1964.

Although James was out of the picture, Pamela was very much in it. She was a fame seeker who achieved some success with her syndicated shows, *The Pamela Mason Show* and *The Weaker (?) Sex.* She had the kind of acerbic wit that passed for urbanity and appealed to viewers with a taste for mordant humor.

Loretta was no match for Pamela Mason, who wanted a career for her daughter and headlines—or at least celebrity—for herself. When Loretta decided to replace Portland, Pamela retaliated, branding Loretta "a dictator . . . shouting orders, running around . . . and doing all manners of things which don't match with her saintly soul." The most damning charge was Pamela's refusal to buy her daughter's wardrobe from the dress store owned by Loretta's half sister, Georgianna. Portland, however, believed that the reason for her dismissal was Loretta's fear that the Masons' marital problems would escalate into divorce and impact negatively on the show. Nothing would stand in the way of Loretta's achieving another record run for her new show, even a child actress. To Loretta, it was all very simple: Portland must be replaced.

Loretta, ever gracious, sent a note to Portland: "Dear Portland—I shall miss you very much." The note was merely a gesture of propriety, the equivalent of a bread-and-butter letter after a dismal dinner party. Determined to keep her name and her daughter's media-fresh, Pamela slapped Loretta with a $138,000 lawsuit, with Portland as plaintiff. Loretta never expected such a brouhaha over a dismissal. But Pamela used the incident to tarnish Loretta's angelic reputation, occasioning a damning headline in the *Los Angeles Times* (3 August 1962 C14): "Is Loretta Young Image Blurred?" It was not so much blurred as questioned, with Loretta emerging as a saint with a tarnished halo.

Historically, even saints have stepped out of the celestial spotlight, casting a dark shadow that makes them more human than statue. St. Martha was jealous of Christ's preference for the company of her sister, Mary; Peter Celestine was a papal misfit who ended up being canonized; the mother of the apostles James and John believed her sons should sit on either side of Christ's heavenly throne, and they thought so, too. Even Christ had a temper: When he saw oxen, sheep, and doves being sold in the temple of Jerusalem, he made a whip of cords and lashed the sellers out of the temple, overturning the tables of the money changers in the process (John 2: 13–16), Hollywood's Catholic elite often appeared without their nimbus. Bing Crosby was an indifferent father and an uncaring husband to his first wife, Dixie. His portrayal of Father O'Malley in both *Going My Way* (1944) and *The Bells of St. Mary's* (1945) was a testimonial to his acting ability; he was certainly not playing himself. Rosalind Russell railed at Jerome Lawrence and Robert E. Lee for converting her stage hit, *Auntie Mame*, into a musical with Angela Lansbury—as if Russell, with her four good notes, could negotiate Jerry Herman's lush score.

Spencer Tracy was an alcoholic who remained faithful to his wife while continuing in a relationship with Katharine Hepburn that may just have been platonic, although few thought so. Frank Sinatra returned to the fold and was buried from the Church of the Good Shepherd, although he was hardly an exemplary Catholic. And Loretta, as we know, had her "mortal sin." Only Joan Leslie and Irene Dunne were seemingly above reproach.

Catholicism, however, had no bearing on Loretta's decision to countersue for $100,000, charging Portland with failing to fulfill her contractual obligations by not supplying a proper wardrobe. The case attracted attention because of its unusual nature: a sixteen-year-old actress suing a movie star pushing fifty. Nothing dramatic happened until 5 April 1965, when Jack Murton, Toreto's casting director, collapsed in the aisle after leaving the witness stand. Loretta bolted from her seat and rushed over, knowing that he carried nitroglycerine tablets for his heart condition. Fumbling around in his jacket, Loretta located them and pressed one under his tongue, but to no avail. Murton was rushed to Santa Monica Hospital, where he died. The case was resolved less than two weeks later in Portland's favor. However, she was not awarded $138,000, but only $2,800. Loretta's countersuit was dismissed.

In 1965, *The New Loretta Young Show* was, if anything, a footnote in television history. Even if Loretta relented and allowed Portland to continue on the show, it would have done nothing for Portland's career, just as it did nothing for the career of Celia Kaye, the actress who replaced her. Both continued to work, with Portland even appearing in Oscar Wilde's *A Woman of No Importance* in London's West End. Sadly, Portland's career was cut short by her death from a stroke in 2004 at the age of fifty-five. Celia Kaye had a more extensive résumé, with appearances on such series as *Little House on the Prairie*, *The Young Lawyers*, and *The Green Hornet*, in addition to a few movies, none of which led to a major career. But at least the two had a life after Loretta.

If Loretta overreacted or became abusive on the set, it was mainly because she was uncomfortable with the sitcom format. With *The Loretta Young Show*, she was on home ground, starring in the equivalent of half-hour movies with a different script each week. Sitcom was terra incognita. If Loretta's story editor and producer believed that viewers would be interested in watching her interact with a bunch of kids as they waited for her to do a star turn in another episode, they must have thought otherwise after the ratings, which were so dismal that the sponsors terminated the show after twenty-six weeks. In the final episode,

Christine married her editor, leaving faithful viewers, few though they were, with the hope that a future series about a writer and editor couple would emerge from the wreckage. It did not. What *The New Loretta Young Show* proved was that audiences wanted Loretta neat, not with children on the side.

Loretta's television career was not entirely over. She would return for two hour-long television dramas—the first in 1986, at seventy-three; the second, three years later.

CHAPTER 22

A New Life

Despite the failure of *The New Loretta Young Show* to repeat the success of the first series, Loretta had not given up on either television or film. In the 1960s, Hollywood's drama queens of yesteryear, eager to continue working, accepted roles requiring them to play grotesques (Bette Davis in *Whatever Happened to Baby Jane?*, *The Nanny*); women entrapped and terrorized by punks (Olivia de Havilland in *Lady in a Cage*), or tormented by relatives (Bette Davis by cousin Olivia de Havilland in *Hush . . . Hush, Sweet Charlotte*; Joan Crawford by sister Davis in *Baby Jane*, and by daughter Diane Baker in *Strait-Jacket*). Strange as it seems, Loretta was thinking of joining the dark sisterhood.

The phenomenal success of *Baby Jane*, legitimized by an Oscar nomination for Davis, led to another film in which Davis and Crawford would costar, this time with Davis as victim, and Crawford as victimizer. The film became Twentieth Century-Fox's *Hush . . . Hush, Sweet Charlotte* (1964), with Davis, but not Crawford, who came down with pneumonia and canceled. Barbara Stanwyck and Loretta were rumored to be possible replacements. Loretta's would have been the better performance, since her character was a woman of charm and poise with an agenda that is only revealed at the end. Basically, she wants to get Davis, her cousin, institutionalized, not knowing that she is not as loony as she seems. Understandably, Fox thought of Loretta for the role of a woman who concealed her malevolence behind a saintly façade. Loretta had never played such a character; after reading the script, she decided she never would: "I don't believe in horror stories for women." Yet it would have been a good role for Loretta, giving her an opportunity to step out of the starlight and into the dark of the moon.

But for Loretta, there was only the bright side of the moon. She was not interested in altering her image, but Olivia deHavilland, also known for her feminine grace and gentility, accepted the challenge, having played twins—one good, the other evil—in *The Dark Mirror* (1946). In 1982, Norman Brokow approached her with the possibility of starring in two television films: The first was fictitious, chronicling the trials of the first female president of the United States; the second was factual, the life of Mother Angelica, the nun who launched the Eternal Word Television Network. Loretta could have managed the first (she ran for Congress in *The Farmer's Daughter* and played a mayor in *Key to the City*), but she was too glamorous to be a convincing Mother Angelica. In the long run, it didn't matter, since neither program came to pass.

Three years later, Loretta was in the news again; she signed on as the lead in the prime time return of ABC's popular daytime serial, *Dark Shadows*, whose ghoulish ambience kept it on the air from 1966 to 1971. The new *Dark Shadows* would be a TV movie that one of the industry's most successful producers, Aaron Spelling, hoped would evolve into an evening series. That Loretta was even interested in starring as the matriarch of a vampire-haunted estate is unusual, but Spelling convinced her that the series would have less of the occult and more of the religious, informing the press that her character, Margaret Drake, is "the fabric that holds two families together [and] fights for morality when others lose theirs." That was Loretta's kind of woman. She did all the screen tests and even had Jean Louis design her gowns. But when it came time to film the pilot, she bowed out, citing "creative differences" with Spelling over the way her character was being developed. Joan Fontaine was announced as her replacement, but also demurred. *Dark Shadows* finally turned up on NBC with Jean Simmons in the lead, lasting only a few months, 13 January–22 March 1991. Vampirism was not as intriguing as it had been in the 1960s, although it made a comeback in 1997 with *Buffy the Vampire Slayer*. But in 1991, viewers with a preference for the flip side of the cheery sitcom preferred *Murder, She Wrote* or *Unsolved Mysteries* to middlebrow gothic.

Loretta may have toyed with the dark side, but, to her, brightness was all. So was her television legacy. Accepting the debacle of *The New Loretta Young Show* as an ill-conceived bid for sitcom fame, she was determined that its failure would not undermine her pioneer work in anthology television. Apart from her Emmys, Emmy nominations, and Golden Globes, *The Loretta Young Show* could rest on its laurels. It was in syndication, both in the States and abroad in thirty-three countries, including Syria, Thailand, Cyprus, Brazil, Hong Kong, and New Zealand. As long as the series remained in syndication, NBC had to honor the terms of her contract, one of which required the deletion of her entrance/welcome and her mini-sermon sign offs, which were abbreviated fashion shows, with wardrobe and hairstyle changing from episode to episode, but always reflecting the styles of the era. Since the series ended in 1961, Loretta did not want to be seen a decade later in anything that had become passé. Her character's costumes were another matter; they were determined by the script. But the entrances and exits were Loretta's way of acknowledging her designers and supplying women with a dream wardrobe that, if nothing else, would make them envious enough to tune in every Sunday night. When NBC failed to eliminate the entrances and exits for foreign syndication, Loretta sued for $1.3 million, including payment for the opening and closing segments. NBC countered, insisting that the accountant, Robert Shewalter, had granted the network oral permission. Although Shewalter was subpoenaed and was in attendance, he was never called to testify. Instead, the litigious footage was shown in the courtroom. A year later, the breach-of-contract suit was resolved in Loretta's favor. She did not get $1.3 million, but $559,000 was not bad take-home money.

One would like to believe that audiences worldwide assumed that Loretta's choice of wardrobe was partially dictated by trends, but more by her instinct for choosing outfits consistent with her image. Fashion can transcend time. The creations of Adrian, Travis Banton, Edith Head, and Jean Louis that adorned the stars of Hollywood's Golden Age can still awe in their unerring ability to capture period, style, and mood, so that when they are seen, even in the twenty-first century, they are timeless, bridging the years between their era and the viewer's. It is the same with television: When a show goes off the air, it moves into history, where it plays a role, however slight, in the development of the medium, studied in depth or relegated to a footnote. To call any show "dated" is to ignore the age in which it is set and the ethos it reflects. Perhaps some of Loretta's costumes seemed quaint, but they suited her hostess image.

In America, viewers seemed less tolerant of the settlement. The *Los Angeles Times* ran a series of letters that were highly critical of Loretta: "I would like to know what Miss Young . . . is going to do with her $559,000—buy new clothes?"; "Did my tax money pay for her jury?"; "I hope that NBC fights to the last penny to get a reversal."; "Loretta underestimates the intelligence of TV viewers." Only one writer expressed sympathy: "NBC shouldn't have made the contract unless it intended to honor it." Loretta may have underestimated the intelligence of her viewers. One can hardly imagine Cyprians, Syrians, or New Zealanders scoffing at her costumes—although maybe at her choreographed entrance.

Since Loretta had programmed herself into a litigious mode, she was even ready to take on her old studio, Twentieth Century-Fox, when she discovered that it planned to use a clip from *The Story of Alexander Graham Bell* (1939) in *Myra Breckinridge* (1970), the execrable film version of Gore Vidal's brilliantly satiric novel. In the film, which was midway between sleaze and low camp, a shot from a film from the past would be edited into a scene for no other purpose than to elicit a cheap laugh. Someone at Fox had selected a shot from *The Story of Alexander Graham Bell*, in which Loretta dreamily beseeched Don Ameche, "Don't move. Don't even breathe. I want to remember this moment all my life," to be intercut with Myra's rape of Rusty with a dildo. When Loretta learned about the context, she was furious. Claiming that the film "depicts unnatural sex acts," she filed for an injunction against the studio, threatening a $10 million lawsuit. Loretta prevailed; she had spent too much time and money creating her image, and had no intention of seeing it sullied. Instead, the victim was the minor Laurel and Hardy film, *Great Guns* (1941), in which the rape was juxtaposed with a shot of Sheila Ryan cheering lustily.

Until an offer she could not refuse came her way, Loretta occupied herself with other activities after the failure of *The New Loretta Young Show*. She spent almost two years traveling around the world. Upon her return, she hit the lecture circuit. The subject? "The subject is me .... What else do I know about?" Loretta knew more than she let on—until it was time for a press release. That she understood fashion was evident to anyone who watched her show. Loretta did not wear a wedding gown when she married Tom Lewis in 1940; it would not have been appropriate for a woman who had been previously married, as the teenage Loretta had been to Grant Withers. But bridal gowns fascinated her, and in 1968, she joined Bridal Showcase International, even allowing her name and photo to be used. Bridal Showcase was a bridal salon franchise and thus not quite so manageable as an autonomous company. Loretta came on board in March 1968; by the end of August, she had resigned, claiming that the company did not measure up to her standards. According to the *Wall St. Journal* (30 August 1968), Bridal Showcase felt otherwise: Loretta's lack of retail experience, the company claimed, did not equip her for the task. Four years later, she was on the verge of launching a cosmetics line, but nothing came of that, either.

For someone with a work ethic, Loretta found little comfort in retirement. If there were gold in the golden years, she had yet to mine it. Loretta became restless, searching for projects but never finding one that would bring either the success or fulfillment she was seeking. She did not despair; in fact, her faith grew stronger. Her piety may have struck scoffers as incipient senility, yet it was not all that different from the spirituality of her youth—except that it had acquired a mystical cast. Churches took on a special aura for her, as if the Holy Spirit brooded over them. She was fond of quoting a childlike prayer, perhaps one she composed herself: "Each time I pass a church / I stop in for a visit. / Comes the day they wheel me in, / the Lord won't say: 'Who is it?'" Once a week Loretta volunteered at hospitals, where she read to patients, who must have felt that they were blessed with a heavenly visitation. On Sundays, she often accompanied a priest friend to Los Angeles's then seedy Skid Row, where he ministered to homeless women, many of whom gravitated to her and felt better about themselves after being in her presence.

But not everyone was impressed by Loretta's religious fervor. When one of Joan Crawford's backgammon partners dropped by her New York condo during a snowstorm and, exhausted, sank down on an antique chair, Crawford snapped, "Oh! Don't sit there! Gretchen just sat there and she left the shape of the cross." It is interesting that Crawford referred to Loretta as "Gretchen." But as she moved into her sixties, Loretta became more like Gretchen and less like Loretta. Loretta Young was one of the wealthiest women in Hollywood, having made some sound investments in real estate, including the elegant Beverly Wilshire Hotel, when Hernando Courtright purchased it for $6 million in 1961. Twenty-five years later, Regent International Hotels bought it from Courtright for $125 million, making the other investors, including Kirk Douglas and Irene Dunne, richer than they were before. Loretta was a woman of wealth, but money without good works does not guarantee salvation. She was determined that the Lord would not ask, "Who is it?" when her casket was brought into the church. To Loretta, even acting was a prayer, a form of repaying God for what had been given her: "God gave me this face . . . and I've made a lot of money with it. I should be grateful and I am."

If Loretta were living in 2007, she also would have been grateful to her son Christopher and his wife Linda when the DVD, *The Road to Lourdes and Other Miracles of Faith* (VCI Entertainment) was released in commemoration of the 150th anniversary of the Virgin's apparitions to Bernadette. In addition to *The Road*, the disc included the three Sister Ann episodes from *The Loretta Young Show*, Christopher Lewis's description of the making of *The Road*, and Linda Lewis's account of the Lourdes miracles. Christopher, relaxed and clearly proud of his mother, emerged as a born storyteller, leaving the viewer with a renewed respect for both mother and son.

Loretta went back to her familiar routine, performing acts of mercy and collecting awards. In April 1981, she was honored with a career retrospective at the Los Angeles International Film Exposition (FILMEX). She had not lost the art of making an entrance. Wearing a sheath dress, her neck bedecked with pearls, Loretta assumed a regal pose in a director's chair. No director ever looked like Loretta. Even as sixty-seven, Loretta was "cherce," as Spencer Tracy called Katharine Hepburn in *Woman of the Year* (1942). Loretta was "cherce" personified, charming her audience as she recounted highlights from her career: Herbert Brenon throwing a chair at her during the filming of *Laugh, Clown, Laugh*; feuding with Darryl Zanuck; winning an unexpected Oscar for *The Farmer's Daughter*; and making her four favorite films: *The Farmer's Daughter, Rachel and the Stranger, Come to the Stable*, and, surprisingly, *The Men in Her Life* (perhaps included because of the discipline it required of the then twenty-seven old actress to give a convincing portrayal of a ballerina).

In 1987, she was given the Golda Meir award. Although Golda Meir had been an Israeli prime minister, Loretta was not singled out for her support of Israel but, according to *Variety* (15 May 1997), for her dedication to human values such as working with the homeless and volunteering at veterans' hospitals. The following year she was one of six recipients of the Women in Film's Crystal Awards, and she received a standing ovation when she was introduced at the awards ceremony. Loretta echoed what some of the other honorees admitted, addressing the paucity of women in high places and the difficulties aspiring female executives faced when they tried to break through the glass ceiling in a male-dominated business, whose motto seems to have been "Separate and unequal." Recalling the Hollywood of her day, Loretta described a business in which, "[O]ther than actresses, there was the script girl, a wardrobe girl, maybe a stand-in . . . . There was one female editor back then, Margaret Booth."

Actually, there were other editors, although none as well known as MGM's Booth. Ten of the sixteen feature films directed by Dorothy Arzner, who managed to break through the glass ceiling and land behind the camera, were edited by women: Doris Drought (*Manhattan Cocktail*), Verna Willis (*Sarah and Son*), Jane Lorring (*Anybody's Woman, Working Girls, Merrily We Go to Hell, Christopher Strong*), Helen Turner (*Honor Among Lovers*), Viola Lawrence (*Craig's Wife, First Comes Courage*), and Adrienne Fazan (*The Bride Wore Red*). Loretta apparently forgot that Viola Lawrence, who joined Columbia in 1933, edited two of her films, *The Doctor Takes a Wife* and *He Stayed for Breakfast*. Like all film editors, Lawrence cut both B movies and classics, including Howard Hawks's *Only Angels Have Wings* (1939) and Orson Welles's *The Lady from Shanghai* (1948). Yet another female editor who may not have been as famous as Margaret Booth was Darryl Zanuck's favorite: Barbara McLean, who won an Oscar for editing a movie that meant more to Zanuck than it did to audiences: *Wilson* (1944). It's difficult to imagine Loretta's not being aware of McLean while she was at Fox. McLean edited three of her films, *The House of Rothschild, Love Under Fire,* and *Suez,* as well as some of Fox's biggest hits, such as *In Old Chicago* (1938), *The Rains Came* (1938), *Jesse James* (1939), and the multi-Oscar winner (best picture, supporting actor, director, screenplay, sound recording, and costume design), *All About Eve* (1950). During the studio years, women were well represented in the editing room, the closest most of them ever got to the executive suite.

Loretta adhered to the theme of the evening: the progress women made in the Hollywood boys club, concentrating on the absence of women in key positions during her tenure. Still, she could not resist giving a homily. Noting the strides women had made since her day, she went into uplift mode: "You bring your sensitivity, intuition and spirit in wanting to create and inspire and educate. Knowingly or unknowingly, you put that in the films you do." That was nothing compared to the homily she delivered three weeks later at the National Conference of Christians and Jews (NCCJ), an organization devoted to promoting racial and religious harmony. Loretta arrived in a wheelchair because of a leg injury, but when Sidney Poitier, who was hosting the event, introduced her, she rose and walked to the podium, which became her pulpit. She acknowledged Christianity's Jewish roots, noting that the religions are "braided, interwoven, intertwined—and never to be separated." She was sincere when she called Christianity a "demanding" religion, but then added: "I don't think I could live one day more—not one day more—without it." She ended with a rousing peroration: "So tonight I boldly and unhesitatingly beg God to bless all of us in all of our efforts and everything that you're trying to do for Him—all of us, all of His children, all over the world."

Loretta's zeal may have struck some as a bid for the title of Our Lady of Hollywood, yet she was as sincere as any missionary who believed that the age of the apostles had not ended, but had evolved into the age of the personal apostolate, in which the individual embarks on his or her own crusade, promoting and defending the faith, whatever it may be. For Loretta, faith was not so much Christian as Catholic, her brand. To Loretta, Catholicism was the true faith, just as the cross the Emperor Constantine's mother, Helena, discovered in Jerusalem in the fourth century (said to be the cross on which Christ was crucified) was known as the true cross. Loretta knew that some scoffed at her commitment to the Church, regarding it as self-canonization, yet whenever she spoke of religion, it was with such conviction that even the most jaded interviewers did not question her belief, even if they could not comprehend the spiritual depths from which it came. Ten years before she died, Loretta, then seventy-eight, spoke philosophically about her religion, which—demanding as it is—establishes limits within which we must live our lives, and beyond which we should not venture: "My belief in God is the main thing . . . . Religion gives us strength. It tells us how far we can and cannot go . . . . Take the qualities you have and build on them and pray to find out what God wants of you. Oh, I know some people think I'm a prude. 'Holier than thou Loretta,' they say . . . . Well, that's their business. *Me?* I believe in establishing limits and setting standards, because you can't be happy without them. And I'm *happy!*" To Loretta, happiness, faith, and prayer were all interconnected. She had much for which to be happy: financial security, and a distinguished career that might have been aborted if Hollywood had not closed ranks and protected her from newshounds and moralists after she bore Judy. Loretta would have argued that her conspirators were really God's emissaries, carrying out a divinely ordained mission on behalf of a repentant sinner, whose faith saved her from the crucifying press. Loretta understood that her transgression caused her to transcend the boundaries set by her religion and career and deviate from their standards. She vowed that she would never again wander into enemy territory.

The 1980s were especially meaningful to Loretta, not just because she was lavished with honors and awards, but because of her triumphant return to television on 22 December 1986 in *Christmas Eve* on NBC's Monday Night at the Movies. Her television career had come full-circle, beginning and ending at NBC—not in a half-hour series but in two two-hour films. *Christmas Eve* could easily have been a tear-duct opener—had it not been for Blanche Hanalis's script with its honest sentimentality, and Stuart Cooper's direction that observed the line of demarcation between poignancy and emotional manipulation. It is easy to understand Loretta's attraction to the script. The character, Amanda Kingsley, was very much like Loretta: a woman of enormous wealth who goes out with her Jeeves-like butler (Trevor Howard) on nightly forays to dispense money, food, and encouragement to the homeless. (They also befriend stray cats and bring them back for rehabilitation.) Learning that she has an inoperable aneurysm, Amanda makes use of what little time she has to locate her three grandchildren, who became so estranged from their coldly indifferent father (Arthur Hill) that they left home without forwarding addresses. Determined to have them back for what might be her last Christmas Eve, Amanda hires a private investigator (Ron Leibman, in a beautifully understated performance) to locate them, enabling Hanalis to intercut the New York sequences with the investigator's trips to Nashville, Los Angeles, and Toronto to track them down.

Hanalis was not an arbitrary choice. She had written the screenplays for *The Trouble with Angels* (1966) and its sequel, *Where Angels Go...Trouble Follows* (1968). Loretta's fascination with angels was not the reason for signing on to *Christmas Eve*; the "angels" in the two movies were rambunctious girls in a convent school. The reason was the films themselves, which were informed by a Catholic sensibility. While Catholicism was not a theme in *Christmas Eve*, Loretta's character was the embodiment of the perfect Christian, as she went about performing spiritual and corporal works of mercy. Loretta was totally believable as a benefactor of the underclass; but so was Leibman, who made the character's investigative technique—a combination of deduction and networking—refreshingly credible. That Hanalis handed Loretta and Leibman a script without loopholes or loose ends made it easy for them to flesh out their characters. Although the terminal illness plot does not allow for a misdiagnosis, *Christmas Eve* is really about the reunion, not Amanda's aneurysm. We know she will not make a pilgrimage to Lourdes; Loretta had already gone down that route in *The Road*. Hanalis sustained audience interest by posing three questions: Will the trio arrive in time? Will the son drop his mental incompetency case against his mother? Will the yuletide spirit bring the family together? The script was not entitled "*Christmas Eve*" for nothing.

It was a perfect role for Loretta. At seventy-three, her cheekbones were still clearly defined, and artfully applied makeup erased time's fingerprints. Having gained ten pounds after breaking her smoking habit, she was less svelte than she had been in her salad days. With hair looking like a swirl of silver, and pastel sheaths flowing down her frame, Loretta appeared to have had a heavenly makeover. Although she had been off the screen for almost a quarter of a century, she was still every inch an actress. She had not lost the art of radiating spirituality, even though she was not playing a nun, just a wealthy liberal with a mission: finding housing for the homeless, including cats. Some of the lines reflected Loretta's philosophy as much as they did Amanda's. In the scene in which Amanda tells a dying woman (Kate Reid) that she is a "child of God who loves you dearly," one could envision Loretta saying the same to a patient in one of the hospitals where she volunteered. When she explains to a group of children how the dove came to symbolize peace, she uses a parable, describing the time a dove alighted on a battlefield, inspiring the combatants to drop their weapons and walk toward each other in a gesture of reconciliation. Significantly, when the Christmas Eve reunion has ended, Amanda notices a dove on her terrace, which then flies off. Amanda is now at peace and ready for what Peter Pan in James M. Barrie's play (act 3) calls "an awfully big adventure."

Loretta held her own, despite formidable competition from Trevor Howard, as the quintessential English butler, who could easily have walked off with the film (as John Gielgud did when he played a similar character in *Arthur*). But like a typical manservant, Maitland knows his place—and it is not in the limelight. Still, it was a rich performance, in addition to one of Howard's last. Trevor Howard died the following year. The script also made demands on Leibman and Hill. Leibman is not a Hollywood "private eye," laconic and dispassionate like Humphrey Bogart in *The Maltese Falcon* and *The Big Sleep*. As he meets each of the three grandchildren, he behaves more like a father figure, making them feel slightly guilty for ignoring the grandmother they claim they adore, but never chastising them for their thoughtlessness. Hill had to project a severe rigidity that his children equated with lovelessness. But, again, Christmas Eve can bring about miraculous changes, with the embittered growing mellow and the loveless dispensing love, as the estranged are reconciled and reptilian eyes give way to pools of compassion.

Loretta also had a challenging role. Amanda may have been an affluent matron, dressed like a grand dame at home, but she wears pants and a working class coat when she and Maitland went about performing nocturnal acts of charity. She knew the difference between eccentric and certifiable, making Amanda's mission more like normal behavior—at least for those with a social conscience. Loretta only made a few films in Technicolor, which was too flamboyant for her delicate features. Color television was more congenial, avoiding the theatricality of a process that called attention to its lush palette. The mellow lighting and the soft colors of the costumes coalesced in a visual style familiar to 1986 viewers, who knew they were not watching a 1940s MGM Technicolor film. Loretta was proud of *Christmas Eve:* "It took out football on Monday night." It also won her a Golden Globe for best actress in a television movie.

Lady in a Corner, her next and last NBC Monday movie, was telecast two weeks before Christmas, on 11 December 1989. In many ways, it was a more contemporary film, reflecting the mergermania and corporate takeovers whereby once freestanding companies—networks, newspapers, publishing houses and movie studios—became subsidiaries of corporations. Paramount was engulfed by Gulf + Western in 1966. In 1985, Twentieth Century-Fox became part of Rupert Murdoch's News Corporation, which also included the *New York Post,* HarperCollins, and Basic Books. Time Inc. acquired Warner Communications in 1989, resulting in Time Warner. The same year, Sony bought Columbia Pictures. A year later, another Japanese company, Matsushita, the world's largest manufacturer of consumer electronic goods, bought MCA, a package that included Universal Pictures, Universal Television, MCA Records, and Universal Tours in Los Angeles and Orlando. And this was just the beginning. Owners would change, subsidiaries would be spun off, and eventually the day would come when even the big three networks, NBC, CBS, and ABC, would become cogs in the corporate wheel: NBC in General Electric's, CBS in Viacom's, and ABC in Disney's.

In *Lady in a Corner,* Grace Guthrie (Loretta), the editor-in-chief of a fashion magazine that bears her name, bucks the trend of showing sullen-looking models with arms crossed on bare breasts. She regards such magazines as pornographic. She meets her match when a hotshot editor, Susan Dawson (Lindsay Frost), becomes the anointed of a Rupert Murdoch-like media tycoon (Christopher Neame), who plans to replace Grace with Susan after taking over the magazine. Will the magazine be swallowed up by a ruthless British empire-builder, or will Grace be able to raise enough money from like-minded millionaires to purchase the company herself? If she succeeds, will Grace work with Susan to bring the magazine into the next century without compromising her values? Will Grace and her partner (Brian Keith) legitimize their autumnal romance in marriage? And did Loretta extract a quarter from Keith for the Swear Box when he said "Hell," as mandated by the script? Again, the show was aired two weeks before Christmas, when media pirates do not hijack decent magazines and turn them into softcore. But it is a time when late-life romances end at the altar, and swear boxes are shelved with other relics of the past. Loretta at least had the satisfaction of knowing that she appeared in a truly contemporary television movie reflecting her own standards of decency, which she assumed were shared by her viewers. But whether the viewers appreciated the intelligence of the script depends on how knowledgeable they were about the corporatization of the media. Probably not too many were. To most of them, it was a Capra upgrade, another individual vs. the establishment movie.

There was nothing simplistic about *Lady in a Corner*. To survive, a magazine might have to become part of a conglomerate. A magazine must also accommodate the evolving taste of its readers. When *The New Yorker*, renowned for its sophistication and stylistic elegance, began printing stories with four-letter words, purists were shocked. Yet there was no lowering of standards; the magazine still printed quality fiction, poetry, criticism, and globe-spanning articles. Viewers were not left with the idea that it would be business as usual at *Grace* magazine. Grace appoints Susan as her successor, and at a staff meeting asks that she sit next to her. Susan declines, choosing to sit opposite her—the young Turk facing the old guard. Is this a face-off or a compromise? Susan sports a triumphant smile, but Grace flashes a wily one. Capitulation or cooperation? Loretta capitulate? Did she ever? Compromise? Every actress does for the sake of the film.

For her final television appearance, Loretta did not look her best. Pants were a mistake; her weight gain left an abdominal bulge and a drooping backside. Suits were no help, either. Sheaths did the trick in *Christmas Eve*, but she needed a different wardrobe to minimize the extra inches that encircled her waist. And there was also the matter of Loretta's voice. She seems to have had some kind of dental problem, creasing the sides of her mouth as she spoke, as if she were going to whistle the lines. She did not sound like the old Loretta, but she was still the pro, always in character, particularly at the end when she had to come to terms with a changing readership and name the former editor from *Foxy Girl* as her successor.

Like Grace Guthrie, Loretta had made peace with the present. She still had more to do as she approached the last decade of her life.

CHAPTER 23

The Last Reel

Early in her career, Loretta was romantically linked with several men, including director Edward Sutherland; actors Spencer Tracy, Clark Gable, and Tyrone Power; a British polo player; and a shady lawyer. All were attracted to her beauty, just as she was to their varying degrees of masculinity: paternal, carnal, androgynous, and protective. Most were older than she; some, significantly so (Gable, twelve years; Tracy, thirteen; Sutherland, eighteen). She and Power were the same age; they would have made a smashing couple, except that during the *Suez* shoot (1938), Power discovered the gamine-like Anabella in the supporting cast and married her the following year.

Tom Lewis was another "older" man—eleven years Loretta's senior, to be exact. It would be simplistic to reduce their courtship to Loretta's quest for a father figure to compensate for the desertion of John Earle Young. Ironically, his desertion brought Loretta to Los Angeles, where she became a bona fide movie star at fifteen. For someone attuned to the divine will, as Loretta was, Young's abandoning his family was providential. Eventually, everyone prospered, which would probably not have been the case if he stayed. Conversely, was Lewis contemplating a brilliant marriage to a Hollywood star? Or was he really in love with Gretchen, saving Loretta for his radio, and later television, productions? Loretta and Lewis were in their late twenties and late thirties, respectively, when they married in 1940. Riotous youth had passed, along with the heyday of the blood. Loretta was no longer a teenage fantasist or a moonstruck ingénue, flaunting convention even by Hollywood's liberal standards and socializing with a married man—much less a married Catholic, like Spencer Tracy. Neither was she reacting to Gable's erotic instant messaging with her easily decodable body language, which William Wellman and some of the *Call of the Wild* cast, particularly Jack Oakie, had no trouble deciphering.

Loretta was a poor judge of men. None of her great loves ever lived up to her expectations. What she experienced with Grant Withers was first love, which when it was over left a void in her life that could never be completely filled. Even at seventeen, Loretta seemed to know that once she really fell in love, as she did with Withers, she might be able to love again, but never in the same way. Loretta was sincere when she admitted that she would always love Withers. First love may be evanescent, but it is not forgotten. The passing years and Withers's suicide may have lessened the intensity of her emotions, but it was still her first encounter with, as Cole Porter put it, "this funny thing called love." She was seventeen when she eloped with Withers, twenty-seven when she married Tom Lewis. "Love is too young to know what conscience is," Shakespeare observes in Sonnet 151. At seventeen, Loretta certainly did not know; at twenty-seven, she did. She knew the distinction between first love, infatuation, and conjugal love. She wanted a stable marriage to make up for her own short-lived one and her mother's two failures.

When Loretta married Lewis, the scenario changed: It was no longer the princess and her betrothed; it was the movie star wife and her radio producer husband, followed by the TV celebrity and her TV producer husband, and ending with the former star and her ex-husband. Undoubtedly, Loretta and Lewis loved each other, but it was not a case of love given unconditionally and selflessly. In 1939, Loretta left Fox despite Zanuck's threat of blacklisting. She had, she believed, survived worse: *l'affaire Gable*, the unplanned pregnancy, the subterfuge. But now it was time for a real marriage, a church wedding even though Loretta would not be wearing white. There should be life after Fox, Loretta reasoned, but where? Harry Cohn, who had no love for Zanuck, offered her a haven at Columbia, but after she fulfilled her five-picture commitment there, then what? A couple of movies at one studio, a couple at another? A stable marriage? That she found, temporarily, in Lewis.

Lewis's pursuit of Loretta was partly motivated by desire but also by his need for her talent—not to mention her contacts—for Screen Guild Theatre, the radio program that he was creating for Young & Rubicam. It was no different when he signed on to Father Peyton's *Family Theatre*, or later, when Loretta ventured into television. The network needed an anthology series, the series needed a star, the star needed a producer. Marriage served a dual purpose. Lewis wanted a family and got one; he wanted producer status, and he received it. Loretta's needs were more complex. If she were to be known as a butterfly, better a rare one with translucent wings, not metallic ones. For a time Loretta was airborne, but as the 1950s approached, the wings began to harden. The star-producer-network relationship began to unravel. Soon it was just the star with a new series, production company, and network.

After her divorce from Lewis, Loretta was rarely seen in the company of eligible men. She was too busy enshrining her image, accepting awards, lecturing, and supporting charities. It was odd, then, to pick up the *National Enquirer* (24 July 1979) and read the headline: "Loretta Young, 66, and Producer—It Looks Like Love." The producer was William Frye (then in his early fifties), who had produced, among other films, the two Rosalind Russell vehicles *The Trouble with Angels* and *Where Angels Go . . . Trouble Follows*, both of which were written by Blanche Hanalis. It may well have been Frye who brought Hanalis's *Christmas Eve* script to Loretta and encouraged her to star in it. The *National Enquirer* was known for sensationalizing even the trivial, which seems to have been the case when the couple was spotted on their way to a dinner party. Frye and Loretta may have been holding hands and smiling at each other, but Loretta insisted they were only "very, very good friends." The friendship continued, but speculation about an upcoming marriage did not. A serious relationship with a younger man would not have been typical of Loretta, who was usually attracted to older ones. In 1979, Frye's being a Presbyterian would not have been an impediment; if their relationship really became serious, Loretta would have done some serious proselytizing to bring him into the fold—her fold. The age disparity was the real obstacle. "[V]ery, very good friends" was all they could be.

However, a sensational bit of news occurred some fourteen years later when the eighty-year old Loretta married one of her favorite designers, Jean-Louis, five years her senior and far from a father figure. The wedding took place at the Church of the Good Shepherd in Beverly Hills, the preferred parish of the Hollywood Catholics. The couple had known each other even before *The Loretta Young Show*, for which Jean Louis designed the gowns for fifty-two of Loretta's entrances. Loretta insisted that his creations were seductive, but never obscene. That was indeed true; the strapless black satin gown that he designed for Rita Hayworth when she sang "Put the Blame on Mame" in *Gilda* (1946) was tastefully sexy—although at the time the question was not how tasteful it was but how Hayworth managed to avoid a wardrobe malfunction while she went through her gyrations. The shimmering gown in which he dressed Marilyn Monroe when she appeared at Madison Square Garden in 1962 to purr "Happy Birthday" to President John F. Kennedy was intended to be so form-fitting she had to be sewn into it. Like Loretta, who could reconcile her faith with her profession, Jean Louis saw no disparity between his deep-rooted Catholicism and his creations, even when they raised eyebrows by their suggestiveness (e.g., Marlene Dietrich's beaded nude-colored gown, which she wore for her Las Vegas debut in 1953). Jean Louis could also design less sensational costumes, as he proved with the stylish ones he created for Judy Holliday in *The Solid Gold Cadillac* (1956), for which he won his only Oscar.

Loretta and Jean Louis's was not a late autumn-early winter romance, but more of an early winter-late winter one. Two octogenarians, Loretta and Jean Louis were both in the winter of their lives; the golden years had turned to silver, and sunset was darkening into evening. Loretta's decision to marry was primarily an act of charity, really a form of love, the greatest of the three virtues, even surpassing faith and hope. It was love that Loretta felt, but of a certain kind: love mingled with compassion. Loretta knew what a staggering loss Jean Louis experienced in 1997 when his beloved wife, Maggy, died. In Jean Louis, Loretta found a man who was content with his own achievements, as she was with hers. Withers fulfilled her romantic longings, however briefly. Tracy could only provide Loretta with fatherly affection that was misinterpreted by a prying press and discouraged by the faith they both practiced. Lewis offered a dual arrangement: a husband-producer who did not feel threatened by her fame until she became a television celebrity with a larger public than she had ever known—and one that she had every intention of retaining regardless of what kind of a turn her health would take. In Jean Louis, she found the companionship she once had with Tracy, except that now she played the dual role of nurturing mother and ministering wife. She was no longer searching for a surrogate father, but rather a lost soul in need of rehabilitation. Although they only enjoyed four years of marriage, Loretta gave Jean Louis as close a reincarnation of Maggie as he would ever find—in addition to being a wife as fashion-conscious as he was. Visitors marveled at Jean Louis's attire. He usually looked as if he were wearing one of his creations, which he probably was. With Loretta and Jean Louis, it was both mutual affection and shared taste.

A new marriage, a new address. Loretta was no stranger to relocation; from her childhood on, she was used to a peripatetic existence. Gladys moved the family from one home to another. Loretta was no different; she lived in a variety of homes in Los Angeles, including a ranch in Beverly Hills, a Santa Monica beach house, and a maisonette that Gladys had designed for her in the North Flores apartment complex. However, her most famous residence was the one in Bel-Air designed by Garrett Van Pelt and decorated by Gladys, where Loretta lived in the 1930s and which was showcased in *Architectural Digest*. It was a ten-room white colonial that featured a dining room with hand-painted wallpaper and some of her mother's collectibles, such as a lacquered screen from Korea and artifacts from the American Southwest and Mexico. In the living room, ivory settees faced each other on either side of a fireplace. Loretta's room was a vision in blue and rose: rose chair and rug, wallpaper in rose and ivory. Hers was not an ordinary bed; it was double-canopied with a ruffled bedspread. Dresden figurines imparted a Victorian femininity to the room, which looked as if Christina Rossetti slept there. If any room could define Loretta, it was the Bel-Air bedroom. It was as much of a paradox as she: innocent yet sensuous, childlike yet sophisticated, luxurious yet simple.

Loretta decided that the ideal place for her and Jean Louis was Palm Springs. She put her last home, a Beverly Hills French Regency model, up for sale. The asking price was $895,000; it sold for slightly less in August 1996. The gated home in Palm Springs, complete with swimming pool, was discreetly opulent. There was no doubt that it was a movie star's home, with Loretta's portrait spotlighted by Tiffany lamps. But it was also the home of a devout Christian, as the four-foot silver crucifix dominating the living room indicated. The cross was both a memorial to her mother, who found it in Mexico, and a reflection of the faith they shared. This was Loretta's last home. In a few years, when she became terminally ill, she would make one last trip to Beverly Hills.

In 1997, death became Loretta's companion, the equivalent of a *memento mori*. Early that year, on 14 January, her sister Polly Ann died of cancer. Next was Jean Louis. On 20 April, the couple was on the way to Mass, when he collapsed and died. No stranger to death, Loretta knew the protocols: First a funeral mass, which took place at St. Louis Catholic Church in Cathedral City, midway between Palm Springs and Rancho Mirage, the latter a resort community and home to the affluent. Loretta's sons delivered the eulogy; after the ceremony, the family returned to Palm Springs for a gathering at the Givenchy Hotel. On 27 August 1997, it was Elizabeth Jane's (Sally Blane) time to die, also from cancer. Loretta had already lost her mother, Gladys, in October 1984 when she suffered a massive stroke. All that remained of her family were her half sister and brother-in-law, Georgiana and Ricardo Montalban.

But to the image-obsessed Loretta, the death that meant as much to her as that of a family member was the death of a myth. In 1994, Judy published *Uncommon Knowledge*, touted as "The heartrending true story of the daughter of Clark Gable and Loretta Young." At eighty-one, Loretta's determination to conceal the truth of Judy's parentage had nothing to do with her professional image. She knew she would never act again, not even on television, where all she would be offered were either cameo spots or character parts. Loretta was STAR in all caps; she had no intention of going lower case. In the last decade of her life, Loretta only cared about her image. A devout Catholic, despite a few early indiscretions, she was in every respect a daughter of the Church—even if maintaining that status meant having Judy's birth and baptismal certificates falsified, and passing Judy off as her adopted daughter, whose father had died. A Jesuit would have understood: Loretta was resorting to the Jesuitical art of equivocation, reasoning that after Judy's birth, her father, Clark Gable, had "died," as someone who enters the religious life "dies" to the world, or, in this case, as someone who *was* but no longer *is*. Loretta had created the myth—with help, of course. It had become a sacred text that had always been suspect but never repudiated. She had no intention of having anyone, much less her daughter, expose her as the mythographer that she was. And yet, as an observant Catholic, what else could Loretta have done, short of holding a news conference, admitting the truth, embarrassing Gable, and endowing Judy with her own epithet: "Loretta Young's illegitimate daughter"? An abortion was out of the question. Loretta was pro-life even in 1935, before the phrase became part of the national vocabulary. It was bad enough that she had committed one mortal sin by engaging in sex outside of marriage; she could not afford another.

By the time Judy set the record straight about her parentage, other movie stars' children had had their say. None of their memoirs was flattering. However, if *Mommie Dearest* (1976), Christina Crawford's devastating account of her life as Joan Crawford's adopted daughter, were juxtaposed with Crawford's films, there would not have been much difference between the actress's screen image and her real self. The same was true of *My Mother's Keeper* (1985), by Bette Davis's daughter, B.D. Hyman, christened Barbara Davis Sherry, whom Bette used to call "B.D." If Crawford was the mother from hell, Davis came from some other infernal region. Neither Crawford nor Davis was meant for motherhood; they were too preoccupied with their careers. But they were meant for the screen, which they honored with some extraordinary films: Crawford's *Grand Hotel, The Women, Mildred Pierce*; Davis's *Of Human Bondage, Dark Victory, Jezebel, Now, Voyager, All About Eve*. Once they discovered that they were mere subjects in a patriarchy, they learned to hide their insecurities by imitating the moguls, thereby acquiring reputations for being demanding and difficult. Another "d" word is also applicable: "driven."

So was Judy, but in a different way. Judy was driven by a need to tell the truth. To her credit, she did not engage in venom spewing. In fact, *Uncommon Knowledge* is temperate compared to Crawford's and Hyman's feeding frenzies. Judy's memoir is a deconstruction of the Celestial Loretta myth that exposes, at its core, a frightened woman, who in 1935 was faced with two choices: to arrange for an abortion through Dr. Holleran (who could have given her a referral, as he supposedly did for other actresses in similar situations), or become a mythmaker with herself at the heart of the myth. Naturally, she chose myth. In July 1936, Judy was placed in a San Francisco orphanage, where she remained for five months. Until Loretta decided upon the next plot point, Judy stayed then with her grandmother. Finally, in June 1937, the next scene was ready: Loretta would adopt Judy. The script conformed to fact, but the facts were founded on myth. The magnanimous Loretta had found fulfillment as a single parent.

As for the circumstances of Judy's birth, it was a matter of expediency. Disclosure of Judy's parentage would have damaged Loretta's career—perhaps irreparably—and tainted Judy's name. Unless she were willing to pull up stakes and head to Broadway, which was more liberal than Hollywood (and where her liaison with Gable would have been dismissed with a shrug), Loretta had no choice but to mythologize. Otherwise, her image would have been shattered so thoroughly as to be beyond restoration. If Loretta had sinned, as she believed she had, she would atone a hundredfold for an act that other actresses would have considered casual sex. And if it led to pregnancy, they knew the route to take. But they also knew how to take precautions. Artificial birth control was alien to Loretta. She probably knew little, if anything, about contraception, especially devices women used to avoid a pregnancy. Contraception was Gable's department, not hers. Unfortunately, Gable assumed she had been around the block and knew the score. At twenty-two, Loretta was still the dewy-eyed romantic. But Gable's potent masculinity was not the stuff of adolescent fantasy; it was fantasy in the flesh, the closest Loretta had come to the carnal. If it was God's will that she continue in her career, so be it. Since there were no repercussions, apparently it was.

Loretta belonged to old Hollywood, where an actress can have five husbands but no illegitimate children, as the Countess (Hildegarde Knef) explains to producer Barry Detweiler (William Holden) in Billy Wilder's *Fedora* (1979). In the New Hollywood, she could have had five illegitimate children and no husband.

The double standard was in full force in 1935. Errol Flynn could engage in his "wicked, wicked ways" (as he entitled his autobiography), even being acquitted of a double rape charge. However, when Clara Bow's personal secretary revealed the names of her employer's multitudinous lovers, the disclosure spelled the end of Bow's career. Gable, who that year was awarded an Oscar for his performance in *It Happened One Night* (1934), was a full-fledged star, bigger than Loretta. He would be protected. He was also a male. In Hollywood, men covered for each other. MGM made sure that the general public remained ignorant of George Cukor's homosexuality; Cukor was the studio's premier director (*Camille*, *The Women*, *The Philadelphia Story*, the Spencer Tracy-Katharine Hepburn films). All that mattered was box office. The days of embroidering an "A" on the dress had passed, but Loretta would have been stigmatized nonetheless. Gable, on the other hand, would just be another male sowing his wild oats.

It was not that different for women fifteen years later. In 1949, Ingrid Bergman—whose image only partly derived from *The Bells of St. Mary's* (1945) and *Joan of Arc* (1948), in which she played a nun and a saint, respectively (she had also played hookers in *Dr. Jekyll and Mr. Hyde* [1941] and *Arch of Triumph* [1948])—went off to Italy to make *Stromboli* (1949) for Roberto Rossellini. When she became pregnant with his child, Louella Parsons broke the news. The headline of her 12 December 1949 column caused a sensation: "Ingrid Bergman Expecting Baby." The following year, Colorado senator Edwin Johnson excoriated the actress on the floor of the senate and called for a resolution forbidding Bergman to return to the States. Bergman played a nun and a saint; therefore, she should behave accordingly. It was specious logic, but characteristic of postwar America. Loretta was blessed; Parsons remained silent about her, but not Bergman. If Loretta had not been a fellow Catholic, one doubts that Parsons would have passed up one of the biggest scoops of her career. The resolution was never passed; Bergman lived abroad, returning to Hollywood in 1955 to make *Anastasia* (1956), for which she deservedly won an Oscar.

Loretta's carefully plotted myth was one of the biggest open secrets in Hollywood. But the knowledgeable realized that it was not just Loretta's reputation that was at stake; it was also Judy's. All one had to do is look at Judy with her prominent ears, Gable's ears. Children giggled about her "elephant ears," calling Judy "Dumbo." Suspecting that others would make the connection between Gable and Judy, Loretta arranged for plastic surgery, even though she had been warned that the procedure was extremely painful. What did it matter if the operation made Judy's ears less prominent and aroused less suspicion? Surgery was not the solution. Judy was bound to learn eventually.

Meanwhile, Judy pursued her dream of becoming a stage actress. She began studying with the well-known stage, screen, and soon television star, Agnes Moorehead, a 1929 graduate of the American Academy of Dramatic Arts and best remembered as Endora in the television series *Bewitched*. Judy knew she was not destined for the movies, just as Loretta knew that while she could play stage actresses, she could never be one. And until Broadway beckoned to Judy, there was always television. Loretta tried to discourage Judy, emphasizing the dark side of a profession that exploits rather than nourishes and forces women to play the irresistible force-meets-immovable-object game with executives: bargaining and negotiating, conceding on some points and remaining adamant on others, but determined to leave the honcho's office with dignity intact, even at the risk of ulcers or colitis (or worse, ulcerative colitis). But as Charley says at the end of Arthur Miller's *Death of a Salesman*, "It comes with the territory."

Judy's territory turned out to be primarily television, starting in 1958 with NBC's daytime soap, *Kitty Foyle*, based on Christopher Morley's bestseller and the 1940 film for which Ginger Rogers won an Oscar. The poor girl-rich boy drama was also a popular radio soap that aired from 1942 to 1944. In the television version, Kathleen Murray starred as Kitty, with Judy in the supporting role of Molly Scharf, which she played for the two seasons the show was on the air. Like other actresses who alternated between television and theatre, Judy became bicoastal, even though she preferred Los Angeles to New York and eventually made it her permanent residence. The prospect of being a regular on NBC's *The Outlaws* brought her back to Los Angeles for the second and last season (1961–62) as Connie Masters, a Wells Fargo employee. Judy preferred live television, but she went where the work was. For the most part, it was filmed television, such as ABC's highly successful *711 Sunset Strip* (1958–64), shot at Loretta's old studio, Warner Bros. in Burbank. Judy was not a regular on the show and only appeared in a few episodes, such as "Eyes of Love" in 1961. Finally, there was an opportunity to replace

Betsy von Furstenberg in Jean Kerr's long running (1961–64) comedy, *Mary, Mary* during the last year of the run. That was the extent of her Broadway career. Judy was meant for the soaps; her life was the stuff of melodrama. Significantly, it was a soap that gave Judy her longest run: CBS's *The Secret Storm*, on which she played Susan Dunbar for seven years, 1965–72, until her character was written out of the plot. In the long run, it didn't matter; *The Secret Storm* went off the air in 1973.

Judy had not given up on television. She approached NBC with the idea for an hour-long soap, *Texas*, which would be the network's daytime equivalent of CBS's nighttime *Dallas*. But there was only one *Dallas*. *Texas* had the misfortune of occupying the same 3:00–4:00 p.m. time slot as ABC's *General Hospital*. Longevity tells the story: *General Hospital* lasted from 1963 to 1981. *Texas* premiered in August 1980. Discouraged by the ratings, NBC moved it to 11:00 a.m. When that didn't work, the network cancelled the series at the end of 1982. At least Judy received a producer's credit. The swift demise of *Texas* forced Judy, then forty-seven, to think more seriously about the future now that her television career seemed to be over. In 1985, Judy made a dramatic career change: She enrolled at Antioch University, where she could receive life experience credit enabling her to complete a B.A. in a year and an M.A. in clinical psychology in two.

Like her grandmother and mother, Judy was not meant for marriage—at least not to Joseph Tinney Jr., a television director. Judy's marriage lasted for thirteen years, 1958–71, three years short of Loretta's to Lewis, which really ended in 1956, even though they were not officially divorced until 1969. But Judy's marriage lasted longer than either of her grandmother's marriages: Gladys was married ten years to John Earle Young, eleven to George Beltzer.

In 1966, Judy decided to wrest the truth from Loretta about her parentage. The celluloid wall of silence had shielded Loretta, but the wall had fissures with conduits for whispered revelations that even reached the ears of Judy's husband, who nonchalantly informed her that he knew she was Clark Gable's daughter. Joe Tinney knew, but Judy didn't. But then, she wondered, how many others did? Judy's divorce from Tinney made her a single parent with a daughter, Maria—a situation Loretta would, or should, have understood. Judy may have hoped that their common bond would bring them closer at a time when neither she nor Loretta had any marital prospects. Loretta is called "Mom" throughout *Uncommon Knowledge*, but on one occasion, Judy called her "Mama," using the childhood vernacular to suggest someone more than a mother:

a source of comfort, assuaging fears, humming lullabies, and bandaging wounds, visible and otherwise. It was "Mama" that Judy needed; it was "Mom" that she usually got.

As she entered her mid forties, Judy was eager to repair the rift in their relationship that occurred when she announced her intention to become an actress. In 1981, Loretta learned that a portrait that Sir Simon Elwes had painted of her was featured in a New York gallery's catalog. Since Judy was then living in New York, Loretta asked her to stop at the gallery and see if it was as good as she remembered it. Judy was practically an expert on the portrait, since she was a frequent visitor at Elwes's studio when he was executing it. The portrait was indeed as Judy remembered. She decided to buy it for Loretta, who was thrilled, convinced that Elwes had captured her essence: eyes coated with a film of tears and a mouth not drooping in defeat but taut with determination—in short, a woman who was neither a stranger to suffering nor a lost lamb in need of a shepherd. Judy agreed with Loretta; it was indeed "the essence of Mama."

The admission that Judy was seeking came during the 1966 Labor Day weekend when Loretta revealed the truth about Gable and the adoption conspiracy. But the story was not intended for public consumption. Loretta had no intention of repudiating the myth. Her mortal sin could not be divulged, or her image defiled. Knowing her mother's obsession with her persona, Judy conceded. But that was 1966. Twenty years later, it was a different scenario. It was also a different Judy. Judy had undergone therapy, and her studies in psychology convinced her that the only way she could exorcise the demons of the past—the "Dumbo" taunts; the cosmetic surgery that was not completely successful and required a hair style that concealed her ears; Tom Lewis's indifference to her after his sons were born; a marriage that began with a church wedding and a Hawaii honeymoon and ended in a Connecticut divorce court—was to write about them. Memoir-as-therapy was the solution. *Uncommon Knowledge* has little in common with the classic autobiography, in which the subject investigating becomes the object investigated. Here the object investigated is not so much Judy as her mother, and, indirectly, her father.

There is a difference between making peace with the past and understanding how it impinges on the present. In *Timebends* (1987), Arthur Miller disentangled a knot of memories—people, events, family members, rooms, clothes, shoes, a piano, a first stage performance in a Harlem theater—that were seemingly insignificant details, except to Miller who, by excavating the past, organized the shards of time remembered into the mosaic of his life and work. *Uncommon Knowledge* is not so ambitious. Judy does not approach the past as a picture puzzle, whose pieces must interlock. Her purpose was simple: to have herself acknowledged, once and for all, as the daughter of Loretta Young and Clark Gable, not the adopted daughter of Loretta Young and an unknown father.

When Loretta learned in 1986 that Judy was writing her memoir, which Loretta considered an exposé, she threatened a lawsuit, not realizing that she did not wield the power she once did. If it was a case of "once a star, always a star," the light had dimmed. Estrangement followed, and when the memoir appeared in 1994, Loretta's name was constantly in the press. She was now eighty-one, the self-appointed keeper of her own flame, which she assumed would not be extinguished in her lifetime. Judy relieved her mother of guarding a shrine with only one votary. It was time to blow out the light; since Loretta would not, Judy did. The myth was extinct. The saint was revealed as a sinner—human, all too human—yet strangely triumphant. The Loretta that emerged from *Uncommon Knowledge* was a vulnerable woman who, in her determination to maintain her star status, resorted to subterfuge and equivocation. One could not help but admire both her inventiveness and her tenacity. An astute reader, as opposed to someone interested only in a sensational read, would have finished *Uncommon Knowledge* with renewed admiration for Loretta—less so for her daughter, who simply resorted to another form of therapy, one that does not require payment to a therapist because the therapist was the author, who was paid in royalties.

In a 1994 interview, Judy hinted at the real reason for writing *Uncommon Knowledge*: to see if by reconstructing the past she could fill the void in her life caused by Gable's disowning her. Loretta would have understood such a void; her father had left one in her life, too, when he disappeared. As Judy told *People* magazine, "If I could talk to him [Gable] now, I'd say, 'Where were you when I needed you? Why did you stay away?' Then, of course, I'd tell him how much I missed him." Had Judy made her ambivalence about Gable a major theme, so that he would have played as significant a role in the memoir as Loretta, she would have emerged as a scarred child bearing wounds inflicted by both parents, perhaps more from her father than her mother. Loretta did not abandon Judy; Gable did. To her credit as an autobiographer, Judy placed her life within the context of her great grandparents, grandparents, and mother. After Gladys's mother died, her father defected, as did Loretta's father, and Judy's as well. It was almost like the ancestral curse in myth, except that no one was murdered or driven mad by the Furies. Still, the women were ill served by men, which, ironically, made them stronger. Like her mother, Judy survived.

To Loretta survival was all. Countless women would have understood—women who turned their indiscretions into myths that they either carried to the grave or admitted when it was safe to do so. So, too, would fellow Catholics who shared Loretta's primitive view of mortal sin, particularly violations of the sixth commandment, and to whom confessing and performing the prescribed penance (which could vary with the confessor) were not enough and, like Loretta, spent a lifetime atoning. Quoting John 6:1–11 would probably not have helped. In that chapter, the Pharisees brought an adulterous woman before Jesus, expecting him to denounce her. Instead, he merely told her to reform her ways. Loretta had done that, but she had to do more. In imitation of Christ, she chose to serve rather than be served.

Most actresses in Loretta's situation would not have regarded *Uncommon Knowledge* as a daughter's betrayal as much as a mother's chance to hit the lecture circuit and tell her side of the story. If Loretta had, feminists would have embraced her, many of them knowing nothing about the restrictive production code, the sanctimonious Legion of Decency, contracts with morals clauses, and the Hollywood patriarchy. It was a perfect opportunity to provide a counter-narrative to Judy's, and given Loretta's ability to sweep onto a stage, she would have found an audience eager to relight her flame. It could have been Loretta *redidiva*. Instead, Loretta dismissed the book as rumor, and went on performing her usual charitable acts. Judy had a secondary career: After Loretta's death, she was booked on cruises to lecture about her movie star parents and show clips from their films.

For four years, mother and daughter were estranged. It took three deaths in a single year—Jean Louis', Polly Ann's, and Elizabeth Jane's (Sally Blane), together with her brother Jack's the following year—to make Loretta realize that it was time to bury the past. Anyway, there was something unseemly about a mother in her eighties harboring a grudge against a daughter in her sixties, particularly when the mother practices a faith based on forgiveness. Besides, Loretta reasoned, some readers may have profited from *Uncommon Knowledge*, particularly those who had to live a lie or work in a profession where, like T.S. Eliot's Prufrock, they were scrutinized and classified like specimens, "pinned and wriggling on a wall." Unintentionally, Loretta became the heroine of *Uncommon Knowledge*; it was one of the best scripts she was ever handed.

Loretta spent the last years of her life putting her faith into action. Loretta had never worked in a film with Jane Wyman, although she knew that Wyman was inspired by her success in television to try her hand in the new medium. In 1955, Wyman became the host of *Fireside Theatre*. While there had been other hosts, she proved the most popular, so much so that *Fireside Theatre* was renamed *The Jane Wyman Show*. Loretta and Wyman had more in common than their professions. After divorcing her husband, Freddie Karger, in 1952, Wyman converted to Catholicism, becoming such a promoter of the faith that she brought Karger back into the fold and even remarried him in 1961. After they separated four years later, Wyman never remarried and moved to Palm Springs. Loretta immediately enlisted her help. They both belonged to St. Louis Catholic Church in Cathedral City. The church carpeting had become so frayed that a heel caught in loose threads could result in an injury. Loretta and Wyman had the church recarpeted; parishioners could now walk to the altar at communion time without fear of tripping.

It is hard to think of two more incompatible types than Loretta and Carol Channing. But when Channing moved to Palm Springs in 1998, Loretta coaxed her into donning a white beard and red cap to impersonate Santa Claus at a children's Christmas party. Knowing Channing was a committed Christian Scientist, Loretta made no effort to convert her. But the affection remained; "She was my fairy godmother growing up," Channing remarked. "Fairy godmother" suited Loretta; one could easily imagine her in a silvery white gown and tiara, brandishing a wand and tapping the original Lorelei Lee in Jule Styne's *Gentlemen Prefer Blondes* and Dolly Gallagher Levi in Jerry Herman's *Hello, Dolly!* for her ministry.

It was a short-lived friendship. In 1999, Loretta was diagnosed with ovarian and stomach cancer. She accepted the inevitable, asking only that she not die in a hospital. Since Loretta could not get the care she needed in Palm Springs, Georgiana and Ricardo brought her to their home in Hollywood Hills. It was there that she died on Saturday, 12 August 2000.

The funeral mass took place the following Wednesday at St. Louis Church in Cathedral City. There was a huge turnout of around four hundred people, including all the remaining members of her family (except Georgiana, who remained in Los Angeles because Ricardo was having surgery). Channing, Wyman, Marlo Thomas, and Norman Brokaw, her agent of fifty years, were there. And, of course, the fans. Casablanca lilies, Loretta's favorite flowers, filled the church. Bishop Gerald Barnes officiated, recalling the last conversation he had with Loretta, in which she said that "she was ready to die and she looked forward to going home." Loretta was cremated; on 7 October, her remains were buried in her mother's grave in Holy Cross Cemetery, Section F, Tier 65. Polly Ann and Sally Blane are also interred at Holy Cross in other sections. Anyone trying to locate Loretta's grave would have to go to her mother's. The design is simple: two hands holding a small cross and the inscription, "Beloved Mother and Grandmother Gladys Belzer 1888–1984." There is no indication that Loretta's ashes lie there. That is what she wanted. Her home was no longer on earth.

The obituaries were lengthy, and the tributes deeply felt—especially Robert Osborne's in his *Hollywood Reporter* column (15 August 2000): "Young was courageous, generous, talented, beautiful, always her own woman—and one of the handful of giants never given her proper due by the industry she leaves behind." At least Loretta knew that she moved effortlessly and gracefully between the two pillars that enclosed her life: her profession and her faith. She did not consider them confining boundaries, but rather defining the space within which she worked and prayed—a space large enough to accommodate her nearly 100 films, close to 260 episodes of her two television shows, two two-hour TV movies, around thirty-five radio appearances, and countless hours spent in charity work. Few stars had racked up as many humanitarian awards as Loretta. But then, few know how to balance their career and their faith. Loretta knew how to integrate her art and her religion. She was living proof that Christ was right when he said, "Render to Caesar the things that are Caesar's and to God the things that are God's" (Matthew 22:21). Loretta would have emended the text to read, "Render to Hollywood the things that are Hollywood's," but she would have retained the rest of the mandate.

NOTES

Chapter 1. Life without Father

3   "in any number of places": Information about Loretta's life and family comes from a variety of sources: the invaluable Gladys Hall Collection, Folder 506, and the Jane Ardmore Papers, Folders 14 and 15, both of which are in Special Collections, Margaret Herrick Library, the Fairbanks Center for Motion Picture Study; the Loretta Young Clippings File, Margaret Herrick; the Constance McCormick Collection, Vols. 1–3 (1935), Cinema–Television Library, University of Southern California; obituaries in the *Hollywood Reporter International Edition*, 15 August 2000, 22; *New York Times*, 13 August 2000, 39; *Daily Variety*, 14 August 2000, 8, 16; *People*, 28 August 2000, 117; Samuel Grafton, "The Loretta Young Story," *Good Housekeeping*, March 1955, 65, 234–40; Dean Jennings, "Indestructible Glamour Girl," *Saturday Evening Post*, 28 May 1960, 20, 108, 111, 113; Judy Lewis, *Uncommon Knowledge* (New York: Pocket Books/Simon & Schuster, 1995); "Loretta Young," *Biography*, A&E, hosted by Peter Graves, first aired 24 February 1995. Loretta wrote an autobiography of sorts, *The Things I Had to Learn, As Told to Helen Ferguson* (New York: Bobbs-Merrill, 1961), in which she says little about her career. Exactly what she had to learn, apart from having to "think" through a role, as Capra taught her, is never clear. The studio biographies in the Loretta Young Clippings File are mostly on target. Joan Wester Anderson's "authorized biography," *Forever Young: The Life, Loves and Enduring Faith of a Hollywood Legend* (Allen, TX: Thomas Moore, 2000) is cloyingly reverential. Anderson became Loretta's biographer because Loretta was taken with her books on angels and wanted such an author to tell her story. Still, there is information in it that is not available elsewhere. Joe Morella and Edward Z. Epstein's popular biography, *Loretta Young: An Extraordinary Life* (New York: Delacorte, 1986), is readable but lacks both notes and a bibliography, in addition to being incomplete.

4   "a large number of businesspersons": Craig Fuller, Associate Editor, Utah Historical Society, email to author, 15 April 2009.

5   "Universal released films": Bernard F. Dick, *City of Dreams: The Making and Remaking of Universal Pictures* (Lexington: University Press of Kentucky, 1997), 40–41.

7   "'one less mouth to feed'": Lewis, Uncommon Knowledge, 47.

7   "according to Loretta's daughter": ibid
8   "she was going to be a movie star": "Loretta Young," *Biography*, A&E, 1995.
8   "priests were frequent dinner guests": "Interview with Ricardo Montalban, Polly Ann Young, Sally Blane," Jane Ardmore Papers, folder 14, Margaret Herrick Library, Special Collections.
9   "steel butterfly": James Robert Parish, *The Fox Girls* (Secaucus, NJ: Castle Books, 1972), 202.

Chapter 2. The Creation of Loretta Young

10 "Norma Jean Baker became Marilyn Monroe": Donald Spoto, *Marilyn Monroe* (New York: Harper Paperbacks, 1993), 140.
10 "the most beautiful little girl I had ever seen": Colleen Moore, *Silent Star* (Garden City, NY: Doubleday, 1968), 162.
11 "I named her": ibid., 163.
11 "as her Paramount salary showed": *The Magnificent Flirt*, Paramount Collection, #101. Margaret Herrick Library, Special Collections.
12 "She was my first discovery": Mervyn LeRoy, *Take One* (New York: Hawthorn Books, 1974), 91
12 "he must have been very surprised": Lewis, *Uncommon Knowledge*, 52.
12 "For *Marry* Loretta received": *Broken Dishes* (*Too Young to Marry*) production file. 2722A, USC, Warner Bros. Archives.
13 "weekly check," "That's up to God," "Interview," Jane Ardmore Papers, box 28, folder 14, Margaret Herrick Library, Special Collections.
14 "her talent as an actress": rev. of *Laugh, Clown, Laugh*, New York Times, 28 May 1928, 23.2.
14 "the finest speaking voice": Hedda Hopper Collection, #3622, USC, Cinema–Television Library.
16 "stupid and useless," "he even threw a chair": Anderson, *Forever Young*, 39.
16 "hot fudge sundae": Loretta Young, "I Like (These) Men," *Movieland*, August 1945, 62.
16 "First National, then Associated First National": David Cook, *A History of the Narrative Film*, 4th ed. (New York: Norton, 2004), 38, 170; Clive Hirschhorn, *The Warner Bros. Story* (New York: Crown, 1979), 59.
17 "often until 3:30 a.m.": Jane Ardmore Papers, Box 28, folder 14, Margaret Herrick Library, Special Collections.

Chapter 3. LORETTA TALKS!

18 "a major player in the movie business": see Cari Beauchamp *Joseph P. Kennedy: The Hollywood Years* (New York: Knopf, 2009).
18 "created his own": ibid., 59.
21 "for which First National paid": *The Squall*, story file, #222A, USC, Warner Bros. Archives.
22 "big bucks for a seventeen-year-old": *Loose Ankles*, ibid.
23 "she received $4500": *The Truth about Youth*, file 2723B, USC, Warner Bros. Archives.

23   "dissatisfied with the way": A. Scott Berg, *Goldwyn: A Biography* (New York: Ballantine, 1989), 141.

Chapter 4. Sacrificial Wives, Shop Girls, and Proud Proletarians

26   "a third of the audience": Eileen Bowser, *The Transformation of Cinema, 1907–1915* (Berkeley: University of California Press, 1990), 2.

26   "free admission to prenoon shows": Russell Merritt, "Nickelodeon Theaters, 1907–1914: Building an Audience for the Movies," *The American Film Industry*, ed. Tino Balio, rev. ed. (Madison: University of Wisconsin Press, 1985), 96.

27   "the woman's picture": On the genre and its broad range of character types, see Marjorie Rosen, *Popcorn Venus* (New York: Avon, 1973), Chapters 3–5; and Molly Haskell, *From Reverence to Rape: The Treatment of Women in the Movies*, 2nd ed. (Chicago: University of Chicago Press, 1987), 153–88.

32   "extreme cruelty": Ronald L. Davis, *The Life and Image of John Wayne* (Norman, OK: University of Oklahoma Press, 1998), 110.

38   "politically confused": Andrew Bergman, *We're in the Money: Depression America and Its Films* (New York: Harper Colophon, 1971), 97.

Chapter 5. Loaned Out

39   "CBC had become Columbia": on CBC's transformation into Columbia Pictures Corporation, see Bernard F. Dick, *The Merchant Prince of Poverty Row: Harry Cohn of Columbia Pictures* (Lexington: University Press of Kentucky, 1993), 31–57.

39   "great cast," "breastworks": Frank Capra, *The Name Above the Title* (New York: Vintage, 1985), 134.

39   "original title": Joseph McBride, *Frank Capra: The Catastrophe of Success* (New York: Simon & Schuster, 1992), 231.

41   "Borzage has been labeled": Herve Dumont, *Frank Borzage: The Life and Films of a Hollywood Romantic*, trans. Jonathan Kaplansky (Jefferson, NC: McFarland, 2006), 10–11.

42   "I don't feel," "Nearly 2000 years ago": *Los Angeles Times*, 18 February 1934, A8.

44   "I proved," "He made you believe": Dumont, *Frank Borzage*, 198.

44   "She was never interested": Judy Lewis interview, 1 June 2008.

46   "The first writer": *Midnight Mary*, MGM Collection, #932, USC, Cinema—Television Library.

Chapter 6. Last Days at Warner's

48   "The new name was": Bernard F. Dick, *Engulfed: The Death of Paramount Pictures and the Birth of Corporate Hollywood* (Lexington: University Press of Kentucky, 2001), 10.

49   "'There was a honeymoon'": Sharon Rich, *Sweethearts: The Timeless Love Affair—On Screen and Off—between Jeanette MacDonald and Gene Raymond* (New York: Donald Fine, 1994), 186.

Chapter 7. Darryl Zanuck's Costume Queen

53   "the studio had suffered a net loss": Clive Hirschhorn, *The Warner Bros. Story* (New York: Crown 1979), 112.

53 "RKO reported a loss": Richard B. Jewell, with Vernon Harbin, *The RKO Story* (New York: Arlington, 1982), 56.
54 "to create a new studio, Twentieth Century": George F. Custen, *Twentieth Century's Fox: Darryl F. Zanuck and the Culture of Hollywood* (New York: Basic Books/Perseus, New York, 1997), 177–78.
63 "In 1932, Fox reported": Glendon Allvine, *The Greatest Fox of Them All* (New York: Lyle Stuart, 1969), 152.
63 "In 1935, Twentieth Century": Custen, *Twentieth Century's Fox*, 194.
63 "mortal sin": Lewis, *Uncommon Knowledge*, 442.

Chapter 8. The Men in Her Life
65 "I have been in love": Gladys Hall, "I Have Been in Love Fifty Times," *Motion Picture*, October 1933, 51.
65 "I like men": Loretta Young, "I Like (These) Men," *Movieland*, August 1945, 38.
66 "alimony suit": *Los Angeles Times*, 9 Feb. 1930, A3.
67 "Loretta initiated divorce proceedings": *New York Times*, 3 July 1931, 26.
67 "I never, I know": Gladys Hall Collection, folder 506 ("Loretta Young"), Margaret Herrick Library, Special Collections.
67 "He has given me," "a rare masculine quality": Jack Grant, "Why Loretta Young Broke Up Her Romance," *Movie Mirror Weekly*, Oct. 1934, 9.
67 "had nothing to do": Gladys Hall, "Spencer Tracy's Love Confession," *Movie Mirror*, March 1934, 11, 72.
68 "I tried to save him": phone interview, 11 May 2008.
68 "there were unconfirmed tales": Michael Sragow, *Victor Fleming: An American Master* (New York: Pantheon, 2008), 37.
68 "never lovers," "common knowledge": Graham Lord, *Niv: The Authorized Biography of David Niven* (New York: St. Martin's, 2004), 62, 71.
68 "fearful of": Marc Eliot, *Jimmy Stewart: A Biography* (New York: Harmony Books, 2006), 116.
68 "beautiful": Jeanine Basinger, *The Star Machine* (New York: Knopf, 2007), 143.
69 "by setting up a romance": Lawrence Guiles, *Tyrone Power: The Last Idol* (New York: Doubleday, 1979), 15.
69 "perfectly terrible": Nancy Nelson, *Evenings with Cary Grant: Reflections in His Own Words and by Those Who Knew Him Best* (New York: William Morrow, 1991), 77.
69 "I don't mind": Warren G. Harris, *Cary Grant: A Touch of Elegance* (New York: Doubleday, 1987), 144.
70 "Loretta idealizes," "I don't blame him": Constance McCormick Collection, Vol. III. USC, Cinema–Television Library.

Chapter 9. Heeding the Call of the Wild
71 "the dominant primordial beast": Jack London, *The Call of the Wild and Selected Stories* (New York: Signet, 1998), 19.
73 "National Legion of Decency": Jack Vizzard, *See No Evil: Life inside a Hollywood Censor* (New York: Pocket Books/Simon & Schuster, 1971), 35.
73 "sex affair," "lady friend," "*The Call of the Wild*," *American Film Institute Catalog*, F3, *Feature Films, 1931–40* (New York: R.R. Bowker, 1971), 272–73.
74 "Studio contracts contained a morals clause": David Bret, *Clark Gable: Tormented Star* (New York: Carroll & Graf, 2007), 24.

74 "George Cukor's homosexuality," "producer Anderson Lawler": Patrick McGilligan, *George Cukor: A Biography of the Gentleman Director* (New York: St. Martin's, 1991), 184.
76 "I thought she knew": Lewis, *Uncommon Knowledge*, 29.
77 "the tomb . . . hewn out of rock": Donald Spoto, *The Hidden Jesus: A New Life* (New York: St. Martin's, 1998), 238–39.
78 "He set a cap": *The Crusades*, folder five, Paramount Collection, Margaret Herrick Library. Subsequent production details derive from this source.
78 "Loretta has been in ill health": *Los Angeles Times*, 22 August 1935, A1.

Chapter 10. The Great Lie

79 "The radio dramatization": Lux Radio Theatre Collection, Margaret Herrick Library.
81 "You are the glory": *Daily Missal of the Mystical Body*, ed. Maryknoll Fathers (New York: P.J. Kennedy, 1956), 1201.
81 "elephant ears": Lewis, *Uncommon Knowledge*, 144.
81 "All I know": "*The Call of the Wild*," American Film Institute Catalog, F3, 273.
81 "She was identified": Lewis, *Uncommon Knowledge*, 71.
82 "On 4 July": *Los Angeles Examiner*, 4 July 1937, I, 3.
82 "I am the happiest girl," "I can't tell," "bring herself to disclose": ibid.
83 "In one version": Box 28, 15, Jane Ardmore Collection, Margaret Herrick Library.
83 "In that account": Scrapbook #2, Jane Ardmore Collection, Margaret Herrick Library.
83 "I don't want them": *Los Angeles Examiner*, 20 June 1937, N5.
83 "she was a lesbian": Samantha Barbas, *The First Lady of Hollywood: A Biography of Louella Parsons* (Berkeley: University of California Press, 2005), 153.
83 "Guests could either receive": ibid., 186–87.
84 "The day that Liza called": Scrapbook #2, Jane Ardmore Collection, Margaret Herrick Library.
84 "Parsons: So you think": Program 71, 27 April 1947, folder 8, Louella Parsons Collection, USC, Cinema–Television Library.
85 "Louella never wrote": Box 15, folder 426, Hollywood Women's Press Club Records, Margaret Herrick Library.
86 "Buckner claimed he was innocent": *Los Angeles Times*, 2 December 1938, 1.
86 "It would be nice": *Los Angeles Times*, 3 December 1938, 2.
86 "I have the fullest expectation": *New York Times*, 24 December 1938, 32.
86 "Am I going to marry": *Los Angeles Times*. 13 January 1939, A1.
87 "in a spot": Box 28, folder 15, Jane Ardmore Collection, Margaret Herrick Library.
87 "iridescent water lily blue": *Los Angeles Times*, 1 August 1940, A1.

Chapter 11. Return from the Ashes

88 "Oh, my child": Charles Dickens, *Bleak House*, Chapter 11 (New York: Signet, 1964), 516.
90 "expecting little, if any, opposition": A. Scott Berg, *Goldwyn: A Biography* (New York: Random House/Ballantine, 1989), 215.
94 "exhaustive tests": *Los Angeles Times*, 1 October 1936, 10.

94 "sunny face," "joyous voice," "blessed child": Helen Hunt Jackson, *Ramona: A Story* (New York: Roberts Brothers, 1886), 45.
95 "but the most beautiful": ibid., 499.
98 "He pared down the budget": Memo from Zanuck to Ed Ebele (Production Dept.), 14 January 1937, *Café Metropole*, Twentieth Century-Fox Collection, USC, Cinema–Television Library.
99 "Eliminate all references": "Conference with Mr. Zanuck on Revised Final Script of 3/10/37, 15 March 1937," *Love under Fire*, Twentieth Century-Fox Collection, USC, Cinema–Television Library. The film's production history can also be found in this file.

Chapter 12. Addio, Darryl
103 "adapted from James M. Cain's": James M. Cain, *Three of a Kind* (New York: Knopf, 1944), 3–118.
104 "To coincide with the remake": James M. Cain, *Everybody Does It* (New York: Signet, 1949).
105 "I just didn't like": Peter Bogdanovich, *John Ford* (Berkeley: University of California Press, 1968), 69.
107 "Once she learned": Fred Lawrence Guiles, *Tyrone Power: The Last Idol* (New York: Doubleday, 1979), 13.
107 "In other words": ibid., 15.
107 "his salary was raised ": Hector Arce, *The Secret Life of Tyrone Power* (New York: Morrow, 1979), 136.
107 "At Power's funeral": Guiles, *Tyrone Power*, 312.
111 "Darryl, I won't": "Loretta Young, 'I'm Still a Ham,'" *TV Guide*, 19 October 1957, 10.

Chapter 13. The Price of Freedom
113 "Loretta insisted": Lewis, *Uncommon Knowledge*, 116.
114 "semi-independent producer": Matthew Bernstein, *Walter Wanger, Hollywood Independent* (Berkeley: University of California Press, 1994), 96.
115 "complete control of all production matters": Tino Balio, *United Artists: The Company Built by the Stars* (Madison: University of Wisconsin Press, 1976), 140.
115 "wounding, but not killing, him": Bernstein, *Walter Wanger*, 275.
116 "drew the line at $50,000": Lewis, *Uncommon Knowledge*, 116.
116 "gleaming white office": Bernard F. Dick, *The Merchant Prince of Poverty Row: Harry Cohn of Columbia Pictures* (Lexington: University Press of Kentucky, 1993), 72.
118 "time and feeding": Charles Dickens, *The Pickwick Papers* (New York: Washington Square Press, 1960), 3.
123 "revenge on Loretta": Bob Thomas, *King Cohn: The Life and Times of Harry Cohn* (New York: Bantam/Putnam's, 1968), 249–50.
123 "came in under budget": *Daily Committee Meeting Reports*, *The Lady from Cheyenne* production file, Universal Collection, USC, Cinema–Television Library.

Chapter 14. Loretta Goes to War
127 "luxury of starting": Paramount Collection, *China* production file, box 21, folder 3, Paramount Collection, Margaret Herrick Library.
128 "military escort": *Los Angeles Times*, 4 August 1943, 10.

128	"greeted on her return": *Los Angeles Times*, 23 February 1943, A3.
128	"$2,500 a week": Thomas Schatz, *The Genius of the System: Hollywood Filmmaking in the Studio Era* (New York: Pantheon, 1988), 350.
128	"he convinced Universal": ibid.
129	"the film became *Ladies Courageous*": Bernstein, *Walter Wanger*, 185–86.

Chapter 15. "Age cannot wither" (but Hollywood Can)

133	"agonizing experience": William Luhr, *Raymond Chandler on Film* (New York: Ungar, 1982), 32.
135	"Goetz turned to Leo Spitz": Bernard F. Dick, *City of Dreams: The Making and Remaking of Universal Pictures* (Lexington: University Press of Kentucky, 1997), 136.
135	"brokered a merger": ibid., 138.
136	"adopted the alias": Bernard F. Dick, *Engulfed: The Death of Paramount Pictures and the Birth of Corporate Hollywood* (Lexington: University Press of Kentucky, 2001), 114.
136	"He operated": Andrew Sinclair, *Spiegel: The Man behind the Pictures* (Boston: Little, Brown, 1987), 37.
137	"When Welles wanted the script changed": Charles Higham, *The Films of Orson Welles* (Berkeley: University of California Press, 1970), 100.
137	"a joyless experience": Sinclair, *Spiegel*, 43–44.
138	"recalled the way": James Naremore, *The Magic World of Orson Welles*, rev. ed. (Dallas: Southern Methodist University Press, 1989), 123.
138	"despite occasional bouts of illness," "having to work": International Pictures Collection, *The Stranger, Daily Production Reports*, USC, Cinema–Television Library.

Chapter 16. Thrice Blessed: A Reunion, a Replacement, and an Oscar

139	"Wallis immediately rose from his seat": Bernard F. Dick, *Hal Wallis, Producer to the Stars* (Lexington: University Press of Kentucky, 2004), 73.
140	"star," "friend": Hal Wallis and Charles Higham, *Starmaker: The Autobiography of Hal Wallis* (New York: Macmillan, 1980), 20.
141	"contracts imply": *The Perfect Marriage* production file, Box 79, #205, Hal Wallis Collection, Margaret Herrick Library.
143	"according to Douglas Dick": personal interview, 11 July 2001.
143	"She now insisted": phone conversation with Douglas Dick, 20 May 2008.
143	"arbitrary stand," "legal steps": letter from Wallis to Loretta, 10 June 1948, *The Accused*, Box 221 (x–y correspondence), Hal Wallis Collection, Margaret Herrick Library.
144	"When you were": phone conversation with Donald Spoto, 11 May 2008.
146	"Selznick came upon an obscure play": Dore Schary, *Heyday: An Autobiography* (Boston: Little, Brown, 1970), 140–46.
146	"sold the rights to RKO": Rudy Behlmer, ed., *Memo from David O. Selznick* (New York: Avon, 1973), 427.
146	"I honestly feel": Schary, *Heyday*, 144; "plunged into the role": ibid., 145.
148	"Her knowledge": Joseph Cotten, *Vanity Will Get You Somewhere* (San Francisco: Mercury House, 1987), 85.
148	"it opened at the Golden": Bernard F. Dick, *Forever Mame: The Life of Rosalind Russell* (Jackson: University Press of Mississippi, 2006), 109.

149   "When Fredric March opened the envelope": Mason Willey and Damien Bona, *Inside Oscar: The Unofficial History of the Academy Awards*, ed. Gail McColl (New York: Ballantine, 1987), 179.
151   "he screened a number of films": Bernard F. Dick, *Claudette Colbert: She Walked in Beauty* (Jackson: University Press of Mississippi, 2008), 15.
151   "which reaped profits": Richard B. Jewell, with Vernon Harbin, *The RKO Story* (New York: Arlington House, 1982), 228, 231.
151   "Fast served three months": Victor Navasky, *Naming Names* (New York: Viking, 1980), 36.
151   "if the hearings had not been": Larry Ceplair and Steven Englund, *The Inquisition in Hollywood: Politics in the Film Community 1930–1960* (Garden City, NY: Anchor/Doubleday, 1980), 283.
153   "How much does Miss Young charge": Lloyd Robson, *Oh Dad! A Search for Robert Mitchum* (Cardigan, Wales: Parthian, 2008), 170.

Chapter 17. The Return to Fox—and Zanuck
156   "a great Catholic," "a great script": Memo from Zanuck to producer Sam Engel, 6 July 1948, folder 1, *Come to the Stable* production file, Twentieth Century-Fox Collection, USC, Cinema–Television Library. Further details about the film's production history derive from this source.
156   "a comedy about faith": Memo to Engel, 1 March 1948, ibid.
157   "an American raised": "A Brief by Oscar Millard, 1/7/48," ibid.
160   "Despite some unfavorable press": Annette Bosco, *Mother Benedict: Foundress of the Abbey of Regina Laudis* (San Francisco: Ignatius Press, 2007), 332.
160   "unreal," "contrived," "crude": Michael Abel to Zanuck, 8 May 1950, #2444-1a, *Half an [sic] Angel* production file, Twentieth Century-Fox Collection, USC, Cinema–Television Library.
160   "totally unacceptable," "without dignity," "breasts," "the unconscious": Letter from Joseph Breen to Jason S. Joy, 12 April 1950.
161   "on 23 April 1951": Eric Bentley, *Thirty Years of Treason* (New York: Viking, 1971), 382.
162   "My only worry": "Transcript of a 2 May 1950 Conference with Mr. Zanuck on Temporary Script, " #2444-2, *Half an Angel* (*Half Angel*) production file, Twentieth Century-Fox Collection, USC, Cinema–Television Library.

Chapter 18. Slow Fade to Small Screen
163   "although he includes it in his filmography": Dore Schary, *Heyday: An Autobiography* (Boston: Little, Brown, 1979), 373.
165   "it was not Loretta": folder 96, Y/Z, Sidney Skolsky Collection, Margaret Herrick Library.
167   "a low-budget production, "time clause": *Because of You* ("Magic Lady") production file, #1708, Universal Collection, USC, Cinema–Television Library.
168   "filmed over twenty-five days": *Daily Production Reports*, *It Happens Every Thursday* production file, #1726, Universal Collection, USC, Cinema–Television Library.

Chapter 19. Radio Days
171   "which aired on CBS": Connie Billips and Arthur Pierce, *Lux Presents Hollywood: A Show-by-Show History of Lux Radio Theatre and Lux Video Theatre, 1934–1957* (Jefferson, NC: McFarland, 1969).

171 "there was a read-through": John Dunning, *On the Air: The Encyclopedia of Old-Time Radio* (New York: Oxford University Press, 1998), 378.
174 "charity children": Charlotte Brontë, *Jane Eyre* (New York: Random House, 1950), 51.
174 "Reader, I married him": ibid., 489.
177 "was broadcast to members of the military": Dunning, *On the Air*, 238.
178 "Bolingbroke (to Gracie)": Irving Sette, *A Pictorial History of Radio* (New York: Grosset & Dunlap, 1967), 81.
179 "LORETTA: George always looked": Script #525, *The George Burns and Gracie Allen Collection*, USC, Cinema–Television Library.
180 "a friend," "do as you truthfully," "beautiful fruition": Loretta Young, folder 502, Gladys Hall Collection, Margaret Herrick Library.
180 "the bleak western part": Father Patrick Peyton, *All for Her: The Autobiography of Father Patrick Peyton, C.S.* (Garden City, NY: Doubleday, 1967), 11.
180 "Joyful," "Sorrowful": *The Holy Rosary: Mysteries and Meditations* (Conception, MO: The Printery House/Conception Abbey, 2004).
181 "a network made up of four stations": Christopher H. Sterling and John M. Kittross, *Stay Tuned: A Concise History of American Broadcasting* (Belmont, CA: Wadsworth, 1990), 157–58.
181 "to kneel and recite": Father Patrick Peyton, *All for Her*, 125.
181 "Gladys advised her": Joan Wester Anderson, *Forever Young* (Allen, TX: Thomas More, 2000), 218.
181 "Loretta presented her": ibid., 41.
182 "Loretta may well have had a vision," "Medjugorje solidified": ibid., 261, 264.
182 "her Noble Contribution": Loretta Young, *The Things I Had to Learn, as Told to Helen Ferguson* (Indianapolis: Bobbs-Merrill, 1961), 249–50.
183 "Then, when you get them": Father Patrick Peyton, *All for Her*, 126.
183 "proved an essential cog": ibid., 129.
183 "The family that prays together": ibid., 144.
183 "The inaugural program": available through *Audio Classics Archive* (www.audioclassics.com). This invaluable archive includes many *Family Theater* broadcast CDs. For specifics, contact terryotr@earthlink.net.
184 "the finest feminine speaking voice": Loretta Young, *The Things I Had to Learn*, 252.
185 "By 1949": Charles Higham, *Hollywood at Sunset* (New York: Saturday Review Press, 1972), 67.

Chapter 20. Another Medium, Another Conquest
186 "*Holiday Hotel*": The title was soon changed to *Don Ameche's Musical Playhouse*; see Tim Brooke and Earle Marsh, *The Complete Directory to Prime Time Network and Cable TV Shows, 1946–Present* (New York: Ballantine, 2007), 621.
187 "never get another script," "next natural step": *Chicago Tribune*, 6 December 1989, 7.
187 "Producer Jerry Wald": *Los Angeles Times*, 10 March 1960, B9.
188 "I can give a better": Dean Jennings, "Indestructible Glamour Girl," *Saturday Evening Post*, 28 May 1960, 108.
188 "Loretta felt they were friends": "Loretta Young and Television," publicity release, n.d., Hal Humphrey Collection, USC, Cinema–Television Library.
189 "[Loretta Young] has succumbed": *Los Angeles Times*, 18 September, 1952, 30.

189	"Loretta and Lewis splitting the stock": Lewis, *Uncommon Knowledge*, 246.
190	"I am not going to interfere": Hal Humphrey, *The Mirror*, 24 June 1953, 35.
190	"It's hard to explain": *Los Angeles Times*, 6 May 1953, 32.
191	"for spiritual reasons": *USA Today*, 11 December 1989, 03D.
191	"tops," "end this affair": *Photoplay*, November 1948, 6, 8.
191	"A producer": ibid.
191	"These letters seemed": *Movieland*, December 1945, 14+.
192	"ambiguous replies": *Movieland*, March 1948, 8+.
201	"Loretta was honored": For a list of her awards, see Loretta Young, *The Things I Had to Learn, as Told to Helen Ferguson* (New York: Bobbs-Merrill, 1961), 246–54.
201	"In fall 1953": William Manchester, *The Glory and the Dream: A Narrative History of America, 1932–1972* (New York: Bantam, 1975), 473–513.
202	"she was rushed to St. John's Hospital": *Los Angeles Times*, 11 April 1955, 1.
203	"abdominal adhesions": ibid., 1 July 1955, 26.
203	"finally discharged": ibid., 2 August 1955, 11.
203	"Finally, I have": Lewis, *Uncommon Knowledge*, 277.
203	"called her own meeting": ibid.
203	"It was awfully hard": Gregory Speck, "Loretta Young," *Interview*, May 1987, 63.284; "her weekly schedule": *Loretta Young Production Schedule, July–March Inclusive*, Helen Ferguson Public Relations, Hal Humphrey Collection, USC, Cinema–Television Library.
205	"seeking control of Lewislor": *Hollywood Citizen-News*, 14 March 1958, 13.
205	"he agreed to relinquish": *Los Angeles Times*, 8 April 1958, 88.
205	"He filed suit": *Los Angeles Mirror*, 14 March 1958, 10.
205	"finally dismissed": *Los Angeles Times*, 16 March 1966, D18.
205	"with Loretta receiving a dollar": *Los Angeles Times*, 21 August 1969, C2.
205	"nice," "tough": Lewis, *Uncommon Knowledge*, 344–45.
205	"dreadful profession": ibid., 296.

Chapter 21. The Road to Retirement

207	"estranged husband, "their estrangement": *Los Angeles Herald Examiner*, 10 September 1962, D1.
208	"front-page news": *Los Angeles Times*, 28 April 1957, 1.
208	"had assumed an aura": Gregory Speck, "Loretta Young," *Interview*, May 1987, 60.
209	"I must say," "One could": ibid., 63.
215	"shouting orders": *Los Angeles Times*, 3 August 1962, C14.
215	"Dear Portland": ibid.
216	"nothing dramatic happened": ibid., 6 April 1965, 3.
216	"The case was resolved": ibid, 17 April 1965.

Chapter 22. A New Life

219	"creative differences": *Los Angeles Times*, 12 April 1985, 22.
220	"$559,000": ibid., 18 January 1972, 3.
220	"a series of letters": ibid., 24 January 1972, B6.
221	"depicts unnatural sex acts": ibid., 2 August 1970, B2.
221	"The subject is me": *Chicago Tribune*, 31 May 1985, 5.

222 "Each time I pass": phone conversation with Donald Spoto, 11 May 2008.
222 "Oh! Don't sit there!": email from Dennis Dolph, former Sony executive and founder of Sony Pictures Classics, 2 January 2010.
222 "God gave me": *TV Guide*, 16 May 1959, 19.
223 "career retrospective": *Los Angeles Times*, 11 April 1981, D7.
223 "other than actresses": *Variety*, 6 June 1988, 8.
223 "Ten of the sixteen": Judith Mayne, *Directed by Dorothy Arzner* (Bloomington: Indiana University Press, 1974), 204.
224 "You . . . bring your sensitivity": *Variety*, 6 June 1988, 8.
224 "braided," "demanding," "So tonight": *Variety*, 27 June 1988, Loretta Young Clippings File, Margaret Herrick Library.
225 "My belief": Peter Swet, "The Secret Strength of Loretta Young," *Parade*, 28 January 1990, 9.
227 "an awfully big adventure": James M. Barrie, *Peter Pan*, in *The Plays of J.M. Barrie* (New York: Scribner's, 1956 rpt.), 308.
228 "It took out": Tom Green, "Loretta Young, Forever a Lady," *USA Today*, 11 December 1989, 3D.

Chapter 23. The Last Reel

232 "strapless black satin gown": Tom Gilatto and Anne Marie Otey, "The Gift of Garb," *People*, 12 May 1997, 44.
234 "designed by Garrett Van Pelt": Donald Spoto, "Loretta Young: The Farmer's Daughter on Sunset Boulevard," *Architectural Digest*, April 1994, 216–19.
234 "Tiffany lamps," "silver crucifix": Lena Williams, "At Home with Loretta Young, Life Waltzes On," *New York Times* 30 March 1995, C3.
236 "supposedly did for other actresses": conversation with former publicist Walter Seltzer, 31 May 2009.
237 "revealed the names," "spelled the end": Donald Stenn, *Clara Bow, Runnin' Wild* (New York: Cooper Square Press, 2000), 217, 222.
237 "The headline," "Colorado senator": Samantha Barbas, *The First Lady of Hollywood: A Biography of Louella Parsons* (Berkeley: University of California Press, 2005), 293, 296.
238 "elephant ears," "Dumbo": Lewis, *Uncommon Knowledge*, 144.
240 "the essence of Mama": Jill Spalding, *Only the Best* (New York: Harry Abrams, 1985), Loretta Young Clippings File, Margaret Herrick Library.
241 "If I could talk," "Daughter of Deception": *People*, 18 April 1994, 54.
243 "Wyman converted to Catholicism": Lawrence J. Quirk, *Jane Wyman: The Actress and the Woman, An Illustrated Biography* (New York: Dembner Books, 1986), 118, 119.
243 "She was my fairy godmother": Bruce Fessier, "Loretta Young remembered as a special friend," *The Desert Sun*, 17 August 2000, 1.
244 "she was ready to die": ibid.
244 "on 7 October": James Robert Parish, *The Hollywood Book of the Dead* (New York: Contemporary Books/McGraw-Hill, 2002), 247.

FILMOGRAPHY

C = Columbia Pictures
FN = First National
FFC = Fox Film Corporation
MGM = Metro-Goldwyn-Mayer
PAR = Paramount Pictures
RKO = RKO Radio Pictures
TC = Twentieth Century
TCF = Twentieth Century-Fox
UA = United Artists
U = Universal Pictures
UI = Universal-International
WB = Warner Bros.
* = uncredited

FILM	STUDIO	DIRECTOR
Sirens of the Sea (1917)	U	Allan Holubar
The Primrose Ring (1917)	PAR	Robert Z. Leonard
The Only Way (1919)	PAR	Unknown
White and Unmarried (1921)	PAR	Tom Forman
The Sheik (1921)	PAR	George Melford
Naughty but Nice (1927)	FN	Millard Webb
Her Wild Oat (1927)	FN	Marshall Neilan
The Whip Woman (1928)	FN	Joseph C. Boyle
Laugh, Clown, Laugh (1928)	MGM	Herbert Brenon
Head Man (1928)	FN	Eddie Cline
Scarlet Seas (1928)	FN	John Francis Dillon
*Seven Footprints to Satan (1929)	FN	Benjamin Christensen
The Magnificent Flirt (1929)	PAR	H. d'Abbadie d'Arrast
The Squall (1929)	FN	Alexander Korda
The Girl in the Glass Cage (1929)	FN	Ralph Dawson
Fast Life (1929)	FN	John Francis Dillon
The Careless Age (1929)	FN	John Griffith Wray

The Forward Pass (1929)	FN	Eddie Cline
The Show of Shows (1929)	WB	John Adolfi
Loose Ankles (1930)	FN	Ted Wilde
The Second Floor Mystery (1930)	WB	Roy Del Ruth
The Man from Blankley's (1930)	WB	Alfred E. Green
Road to Paradise (1930)	FN	William Beaudine
The Truth about Youth (1930)	FN	William A. Seiter
The Devil to Pay (1930)	Goldwyn/UA	George Fitzmaurice
Kismet (1931)	WB	John Francis Dillon
Right of Way (1931)	FN	Frank Lloyd
Beau Ideal (1931)	RKO	Herbert Brenon
Too Young to Marry (1931)	FN	Mervyn LeRoy
Big Business Girl (1931)	FN	William A. Seiter
I Like Your Nerve (1931)	FN	William McGann
The Ruling Voice (1931)	FN	Rowland V. Lee
Three Girls Lost (1931)	FFC	Sidney Lanfield
Platinum Blonde (1931)	COL	Frank Capra
Taxi! (1932)	WB	Roy Del Ruth
The Hatchet Man (1932)	FN	William Wellman
Play-Girl (1932)	WB	Ray Enright
Week-end Marriage (1932)	FN	Thornton Freeland
Life Begins (1932)	FN	James Flood
They Call It Sin (1932)	FN	Thornton Freeland
Employees' Entrance (1933)	FN	Roy Del Ruth
Grand Slam (1933)	WB	William Dieterle
Zoo in Budapest (1933)	FFC	Rowland V. Lee
Heroes for Sale (1933)	FN	William Wellman
The Life of Jimmy Dolan (1933)	WB	Archie Mayo
Midnight Mary (1933)	MGM	William Wellman
She Had to Say Yes (1933)	FN	Busby Berkeley and George Amy
The Devil's in Love (1933)	FFC	William Dieterle
Man's Castle (1933)	COL	Frank Borzage
The House of Rothschild (1934)	TC/UA	Alfred Werker
Born to be Bad (1934)	TC/UA	Lowell Sherman
Bulldog Drummond Strikes Back (1934)	TC/UA	Roy Del Ruth
Caravan (1934)	TC/UA	Eric Charrel
The White Parade (1934)	FFC	Irving Cummings
Clive of India (1935)	TC/UA	Richard Boleslawski
Shanghai (1935)	Walter Wanger/PAR	James Flood
The Call of the Wild (1935)	TC/UA	William Wellman
The Crusades (1935)	PAR	Cecil B. DeMille
Ladies in Love (1936)	TCF	Edward H. Griffith
Private Number (1936)	TCF	Roy Del Ruth
Ramona (1936)	TCF	Henry King
The Unguarded Hour (1936)	MGM	Sam Wood
Café Metropole (1937)	TCF	Edward H. Griffith

Love Is News (1937)	TCF	Tay Garnett
Love under Fire (1937)	TCF	George Marshall
Second Honeymoon (1937)	TCF	Walter Lang
Wife, Doctor and Nurse (1937)	TCF	Walter Lang
Four Men and a Prayer (1938)	TCF	John Ford
Kentucky (1938)	TCF	David Butler
Suez (1938)	TCF	Allan Dwan
Three Blind Mice (1938)	TCF	William A. Seiter
Daytime Wife (1939)	TCF	Gregory Ratoff
The Story of Alexander Graham Bell (1939)	TCF	Irving Cummings
Wife, Husband and Friend (1939)	TCF	Gregory Ratoff
Eternally Yours (1939)	Walter Wanger/UA	Tay Garnett
The Doctor Takes a Wife (1940)	COL	Alexander Hall
He Stayed for Breakfast (1940)	COL	Alexander Hall
The Men in Her Life (1941)	COL	Gregory Ratoff
The Lady from Cheyenne (1941)	U	Frank Lloyd
Bedtime Story (1941)	COL	Alexander Hall
A Night to Remember (1943)	COL	Richard Wallace
China (1943)	PAR	John Farrow
And Now Tomorrow (1944)	PAR	Irving Pichel
Ladies Courageous (1944)	Walter Wanger/U	John Rawlins
Along Came Jones (1945)	International/RKO	Stuart Heisler
The Stranger (1946)	International/RKO	Orson Welles
The Farmer's Daughter (1947)	RKO	H. C. Potter
The Bishop's Wife (1947)	Goldwyn/RKO	Henry Koster
The Perfect Marriage (1947)	PAR	Lewis Allen
Rachel and the Stranger (1948)	RKO	Norman Foster
The Accused (1948)	PAR	William Dieterle
Mother Is a Freshman (1949)	TCF	Lloyd Bacon
Come to the Stable (1949)	TCF	Henry Koster
Key to the City (1950)	MGM	George Sidney
Cause for Alarm! (1951)	MGM	Tay Garnett
Half Angel (1951)	TCF	Richard Sale
Paula (1952)	COL	Rudolph Maté
Because of You (1952)	UI	Joseph Pevney
It Happens Every Thursday (1953)	UI	Joseph Pevney

MAJOR RADIO APPEARANCES

**Margaret Herrick Library,
Fairbanks Center for Motion Picture Study, Beverly Hills**
Lux Radio Theatre (tapes)
Jezebel (25 November 1940)
The Lady from Cheyenne (16 June 1941)
The Great Lie (2 March 1942)
Algiers (14 December 1942)
The Philadelphia Story (14 June 1943)
And Now Tomorrow (21 May 1945)
Love Letters (22 April 1946)
The Barretts of Wimpole Street (9 September 1946)
The Farmer's Daughter (5 June 1948)

Paley Center for Media, Beverly Hills
Theodora Goes Wild (*Campbell's Playhouse*, 14 June 1940)
Jane Eyre (*Lux Radio Theatre*, 5 June 1944)

**Audio Classics Archive (Terry Salomonson, Audio Classics Archives,
P.O. Box 347, Howell MI, 48884-0347)**
The Perfect Marriage (*Screen Directors' Playhouse*, 20 March 1947)

Family Theatre
   "Flight from Home" (13 February 1947)
   "Dear Mr. American" (4 March 1948)
   "The Happy Prince" (12 October 1949)
   "The Littlest Angel" (21 December 1949, repeated 27 December 1950)
   "The Treasury of Holmes" (14 February 1951, repeated 13 February 1957)
   "Talk about the Weather" (24 October 1951)
   "Heritage of Home" (13 February 1952, repeated 18 February 1953)
   "Just for Tonight" (19 November 1952)
   "The Longest Hour " (1 July 1953)
   "The Man Who Bought the Phone Company" (3 February 1954)

"The Hound of Heaven" (27 October 1954)
"The Outing" (9 September 1956)

OTRCAT.com *(Old Time Radio Show Catalog). Note: MP3 format.*

Lux Radio Theatre
Polly of the Circus (30 November 1936)
The Old Maid (30 October 1939)
China (22 November 1943)
The Farmer's Daughter (5 January 1948)
The Accused (28 March 1949)

Everything for the Boys

Blithe Spirit (1943 or 1944)

MAJOR TELEVISION APPEARANCES

www.videocollection.com

The Loretta Young Show, Season 1 (1953–54). 30 episodes. 3 DVDs. KKMDY064433.

The Loretta Young Show, Season 2 (1954–55). 30 episodes. 3 DVDs. KKMDY067293.

The Loretta Young Show, Seasons 3 and 4 (1955–57). 30 episodes. 3 DVDs. KKMDY063445.

The New Loretta Young Show. 26 episodes (1962–63). 4 DVDs. KKVC1008453.

The Road to Lourdes and Other Miracles of Faith ("The Road," "Three and Two Please," "Sister Ann," "Faith, Hope and Mr. Flaherty") VCI Entertainment, 2007.

The Paley Center for Media, Beverly Hills, CA
The Loretta Young Show
"I Remember the Rani" (Season 1, 1 May 1955)
"The Pearl" (Season 3, 12 February 1956)
"Incident in India" (Season 6, 25 January 1959)
"The Prettiest Girl in Town" (Season 6, 6 March 1959)

INDEX

Abbey of Regina Laudis, 155, 159–60
Abel, Michael, 160
Accused, The (1948), 141–43, 167
Aherne, Brian, 122, 132
Akins, Zoë, 90–91
Albert, Eddie, 141
Alfred Hitchcock Presents, 212
Algiers (radio version), 174–75
Along Came Jones (1945), 124, 135–36, 146, 152
Ameche, Don, 65, 94–95, 96, 99–100, 109, 183, 186
And Now Tomorrow (1944), 133–34
Annabella, 69, 107
Arbuckle, Fatty, 74
Arliss, Florence, 60
Arliss, George, 58
Arthur, Jean, 141, 213
Arzner, Dorothy, 186, 223
Asther, Nils, 15, 16
Astor, Mary, 79
Awful Truth, The (1937), 120, 192

Baker, Norma Jean. *See* Monroe, Marilyn
Ball, Lucille, 186, 189
Barnes, Binnie, 104
Barrymore, Ethel, 146
Barthelmess, Richard, 36, 65
Baxter, Warner, 100, 101, 103, 104
Beau Ideal (1931), 24
Because of You (1952), 167–68

Bedtime Story (1941), 120–21
Belcher, Ernest, 119
Bells of St. Mary's, The (1945), 157, 237
Belzer, George, 8–9
Belzer, Georgiana (half sister), 8; as Mrs. Ricardo Montalban, 111, 192
Bennett, Constance, 90
Bennett, Joan, 115, 129
Benson, Sally, 156
Bergman, Ingrid, 146, 237
Berkeley Square (1933), 44, 48
Beverly Wilshire Hotel, 222
Bickford, Charles, 147
Big Business Girl (1931), 28–29
Bishop's Wife, The (1947), 69, 143–46; as postwar spiritual renewal film, 144–45
Blane, Sally, 3, 8–9, 11–12, 13, 111, 149, 150, 234, 244
Bleak House (Dickens), 86
Blithe Spirit (radio version), 177
Born to Be Bad (1934), 55–56, 69
Borzage, Frank, 3, 41–44, 115, 195
Bosco, Antoinette, 158
Bow, Clara, 237
Boyer, Charles, 57, 63, 65, 115, 175, 204
Breen, Joseph Ignatius, 73–74, 160–61
Brennan, Walter, 108, 109
Brenon, Herbert, 14, 15–16, 24, 222
Brent, George, 30, 79
Bridal Showcase International, 221–22
Brokow, Norman, 167, 203, 212, 219, 243

INDEX

Brower, Otto, 107
Bruce, Virginia, 100–101, 132
Buckner, William R., 85–86
Bulldog Drummond Strikes Back (1934), 56–57
Burns and Allen Show, The (radio), 178–79
Busch, Niven, 194

Café Metropole (1937), 97–98
Cagney, James, 33, 34
Cain, James M., 103–4, 133
Calhern, Louis, 30
Call of the Wild, The (1935), 71–74, 163, 164, 209, 230
Campbell's Playhouse, 173–74
Capra, Frank, 39–41, 43, 162, 194
Caravan (1934), 57–58
Career in C Major (Cain), 103–4
Casablanca (1942), 139
Cause for Alarm! (1951), 165–66
Champion, Marge, 119
Chandler, Jeff, 167, 168
Chandler, Raymond, 132–33
Chaney, Lon, 14–16
Channing, Carol, 243
Charral, Erik, 57
Cheat, The (1915), 6
China (1943), 126–27, 132
Christmas Eve (TV movie), 225–28
Christmas Holiday (radio version), 175–76
Church of the Good Shepherd, 183, 216, 232
Citizen Kane (1941), 137–38, 151
Clive of India (1935), 61–62
Cohn, Harry, 39, 42, 43, 54, 116, 231; relationship with Loretta, 116–17, 123
Colbert, Claudette, 6, 125, 127, 150, 153, 171, 203, 204
Colman, Ronald, 23, 61, 65, 143, 166
Columbia Pictures, 39, 41, 166, 186, 224, 231
Come to the Stable (1949), 125, 154–60; radio version, 185
Cooper, Gary, 65, 135
Cooper, Gladys, 145, 146, 155
Corey, Wendell, 140, 142
Cotten, Joseph, 138, 146, 148, 161, 162

Coward, Noël, 100, 177
Crain, Jeanne, 115
Crawford, Joan, 45, 127, 148, 168, 192, 213, 218, 222, 235–36
Crosby, Bing, 215
Crowther, Bosley, 123
Crusades, The (1936), 76–78; historical accuracy of, 76–77
Cukor, George, 74, 237
Cummings, Constance, 23, 143
Cummings, Robert, 142

Daniell, Henry, 89
Dark Shadows, 219
Dassin, Jules, 161, 186
Davis, Bette, 47, 79, 125, 127, 135, 150, 168, 170, 172, 213, 218, 235–36
deHavilland, Olivia, 218, 219
DeMille, Cecil B., 6, 75–78, 171
Desilu, 189
Devil to Pay, The (1930), 23, 143
Devil's in Love, The (1933), 50–51
Dick, Douglas, 139, 142
Dieterle, William, 50, 51
Dietrich, Marlene, 143, 233
Dinelli, Mel, 163
"dish night," 26
Dmytryk, Edward, 161
Doctor Takes a Wife, The (1940), 117–18
Double Indemnity (1944), 132, 133
Douglas, Melvyn, 17–18
Dunne, Irene, 156, 168, 173, 192, 203, 207, 213
Durbin, Deanna, 175–76
Dwan, Allan, 14, 107

Eagle Squadron (1942), 128–29
Elwes, Sir Simon, 240
Employees Entrance (1933), 35–36
Erwin, Stuart, 91, 92, 100
Everybody Does It (film and novella), 104
Everything for the Boys (radio show), 177

Fairbanks, Douglas, Jr., 22, 24, 32, 65
Family Theatre, 181–85, 190–91, 231
Famous Players-Lasky, 5, 6, 48

Farmer's Daughter, The (1947), 125, 146–48, 159, 168
Farrell, Glenda, 31
Fast, Howard, 151
Faye, Alice, 113
Ferguson, Helen, 187–88, 203
Field, Rachel, 132
Field, Virginia, 116, 141
Film Booking Office, 18–19
film editors, female, 223–24
First National, 10, 13, 16, 19, 20, 22
Fitzgerald, Geraldine, 129
Florey, Robert, 193–94, 195
Flynn, Errol, 237
Fonda, Henry, 109–10
Fontaine, Joan, 174, 202, 219
Ford, John, 105, 115
Forsythe, John, 169
Foster, Norman: as actor, 28, 150; as director, 150–51, 195
Four Men and a Prayer (1938), 105–6
Four-Star Playhouse, 185, 204
Fox, William, 63
Fox Film Corporation, 53
Freeland, Thornton, 29–30
Frings, Ketti, 142, 168
Frost, Lindsay, 228
Frye, William, 232

Gable, Clark, 29, 34, 65–66, 71–74, 76, 78, 92, 163, 164, 171, 209, 235, 236, 237, 241
Gabriel over the White House (1933), 114
Garbo, Greta, 20, 47, 135
Garnett, Tay, 96, 165, 196
Garson, Greer, 125, 127, 155
Gaynor, Janet, 90
George Burns and Gracie Allen Show, The (TV), 200–201
Goetz, Edith, 135
Goetz, William, 54, 135
Going My Way (1944), 157, 199
Goldwyn, Samuel, 23, 24, 90, 138, 143
Grable, Betty, 112, 113
Grand Slam (1933), 51
Grant, Cary, 55, 69, 135, 144, 145, 192

Great Guns (1941), 221
Great Lie, The (radio version), 79
Greeks Had a Word for It, The (play and film), 90–91
Greene, Richard, 105, 108, 109

Half Angel (1951), 148, 154, 160–62
Hall, Alexander, 119, 120, 121
Hall, Gladys, 67
Hanalis, Blanche, 225–26, 232
Harlow, Jean, 40, 41
Hatchet Man, The (1932), 34–35, 199
Haver, June, 113
Hays, Will, 90–91
Hayward, Susan, 115, 129, 134, 148
Hayworth, Rita, 232
He Stayed for Breakfast (1940), 118–19
He Who Gets Slapped (1924), 14–15
Head, Edith, 126, 133, 142
Head Man (1928), 13, 14
Henie, Sonja, 69, 93–94, 107, 146
Hepburn, Audrey, 155
Hepburn, Katharine, 170, 172, 173
Her Wild Oat (1927), 10
Heroes for Sale (1933), 36–38, 45
Hill, Arthur, 226, 227
His Girl Friday (1940), 120
Hitchcock, Alfred, 136, 138, 212–13
Holden, William, 150, 151, 175
Holleran, Dr. Walter, 80, 81, 88
Holliday, Judy, 150, 233, 237
Hollywood, corporate, 228
Hollywood Hotel (radio show), 83
Holm, Celeste, 155, 157
Holy Cross Cemetery, 244
Hopkins, Miriam, 140
House Committee on Un-American Activities (HUAC), 151
House of Rothschild, The (1934), 59–61
Howard, Trevor, 226, 227
Hughes, Howard, 163
Hussey, Ruth, 183
Huston, John, 137, 138
Huston, Walter, 65

I Like Your Nerve (1931), 24–25
I Love Lucy, 186

International Pictures: films of, 135; merger with Universal, 135
It Happens Every Thursday (1953), 168–69

Jack Benny Show, The, 187
Jackson, Helen Hunt, 94–95
Jane Eyre (radio version), 174
Jane Wyman Show, The, 243
Jean-Louis, 232–34
Johnson, Nunnelly, 136
Johnson, Van, 154, 155, 202
Jones, Jennifer, 125, 155, 175
Jory, Victor, 50, 140
June Allyson Show, The, 214

Karloff, Boris, 59, 63
Kaye, Celia, 216
Keith, Brian, 223
Keller, Harry, 195–96
Kennedy, Joseph P., 18–19, 20
Kentucky (1938), 108–9
Key to the City (1950), 163–64
Kibbee, Guy, 32, 33
King, Henry, 94, 95
Kingsley, Dorothy, 165
Koster, Henry, 69, 147

Ladd, Alan, 65, 125, 126, 127, 128, 132, 134
Ladies Courageous (1944), 129–31
Ladies in Love (1936), 90
Lady from Cheyenne (1941), 123–24, 129
Lady in a Corner (TV movie), 228–29
Lake, Veronica, 125, 127, 130
Lamarr, Hedy, 175
Lanchester, Elsa, 145, 146, 157
Lasky, Jesse, 48
Laugh, Clown, Laugh (1928), 13, 14–15
Leave Her to Heaven (1945), 112
Lee, Roland V., 49
Leibman, Ron, 226, 227
Leonard, Robert Z., 6, 7
LeRoy, Mervyn, 11–12
Lewis, Christopher Paul, 87, 181, 222–23
Lewis, Judy, 7, 203, 205; "adoption" of, 81–83; appearance of, 239, 240; birth of, 80; childhood of, 80, 87; as cruise ship lecturer, 242; estrangement from Loretta, 241; falsified background of, 81; as graduate of Antioch University, 239; inspiration for name, 80–81; learns truth about birth father, 209; marriage and divorce of, 239–49; as radio actress, 238; as stage actress, 239; as television actress, 238; as television producer, 239
Lewis, Peter Charles, 87, 183
Lewis, Tom: attempt to cancel *The Loretta Young Show*, 203; and *Cause for Alarm!*, 165; courtship and marriage to Loretta, 186–87, 231; estrangement and divorce from Loretta, 204–6; and Father Peyton, 181, 183, 231; as radio producer, 86, 177, 231; as TV producer, 189–90
Lewislor Productions, 189
Life Begins (1932), 30–31
Life of Jimmy Dolan, The (1933), 31–32
Lindley, Angus and Ida, 7
Lombard, Carole, 173
London, Jack, 71–72
Longenecker, Robert, 183
Lonsdale, Frederick, 23
Loos, Anita, 46
Loose Ankles, 21–22
Lord, Robert, 37, 38
Loretta Young Show, The, 13, 69, 188–200, 206, 212, 219–21, 232
Los Angeles Film Exposition (FILMEX), 223
Lourdes, 210–12
Love Is News (1937), 96–97, 112
Love Letters (radio version), 175, 176
Love under Fire (1937), 98–100
Loy, Myrna, 21, 22, 23
Lucas, Paul, 51
Luce, Claire Boothe, 155, 156
Lucky Jordan (1942), 126
Lux Radio Theatre, 79, 86, 171–73, 174–76, 190
Lyons, Ben, 10

MacDonald, Jeanette, 49
MacMahon, Aline, 32, 36

MacMurray, Fred, 171, 213
Magnificent Flirt, The (1928), 11, 13
Manners, David, 22, 23, 30, 50
Man's Castle (1933), 41–44
Mansfield, Jayne, 113
March, Fredric, 120–22, 123, 149
Marcus, Larry, 166
Markey, Gene, 46
Marusia, 190
Mason, James, 214
Mason, Pamela, 214, 215
Mason, Portland, 214, 216
Maté, Rudolph, 211
Mayer, Louis, 139, 154, 163, 187
Mayo, Archie, 31
McCrea, Joel, 91–92
McNeile, H. C. ("Sapper"), 56
Medjugorje, 182
Men in Her Life, The (1941), 119–20
Menjou, Adolphe, 97
Metro-Goldwyn-Mayer (MGM), 14, 44, 47, 89, 163, 165, 186, 223
Midnight Mary (1933), 44–46
Milland, Ray, 117–18, 123
Millard, Oscar, 157
Miller, Arthur, 240–41
Miller, Marilyn, 10
Mitchum, Robert, 152–53
Mohr, Hal, 50
Mommie Dearest, 235
Monroe, Marilyn, 10, 113, 232
Moore, Colleen, 10–12, 16, 19
Moore, Pauline, 91, 92
Moorehead, Agnes, 137, 237
Morris, Richard, 210, 211
Montalban, Georgiana, 192, 215, 243
Montalban, Ricardo, 192, 203, 243
Mother Benedict Duss, 157, 158–60
Mother Dolores Hart, 160
Mother Is a Freshman (1949), 154–55
Mourning Becomes Electra (1947), 148–49
Movieland magazine, 191, 192
Mr. Smith Goes to Washington (1939), 147
Murray, Ken, 188
Murray, Mae, 6–7
Mutual Broadcasting System, 181, 183
My Mother's Keeper, 235

My Three Sons, 213
Myra Breckinridge (film), 221

Nader, George, 192, 193
Nagel, Conrad, 25
Naish, J. Carrol, 34, 50
National Conference of Christians and Jews, 224
National Legion of Decency, 73, 74, 80
Naughty but Nice (1927), 11
Neame, Christopher, 228
Neuman, Theresa, 208
New Deal, 38
New Loretta Young Show, The, 213–19
Niblo, Fred, 183
Nichols, Dudley, 148
Nicol, Alex, 167
Night to Remember, A (1943), 122–23, 132, 213
1950s popular culture, 202
Niven, David, 68, 91, 116, 140, 141, 144, 145
Normand, Mabel, 74
North, Sheree, 113
nuns in films, 155, 157

Oakie, Jack, 231
Oland, Warner, 56, 63
Old Maid, The (radio version), 172
O'Neill, Eugene, 148
Only Way, The (1919), 6
Osborne, Robert, 244

Padre Pio, 208, 209
Pagliacci (opera), 15
Palette, Eugene, 118
Paramount Pictures, 53, 125, 139, 144
Paramount Publix, 48
Paramount-Famous Players-Lasky, 48
Parsons, Louella, 83–85, 178, 237
Partos, Frank, 132
Paula (1952), 123, 166–67
Perfect Marriage, The (1947), 140–41
Perry, Fred, 78
Perry, Joan, 116
Peyton, Father Patrick, 179–81, 207
Philadelphia Story, The (radio version), 173

INDEX

Photoplay magazine, 26–27, 193
Pichel, Irving, 134
Pitts, Zazu, 14, 156
Platinum Blonde (1931), 39–41
Play Girl (1932), 28–29
Poe, James, 166
Poitier, Sidney, 189, 224
Pope John Paul II, 208
Pope Pius XII, 208, 209
Potter, H. C., 147
Power, Tyrone, 65, 68–69, 90, 93, 100, 106–8, 112, 230
President Vanishes, The (1935), 14
Preston, Robert, 124
Primrose Ring, The (1917), 6
Priory of Regina Laudis, 156, 159
Private Lives (film), 100
Private Number (1936), 92–93
Production Code, 44–45, 63
Production Code Administration (PCA), 73

Radio City Music Hall, 19–20, 120, 149
Raft, George, 33
Ramona (1936), 94–95, 199
Rank, J. Arthur, 135
Raphaelson, Samson, 140, 141
Rappe, Virginia, 147
Rathbone, Basil, 93
Raymond, Gene, 48–49
Reed, Donna, 155
Rettig, Tommy, 166, 167
Right of Way, The (1931), 25
Riskin, Robert, 39, 40, 41, 162
RKO Radio Pictures, 19–20, 24, 47, 53, 135, 146, 148, 151, 163
Road, The, 211–12
Road to Lourdes and Other Miracles of Truth, The (DVD), 222
Road to Paradise, The (1930), 22
Roberts, Ruth, 195, 213
Robinson, Edward G., 32, 35, 135, 137
Rogers, Buddy, 49
Rogers, Ginger, 127
rosary, 180–81
Rossellini, Roberto, 237
Royal, Fanny (grandmother), 4, 8

Royal, Robert (grandfather), 4, 8
Ruling Voice, The (1931), 65
Ruskin, Harry, 189
Ruslew Productions, 189
Russell, Rosalind, 116–17, 130, 148, 149, 155, 202, 207, 215, 232
Ryan, Sheila, 221

Sachem, William, 166
Saenz, Josephine, 32
Sale, Richard, 161
Salida, Colo., 3
Salt, Waldo, 151–52
Salt Lake City, Utah, 3, 4, 5
Sarnoff, David, 18
Scalpone, Al, 183
Scarlet Seas (1928), 13
Schary, Dore, 146, 147, 157, 163, 165, 166
Schenck, Joseph, 54
Shanghai (1935), 62–63
Sheen, Bishop Fulton J., 179–80, 202, 208
Shewalter, Robert F., 189, 205
Schumann, Robert and Clara, 194
Scola, Kathryn, 46, 99, 100
Scott, Lizabeth, 139
Screen Guild Theatre (radio show), 86
Second Floor Mystery (1930), 66
Second Honeymoon (1937), 100
Selznick, David, 135, 146
Sersen, Fred, 107
Shadow of a Doubt (1943), 138
She Had to Say Yes (1933), 51–52
Sheik, The (1921), 6
Sheridan, Ann, 127
Show of Shows (1929), 11
Sidney, George, 163
Sirens of the Sea (1917), 5
Sister Mary Rose, 198
sitcoms, 187, 202
Skelton, Red, 186
Skylark (1941), 140, 141
Smith, Kent, 166
Spanish Civil War, 98–100
Speck, Gregory, 209–10
Spelling, Aaron, 219

Spiegel, Sam, 136–37
Spitz, Leo, 135
Spoto, Donald, 68
Squall, The (1929), 20–21
St. Anne's Foundation, 82
St. Elizabeth's Hospital, 81–82, 88, 92, 93
Stanwyck, Barbara, 202, 215
Stewart, James, 68
Story of Alexander Graham Bell, The (1939), 109–11, 221
Stranger, The (1946), 136–38, 140, 146
Stromboli (1949), 237
Suez (1938), 106–7
Sullivan, Barry, 166
Sutherland, Edward, 69–70, 239
Swanson, Gloria, 150

Taylor, Robert, 92, 93
Taylor, William Desmond, 74
Taxi! (1932), 33–34
Tearle, Conway, 22
Temple, Shirley, 93
Thalberg, Irving, 74
That Wonderful Urge (1948), 112
Theodora Goes Wild (radio version), 173–74
They Call It Sin (1932), 29–30
Thomas, Marlo, 181, 243
Three Blind Mice (1938), 93–94
Three Girls Lost (1931), 32
Tierney, Gene, 112–13, 123, 127
Tinney, Joseph, Jr., 239
Tone, Franchot, 46, 89
Tong Wars, 34
Too Young to Marry, 12
Toretto Enterprises, 212, 216
Tracy, Spencer, 42, 43, 67–68, 216, 230
Traxler, Charlene (aunt), 5, 18
Traxler, Ernest (uncle), 5, 17
Trotti, Lamar, 94, 110
True Confession (radio version), 173
Truth about Youth (1930), 22–23
Twelve O'Clock High (1949), 155
Twentieth Century Pictures, 53, 54, 62, 63, 224, 231
Twentieth Century-Fox, 33, 62, 63, 84–85, 93, 94

Uncommon Knowledge, 235–36, 239, 241, 242
Unguarded Hour, The (1936), 89–90
United Artists, 54, 115
Universal International, 136
Universal Pictures, 5, 18, 123, 128

Vallee, Rudy, 155
Van Trees, James, 46, 47
Veiller, Anthony, 137
Venice, Calif., 80, 88
Vertigo (1958), 135
Vidal, Gore, 221
Vidor, Florence, 11

Wald, Jerry, 187
Wallis, Hal, 138, 139–43, 195
Wanger, Walter, 114–16, 128–30
Ward, Fanny, 6
Ward, Father John, 8
Ware, Darrell, 99, 100
Warner, Jack, 139
Warner Bros., 129, 139, 193. *See also* First National
Washburn, Beverly, 214
Wayne, John, 32
Weaver, Marjorie, 91, 92, 100
Webb, Millard, 12
Weekend Marriage (1932), 29
Welles, Orson, 135, 137, 138, 173–74
Wellman, William, 34, 35, 36–38, 45, 46, 47, 73, 195, 230
Werker, Alfred, 59
Werlé (Daniel), 195
Westley, Helen, 59
Whip Woman, The (1928), 13
Wife, Doctor and Nurse (1937), 100–101
Wife, Husband and Friend (1939), 103–4
Wilcoxon, Henry, 76
Wilder, Billy, 133, 237
William, Warren, 12–13, 35–36
Williams, Robert, 40
Wilson, Liza, 84
Withers, Grant, 9, 12, 66–67, 231
woman's picture, 27–28, 30
Women in Film's Crystal Awards, 223–24

Wood, Sam, 89–90
Woolley, Monty, 145, 146
Wright, Teresa, 135, 138, 143–44
Wyman, Jane, 193, 243

Young, Elizabeth Jane (sister). *See* Blane, Sally
Young, Gladys Royal (mother): as boarding house owner, 7; burial place of, 244; conversion to Catholicism, 3; death of, 244; devotion to Virgin Mary, 181; divorce from John Earle Young, 8; as interior decorator, 17, 92, 190; marriage to, and divorce from, George Belzer, 8–9; marriage to John Earle Young, 3, 4; parents of, 4; phone call from Mervyn LeRoy, 11–13; reaction to Loretta's first marriage, 66; role in "adoption" scenario, 78, 79
Young, Gretchen. *See* Young, Loretta
Young, John Earle, 3, 5, 8, 149, 150, 230
Young, John Royal (brother), 5, 7; as John Lindley, 7, 87, 242
Young, Loretta: on acting, 205; "adoption" of Judy, 74, 81–83; affair with Clark Gable, 74; appearances on *Family Theatre*, 283–85; as Asian characters, 190, 191; attraction to older men, 230; awards of, 200, 201, 223–24; birth of Judy and subsequent cover up, 80–81; burial place of, 244; children by Tom Lewis, 87; contract with morals clause, 74; death and funeral of, 243–44; departure from Fox, 111; devotion to Virgin Mary, 181–82; early interest in television, 185–89; education of, 7–8; fascination with stigmatists, 208–9; favorite films of, 222; filmography of, 256–58 (*see also individual films*); as Gretchen, 2, 4; guest on Louella Parsons radio show, 84–85; homes of, 4–5, 7, 221–22; hospitalization of, 202–3; and Jean-Louis (*see* Jean-Louis); marriage to Tom Lewis, 87; marriages of, 66–67; multipicture deal with Harry Cohn, 116–17, 123; name change from Gretchen, 10–12; as observant Catholic, 44, 67, 80, 86, 222, 224, 225, 235; obsession with image, 220, 235; post-career activies, 221, 222; and Tyrone Power (*see* Power, Tyrone); as radio actress, 170–85; recipient of Louella Parsons award, 85; reconciliation with Harry Cohn, 166; refuses *Lloyds of London* role, 101–2; return to Zanuck, 138, 154–62; roles rejected, 101, 187, 218, 219; salaries of, 11, 12, 13, 22, 23, 69, 110, 141, 167; as screwball heroine, 122, 174; smoking habit of, 76; on stardom, 142; and James Stewart (*see* Stewart, James); suit against NBC, 220; and Edward Sutherland (*see* Sutherland, Edward); "swear box" of, 82, 153; as television actress, 206, 210–17, 225–29; as visitor of churches, 222; and Hal Wallis, 140–43; and Grant Withers (*see* Withers, Grant)
Young, Polly Ann (sister), 3, 12, 111, 149, 234, 244
Young, Robert, 58, 60, 179, 183
Young and Rubicam, 86, 185

Zanuck, Darryl: background of, 53–54, 57–58; on *Café Metropole*, 98; on *Come to the Stable*, 156; as controversial producer, 58; favorites of, 93–94, 112–13; and *Half Angel*, 162; notes on *Love Under Fire*, 99; on Louella Parsons radio show, 84–85; Tyrone Power–Loretta romance, 68–69, 97, 107; role in "adoption" scenario, 80; strained relationship with Loretta, 102, 107, 111, 123; and at Warner's, 53; and *Wilson*, 224
Zoo in Budapest (1933), 48–49
Zukor, Adolph, 48

www.ingramcontent.com/pod-product-compliance
Lightning Source LLC
Chambersburg PA
CBHW051720300325
24211CB00005B/22